LIFE AND DEATH IN PRIVATE LAW

Private law regulates life; this is self-evident, but how does it regulate death? This edited collection explores this question.

Life and death are the beginning and end of the legal person: the instigator and terminator of rights, interests and obligations. They are also the nominal separator of particular fields of law (medical law from succession law, for example). As such they act as fault lines that can test the limit of private law principles and norms. This book explores what life and death tell us about private law and what private law can tell us about the meaning and value of life and death.

Volume 50 in the series Hart Studies in Private Law

Life and Death in Private Law

Edited by
Kate Falconer
Kit Barker
and
Andrew Fell

•HART•
OXFORD • LONDON • NEW YORK • NEW DELHI • SYDNEY

HART PUBLISHING

Bloomsbury Publishing Plc

Kemp House, Chawley Park, Cumnor Hill, Oxford, OX2 9PH, UK

1385 Broadway, New York, NY 10018, USA

29 Earlsfort Terrace, Dublin 2, Ireland

First published in Great Britain 2024

A catalogue record for this book is available from the British Library.

A catalogue record for this book is available from the Library of Congress.

Library of Congress Control Number: 2024944072

ISBN: HB: 978-1-50996-932-6
ePDF: 978-1-50996-934-0
ePub: 978-1-50996-933-3

Typeset by Compuscript Ltd, Shannon

FOREWORD

An assumption readily made by a lawyer is that life has a beginning and an end. A theologian or philosopher, focused on the meaning of life, may beg to differ. Perspective is important.

Another assumption of lawyers, perhaps more widely shared, is that life has a middle between a beginning and an end, however blurred boundaries may be in a particular case. With the prolongation of life, supported by modern medicine, a person unable to manage his or her own affairs because of a loss of mental capacity is commonly thought to suffer a form of 'living death' which calls for another person (often called a guardian), within a legal framework, to manage 'the person' (body) and 'the estate' (property) of the incapable person.

Increasingly, the lives of every person in a modern state are managed, more or less, from cradle to grave, by somebody other than themselves: often a public authority or a large corporation. Simple illustrations of this are requirements that births, deaths and marriages be registered; that drivers be licensed; and that recipients of public medical benefits carry an identification card. In this environment, public regulation of private lives increasingly engages with the specific events of birth (eg *inter vivos* fertilisation, surrogacy, birth control measures, abortion) and death (suicide, euthanasia), providing health care, and engaging public institutions such as hospitals and publicly licensed professionals such as doctors, nurses and pharmacists. The law (represented by the State) routinely seeks to regulate social conduct by means of a blanket prohibition qualified by a revocable grant of permission, subject to conditions, in the form of a 'licence' issued by a government agency.

For a lawyer 'birth' and 'death' often present themselves in the form of a process, not a single event. A lawyer officiating as such is rarely present at the point of birth or death, even in the execution of a 'death bed will'. Medical professionals are more commonly on hand at critical times. It is the fate of a lawyer's client to celebrate a birth or mourn a death. Yet lawyers are often called upon to assist management of a process associated with birth or death before or after the event. By their intervention, and that of the courts, in the periphery of a birth or death, their major role may be indirectly to supervise the medical profession by holding hospitals and staff to account for breaches of duty of care.

The process of birth might, for example, commence with a surrogacy agreement or an IVF contract in anticipation of a birth. It might not end until arrangements are in place for the custody or adoption of a baby child.

The process of death might, for example, begin when a person, in anticipation of incapacity preceding death, executes (by whatever name known) an enduring power of attorney, an enduring guardianship appointment and a will. It might not end until a court has issued a grant of probate or administration in a deceased estate, the estate has been fully administered and distributed and any time for claims to be made against the estate has expired. If cryonics becomes a popular practice the administration of a deceased estate might never end.

A quirk of the law may be that 'rights' of an unborn person are not recognised even during the process of birth unless they may have an interest in property which requires an order that their interests be represented in an equity suit about property. Any inconsistency of approach finds its explanation in the purposive operation of law in each case.

A lawyer's life is dominated by rules, boundaries and the characterisation of facts and circumstances for a purpose served by law even though 'law' defies any all-purpose abstract definition. It shares that elusive quality with the bookends of life. Its meaning often depends upon the procedural framework for dispute resolution and problem solving of the particular society it serves.

A common, flexible paradigm within which 'law' is found and applied in a private law setting is, at least implicitly, that of an autonomous individual living, and dying, in community. 'The individual' and 'the community' are interdependent. It is difficult to conceive, or to give practical meaning, to one without the other. At different times and in different places society might strike a different balance between them, and at different times in one person's lifetime the balance might shift. Shakespeare's *Seven Ages of Man* illustrates the point.

Respect for the law requires that it be accepted by the community it serves and be applied with discretion as opinions within the community ebb and flow as, inevitably, they do. A temptation for those who have strong personal views about the province of birth and death in their community is to seek to entrench their particular views in 'law', whether by constitutional amendment, legislation or judicial fiat. This can be counter-productive as the persuasive enthusiasm of reformers hardens in coercion of the unpersuaded. Entrenchment of a contested 'private right' (especially if contested on 'moral' grounds) may be an invitation to civil disorder. The USA's experiences of civil war (over a contested private right to ownership of slaves), prohibition (over a person's contested right to consume alcohol) and abortion (over a woman's contested right to abortion 'on demand') provide historical examples.

In legal practice the paradigm of the 'autonomous' individual is a genuflection in the direction of a need to recognise that some individuals lack capacity to conform to social norms or to manage their own affairs in the middle to late term of their lives.

A major difficulty for a judge dealing with the affairs of a person who (by reason of incapacity or death) is unable to manage his or her affairs is in deciding who may have standing to be heard or to whom notice of proceedings should be given. In short, this involves identification of the individual and his or her community and consultation with proximate community members in management of the individual's affairs. In dealing with a living person management of the person and the estate must generally be seen holistically, and the welfare of the incapable person is the paramount consideration. Interested parties are those significant others who may assist the court with information about the best interests of an incapable person. Disposal of a dead body is in a class of its own as a court looks to respect known wishes of the deceased, to consult significant others experiencing grief and to have regard to the public interest in whatever arrangements are made. After death and disposal of a body, in the absence of children or other dependants in need of protective care, interested parties are those concerned with the due administration of an estate or an interest in property.

The focus of law encountered at and about the time of a birth, death and incapacity must be on respect for the dignity (worth) of an individual person. There are times of vulnerability for every person at birth and sooner or later thereafter. A failure to recognise that vulnerability in one person, or many, may place at risk others, or all of us, whose time has yet to come. In the interests of a free, open and safe society a veil of protective care may need to be thrown over the vulnerable. This must be done in prudent consultation with their significant others, including but not limited to, 'family' (however defined). To privilege 'community' over the individual at those times potentially places everybody at risk.

The secular and divine are not easily disentangled in the practice of law governing life and death. As always, in practice, the text, context and purpose of law must be consulted in dealing with an individual case. Whatever views one might have about controversial questions such as abortion or euthanasia, the starting point for legal analysis in a secular system for the administration of law must be an appreciation that each life is precious and worthy of respect, not readily to be diminished or denied. Any other starting point in the practical administration of law may place too much power in the hands of a judge and (especially if administered without empathy or arbitrarily) undermine the integrity of a legal system.

If, as some philosophers imagine, 'God' (however conceived) is truly 'dead' and 'self' is paramount against all competing interests, without constraints (other than standards imposed by 'law') external to 'self', the sense of community upon which self itself depends and the legal system that services individuals in community are both at risk of a breakdown. The effective administration of law requires a flexible balance, with tolerant give and take, between both the 'individual' and 'the community'.

One of the blurred boundaries commonly encountered by lawyers is the distinction between 'public' and 'private' law. There is much to be said for this distinction as a working rule of practice. However, it is not always helpful. Perhaps the clearest illustration of this, in the middle term of life, is when the law encounters 'insanity' in the context of a criminal trial or upon an exercise of guardianship jurisdiction. The law may seek to protect the mentally ill from self-harm, and to protect others, if necessary by institutional confinement.

In a managed society 'public' and 'private' forms of law coalesce. An example of this coalescence is the intrusion of private 'fiduciary law' reasoning in supervision of public officials, perhaps extending to protection of the interests of a vulnerable person at the time of contemplation of a process of 'voluntary assisted dying' (VAD) (euthanasia). Legislation authorising VAD embodies concepts drawn from the law of trusts, equity and the guardianship jurisdiction of courts about the need for fully informed consent and protections against undue influence and conflicts between interest and duty.

Whatever polemicists might say, on one side of a debate or another, there is generally an individual interest and a public interest in the management of a life before, during and after birth, as there is in the shadow of death, at the time of death and in the aftermath.

There are often two ways of thinking encountered by a judge called upon to intervene in lives affected by the trauma of a birth or death. One peers through a prism of competing claims of right and correlative obligations, whether personal or proprietary in nature. The other looks to management of people, property and relationships: identifying a problem and associated risks, potential solutions and prudent paths to action. They are commonly reflected in different styles of advocacy.

Both mindsets might appeal to 'rules' that bind, or 'principles' that guide, decision-makers. Ultimately, they are both governed by a purpose served by the law and that of the jurisdiction of any court or tribunal entrusted with authority to administer law.

Difficult problems and controversial solutions in the realm of a birth or a death are generally, by nature, such as to engage the conscience of each person directly affected and that person's community. When difficult choices must be made the law, at its best, endeavours to allow all concerned respect, space for reflection and opportunities for material support. Where the burden of a decision can be constructively shared between affected persons or interests judges generally lean towards that objective.

A striking feature of legal practice involving dispute resolution and problem-solving in management of the affairs of a vulnerable person is that experience teaches that cases are routinely fact-sensitive, wisdom resides in no one person, and prudence is required in the management of risk, uncertainty and the profound. Importance therefore attaches to serious conversations about rights and obligations, foreseeable risks and prudential management.

The chapters in this book cover a wide range of problems encountered at the intersection of law, birth, death and incapacity in several jurisdictions. The book offers insight into how lawyers deal with practical problems. It recognises that answers to questions often produce further questions in need of answers. It is much to be commended for its topicality, breadth of learning and academic rigour.

(Justice) Geoff Lindsay AM
Equity Division
Supreme Court of NSW
12 March 2024

ACKNOWLEDGEMENTS

The idea for this collection came out of a casual conversation between the three editors in early 2022. In response to Kate's insistence that 'Private Law and Death' would make a fantastic book title, Kit rightly pointed out that, as far as titles go, 'Life and Death in Private Law' is punchier. Not content to let such a title go to waste, all that remained for us to do was to put the collection together.

With this in mind, we are thankful to the TC Beirne School of Law at the University of Queensland, as well as the Australian Centre for Private Law, for supporting a workshop held in September 2022 at which several of the chapters found in this collection were presented in draft form. Our thanks also to the Bar Association of Queensland for hosting the event, and to all those who attended for their insightful comments on the papers.

We are grateful to Edward Spinks for his valuable research assistance throughout the duration of this book's production, and to Hart Publishing for their enthusiasm for the project and their patience as it was completed. We would also like to express our gratitude to the Hon Justice Geoff Lindsay for kindly agreeing to write the Foreword. As a highly respected jurist who has first-hand experience of many of the types of disputes discussed in these chapters, we are delighted that he has introduced the collection.

TABLE OF CONTENTS

CONTRIBUTORS

Kit Barker is Professor of Law at the TC Beirne School of Law, The University of Queensland, Australia.

Anna Broadmore is a Lecturer in Law at the Faculty of Law, University of Auckland, New Zealand.

Heather Conway is Professor of Property Law and Death Studies at Queen's University Belfast.

Kate Falconer is a Lecturer at the School of Law and the Radical Humanities Laboratory, University College Cork, Ireland.

Andrew Fell is a Lecturer in Law at the TC Beirne School of Law, The University of Queensland, Australia.

Jonathan Herring is Professor of Law at the University of Oxford, and the DM Wolfe-Clarendon Fellow in Law at Exeter College.

Mark Lunney is Professor of Tort Law at the Dickson Poon School of Law, King's College London and Adjunct Professor at the School of Law, University of New England, Australia.

Stephen Todd is Professor Law at the Faculty of Law, University of Canterbury, New Zealand.

Prue Vines is Professor of Law at the School of Private and Commercial Law, UNSW Sydney, Australia.

Jesse Wall is Associate Professor at the Faculty of Law, University of Auckland, New Zealand.

Danaya Wright is the T Terrell Sessums and Gerald Sohn Professor in Constitutional Law at the Levin College of Law, University of Florida.

TABLE OF CASES

Australia

Canada

European Court of Human Rights

France

Germany

Israel

New Zealand

Northern Ireland

Scotland

Singapore

United Kingdom

United States of America

TABLE OF LEGISLATION

Australia

Canada

France

New Zealand

Scotland

United Kingdom

United States of America

TABLE OF STATUTORY INSTRUMENTS

1

Life and Death in Private Law

ANDREW FELL AND KATE FALCONER

I. Introduction

Life begins, and then ends. For most of its duration, its edges are out of view and forgotten, or perhaps ignored. Our focus on day-to-day concerns predominates. Occasionally, however, we are reminded that life is both contingent and fleeting. The probability that any of us would ever be born is incomprehensibly small, depending on such a perfect combination of events that could not have differed except in the most minute ways. The creation of new life is the closest thing to supernatural that most of us are likely to witness. It is certain, in contrast, that all life will eventually come to an end in death.

Private law must respond to life and death, and the complications to which they give rise. Sometimes, the issues are predictable; people die every day, and something must be done with their property. Sometimes, they are not; when a person dies unexpectedly, should their partner be allowed to harvest gametes from their body to conceive a child? As the various chapters of this book demonstrate, life and death cases can provide merely a different context for familiar issues that arise across private law, but they can also raise entirely distinct questions and concerns. The issues are often more intense and personal than their quotidian counterparts, and test the limits of established doctrines and principles.

The purpose of this book is to consider how life and death are relevant in or to private law, whether it deals with them consistently with other disciplines or areas of law, whether life and death offer any distinctive contributions to our understanding of private law and perhaps even whether private law offers any distinctive contributions to our understanding of life and death. In considering these questions, the chapters that make up this collection present a number of recurring themes that we will attempt to draw out and expand upon here.

II. Private Law Values

Life and death, perhaps more than any other subjects, invite us to confront and reflect upon what we truly value. In turn, we can consider the extent to which the same or different values are at the heart of private law. The question of private law's own values is one about which there is a large body of contemporary thought from a variety of theoretical perspectives. One popular theory draws explicitly on the philosophy of Immanuel Kant, appealing to the value of being independent of the choices of others and free to determine one's own ends.[1] An opposing, 'economic' view sees private law as an instrument for achieving efficiency, or wealth maximisation.[2] A third, more diffuse strand rejects both the Kantian and economic approaches. Unlike economic theories, it understands private law as reflecting a distinctive interpersonal morality, but it rejects Kant as advancing too thin a conception of the duties we owe to others in our interactions with them.[3] There is obviously a variety of views about what values might be substituted instead.[4] One possible value, which is prominent in much private law theorising, is autonomy.[5] Although autonomy can be understood in a thin sense as requiring respect for any and all of the choices that a person happens to make, without regard to their content or the context in which they are made, a richer (and more attractive) conception of autonomy gives more significant weight to choices 'that are informed by one's personal beliefs, ethics, values, attitudes and world view, or which have a significant bearing on the way on leads one's life'.[6] The value of autonomy in this 'thick' sense is widely recognised in political philosophy.[7]

It is perhaps unsurprising that economic theories do not feature prominently (if at all) in this book. Quite apart from the relative lack of influence of law and economics outside the United States, matters of life and death are often simply not amenable to economic analysis. They remind us (sometimes happily, sometimes not) that much of what gives life its value and meaning is beyond price and resistant to trade-off within an instrumental calculus.

As Herring argues in Chapter 2, matters of life and death also expose the potential inadequacy of legal and moral theories that focus narrowly on the Kantian values of self-contained individualism and freedom from the will of others. While such theories might (appear to) work for most of our lives,[8] they fail to map reality at its edges, where

[1] See EJ Weinrib, *The Idea of Private Law*, rev edn (Oxford, Oxford University Press, 2012); EJ Weinrib, *Corrective Justice* (Oxford, Oxford University Press, 2012); A Ripstein, *Private Wrongs* (Cambridge, Harvard University Press, 2016); A Beever, *A Theory of Tort Liability* (Oxford, Hart Publishing, 2016). See also A Ripstein, *Force and Freedom: Kant's Legal and Political Philosophy* (Cambridge, Harvard University Press, 2009).

[2] See, eg, RA Posner, *Economic Analysis of Law*, 9th edn (New York, Wolters Kluwer, 2014).

[3] See, eg, H Dagan and A Dorfman, 'Just Relationships' (2016) 116 *Columbia Law Review* 1395.

[4] See, eg, N McBride, *The Humanity of Private Law: Part II: Evaluation* (London, Hart Publishing, 2020).

[5] See, eg, H Dagan and M Heller, *The Choice Theory of Contracts* (Cambridge, Cambridge University Press, 2017); H Dagan, *A Liberal Theory of Property* (Cambridge, Cambridge University Press, 2021). Ripstein suggests that 'autonomy' in the sense described in the text is distinct from Kant's notions of freedom and independence: *Force and Freedom* (n 1) 15.

[6] T Keren-Paz, 'Compensating Injury to Autonomy: A Conceptual and Normative Analysis' in K Barker, K Fairweather and R Grantham (eds), *Private Law in the 21st Century* (London, Hart Publishing, 2017) 413.

[7] See J Raz, *The Morality of Freedom* (Oxford, Clarendon Press, 1986); R Dworkin, *Justice for Hedgehogs* (Cambridge, Belknap Press, 2011), although Dworkin does not refer to it as 'autonomy' as such.

[8] This appearance is misleading. See J Herring, *Law and the Relational Self* (Cambridge, Cambridge University Press, 2020) 30: 'Society has built up a wide range of structures and forms of assistance which disguise our vulnerability. We rely on others and social provision for survival … No one can get up to the second floor of a building without an accommodation. You might need stairs or you might need a lift, but we

the centrality of our relationships and connections with others, indeed our dependence on them, is most explicitly revealed.

Consider Herring's example of the unborn fetus. Legal theories based on the 'individualised self' cannot adequately come to grips with the fetus, seeing it as either separate from or subsumed within the mother, neither perspective capturing the full picture. The preferable legal focus, he suggests, is on the pregnancy *relationship* itself, which should be protected both through criminal and tort law. This relational approach also has profound implications at the other end of life, going to the root of how the law should conceptualise 'death'. Rather than defining death in purely biological terms, Herring argues that a better understanding would focus more on the way in which biological processes affect the nature of our relationships with others. This approach would also emphasise the role and value of those relationships in making any treatment or other decisions on our behalf, as in cases involving children or where capacity has been permanently lost.

This is not to say that a Kantian approach has nothing to add. Freedom and independence represent forceful and compelling values that should rightly feature in any system of private law. In Chapter 4, Broadmore draws on these values to argue that private law should recognise a person's distinct interest in their reproductive autonomy – that is, the freedom to decide whether and with whom to have a child. There is certainly support for this position in the existing law. Although loss of autonomy (without more) is not a standalone harm,[9] private law is arguably moving towards recognising the value of *reproductive* autonomy specifically across 'unplanned birth' cases,[10] including those where a child is conceived after a negligent sterilisation procedure,[11] where a fertility clinic uses incorrect sperm or eggs[12] or where a wrongful injury reduces a person's capacity for reproduction.[13] Broadmore argues that this development is consistent with Kantian principles, given that reproductive choices substantially affect our freedom to determine the shape of our lives and can properly be protected from interference without depriving others of their corresponding freedom. Reproductive choices would likely also be encompassed within a thick conception of autonomy of the kind mentioned earlier, as they reflect values and desires that are central to a person's life. The value of reproductively autonomy could therefore be supported from a variety of moral perspectives.

Broadmore focuses specifically on how this interest in reproductive autonomy should be protected in cases involving reproductive deceit, as where one partner deceives another into sexual intercourse by, for example, lying about their fertility or use of contraception, and a child is conceived. As she explains, courts are currently reluctant

need something to assist us to get up there'. In this light, the emphasis on freedom and independence seems artificial and detached, ignoring the conditions that are necessary to enjoy it.

[9] *ACB v Thomson Medical Pte Ltd* [2017] SCGA 20, [2017] 1 SLR 918, [115]–[124]; *Shaw v Kovac* [2017] EWCA Civ 1028, [2017] 1 WLR 4773, [46]–[84].

[10] S Todd, 'Common Law Protection for Injury to a Person's Reproductive Autonomy' (2019) 135 *LQR* 635. On reproductive autonomy generally, see E Nelson, *Law, Policy and Reproductive Autonomy* (Oxford, Hart Publishing, 2013).

[11] *Rees v Darlington Memorial Hospital NHS Trust* [2003] UKHL 52, [2004] 1 AC 309.

[12] *ACB* (n 9). The loss in *ACB* was characterised as a loss of 'genetic affinity' rather than reproductive autonomy as such, although autonomy was nevertheless an 'important background consideration': at [125].

[13] *XX v Whittington Hospital NHS Trust* [2020] UKSC 14, [2021] AC 275.

to award compensation that goes beyond any physical interference to female claimants resulting from the pregnancy, mainly due to confusion about the appropriate cause of action. In Broadmore's view, recognising reproductive autonomy as a distinct interest opens the way to protecting it through the tort of deceit, rather than through battery or intentional infliction of emotional distress, which do not capture the essence of the harm done in such instances.

There is another, what might be called 'meta-value' at stake in life and death cases, upon which courts rarely need to adjudicate in other contexts, and which is not mentioned in general private law theorising: the value of life itself. The value of life is generally assumed or taken for granted, but must be confronted directly in many cases of the kind discussed in this collection. As Todd highlights in Chapter 5, it can arise in a particularly acute way in unplanned birth cases, where the success of the claim may depend on identifying the existence (birth) of a human being as being either damage itself, or the direct cause of such damage – a parent might claim, for example, that they have suffered loss due to the birth of their child, or a child might claim that they were harmed by their own birth, particularly where they are born with a disability. A fundamental question is whether the birth of the child can itself be regarded as harmful in such cases without undermining the value of human life? Todd gives a simple answer: it cannot. He therefore argues, for example, that parents should not be able to recover the costs of raising their child, whether the 'ordinary' costs or any additional costs arising from some disability suffered by the child. The child must be regarded as a benefit to the parents that outweighs all costs. For the parents or the court to claim otherwise would be 'morally offensive'.[14]

The view that life should be regarded as inherently beneficial is intuitively appealing and accords with prevalent community values. Yet, in other contexts, the value of life is not always paramount. As Barker highlights in Chapter 8, both courts and legislatures now accept that a person's decision to end their own life can be fully informed and autonomous, and should therefore (where these conditions obtain) be free from state interference. This new tolerance for suicide reflects societal permission for a personal judgement that one's own life is sometimes not worth living. In similar vein, Herring refers to the idea of a 'good death' – such as one in the arms of family, in contrast to being wired to a machine in isolation – as potentially having value even at the expense of prolonged life. Some philosophers even question whether life is *ever* valuable, suggesting that life is always harmful to the person whose life it is, and that it is consequently better for them never to be born.[15] At the other end of the lifecycle, there is also significant debate about whether and why death is a harm.[16]

Whatever one's philosophical views, there are valid policy reasons why a court might be reluctant to declare that the birth of a particular child is more harm than good, or

[14] On the other hand, Todd does not necessarily argue that no compensation should be available. For example, he suggests that compensation for loss of reproductive autonomy, or for the physical pain of pregnancy and childbirth, should be available, since it does not go to the value of the child's life as such.

[15] D Benatar, *Better Never to Have Been: The Harm of Coming into Existence* (New York, Oxford University Press, 2006).

[16] See E Gamlund and CT Solberg (eds), *Saving People from the Harm of Death* (Oxford, Oxford University Press, 2019).

that their life is worse than non-existence: it might be understood as conveying, in a very public way, that the child is worthless, unwanted, or unloved. In cases involving disabled children, it might be interpreted as a statement about the worth of disabled people more generally – which (as Todd points out) was the French experience following a successful claim by a disabled child. A similar hesitancy, Herring suggests, is implicit in *Airedale NHS Trust v Bland*,[17] where the court avoided having to decide that life in a persistent vegetative state is not worth living, preferring instead to resolve the case on the less controversial basis that it could not positively conclude that continuing treatment *was* in the patient's interests. All of these instances suggest significant divergence in perceptions of the value of human life, and speak to the frailty of the boundary between public and private.

III. The Public–Private Divide

Life and death are frequently the battleground of various public and private forces. There is, in a sense, nothing more personal than a person's own life and death, but it is never really theirs alone, as far as the public is concerned. The regulation of the creation and cessation of life is never far from the legislative agenda, and has long been a subject on which the church has exerted its influence and authority. At the same time, various human rights instruments attempt, in the modern day, to reclaim a measure of both protection and control for individuals, particularly through rights to life and privacy. Any remaining gaps are filled by the common law courts, which are institutionally attuned to the private interests at stake.

The relationship and tension between public and private law arises in various other ways in the life and death context. In fact, it may be that there is no single public–private dichotomy, but a number of possible distinctions that are made depending on the context and the specific purpose for which the distinction is being made.[18] A law can be described as either public or private based on a variety of factors, such as who creates the law (the legislature or the courts), who enforces it, who it is enforced against, or the values or purposes to which it gives effect. There is nevertheless a group of legal categories that are generally understood as constituting the core of 'private law' and which are regarded as its paradigm instances; tort, contract, and property law are the first examples to come to mind. In terms of the factors mentioned above, these areas of law all contain public and private elements to varying extents. For some, this is not an entirely satisfying conclusion. Perhaps there is some overarching, defining and conclusive factor that we have missed, which can only be brought to our attention by a novel case that goes far beyond our normal expectations?

This is Wall's approach in Chapter 3, where he considers the well-known law enacted by the Texas legislature, often referred to as 'SB-8', which attempts to regulate abortion through private law as a means of avoiding the constitutional hurdles

[17] *Airedale NHS Trust v Bland* [1993] UKHL 17, [1993] AC 789.

[18] See K Barker, 'Private Law: Key Encounters with Public Law' in K Barker and D Jensen (eds), *Private Law: Key Encounters with Public Law* (New York, Cambridge University Press, 2013) 19–25.

(now controversially rescinded) to enforcing it through normal public law mechanisms.[19] The law enables any citizen to commence a civil action against a person who performs or induces an abortion where a fetal heartbeat has been detected (or no attempt is made to detect one), knowingly aids or abets the performance or inducement of such an abortion, or intends to engage in any such conduct. If the action is successful, the court must award statutory damages of not less than $10,000 to the claimant.

It is not a coincidence that this example was generated in the context of decisions about life and death. The intensity of the values and convictions at stake is perhaps the only reason why a legislature would attempt to enact such an extraordinary and unprecedented law. The purpose of Wall's chapter is to vindicate the intuition that SB-8 is nevertheless not *really* private law, or that it is an aberrant instance of it, and that regulating abortion is the task, if at all, of public law. Wall considers a number of possible objections that might come to mind (such as the absence of 'relationality' between the claimant and defendant) but rejects them all as the fundamental explanation of the law's impropriety. The values inherent in SB-8 ground one such objection, which sees those values – particularly our 'shared and mutual concern for the interests of the fetus' – as distinctly public values, which concern the entire community, and which therefore should be enforced on its behalf by a public official through a public law process. These public values, the objection goes, can be contrasted with the narrow set of private values to which private law gives effect, such as freedom and autonomy.

Our discussion in section II suggests that this is not the only possible conception of private law's values. Wall is also sceptical of it, and indeed of any dichotomy between public and private values more generally. He observes that many criminal (public law) wrongs have a private law analogue – battery, trespass to property, and so on – both of which can be understood as directed to protecting the same private values and interests. And much of ordinary private law protects interests in which the community has a shared and mutual concern. The difference between the two areas of law cannot therefore be found in the values that animate them, but rather, Wall suggests, in the ways the respective areas of law relate to those values. Private law responds to and repairs infringements or setbacks to a person's interests, whereas the criminal law responds to *disrespect* for (that is, failure to be sufficiently guided by) those interests. This corresponds to what Wall sees as the fundamental distinction between private and public law: private law protects what people have, while public law limits what they can do. The core objection to SB-8, then, is that it allows a private individual to limit the freedom of other persons, beyond what is necessary to protect the individual's own interests. Such norms are appropriately enforced only by public officials who are guided by and subject to public law norms and standards.

The relative role of the individual and the state in decisions about life and death is also at the core of Barker's discussion in Chapter 8, which considers the nature and extent of the state's duty to take reasonable care to prevent an individual from committing suicide. This issue is bound up with the more general question of when public

[19] See *Dobbs v Jackson Women's Health Organization* 597 US 215 (2022). However, SB-8 remains in force, so it is still a worthy subject of analysis in its own right, not merely as what would otherwise appear to be a contrived hypothetical example.

bodies owe duties of care to individuals to exercise their statutory powers, which is difficult in its own right, but is further complicated in the context of suicide. One reason for this is that the extent of the state's obligation to intervene is inevitably shaped by public attitudes toward the deed itself, which, until recently, was viewed not merely as something that the state committed no wrong in failing to prevent, but as a wrong by the suicide themselves to the state and to God. Tracing the history of English legal and social attitudes to suicide, Barker notes that early tolerance increasingly gave way to a condemnation that peaked in the sixteenth century as a product of Christian influence. Thereafter, public attitudes began to soften, with the issue becoming increasingly 'secularised', and suicide itself eventually being decriminalised in 1961. It was only at this late stage, Barker suggests, that a duty of care on the part of the state to protect its citizens against suicide became a realistic normative possibility.

As Barker explains, there are now several categories of case in which the existence of a duty of care is uncontroversial, such as within professional doctor–patient relationships in the public health system, or where an individual has been taken into state custody. A more difficult question, at the heart of the controversial decision of the High Court of Australia in *Stuart v Kirkland-Veenstra*,[20] is whether a state agent can owe a duty of care to prevent a person from committing suicide where it has a statutory power to detain them which it fails to properly exercise. In that case, the High Court unanimously held that, on the facts in question, the police officers owed no duty of care to either a suicide victim, or his family, in determining whether to exercise their power – a result that Barker considers to be unacceptable where an identified individual is a foreseeable suicide risk.

One of the arguments deployed by the High Court of which Barker is particularly critical appealed to the need for state actors to respect the value of a suicide's personal autonomy – a fundamental value recognised by both the common law and the relevant mental health legislation. As Barker point outs, although a person's decision to end their own life can certainly be the product of rational and informed deliberation, the empirical evidence suggests that up to 90 per cent of those who attempt suicide are in fact affected by some mental or behavioural disorder, or by a psychosocial risk factor, and may therefore not be fully 'autonomous' (particularly in the thick sense described earlier).[21] This being the case, state duties to take reasonable care in the use of its intervention powers (which are clearly premised on the recognition that freedom of choice can be undermined by mental incapacity), while potentially impinging on a person's choices in a particular moment, actually promote their autonomy at a deeper level.

In this way, Barker's chapter highlights the immensely difficult relationship between autonomy, suicide, and state power. A person's decision to end their own life can be an important expression of their autonomy (and dignity, on which see section VIII below), but it can also be the most potent way of undermining it – after all, in death, there is no more autonomy to be had. Left to our own devices, humans are prone to a variety of cognitive biases, deficits, and errors that prevent us from properly assessing information

[20] *Stuart v Kirkland-Veenstra* [2009] HCA 15, (2009) 237 CLR 215.

[21] See also J Herring, *The Right to be Protected from Committing Suicide* (Oxford, Oxford University Press, 2022) chs 3–5.

and making decisions that give best effect to our values.[22] Many of the autonomy-inhibiting risk factors, such as mental health conditions and social inequality, are ones that individuals also cannot eliminate on their own, or cannot manage without the assistance of public welfare programmes. In this light, then, there is much to be said for the role of the state in suicide prevention, not as a burden on autonomy, but as a proper means of enhancing it.[23]

A final, much more literal sense in which life and death cases cross the public–private boundary is in bringing private life into the public domain. At its core, each type of private law dispute addressed in this collection is a 'highly individualised [experience] within a collective setting'.[24] As Broadmore notes, for example, reproductive deceit claims arise in the context of the intensely intimate experience that is the creation of new life by way of sexual intercourse, and the burial disputes discussed by both Conway and Falconer (see section VI below) can involve the very public airing of very private dirty laundry. Any women who wanted, and perhaps even sought, abortions in the face of SB-8 experienced what were likely some of the most desperately personal moments of their lives in the harsh knowledge of potential public outing. And *Stuart v Kirkland-Veenstra*, under its legal covering, is really just another sad story of a family grappling with the grief and loss of suicide. In these, and other, ways, the unique nature of each conception, pregnancy, birth, life and death presents a set of facts, and in many cases, a species of pain, specific to the individuals at the heart of the dispute. At the same time, each dispute, private in content as well as in legal nature, becomes public when brought to law.

IV. Biological and Legal Personhood

Any book about life and death will inevitably give rise to questions about the meaning and definition of those concepts.[25] At times, the meaning ascribed to life and death within (private) law aligns with the definitions provided by other disciplines. In deciding when death occurs, for example, Herring observes that law is generally content to defer to medicine. In the UK, which is Herring's focus, death occurs when there is an irreversible loss of brain stem function.[26] In Australia, there is a slightly different test, according to which death occurs when there is either an irreversible cessation of blood circulation or of all brain (as opposed to brain stem) function.[27] Both definitions nevertheless reflect widespread medical opinion and practice in their respective jurisdictions.

In other areas, however, the medical and legal (and indeed social) conceptions of life and death seem to come apart. An example is the so-called 'born alive' rule, which is

[22] S Conly, *Against Autonomy: Justifying Coercive Paternalism* (Cambridge, Cambridge University Press, 2012). For another argument against the paramount value of autonomy, see C Foster, *Choosing Life, Choosing Death: The Tyranny of Autonomy in Medical Ethics and Law* (Oxford, Hart Publishing, 2009).

[23] See Herring's powerful conclusion to this effect: *The Right to be Protected* (n 21) ch 10.

[24] Conway, ch 10 of this volume.

[25] For a comprehensive discussion of this issue in the legal context, see EP Foley, *The Law of Life and Death* (Cambridge, Harvard University Press, 2011).

[26] See, eg, *Bland* (n 17).

[27] See, eg, Human Tissue Act 1983 (NSW) s 33.

mentioned in several chapters throughout the book, according to which 'a foetus enjoys, while still a foetus, no independent legal personality'.[28] This rule has a number of legal consequences; for example, a wrong to an unborn child is not actionable in tort, unless the child is subsequently born alive.[29] A fetus has no right to prevent its mother from terminating the pregnancy.[30] No claim is available to the parents of an unborn child under the Fatal Accidents Act 1976 (UK).[31] And in the criminal law, no liability arises for killing an unborn child, unless there is a specific offence to that effect.[32]

As Spigelman CJ noted in *R v Iby*,[33] the born alive rule can be traced to the early seventeenth century.[34] It is based on what he describes as 'two anachronistic, indeed antiquated, factors'.[35] The first is that, based on the 'primitive state of medical knowledge' at the time, it was difficult to prove that a fetus was alive (or alive at a particular moment) before its birth, or that a particular event caused its death.[36] The second is that the rate of stillbirth due to natural causes was much higher than it is today.[37] Spigelman CJ suggests that there may be a 'strong case' for abandoning it (given the significant advances in both medicine and technology),[38] but until it is reformed, its consequence is that the legal definitions of life and death appear not to align: the law considers a fetus not to be 'alive' despite it not satisfying the requirements for it to be considered 'dead' – and indeed despite it demonstrating many other indicia to be recognised, both biologically and socially, as alive (such as movement, response to touch and the voice of loved ones, etc). Spigelman CJ's suggestion that, in contrast to its approach to death, the law 'adopts an artificial and non-scientific standard of when life begins, that is, after delivery', is therefore understandable.[39]

With that said, the content of any definition is inevitably influenced by the purpose for which that definition is being formulated. Seen in this way, the divergence between the medical and legal definitions of life is less stark, or at least more explicable. In the case of death, medicine and law are generally using the definition to answer the

[28] *Burton v Islington Health Authority* [1993] QB 204 (CA) 226.

[29] Congenital Disabilities (Civil Liability) Act 1976 (UK). See also *Montreal Tramways Co v Léveillé* [1933] SCR 456; *Watt v Rama* [1972] VR 353; *Burton* (n 28).

[30] *Paton v British Pregnancy Advisory Service Trustees* [1979] QB 276 (QB); *Attorney-General (Qld); Ex rel Kerr v T* (1983) 46 ALR 275 (HCA).

[31] Although some US states take a different approach: see Foley (n 25) 29–30. In a recent high-profile case, the Supreme Court of Alabama decided that its Wrongful Death of a Minor Act 1872 (see AL Code § 6-5-391) extended even to frozen embryos: *LePage v Center for Reproductive Medicine, PC* (Supreme Court of Alabama, 16 February 2024).

[32] *Attorney-General's Reference (No 3 of 1994)* [1998] AC 245 (HL) 254 (Lord Mustill). Specific offences were created in New South Wales in 2021 for causing the loss of a fetus: Crimes Legislation Amendment (Loss of Foetus) Act 2021 (NSW).

[33] *R v Iby* [2005] NSWCCA 178, (2005) 65 NSWLR 278. See also CD Forsythe, 'Homicide of the Unborn Child: The Born Alive Rule and Other Legal Anachronisms' (1987) 21 *Valparaiso University Law Review* 563.

[34] *Iby* (n 33) [25].

[35] ibid [32].

[36] ibid [33]–[36].

[37] ibid [37]–[39].

[38] ibid [63]. Cf K Savell, 'Is the "Born Alive" Rule Outdated and Indefensible?' (2006) 28 *Sydney Law Review* 625. On the impact of other technological developments, see EC Romanis, 'Challenging the "Born Alive" Threshold: Fetal Surgery, Artificial Wombs, and the English Approach to Legal Personhood' (2019) 28 *Medical Law Review* 93. Similar difficulties may arise in defining death: see K Falconer, 'Cryopreservation and the Death of Legal Personhood' (2023) *Mortality* (forthcoming).

[39] *Iby* (n 33) [74].

same questions – for example, when medical treatment can be discontinued, or organs removed from a body. These purposes are confined and, speaking broadly, uncontentious in the minds of both doctors and lawyers, allowing for an easy alignment of the medical and legal. The definition of life, on the other hand, is of (perhaps more frequent) concern to both doctors and lawyers, but in potentially very different contexts. A definition whose purpose is to determine whether a medical professional should, as a matter of medical practice or ethics, provide care or treatment for an unborn fetus is likely to have very different content, for example, to one whose purpose is to determine whether a fetus is capable of bringing a legal action for negligence. The definition might differ further still in the context of whether to impose criminal liability for murdering a fetus (which would undoubtedly be complicated by its perceived moral implications for the regulation of abortion), or whether a child *en ventre sa mère* should be treated as living for the purpose of a testamentary gift.[40] Perhaps what this shows is that a single legal definition of 'life' is impossible, given the different moral purposes to which the definition is put in different medico–legal contexts.[41]

Indeed, it is not even clear that the born alive rule is or purports to be a definition of 'life' at all. In requiring the fetus to be 'alive' at the time of birth, the rule presupposes a conception of life that the rule does not itself specify. As Spigelman CJ observed, '[t]he case law does not suggest that there is a common law definition of what constitutes "life" for the purpose of the born alive rule'.[42] The rule is perhaps better understood, then, not as a definition of life, but as a test of legal personhood – of when a person becomes *legally* alive, rather than biologically. It therefore cannot be criticised simply because it does not align with medical or biological definitions of life, since they are not necessarily what it is trying to capture.

In broad terms, 'legal personhood' is 'a boundary, identifying … entities (for lack of a better word) capable of holding rights, owing duties, and entering into legal relations with others'.[43] There are a range of views about which entities should be recognised as legal persons, which Naffine suggests can be broadly classified as either 'legalist' or 'realist'.[44] According to realism, the recognition of legal personhood should be based on some defining attribute of the subject on which it is conferred, which might be the subject's rationality, sentience, divine sanctity or something else.[45] On this approach, the law 'finds its subject beyond the legal realm and … is to be judged by its success at finding and rendering this subject faithfully'.[46] The view that legal personhood should align with biological personhood (the boundaries of which are biological life and death) would be an example of realism.

[40] See *Burton* (n 28) 227: 'where there is a gift to a class of children living at a particular date, a child en ventre sa mère at that date but later born alive will be treated as having been living at the date and thus included in the class'. This is an example of 'the English courts [having] adopted as part of English law the maxim of the civil law that an unborn child shall be deemed to be born whenever its interests require it': at 226.

[41] See generally Foley (n 25) ch 1. See also P Stewart and A Stuhmcke, 'Legal Pragmatism and the Pre-Birth Continuum: An Absence of Unifying Principle' (2007) 15 *Journal of Law and Medicine* 272.

[42] *Iby* (n 33) [40].

[43] Falconer (n 38) 3.

[44] N Naffine, *Law's Meaning of Life: Philosophy, Religion, Darwin, and the Legal Person* (London, Hart Publishing, 2009) ch 2.

[45] ibid 22–24.

[46] ibid 22.

In contrast, according to legalism, 'the concept of the person is internal to law and essentially a matter of formal legal definition', 'an artificial legal device created for legal purposes'.[47] In his recent book, Kurki favours a legalist view, arguing that

> legal personhood is not an intrinsic attribute of an entity; rather, a necessary condition for the legal personhood of any entity is that that entity is treated as a legal person by the prevailing legal system. Whether or not X is a legal person is thus an *institutional fact*.[48]

This is the only way, he points out, to account for the existence of 'artificial' legal persons such as corporations. Others have relied on this kind of legalism to argue for the legal personhood of animals, trees, rivers and other non-human entities, as a basis for conferring a variety of private rights on them.[49]

According to Kurki, legal personhood is best understood as a cluster property with various 'interconnected but disseverable' incidents, which can be possessed by a certain entity to a greater or lesser degree.[50] These incidents include protection of the entity's liberty and bodily integrity, its capacity to own property, its standing to enforce legal rights, its victim status in criminal law, its legal responsibility for its actions, and so on.[51] Recognising one or more of these incidents would not constrain the law into recognising them all.[52] Kurki describes this approach as a 'bundle theory' of legal personhood, highlighting its similarity to bundle-of-rights theories of property ownership.

On this approach, there is no conceptual reason why legal personhood cannot be possessed by biological non-persons, or on the other hand, why it must be possessed by all biological persons. Herring argues, for example, that restrictions on the legal personhood of fetuses can be supported on his relational approach, given the difference in the nature of their relationships with others before and after their birth. And even if an entity were recognised as possessing legal personhood in one respect, it does not follow that they must be recognised as a legal person in other respects as well. The only question is whether it is appropriate for that particular incident of legal personhood to be recognised in relation to that entity.

At the same time, there are several notable examples throughout history of legal personhood, or certain incidents of it, being denied to biological persons. It is striking how often the metaphor of death is invoked to describe their status. Persons held under conditions of slavery held very limited legal rights and in Kurki's view are rightly called legal non-persons, for example.[53] An attainted person, convicted of a capital felony or treason, also 'was deprived of status as a person'; their property was liable to forfeiture to the Crown, their land could not be transmitted to heirs, and their legal right to sue was extinguished, an incident described as 'civil death'.[54] As Gibbs J put it, 'it was as though he had in fact suffered the penalty of death which had been imposed on him'.[55]

[47] ibid.
[48] VAJ Kurki, *A Theory of Legal Personhood* (Oxford, Oxford University Press, 2019) 93.
[49] CD Stone, *Should Trees Have Standing?: Law, Morality, and the Environment* (Oxford, Oxford University Press, 2010). Kurki argues that animals, but not non-sentient natural objects, can be legal persons: (n 48) ch 4.
[50] Kurki (n 48) ch 3.
[51] ibid.
[52] ibid 197.
[53] Kurki (n 48) 121: 'The number of incidents [slaves] were endowed with was simply too limited to warrant classifying them as legal persons *tout court*'.
[54] *Dugan v Mirror Newspapers Ltd* (1978) 142 CLR 583, 609–10 (Murphy J).
[55] ibid 588.

Another clear example is coverture, which is the subject of Wright's Chapter 7. Wright sets out in detail what this form of 'legal death' looked like in reality for many married women, the attenuation of which only began in the second half of the nineteenth century. According to Blackstone:

> By marriage, the husband and wife are one person in law: that is, the very being or legal existence of the woman is suspended during the marriage, or at least is incorporated and consolidated into that of the husband: under whose wing, protection, and *cover*, she performs every thing; and is therefore called in our law-french a *feme-covert*; is said to be *covert-baron*, or under the protection and influence of her husband, her *baron*, or lord; and her condition during her marriage is called her *coverture*.[56]

A number of consequences followed from this 'condition', some of the most significant being that the woman's personal property vested in her husband,[57] and that she could not sue (except in ecclesiastical courts) without her husband's consent.[58] In return, the husband was bound to provide his wife with necessaries such as food and shelter.[59] As this indicates, the woman did not lose *all* incidents of legal personhood: 'But, though our law in general considers man and wife as one person, yet there are some instances in which she is separately considered'.[60] Like slaves, women could still be indicted and punished separately in criminal prosecutions, for example.[61]

Coverture rendered the married women held under its supposedly protective wing, in Wright's terms, 'legally extinct'; the removal of the incidents of legal personhood placed them in a liminal state that rendered them biologically alive but, in nearly all circumstances, legally dead. As Wright demonstrates, making powerful use of women's stories, often drawn directly from the court records, this liminal space was one of dependency, vulnerability and exploitation, within which women were routinely taken advantage of by their husbands and others. Many women were unable to sue for wrongs done to them, had difficulty securing credit or, if they did succeed in making a life of their own, saw their hard-earned financial gains claimed by their husband. The control of a husband over his wife extended beyond her financial resources, however, to include her children, domicile and body. As the first-hand accounts marshalled by Wright illustrate, this physical control extended to the power to have an intransigent wife committed to an asylum, a threat that could be realised with scarce little provocation.

The message of Wright's chapter is that, while the incidents of legal personhood *can* be taken away from living persons, they should not be, unless there are clear reasons for doing so and sufficient protections are put in place. In this sense, the realist perspective mentioned earlier does capture an important insight: legal personhood is an important marker and protection of the value of the actual entities on which it is conferred.[62]

[56] 1 Bl Comm 430.

[57] 2 Bl Comm 433.

[58] 1 Bl Comm 431. As an exception, Blackstone referred to another example of a living person losing legal personhood: 'where the husband has abjured the realm or is banished … he is dead in law': at 431. In such cases, the woman could sue without her husband's concurrence.

[59] ibid 430.

[60] ibid 432.

[61] ibid 431.

[62] See also Kurki (n 48) 194–95.

The denial of legal personhood to slaves and attained felons can be understood as an expression of their (perceived) inferiority or worthlessness. As the example of coverture shows, however, even where such an expression is not intended (we might charitably presume), the consequences are just as real, entailing the loss of identity and agency in the legal world, as well as dignity and autonomy in the social one.

V. Rights and Non-Living Persons

As we saw above, legal personhood is closely tied to the concept of rights – having them, enjoying them, enforcing them. On a legalist approach to personhood, there is no reason why these rights must be limited to living persons. The question of whether non-living persons – be they pre-life or post-death – are even *capable* of holding rights, and if so, whether such rights should be legally recognised, is therefore one of both doctrinal and practical significance.

The idea that the dead might be capable of holding rights sits well with disciplines outside law. Indeed, the ongoing presence and ongoing power of the dead in the lives of the living is acknowledged across the social sciences. In his cultural history of death, for example, Thomas Laqueur refers to the dead as 'social beings' who 'creat[e], recreat[e], [represent and disrupt] the social order of which they had been a part'.[63] Their ability to do this work is premised on the fact that the dead live on, at least socially, following their biological death. In Chapter 12, following Laqueur, Falconer demonstrates the power of the dead to ensure that their wishes regarding the disposal of their body are complied with, and even to 'demand' the living to take litigation on their behalf. If we take a socio-legal approach to private law, then, and accept the hold of our ongoing relationships with the dead, and their power over us, we might be willing to accept the dead as having significant legal rights already.

Whether we should formally recognise the dead as holding legal rights (in a traditional sense) is more controversial. In *R v Stewart*, for example, Lord Denman CJ referred to the established rule of English ecclesiastical law that '[e]very person dying in this country … has a right to Christian burial' in their local parish churchyard,[64] and their simultaneous right to be taken to that churchyard in an appropriately dignified way.[65] Yet other judges have had no patience with this description; rejecting an understanding of the deceased as rights-bearer, Stephens J suggested that 'the Court speaks of "rights" of a dead body, which is obviously a popular form of expression – a corpse not being capable of rights'.[66]

This reluctance to view the dead as rights-holding entities is the subject of Fell's contribution in Chapter 6. He argues that, on several prominent theories of rights, it is in fact possible for the dead to have rights – they can have interests that justify

[63] TW Laqueur, *The Work of the Dead: A Cultural History of Mortal Remains* (Princeton, Princeton University Press, 2015) 10.
[64] See *R v Stewart* (1840) 12 Ad & E 773, 777–78; 113 ER 1007, 1009.
[65] ibid. See also *Gilbert v Buzzard* (1820) 3 Phil Ecc 335; 161 ER 1342.
[66] *R v Price* (1884) 12 QBD 247, 253 (Stephens J).

imposing duties on others, and can have the power to waive or enforce those duties exercised on their behalf by a representative. The question of whether the dead have interests that are capable of being harmed has been debated for millennia. Although some philosophers suggest that such interests are impossible because the dead cannot have subjective experiences, most accept that a person can be benefited or harmed even if they do not experience it; no one wants their colleagues to ridicule them behind their back, for example. A more formidable obstacle is the argument that a person must currently exist in order to have interests, but Fell concludes that there is no convincing reason for this requirement, and that a person can have interests that continue after their death.

This does not mean that the dead have the same interests as living persons; for example, the dead cannot feel pain (at least on the Western, rationalist view),[67] and have no interest in avoiding it. There are nevertheless some interests that can continue post-death, including a person's interests in the satisfaction of the goals and desires that they formed during their life, and in their dignity. Fell argues that private law already protects these interests in a variety of ways – for example, by enforcing the deceased's wishes in relation to who receives their property, enforcing their contractual rights (at least, those that are not frustrated by their death), their moral rights as authors of copyright works, their right to the confidentiality of private information, and their right to bodily integrity. One exception is their interest in their reputation – the tort of defamation is generally held not to extend to defamatory statements about a person after their death. Fell argues that this rule is anomalous, and that the deceased's continuing interest in dignity justifies restraining even post-death defamation.

There is also emerging acknowledgement of the rights of those persons who do not yet exist but may come into being in the future. The literature on the rights of future persons or generations is large, particularly in the human rights and environment context.[68] Their status is somewhat controversial, since they are not generally given explicit legal protection in human rights instruments or elsewhere. Their existence was nevertheless asserted in the recent *Maastricht Principles on the Human Rights of Future Generations*, which were developed and endorsed by a number of legal academics and stakeholders.[69] The specific rights that were recognised include, but are not limited to, rights to the protection of the environment and natural resources against depletion, pollution and degradation, particularly to the extent that it is caused by anthropogenic climate change.

[67] This view is both a local (to the Global North) and recent understanding of the dead, and one that is not shared by many cultures around the globe. The same is arguably true of the view, mentioned in the text below, that the reputation of the dead is not worthy of continuing protection. We return to the theme of cultural divergence in section VII below.

[68] See, eg, L Westra, *Environmental Justice and the Rights of the Unborn and Future Generations: Law, Environmental Harm and the Right to Health* (London, Routledge, 2006); RP Hiskes, *The Human Right to a Green Future: Environmental Rights and Intergenerational Justice* (New York, Cambridge University Press, 2008); J Thompson, *Intergenerational Justice: Rights and Responsibilities in an Intergenerational Polity* (New York, Routledge, 2009); M Düwell, G Bos, and N van Steenbergen (eds), *Towards the Ethics of a Green Future: The Theory and Practice of Human Rights for Future People* (London, Routledge, 2018); SM Gardiner (ed), *The Oxford Handbook of Intergenerational Ethics* (Oxford, Oxford University Press, forthcoming).

[69] *Maastricht Principles on the Human Rights of Future Generations* (3 February 2023) www.rightsoffuture-generations.org/home.

While this might appear to be a public law development (in that human rights provisions bind states, not individuals) the analogy between human rights and private law rights is strong, not least because human rights law protects a core range of fundamental, private interests, as well as political and social rights.[70] In any case, the rights of future persons arguably receive some recognition and protection already in more traditional private law domains. For example, a child can sue for damage caused by conduct that occurred before they were born (or even conceived). In *Burton v Islington Health Authority*, Dillon LJ gave the example of a negligently manufactured drug, which the child later consumes.[71] The fact that the child did not exist when the negligence occurred would be no defence. In the law of trusts, a trust can only be terminated or varied with the consent of unborn future beneficiaries, which may be given by the court on their behalf if this is in their interests.[72] A court can also appoint a person to represent the interests of an unborn person in litigation in certain scenarios.[73] The court would arguably have inherent jurisdiction to make similar orders in cases not covered by the statute.[74]

In these (and perhaps other) ways, the law already imposes various duties that protect the interests of future persons, and allows those duties to be enforced on their behalf by a representative. To this extent, it is arguable that those future persons can be described as having corresponding 'rights'. There is nevertheless an important feature of these duties that distinguishes them from any duties that we owe to the dead: they are fundamentally still duties owed to living persons, in that their purpose is to protect the interests of living persons. Although the persons whose interests are being protected are currently non-living, it is their interests as future *living* persons that are being protected. This is different to our duties to the dead, which protect the interests of non-living (and, at least for now, never again to be living) dead persons. In this sense, at least, the notion of duties owed to future persons is far less radical and challenging to our thinking on legal rights, and on life and death more generally.[75]

Duties to future persons nevertheless give rise to an entirely separate philosophical conundrum, which Parfit (who first identified the issue and discussed it at length) labelled the 'non-identity problem'.[76] The non-identity problem arises from the fact that our present actions can change the identity of the people who will exist in the future, in combination with our ordinary conception of harm, according to which a person is harmed only if they are made worse off than they otherwise would have been. Accordingly, if, by some ostensibly harmful conduct, we cause a person to exist who would otherwise not have existed, it seems to follow that the conduct cannot actually have harmed them (assuming that their life is still worth living overall).

[70] Varuhas argues that human rights are more analogous to private law rights than public law rights: J Varuhas, *Damages and Human Rights* (London, Hart Publishing, 2016) ch 4.

[71] *Burton* (n 28) 225–26.

[72] See, eg, Variation of Trusts Act 1958 (UK) s 1.

[73] See, eg, The Civil Procedure Rules 1998, SI 1998/3132 (UK) r 19.9.

[74] On the inherent jurisdiction of courts to regulate their procedures, see *Al Rawi v Security Service* [2011] UKSC 34, [2012] 1 AC 531.

[75] On the other hand, the reverse argument might also be made, given the greater social existence and power of the dead (who so recently *were*, and in many respects still are), compared to that of future persons, who might never come into being.

[76] See D Parfit, *Reasons and Persons* (Oxford, Oxford University Press, 1986) chs 16–19.

This argument applies in a surprising number of practical scenarios. Parfit gives the well-known example of a young teenage girl who wants to conceive a child.[77] Most people would intuitively suggest that she should wait until she is older, when she would be better able to care for the child, since this would be in the child's interests. But if she waits, the child that she eventually conceives will be a different child.[78] So, if she does conceive now, the child would not be worse off than it otherwise would be, because it would otherwise not exist. On our ordinary conception of harm, the child is therefore not harmed; if anything, the mother has benefited the child by causing it to exist. The same reasoning could apply to cases of reproductive deceit, drawing from Broadmore's discussion. Most readers would suggest that a person should wait until their partner is willing to become a parent before conceiving, as having two consenting parents (rather than one willing and one deceived parent) would be in the child's interests. Again, however, the child would not exist if the parents were to wait, so it seems to follow that any reproductive deceit does not harm the child.

These are moral, rather than legal examples, since legal duties of care owed by parents to their unborn children have generally not been recognised (outside the context of negligent driving causing injury to an existing fetus).[79] The non-identity problem is nevertheless relevant in a variety of private law contexts.[80] As mentioned earlier, it has been argued that we owe legal duties of care to future generations to take measures to limit the harmful effects of climate change.[81] But if we take such measures, this would very likely change the identity of the people who will exist in the future. It would lead to the existence of different modes of transportation and different employment opportunities, which would lead people to live in, and travel to, different locations, which would in turn lead them to meet different people at different times, and therefore to conceive different children. It therefore appears that, if we take no preventative measures, no future person would be harmed, because those people would, in all likelihood, not otherwise exist. This would rule out liability on ordinary private law principles. Similarly, extrapolating from Todd's arguments, it could be argued that a doctor owes a duty to a patient's future child to advise the patient to wait a minimum amount of time (likely several weeks) between receiving a rubella vaccine and conceiving a child, to prevent the child from becoming infected by rubella. However, waiting this period would almost certainly result in a different child being conceived, and subsequently born, such that the doctor would appear to cause no harm to the child by failing to give this advice, for the reasons given above. This conclusion is intuitively unsatisfying.

It is not possible here to provide a definitive solution to such a widely debated philosophical puzzle, but a few points can be made. The first is that, even if we accept the conclusions mentioned above, this would not rule out the possibility of duties to future persons entirely, since not all duties relevantly cause different people to exist when they

[77] ibid 358.

[78] Since it would almost certainly be the product of a different sperm–egg combination.

[79] Congenital Disabilities (Civil Liability) Act 1976 (UK) s 2. See also R Scott, *Rights, Duties and the Body: Law and Ethics of the Maternal–Fetal Conflict* (London, Hart Publishing, 2002) ch 6.

[80] Similar examples to those in the text are mentioned in D Boonin, *The Non-Identity Problem and the Ethics of Future People* (New York, Oxford University Press, 2014) ch 1.

[81] Although the existence of such duties has been rejected by some courts, for a variety of reasons: see, eg, *Minister for the Environment v Sharma* (2022) 291 FCR 311.

are performed. To use another of Parfit's examples, suppose that I leave broken glass exposed in the undergrowth of a wood instead of safely burying it, wounding a child a hundred years later.[82] While my actions might change which child I will later conceive, they more likely than not would not affect the identity of the injured child, who we can therefore conclude was harmed by my actions. Similarly, it is unlikely that taking reasonable care when manufacturing medicine for children would cause an entirely different set of children to exist, although it would have some coincidental effects.

Even where the non-identity problem does arise, it might be possible to reject the (seemingly implausible) conclusions it requires. There are several possible ways of doing this,[83] but the most straightforward for present purposes is to reject the conception of harm on which it is based, which assumes that a person is harmed only if they are made worse off by some action than they would otherwise have been, which they cannot be if the action causes them to exist. Parfit himself rejects this account of harm, arguing that 'most harms are intrinsic' rather than 'comparative' – '[t]he badness of these harms does not consistent in their being in some way worse than some alternatives'.[84] In his view, for example, 50 years of intense suffering is intrinsically bad, regardless of what alternatives were available. A life of such suffering might be worse than non-existence, but this relative worseness is not what makes it bad; the suffering is bad in itself.[85] Similarly, 50 years of suffering is still bad, even if the alternative is one hundred years of suffering.

Understanding the concept of harm (or damage or loss) in this way would allow for private law liability in the cases mentioned earlier. Even if a person would not exist if measures were taken to prevent climate change, for example, this would not mean that the consequences suffered if such measures were not taken (arising from extreme heat, flooding, etc) were any less harmful. Of course, more would be needed to defend this kind of non-comparative account of harm than is possible here, but it shows that the obstacles to recognising duties to future persons may not be insurmountable.

VI. The Physical Corpse

The human body is notoriously leaky, and as a result, the coming into life and the going out of it are messy matters. The dead leave much behind them, and whilst various legal processes begin almost immediately once a death occurs to manage the deceased's material belongings, death also leaves behind a very real physical body that requires a very real and pragmatic response. Simply put, the corpse must be dealt with.

The normative power of the physical corpse is an essential theme in the field of death studies. Scholars writing in this area have noted the various meanings that can attach to a dead body – as a conveyer of disease and decay, a reminder of our own

[82] Parfit (n 76) 356.

[83] As Boonin points out, the argument that leads to the apparently implausible conclusions mentioned above has a number of distinct premises, each of which one might attempt to reject: (n 80) chs 2–6. Boonin himself nevertheless accepts all of those premises and the conclusions to which they give rise: see ch 7.

[84] D Parfit, 'Future People, the Non-Identity Problem, and Person-Affecting Principles' (2017) 45 *Philosophy and Public Affairs* 118, 133.

[85] ibid 132–33.

mortality or the symbol of a specific loss. In Chapter 12, Falconer draws on this literature to reveal the power of the corpse in private law. In her discussion of the decision in *Oldham Metropolitan BC v Makin*,[86] for example, she examines the fear and anger espoused by several local authorities in England at the possibility that the executor of Ian Stewart-Brady (the notorious Moors murderer) would dispose of his body within their jurisdictional boundaries. Identifying the ability of this particular corpse to negatively affect the living, the court effectively treated Stewart-Brady's body as a form of 'toxic necro-waste' and used its disposal as a means to decimate his ongoing social existence. In doing so, the court took the rare step of explicitly stating how the body was to be disposed of – after hours in a spare cremator that was to be deep-cleaned after use, his ashes to be scattered at sea with none beyond those necessary to be present – showing how the bodies of the 'difficult dead' can require extraordinary legal responses.

Even a conventional corpse can create tension in the law, however. Private law in particular has struggled to contain the corpse within a taxonomic legal boundary. As mentioned earlier, some courts have been willing to the accept that the dead can hold enforceable rights. Yet, the unavoidable physicality and materiality of the corpse may suggest to others that, rather than 'right-holder' or 'legal person', the more appropriate label to attach to a dead body is 'property'. The extent to which a body, or any part thereof, is (or should be) capable of being the subject of property rights is not discussed in detail in this book, since it has been covered exhaustively elsewhere.[87] For present purposes, it is sufficient to note the fundamental principle that the body (or material derived from the body) of the deceased is not capable of being the subject of property rights.[88] A small number of exceptions have nevertheless developed to this 'no property' rule, the most well-known of which was formulated by Griffith CJ in *Doodeward v Spence*:

> [W]hen a person has by the lawful exercise of work or skill so dealt with a human body or part of a human body in his lawful possession that it has acquired some attributes differentiating it from a mere corpse awaiting burial, he acquires a right to retain possession of it, at least as against any person not entitled to have it delivered to him for the purpose of burial, but subject of course, to any positive law which forbids its retention under the particular circumstances.[89]

This 'work or skill' exception leaves much unanswered: how much work or skill is needed to turn the body into property? Is the identity or intention of the person performing the work or skill relevant? Just how different does the end result need to be from an 'unworked' dead body to enliven the exception? This uncertainty has led to calls for the exception to be abolished altogether.[90]

[86] *Oldham Metropolitan BC v Makin* [2017] EWHC 2543 (Ch), [2018] Ch 543.

[87] See, eg, R Hardcastle, *Law and the Human Body: Property Rights, Ownership and Control* (London, Hart Publishing, 2007); I Goold et al (eds), *Persons, Parts and Property: How Should We Regulate Human Tissue in the 21st Century?* (London, Hart Publishing, 2014); J Wall, *Being and Owning: The Body, Bodily Material, and the Law* (Oxford, Oxford University Press, 2015).

[88] *Williams v Williams* (1882) 20 Ch D 659, 662–63.

[89] *Doodeward v Spence* [1908] HCA 45, (1908) 6 CLR 406, 414.

[90] See, eg, K Falconer, 'Dismantling *Doodeward*: Guided Discretion as the Superior Basis for Property Rights in Human Biological Material' (2019) 42 *University of New South Wales Law Journal* 899, especially at 924–26.

Apart from the work or skill exception,[91] however, the general rule remains that a person has no property in their own body, from which 'it follows' (as a little-known, but much-criticised, byproduct)[92] that they cannot dispose of it by will,[93] or direct how it must be buried, although a small number of statutes allow otherwise in specific cases.[94] Instead, the power to decide by what method a body will be disposed of is in the hands of the living. Private law recognises that certain persons hold a right to possession of the body for this purpose, which (as Griffiths CJ recognised in *Doodeward*) has priority over any property rights in the body obtained through work or skill, and confers on the right-holder the legal ability (and a corresponding duty) to dispose of the body in the manner of their choosing. Disputes can arise, however, about who holds the right to possession in a particular case, which are generally referred to as 'burial disputes'. The basic legal framework for the resolution of such disputes is relatively fixed, even if controversial in some respects. In the first instance, the right to possession is vested in the deceased's named executor to the exclusion of all others.[95] Where no executor is named, the court will turn next to the person with the highest right to administer the estate.[96] In either case, however, a variety of other factors may also be relevant, especially where the respective claimants have an equal right to administration.[97]

In Chapter 10, Conway offers a fresh perspective on burial disputes, identifying what the law's purposes should be in such cases and how those purposes can best be achieved. As she explains, burial disputes can be especially challenging for courts, for two reasons. The first is that they are time-sensitive, given the biological realities of decay and decomposition that flow from the physicality of the corpse, but also because of the need to respect the deceased by ensuring that burial occurs as quickly as possible without long periods of storage. The second is that such disputes are often emotionally charged. The competing parties are generally close family members of the deceased, who have equally strong views about how the deceased's body should be dealt with. Their feelings of grief and upheaval can reopen old wounds. The decision of the court can easily inflame the

See also *Yearworth v North Bristol NHS Trust* [2009] EWCA Civ 37, [2010] QB 1 [45](d) (rejecting the work or skill principle as 'not entirely logical').

[91] A possible further exception was recognised in *Yearworth* (n 90), although in relation to material from a *living* person. The court held that ownership attaches to 'products of a living human body intended for use by the persons whose bodies have generated them': see [45](b). On this basis, several men were held to be the owners of sperm they had produced and which was being stored for the purpose of enabling them to conceive children in the future.

[92] See, eg, S McGuinness and M Brazier, 'Respecting the Living Means Respecting the Dead Too' (2008) 28 *Oxford Journal of Legal Studies* 297; H Conway, 'Burial Instructions and the Governance of Death' (2012) 12 *Oxford University Commonwealth Law Journal* 59; RN Nwabueze, 'Legal Control of Burial Rights' (2013) 2 *Cambridge Journal of International and Comparative Law* 196; TL Muinzer, 'The Law of the Dead: A Critical Review of Burial Law, with a View to its Development' (2014) 34 *Oxford Journal of Legal Studies* 791; H Conway, *The Law and the Dead* (Abingdon, Routledge, 2016) ch 5; R Croucher, 'Families in Conflict over Their Dead' in I Freckelton and K Peterson (eds), *Tensions and Traumas in Health Law* (Annandale, Federation Press, 2017) 551. See also Victorian Law Reform Commission, *Funeral and Burial Instructions* (Report, 2016) 48.

[93] *Williams* (n 88) 665.

[94] See, eg, Cremations Act 2003 (Qld) s 7.

[95] *Williams* (n 88) 664–65.

[96] *Smith v Tamworth City Council* (1997) 41 NSWLR 680, 694.

[97] *South Australia v Smith* [2014] SASC 64, (2014) 119 SASR 247 [22]–[34], [46]–[72].

situation if not delivered with care, which is all the more difficult given the urgency with which the dispute must be resolved.

The purpose of Conway's chapter is to analyse and evaluate the extent to which the existing legal principles effectively manage these concerns, or how they might manage them better. To the extent that burial disputes are resolved by the application of fixed rules, Conway argues that this kind of 'formalist' approach has several advantages, in that it allows the dispute to be resolved quickly, easily and in a detached way, avoiding the need for the court to make sensitive value judgements. This might assist the parties to accept the court's decision and to defuse any emotional charge, but at the expense of the court being able to consider the full range of interests at stake. This in turn may increase the emotional fallout if the outcome jars with the realities of the situation, as, for example, where an estranged wife is granted possession of the deceased's body in priority to a long-term current partner.

These are highly sensitive issues, and Conway suggests a number of ways for the court to limit the emotional damage to the parties. In addition to courtroom management strategies, the manner in which the court communicates its decision can be significant. Instead of criticising the parties for having a dispute or failing to resolve it privately (as some courts have done), acknowledging their pain, the difficulty of their situation and their good intentions is (she suggests) surely a more effective way of cooling their emotions and bringing their background dispute to an end.

Both Conway and Falconer's chapters speak to a broader phenomenon within private law, which is the need to contain the dead and their effects on the living, both physically and socially. Thus, in burial dispute cases, courts are as alive to the issues presented by decaying bodies as they are to the potentially damaging emotions of death that those bodies can invoke. The need to keep a body in a hermetically sealed bag to prevent fluid seepage, the health and safety risks (not to mention the anxiety) posed to those handling a decomposing body, and the need for hospitals and other institutions to free up mortuary space, for example, are concerns that courts can and do consider.[98] That these factors are relevant to the resolution of burial disputes is no surprise; the unavoidable physicality of death is a reality to which private law must accommodate itself.

VII. Divergence in Life and Death

It is a truism that there is a wide variety of customs and practices relating to death across both time and geography. The deep commitment and attachment of each culture to its own customs is nevertheless striking, especially given the extent to which those customs not merely differ from, but often oppose those found in other cultures. Herodotus illustrated the point with the following well-known example:

> When Darius was king, he summoned the Greeks who were with him and asked them for what price they would eat their fathers' dead bodies. They answered that there was no price for which they would do it. Then Darius summoned those Indians who are called Callatiae,

[98] For recent examples, see *Re Ghosh* [2022] VSC 410 [2]–[3]; *State Trustees Ltd v Wu* [2022] VSC 756 [4]–[6]; *Eastern Health v Bruinink* [2022] VSC 772 [15]–[16].

> who eat their parents, and asked them (the Greeks being present and understanding through interpreters what was said) what would make them willing to burn their fathers at death [a common practice of the Greeks]. The Indians cried aloud, that he should not speak of so horrid an act.[99]

As Metcalf and Huntington argue, the way that each culture responds to death is 'not merely random', but reflects the basic values of that culture in relation to life more generally.[100] In other words, diversity in responses to death is merely the observable consequence of diversity in approaches to life.

It is not surprising, then, that such differences can lead to divergence between jurisdictions in how their private law responds to life and death – the need to reflect local circumstances and values has always been a powerful driving force for divergence throughout the law of obligations.[101] Even *within* particular jurisdictions, private law will often need to serve a community whose members have vastly different approaches to life and death. Both themes are highlighted by Vines in Chapter 11 in the specific context of succession law, where she considers the extent to which different cultural approaches to inheritance can be accommodated in a single legal system, using Australia as a case study. As she points out, Australian succession law is highly Anglo-centric, being derived substantially from the English common law and embedded in a general political culture with English roots. With that said, in allowing substantial freedom of testamentary disposition, it enables individuals from different cultural or religious backgrounds to implement their preferred customs – at least ostensibly. As Vines demonstrates by reference to Islamic and Jewish practices, implementing one set of customs in the context of a succession law dominated by a different set of cultural values is not this simple, as it depends on practitioners having sufficient knowledge of two (often complex) regimes in order to draft a will that is consistent with both. And even if the will successfully meets the deceased's requirements, it may still be defeated by family provision legislation, which is often applied in a way that reflects particular value assumptions – such as the equal rights of daughters and sons to a share of the estate – that diverge from those underpinning the customs on which the will is based.

In other cultural contexts, on the other hand, Australian succession law has deliberately departed (albeit to a limited extent) from its Anglo-centric roots. As Vines highlights, the norms and values at the centre of Australian succession law pose significant problems for Indigenous Australians. The rate of will-making among Indigenous people is incredibly low, and the intestacy rules often do not align with their customary laws. Terms such as 'child' are often used more expansively to include nieces and nephews, and others to whom kinship obligations are owed. Formal adoption procedures are often not followed, and, as a result, adopted children may not take under class

[99] Herodotus, *Histories* 3.38.

[100] P Metcalf and R Huntington, *Celebrations of Death: The Anthropology of Mortuary Rituals*, 2nd rev edn (Cambridge, Cambridge University Press, 1991) 24–25.

[101] A Robertson and M Tilbury, 'Unity, Divergence and Convergence in the Common Law of Obligations' in A Robertson and M Tilbury (eds), *The Common Law of Obligations: Divergence and Unity* (Oxford, Hart Publishing, 2016) 5. See also A Robertson and M Tilbury (eds), *Divergences in Private Law* (Oxford, Hart Publishing, 2016); M Lunney, *A History of Australian Tort Law 1901–1945: England's Obedient Servant?* (Cambridge, Cambridge University Press, 2018).

gifts or intestacy rules. Alive to these issues, some jurisdictions (as Vines points out) have legislated to allow the estate of an intestate Indigenous person to be distributed in accordance with the customary law of the community or group to which the person belonged.[102] Here, then, we see a departure from traditional private law principles as a result of their inappropriateness to local conditions – a clear example of the kind of divergence mentioned above.

Lunney discusses another such example in Chapter 9, in this case between the survival of actions legislation in the United Kingdom and Australia respectively. As Lunney points out, this appears on its face to be a straightforward example of an English reform being adopted uncritically by a faithful Dominion, but this is not an accurate representation. The Law Reform (Miscellaneous Provisions) Act 1934 (UK) abolished (except in defamation cases) the rule that personal actions are extinguished by the plaintiff or defendant's death, allowing claims to survive for or against their estate. Soon after, in a perhaps unforeseen development, the House of Lords recognised 'loss of expectation of life' as a compensable head of damage for the first time,[103] allowing claims by those whose lives were shortened by the defendant's wrong, or (under the survival of actions legislation) by their estates after their deaths. Lunney considers the effect of this development on the incorporation of the UK legislation in Australia, focusing on Queensland and New South Wales as examples. Although Queensland originally enacted the UK legislation in full, ultimately, both States (along with all other Australian jurisdictions) rejected the possibility of claims for loss of expectation of life and other non-pecuniary losses surviving to the claimant's estate.[104]

A variety of arguments both ways appear in the parliamentary debates. One, predictable line of attack was based (if not always explicitly) on the increased cost to insurers of allowing damages for loss of expectation of life. Another focused on fundamental issues about the connection between private law, life and death: is the mere deprivation of life a compensable harm, as opposed to the subjective distress of appreciating the deprivation (which a deceased person clearly would not experience)? Is it possible for the deprivation of life to be valued in money terms? Does it matter that the plaintiff themselves would not benefit from the damages, which would go instead to the beneficiaries of their estate (or their creditors)? Is it perverse for the beneficiaries to 'profit' from the deceased's death? Should it be cheaper to kill than to maim? The difficulty of these questions is typical of those to which life and death give rise, and the answers are contestable. The opposing (diverging) views of various judges and lawyers played a significant role in the debates, even if by that stage they had been co-opted to suit the legislators' political ends.

A third debate, relevant to the issue of divergence between jurisdictions more generally, was about the relative merits of deference to English law. Lunney's detailed historical analysis shows that, whilst the lawyers and legislatures in Queensland and New South Wales might have begun their analysis with the English law, this was merely a point of departure from which to draw their own independent conclusions as to the

[102] Succession Act 2006 (NSW) pt 4.4.

[103] *Rose v Ford* [1937] AC 926 (HL).

[104] At least where the plaintiff's death is caused by the wrong. As Lunney points out, in some jurisdictions, damages for non-pecuniary loss are denied even where the death is not caused by the wrong.

needs of their own jurisdictions. The Australian states had their own unique legal and political contexts, and both felt entirely confident in going their own way when and as those contexts required, no matter that British law might be 'the light of the world'.[105]

The divergence between the UK and Australia on this issue still persists, although in a somewhat different form. In the UK, damages for the plaintiff's loss of expectation of life were abolished entirely (including for living claimants) in 1982,[106] and replaced by a conventional award of damages for bereavement for spouses and parents under section 1A of the Fatal Accidents Act 1976 (UK), with any loss to living claimants being compensable only to the extent that it constitutes pain and suffering and therefore falls within that separate head of damages. This was in reliance on a report of the Law Commission, which argued that damages for loss of expectation of life were practically insignificant,[107] but that some compensation for non-pecuniary loss arising from the death of a spouse or child was nevertheless justified.[108] The result was to create a further exception to the rule that the death of a third party cannot constitute loss or damage to a claimant.[109] Apart from South Australia and the Northern Territory,[110] a similar reform has not been taken up in Australia, and was rejected recently by the Law Reform Commission of Western Australia.[111] The Commission noted that the question of whether damages should be available for non-economic loss resulting from wrongful death 'may ultimately be [one] of policy for the Government' informed by a balancing of financial, legal, and policy considerations.[112] That this calculus might lead an Australian jurisdiction to a different outcome than that reached in the UK is entirely unsurprising.

All of this illustrates that laws are driven by the unique culture of each jurisdiction, just as that culture is influenced by law; and that whilst most cultures regard life as a good and death as a harm, there are significant divergences in both the extent of these commitments and in the way that are implemented in law, for reasons both moral and pragmatic.

VIII. Dignity

Although dignity is not the sole focus of any single chapter, it is mentioned repeatedly through the book. In the Foreword, Justice Lindsay argues that the worth and dignity of the person must be the law's focus in this area, that 'each life is worthy of respect'. Fell suggests that a person's dignity continues to ground a number of their most important interests after their death, including their reputation, privacy, and bodily integrity.

[105] As one Victorian lawyer mentioned by Lunney put it.

[106] See Administration of Justice Act 1982 (UK) ss 1, 3.

[107] Law Commission, *Personal Injury Litigation: Assessment of Damages* (Law Com No 56, 1973) para 99.

[108] ibid paras 172–80.

[109] This is known as the rule in *Baker v Bolton* (1808) 1 Camp 493; 170 ER 1033. The rule and its exceptions were summarised in *Paul v Royal Wolverhampton NHS Trust* [2024] UKSC 1, [2024] 2 WLR 417 [1]–[4].

[110] Civil Liability Act 1936 (SA) ss 28–29; Compensation (Fatal Injuries) Act 1974 (NT) s 10(3)(f).

[111] Law Reform Commission of Western Australia, *Claims for Non-Economic Loss for Wrongful Death under the Fatal Accidents Act 1959 (WA)* (Report No 109, September 2020) 22–29. There is nevertheless academic support for such a reform: I Field, 'In Mourning of Bereavement Damages' (2014) 22 *Torts Law Journal* 95.

[112] *Claims for Non-Economic Loss* (n 111) 22.

As Todd observes, the concept is also regularly used in judgments to refer to the 'dignity' of a person's life or existence. Barker mentions an autonomous decision of a person to end their life in their own way as one (or perhaps even the ultimate) expression of their dignity. Herring likewise refers to the dignity of a 'good death', and Falconer considers the role of particular funeral practices in affording dignity to a deceased person. Even where dignity is not referred to by name, it is nonetheless present.

Dignity is invoked in disciplines other than (private) law, particularly in theology and bioethics.[113] In legal contexts, it is most often referred to in discussions of constitutional and human rights law,[114] where it appears explicitly in a number of international human rights instruments and domestic constitutions.[115] The references throughout this book indicate that dignity has an important role to play in private law as well. Its utility as a normative concept has nonetheless been called into question, on the basis that it is overly vague or even vacuous, and adds nothing to other values such as autonomy or equality.[116] Those invoking dignity often do not define it explicitly.

Rosen identifies at least three different senses in which the word 'dignity' or its variants have been used historically.[117] The first is to refer to a high ranking or status, particularly one which derives from a person's occupation of a particular social role.[118] Slightly differently, it has also been used to denote the ranking of humans above other species – the idea is that humans, as rational agents, have a dignity that 'mere' animals do not.[119] Secondly, it can refer to a kind of worth or value, particularly one that is intrinsic. As Rosen points out, this conception of dignity is most often associated with the philosophy of Immanuel Kant,[120] but it is also prominent in Catholic doctrine and teachings.[121] Thirdly, certain kinds of behaviour are referred to as 'dignified' or expressing dignity – composure in the face of adversity, strength of moral character, humility and so on.[122]

To these three senses of 'dignity', Rosen himself adds a fourth, which applies to our treatment of others. 'To treat someone *with dignity* is (it seems natural to say) to *respect* their dignity … To respect someone's dignity by treating them with dignity requires that one *shows* them respect, either positively, by acting toward them in a way that gives expression to one's respect, or, at least, negatively, by refraining from behaviour

[113] C McCrudden (ed), *Understanding Human Dignity* (Oxford, Oxford University Press, 2013). See also C Foster, *Human Dignity in Bioethics and Law* (London, Hart Publishing, 2011).

[114] See, eg, D Feldman, 'Dignity as a Legal Value: Part I' [1999] *PL* 682; D Kretzmer and E Klein (eds), *The Concept of Human Dignity in Human Rights Discourse* (New York, Kluwer, 2002); E Daly, *Dignity Rights: Courts, Constitutions and the Worth of the Human Person* (Philadelphia, University of Pennsylvania Press, 2013); A Barak, *Human Dignity: The Constitutional Value and the Constitutional Right* (Cambridge, Cambridge University Press, 2015).

[115] See C McCrudden, 'Human Dignity and Judicial Interpretation of Humans Rights' (2008) 19 *European Journal of International Law* 655, 664–73.

[116] R Macklin, 'Dignity is a Useless Concept' (2003) 327 *British Medical Journal* 1419; M Bagaric and J Allan, 'The Vacuous Concept of Dignity' (2006) 5 *Journal of Human Rights* 257.

[117] M Rosen, *Dignity: Its History and Meaning* (Cambridge, Harvard University Press, 2012) ch 1.

[118] ibid 11.

[119] ibid 12.

[120] ibid 19–31.

[121] ibid 48–53.

[122] ibid 31–36.

that would show disrespect',[123] such as humiliating or degrading them, for example.[124] Importantly, as Rosen explains, the kind of 'respect' that is relevant here is not mere 'respect as observance', in the sense that we might respect the road rules by following them, but 'respect as respectfulness', which involves acting with respect towards some object.[125]

Each writer will emphasise certain aspects of dignity more than others.[126] This chapter is not the place to adjudicate between the different meanings (if that is even necessary). It is possible simply to accept that they all capture important features of the way in which the concept is often used and understood; and that each of them plays a part in mediating the way we understand appropriate behaviours in respect of life and death. The idea of *respect* for the value or status of a person or their life is nevertheless central to most accounts.[127] That core idea is sufficient, at least as a starting point, in attempting to understand appeals to dignity both in this book and elsewhere. There is likely to be disagreement about how it should be applied in specific cases, but this is true of any value. Barker's example of suicide is particular striking: should we respect a person by preserving their life, or by allowing them to end it? Is this simply another manifestation of the interplay between autonomy and welfare, or something else?

A remaining issue, which is important in the context of this book, is whether we should respect the dignity of non-living persons, which a number of chapters appear to suggest that we should. The various legal and social norms, across both time and cultures, relating to the respectful treatment of deceased persons and their bodies, indicate that this intuition is widely held. Indeed, in resolving burial disputes, courts repeatedly mention the need to 'maintain the dignity of the deceased'.[128] It is not possible to resolve this issue here, and different readers will have different opinions. But the past is full of people who lived good, decent lives, and that is surely worth something.

IX. Conclusions

To the question of how life and death are relevant to private law, it is clear that there is no single answer. Life and death arise in different ways in different legal contexts, and it is difficult to say anything about them without a counterexample coming immediately to mind.

Life and death are not simply legal on and off switches, with the law turning on when a person is born and turning off when they die. Certainly, the beginning and end of life are events around which various changes in our legal rights and duties cluster, but they are more inflection points than sharp boundaries. All unborn persons arguably have some minimal legal rights, which expand when the person is conceived and again when the person is born, and which contract when the person dies. These events

[123] ibid 58.
[124] ibid 58–61.
[125] ibid 57–58.
[126] See, eg, Dworkin (n 7); J Waldron, *Dignity, Rank, and Rights* (New York, Oxford University Press, 2012).
[127] See also the 'minimum core' identified in McCrudden, 'Judicial Interpretation' (n 115) 679.
[128] *South Australia v Smith* (n 97) [21]. See also *Bertani v Bertani* [2017] WASC 78 [19].

are sometimes biological, sometimes social, and sometimes legally constructed, as the examples of living persons being deprived of legal personhood show.

Life and death play various roles in private law other than as marking stages of personhood. Life can be a value for private law to uphold and preserve, and death a harm that it seeks to prevent or redress. Life and death can be the subject matter of choices that private law protects from interference, including our choices about whether to create new life, and in some instances our choice to end our own life. The processes by which life is created and ends are often medical processes that must be appropriately regulated. Life and death are also events that impose obligations on others; when a person dies, for example, they leave behind property, debts and a body, the benefits and burdens of which must be distributed among the living.

Many of the issues to which life and death give rise in private law are unique, with no obvious counterpart in other areas of law. This is not surprising – if there were nothing at all distinctive about private law, there would be no reason to have it, or to study it! Although some issues appear to raise general questions, they do not necessarily have general answers. The variation in the law's definition(s) of 'life' is a particularly good example, as is the question of whether certain rights are possessed by unborn or deceased persons, the answer to which depends on the nature and content of the relevant rights.

This is not to say that the issues discussed in this book have no resonance outside private law or in other disciplines. This chapter has referred to insights from biology, medicine, history and sociology, but the most prominent disciplinary crossover is perhaps with moral philosophy. The facts in cases relating to life and death are often perfectly straightforward, with the only question of any difficulty being their moral significance. Life and death have a unique tendency to intensify the values at stake, test their limits and bring them into conflict. Although many of the moral debates will never be fully settled, the law must still come down on one side or the other. In doing so, it will never satisfy everyone. All it can do is what it thinks best as it strives to resolve the impossible.

In giving rise to hard cases, matters of life and death also help us reflect on easier cases. It often does not matter what underlying moral theory is applied to resolve easy cases, since it will reach the right outcome regardless. But in hard cases, the competing theories will pull in opposite directions, forcing us to choose between them, and in turn to reconsider our understanding of those easy cases in which a now-discarded theory had been applied. The various contributions to this book suggest a number of possible lines of inquiry, including the adequacy of individualism as a unified normative foundation for private law, and the role of dignity as a source of private interests.

The collection contains many valuable insights about private law, but has private law taught us anything about life and death? There is no reason why it has to, although it would be a shame if it did not. To us, one of the clear messages of the book is that life and death are not solely matters of concern to the person who experiences them. They have profound and cascading ripple effects on others of a kind that few other events are capable of. The creation of life imposes a relationship on others that, regardless of its status as planned, desired or valued, fundamentally alters the course of their lives. The same is true of death, which, as well as causing deep psychological or emotional suffering to others, can deprive them of their most important source of value and meaning.

The point is not that this fact was previously unknown, or that we needed private law to see it. But private law brings it into view in a distinctive way. Much of the private law of life and death is really about the effects of life and death on others. Private law cases always involve at least two parties, one of whom (and sometimes both) must therefore be someone other than the person whose life or death is in issue, but who is nevertheless affected by it in some way. This effect is sometimes the central focus, but even when it is not, it is always present – even the defendant in a wrongful death case has to live with what they have done. Private law brings these effects to the surface and gives them public acknowledgement, not just through a set of technical rules, but in a series of narratives that could just as easily have happened to any of us. It offers a valuable window into the human experience, through which it is clear that our lives are interconnected, and our fates intertwined.

2

How Private Law Regulates Intimacy and Relationships at the Edges of Life

JONATHAN HERRING

I. Introduction

For much of life, some people can pretend they are independent, autonomous, self-sufficient individuals, of the kind promoted in legal thought. But it is at the edges of life, in birth and death, that this pretence is revealed. The reality, that we are held together by others, is laid bare for all to see. It is then that the intertwined nature of our humanity is most manifest.[1] Our true nature can no longer be disguised.

It is at these boundaries of life that the rights promoted by the torts of trespass to the person, privacy and negligence, namely rights of bodily integrity, individualised autonomy, privacy and self-sufficiency ring so hollow. We come into the world in relational care, bodily intrusion and mutuality; and often end our lives with those same features. In the ending and in the beginning there is blood; excreta; crying; bodies' boundaries crumbling. The legal image of the self-contained body is in ruins and the law looks away, unable to talk or comprehend what is happening. It can relax when the deed is done: we have a baby: we have a legal person; we have a corpse: there is no legal person. But in the very process of the beginning and the end the legal vocabulary fades to a gasp. This chapter seeks to explore why this is so and how the law could do better. Private law, in particular, focuses on individual interests, resting in an identified person, in a way which often fails to capture the importance of relational interests.

As Hilde Lindemann writes, our beginnings and endings involve holding on and letting go.[2] In death and birth we are both being held on to and holding on; letting go and being let go. This language captures the deeply relational nature of the starting and ending of life: the 'essentially interpersonal nature of being human'.[3] Our entry and exit

[1] See H Lindemann, *Holding and Letting Go: The Social Practice of Personal Identities* (Oxford, Oxford University Press, 2014).

[2] (n 1). The book is helpfully reviewed in J Christman, 'Review of Hilde Lindemann, *Holding and Letting Go: The Social Practice of Personal Identities*' (2015) 15(8) *American Journal of Bioethics* W8.

[3] Lindemann (n 1) 202.

from this world is achieved in, through and with others. We are both 'inducted into personhood'[4] and released from it through our relationships.

This chapter will start with a brief overview of how the law tends to understand the self in individualised terms. It will then focus on birth and death as examples where these profoundly relational events leave the law struggling to provide a coherent account. It will be argued that, in fact, the truths about human nature, open for all to see at birth and death, are true throughout the life course. We need to be more honest about the frail, ignorant, deeply interconnected nature of humanity.

II. Individualised Autonomy and Values

In this section, I draw a distinction between the image of the self that the law generally promotes, a highly individualised one, and the reality of the deeply relational self, made most manifest in death and birth. At birth and death, the law's individualised understanding of the self becomes problematic.[5] The law and many ethical theories assume that we are competent, detached, independent people who are entitled to have our rights of self-determination and autonomy fiercely protected by the courts.[6] These key rights (protected by the boundaries of tort, contract and property law in particular) secure the individual from interference from others.[7] Further, the individualised notion of the self, as bounded and self-contained, encourages the promotion of self-reliance and independence. The self should be directing his efforts to doing all he can do to maximise personal gain.[8] The law's role is to provide parameters and regulations within which a fair competition can take place to enable people to maximise their profit. As Linda Barclay puts it:

> Numerous moral and political theories promote a vision of the autonomous self as essentially independent and self-sufficient, a vision that denies the inescapable connectedness of selves and the fact that their immersion in networks of relationships forms their desires, aspirations, indeed their very identities. In other words, what is denied is that the self is essentially social.[9]

Such an individualised understanding of the self is unrealistic and undesirable. The reality is that caring relationships are central to our emotional and physical well-being.[10] No one can, in fact, survive without the practical, emotional and psychological support

[4] ibid.

[5] See J Herring, *Law and the Relational Self* (Cambridge, Cambridge University Press, 2019) ch 2.

[6] See J Herring, *Vulnerable Adults and the Law* (Oxford, Oxford University Press, 2016) ch 2.

[7] This is made explicit in theories of private law which seek to rely on Kantian ethics, such as E Weinrib, *The Idea of Private Law*, revised edn (Oxford, Oxford University Press, 2012).

[8] L Code, *What Can She Know?: Feminist Theory and the Construction of Knowledge* (Ithaca, Cornell University Press, 1991) 77–78.

[9] L Barclay, 'Autonomy and the Social Self' in C Mackenzie and N Stoljar (eds), *Relational Autonomy: Feminist Perspectives On Autonomy, Agency, and the Social Self* (New York, Oxford University Press, 2000) 52 (as cited in JA Parks and M Howard, 'Dying Well in Nursing Homes During COVID-19 and Beyond: The Need for a Relational and Familial Ethic' (2021) 35 *Bioethics* 589, 590).

[10] C Willett, E Anderson and D Myers, 'Feminist Perspectives on the Self' (*Stanford Encyclopaedia of Philosophy*, 19 February 2020) www.plato.stanford.edu/entries/feminism-self/.

of others. Yet, care work, which is key to humanity, is rendered largely invisible to the law, or even a threat to the self-sufficient self. It means that legal interventions which are designed to restore a person's self-sufficiency will work to the disadvantage of those who care.[11] Yet, at the time of birth and death, we are nowhere near self-sufficiency. Birthing and, nearly always, dying are profound moments of care and deeply relational.

A very different understanding of the self and legal regulation would start by appreciating that we are all ignorant, vulnerable, interdependent individuals, whose strength and reality is found not in our autonomy, but our relationships with others. It would ensure that legal interventions are built around the maintenance and preservation of caring relationships, rather than the image of the independent individual person. As Catriona Mackenzie, Wendy Rogers and Susan Dodds explain: 'To be vulnerable is to be fragile, to be susceptible to wounding and to suffering; this susceptibility is an ontological conditional of our humanity'.[12] This is the kind of language that resonates with the realities of birth and death.

Vulnerability is commonly discussed in the media and by politicians. But when it is discussed then, it comes with heavily negative connotations. Particular groups are defined as vulnerable and in need of care and protection. By contrast, the claim of universal vulnerability theorists is that vulnerability is an inevitable part of the human condition. And as a result, care is an essential part of being a human being. If we are all vulnerable, then our caring relationships are essential to our survival. Yet, similarly, our caring relationships are part of what make us vulnerable.

Martha Fineman has done more than anyone to develop the concept of universal vulnerability and she explains it in this way:

> The vulnerability approach recognizes that individuals are anchored at each end of their lives by dependency and the absence of capacity. Of course, between these ends, loss of capacity and dependence may also occur, temporarily for many and permanently for some as a result of disability or illness. Constant and variable throughout life, individual vulnerability encompasses not only damage that has been done in the past and speculative harms of the distant future, but also the possibility of immediate harm. We are beings who live with the ever-present possibility that our needs and circumstances will change. On an individual level, the concept of vulnerability (unlike that of liberal autonomy) captures this present potential for each of us to become dependent based upon our persistent susceptibility to misfortune and catastrophe.[13]

It is because we are vulnerable beings that care is central.[14] We all have needs and the meeting of needs in caring relationships is a universal experience. Wendy Holloway

[11] See J Herring, 'The Caring Subject' in S Vauchez and R Rubio-Marin (eds), *The Cambridge Companion to Gender and the Law* (Cambridge, Cambridge University Press, 2023).

[12] C Mackenzie, W Rogers and S Dodds, 'Introduction: What is Vulnerability and Why Does it Matter for Moral Theory?' in C Mackenzie, W Rogers and S Dodds (eds), *Vulnerability: New Essays in Ethics and Feminist Philosophy* (New York, Oxford University Press, 2014) 4.

[13] M Fineman, 'The Vulnerable Subject: Anchoring Equality in the Human Condition' (2008) 20 *Yale Journal of Law & Feminism* 1, 12.

[14] In several jurisdictions vulnerability is used as a concept to justify novel duties of care: see, eg, duties to those with suicidal ideation, discussed in J Herring, *The Right to be Protected from Committing Suicide* (Oxford, Hart Publishing, 2022). But these developments are not based on a model of universal vulnerability, but rather that particular groups of people are vulnerable.

argues that 'care is the psychological equivalent to our need to breathe unpolluted air'.[15] There will be few, if any, stages during anyone's life when they are not in caring relationships. Eva Feder Kittay, Bruce Gennings and Angela Wassuna explain:

> People do not spring up from the soil like mushrooms. People produce people. People need to be cared for and nurtured throughout their lives by other people, at some times more urgently and more completely than at other times.[16]

So, let us turn next to look more precisely at birth and death, how they reveal our vulnerable and caring nature and how the law struggles to respond to these events.

III. Birth

The law struggles with the beginning of life. In many legal systems the legal status of the fetus is opaque. English law, as in many legal systems, is more confident about declaring what a fetus is not than what it is. It is clearly not a person until it is born.[17] In *St George's Healthcare NHS Trust v S*, Judge LJ stated that a 36-week-old fetus is 'not nothing: if viable it is not lifeless and is certainly human'.[18] But that does not really get us very far in terms of its legal standing. The most authoritative discussion is found In *Attorney-General's Reference (No 3 of 1994)*,[19] where the House of Lords rejected an argument proposed by the Court of Appeal that a fetus should be regarded as part of the mother, equivalent to a leg or an arm. Instead, Lord Mustill declared

> the foetus does not (for the purposes of the law of homicide and violent crime) have any relevant type of personality but is an organism sui generis lacking at this stage the entire range of characteristics both of the mother to which it is physically linked and of the complete human being which it will later become … I would, therefore, reject the reasoning which assumes that since (in the eyes of English law) the foetus does not have the attributes which make it a 'person' it must be an adjunct of the mother. Eschewing all religious and political debate I would say that the foetus is neither. It is a unique organism.[20]

Similarly, in the European Court of Human Rights in *Vo v France*[21] it was confirmed, as had been held in previous cases, that the fetus was not a person and so was not directly protected by the right to life in Article 2 of the European Convention on Human Rights. However, it was left as an open question whether the fetus could claim a version of the right to life. Again, the court was able to state what a fetus was not, but words failed when describing the actual legal status of the fetus.

[15] W Holloway, *The Capacity to Care: Gender and Ethical Subjectivity* (Hove, Routledge, 2006) 11.

[16] E Feder Kittay, B Jennings and A Wassuna, 'Dependency, Difference and the Global Ethic of Longterm Care' (2005) 13 *Journal of Political Philosophy* 443, 443.

[17] *Re An Application by the Northern Ireland Human Rights Commission for Judicial Review (Northern Ireland)* [2018] UKSC 27 [92].

[18] *St George's Healthcare NHS Trust v S* [1998] 3 WLR 936 (CA) 952.

[19] *Attorney-General's Reference (No 3 of 1994)* [1998] AC 245 (HL).

[20] ibid 255–56. This approach was approved by the Court of Appeal in *CP (A Child) v First-tier Tribunal (Criminal Injuries Compensation)* [2014] EWCA Civ 1554, [2015] QB 459.

[21] *Vo v France* (2005) 40 EHRR 12.

The issue of the status of the fetus is, of course, key for a whole set of legal issues: whether the fetus is a legal person protected by human rights and criminal law; whether it has standing to bring claims in tort or contract law; or whether harm to it can be recognised through claims in private law. This can lead the law to tie itself in knots. A fetus which is injured pre-birth can sue for injuries, but only if she is born alive.[22] A fetus cannot be the victim of a crime, but if born and then dies, a manslaughter charge can be brought.[23] These are examples of the law's deep discomfort with the description of pregnancy and its futile attempts to define the fetus reflects the individualistic understanding at the start. The core difficulty is trying to identify the status of 'the fetus' as something in isolation from the woman. It is trying to separate the inseparable.

We see the same individualised approach in a fascinating philosophical discussion of whether a fetus should be regarded as part of a mother or a separate organism. Kingma, for example, contrasts the containment view: that the fetus is contained within the 'gestating organism', and the parthood view: the fetus is part of the gestating organism. She claims that the containment view is the received view, but that the parthood view is more convincing.[24]

Yet both these philosophical views[25] and the legal approach are a million miles away from the lived reality, where the fetus is meaningless outside of its relational context. An unwanted miscarriage is utterly different from a wanted termination. The truth is that pregnancy can only be understood in relational terms. The legal response should be to the pregnancy relationship, not to the status of an imagined isolated fetus. The deeply relational experience of pregnancy, which is invisible to the law, needs further unpacking.

The creative process of pregnancy is deeply relational. In pregnancy, a woman taking on the gestational role is starting the process of holding her fetus which will lead to personhood, but she is also taking on for herself the role of pregnant woman.[26] This is a process of what Lindemann describes as 'entwinement'.[27] It is not just that the woman creates the fetus as a potter may create a pot through skill and care. It is she herself, her body and her identity, which becomes entwined with the fetus. The creative process changes her identity, along with that of the fetus. The lines the law draws between people cannot capture this merging of the selves.

Martha Nussbaum explains why she believes the individual should be the basic unit for political thought:

> It means, first of all, that liberalism responds sharply to the basic fact that each person has a course from birth to death that is not precisely the same as that of any other person; that each person is one and not more than one, that each feels pain in his or her own body, that the food given to A does not arrive in the stomach of B.[28]

[22] Congenital Disabilities (Civil Liability) Act 1976 (UK) s 1(1).

[23] *CP (A Child)* (n 20).

[24] See E Kingma, 'Were You a Part of Your Mother?' (2019) 128 *Mind* 609.

[25] See, eg, J Grose, 'How Many Organisms During a Pregnancy?' (2020) 87 *Philosophy of Science* 1049; E Kingma, 'Nine Months' (2020) 45 *Journal of Medicine and Philosophy* 371; E Kingma, 'Lady Parts: The Metaphysics of Pregnancy' (2018) 82 *Royal Institute of Philosophy Supplement* 165.

[26] Lindemann (n 1).

[27] ibid.

[28] MC Nussbaum, *Sex and Social Justice* (New York, Oxford University Press, 1999) 62.

Whatever is thought of this argument generally, it is clearly untrue of the fetus. The pain of the mother affects the fetus, and the food given to the mother can arrive in the stomach of the fetus. The individual person model, which is relied upon in traditional liberal thinking, breaks down when thinking about pregnancy: a relationship of profound interconnection.[29]

As a matter of biology, the pregnant woman and the fetus cannot be neatly divided into two people.[30] There is no clear point at which fetal tissue ends and the woman's tissue begins. They share fluids and space. The health and well-being of the woman profoundly affect the fetus, and vice versa.[31] As Iris Marion Young puts it: 'Pregnancy challenges the integration of my body experience by rendering fluid the boundary between what is within, myself, and what is outside, separate. I experience my insides as the space of another, yet my own body'.[32]

The fetus, therefore, cannot be assessed on its own terms. It exists in, through and with the mother. The options on an individual model are either some kind of fairy tale image that the woman provides a cosy sitting room for the fetus to live in, awaiting birth; or the fetus is part of the mother's body, just as a toenail may be. Both of these are clearly false. The woman is not simply a 'fetal container'.[33] Barbara Katz Rothman writes:

> [T]he medical model of pregnancy, as an essentially parasitic and vaguely pathological relationship, encourages the physician to view the fetus and mother as two separate patients, and to see pregnancy as inherently a conflict of interests between the two. Where the fetus is highly valued, the effect is to reduce the woman to what current obstetrical language calls the 'maternal environment'.[34]

The reality is that all interaction and dealings with the fetus must be mediated through, and with, the woman. Pregnancy is utterly relational. Rothman suggests an acknowledgement that '[m]otherhood is an experience of interpersonal connection. The isolated, atomistic individual is an absurdity when one is pregnant: one is two, two are one'.[35]

The interconnection is not simply a biological one, but also a psychological one. Under the traditional individualised approach complex issues around pregnancy are presented in terms of a maternal/fetal conflict. While that might be an appropriate conception of pregnancy in a few cases, it fails to capture the interconnected reality for many. As Anne Elvey explains:

> The pregnant body … calls into question these assumptions of separateness and sameness. When I am pregnant, 'my' body is both 'I' and 'not I', mine and not mine. The boundaries of the body shift as the pregnant body creates its own expanding space. While the skin stretches the boundary between the body and its outside is continually renegotiated, until in birth the

[29] See J Herring, 'Ethics of Care and the Public Good of Abortion' (2019) 1 *University of Oxford Human Rights Hub Journal* 1.

[30] See J Herring, 'The Loneliness of Status: The Legal and Moral Significance of Birth' in F Ebtehaj et al (eds), *Birth Rights and Rites* (Oxford, Hart Publishing, 2011).

[31] See J Herring and P-L Chau, 'My Body, Your Body, Our Bodies' (2007) 15 *Medical Law Review* 34.

[32] IM Young, *On Female Body Experience: 'Throwing Like a Girl' and Other Essays* (New York, Oxford University Press, 2005) 49.

[33] See GJ Annas, 'Pregnant Women as Fetal Containers' (1986) 16(6) *Hastings Centre Report* 13.

[34] BK Rothman, 'Commentary' (1986) 16(1) *Hastings Center Report* 25, 25.

[35] BK Rothman, *Recreating Motherhood: Ideology and Technology in a Patriarchal Society* (New Brunswick, Rutgers University Press, first published 1989, 2000 reprint) 55–56.

> inside enters the outside. The pregnant body is, moreover, two or more under the influence of a third, the placenta, through the agency of which self and other are interconnected.[36]

The standard approach in the legal and much philosophical literature seeks to determine the status of the fetus, and to determine the responsibilities that are owed by the woman (or doctors) to the fetus as a result. A different approach is offered by a relational ethics of care approach, which argues that, rather than asking what rights or responsibilities are owed to an individual in response to their status, we ask what the responsibilities and rights are owed in relation to a relationship.[37] The argument is that, in order to determine what are the legal rights and responsibilities between person A and B, we need to know what their relationships is. In brief, where a relationship is marked by care, I would advocate that the law should allocate rights and responsibilities to ensure that the relationship is upheld and maintained.[38] Where, however, that relationship is not marked by care, then it does not have moral value, and the law should enable the parties to find other caring relationships. The relational approach sees our obligations and rights emerging from our relationship, rather than our legal status. It is not as if private law ignores these altogether. Indeed, John Gardner has written of the importance of 'strictly relational rights' which are justified by the value of the relationship. He explains:

> A strictly relational duty is a duty that one has for the reason that one stands in some special relationship with the person to whom the duty is owed. By a 'special relationship' I mean, in turn, a relationship other than the relationship that we are all said to have with each other simply as persons or human beings or God's creatures, etc. A special relationship, we might say, is not just a relationship with someone but a relationship with someone in particular, from which others must inevitably be left out.[39]

In her powerful writing on personhood Lindemann writes that we should understand personhood as an 'interpersonal achievement'.[40] In cases where the pregnancy is wanted 'there is an expectation that the fetus will become a born child, and identity construction is a way of anticipating the child's personhood'. This is part of holding the fetus into personhood. Of course, as she says in other cases 'the woman carrying the fetus might refrain from weaving narratives of personal identity around the fetus, because she doesn't want the fetus to become her child'.[41] She explains that 'calling a fetus into personhood centrally involves forging an identity for the child the fetus will become and that this is typically the responsibility in particular of the gestating woman'.[42]

Developing a relational approach to pregnancy and birth offers many advantages. I will explore three.

[36] A Elvey, 'The Material Given: Bodies, Pregnant Bodies and Earth' (2003) 18 *Australian Feminist Studies* 199, 203.

[37] See J Herring, *Caring and the Law* (Oxford, Hart Publishing, 2016) ch 2.

[38] ibid.

[39] J Gardner, *From Personal Life to Private Law* (Oxford, Oxford University Press, 2018) 23–24. Although James Penner argues Gardner here is over-stating the significance of relational right in current private law: 'Book Review: From Personal Life to Private Law' (2019) 10 *Jurisprudence* 300.

[40] Lindemann (n 1) 21.

[41] ibid 18.

[42] ibid 53.

A. Wanted and Unwanted Pregnancies

A relational approach offers a far more effective language for the law to discuss pregnancy and abortion. Catriona Mackenzie has written of the way those academic discussions on abortion:

> [H]ave focused philosophical and moral reflection away from the contexts in which deliberations about abortion are usually made and away from the concerns and experiences which motivate those involved in the processes of deliberation. The result is that philosophical analyses of abortion often seem beside the point, if not completely irrelevant, to the lives of the countless women who daily not only have to make moral decisions about abortion but, more importantly, who often face serious risks to their lives in contexts where abortion is not a safe and readily accessible procedure.[43]

Much the same could be made about the legal regulation of pregnancy and parenthood generally. It is this that, for me, most strongly calls for a relational approach. The abstracted weighing of the interests of the fetus/baby and woman pays no account of the complex interactions between them; and between them and those who are in relationship with them; not to mention to the broader social context which has such an impact on the actual and perceived moral and legal obligations that are imposed. We need to move from an idealised analysis and listen to voices of women faced with pregnancy decisions and decisions concerning birth and children. There we usually find not the language of status, rights, viability or choice: but the language of despair; ecstasy; interconnection; and guilt. The language is that of relationships: seeking to do the right thing 'for everyone'. It is there we need to start the legal and moral analysis of pregnancy and find the significance of birth.[44]

The relational approach offers a way of presenting a powerful case in favour of abortion, while recognising the importance of treasuring wanted pregnancies and birth.[45] Wanted pregnancies are caring, and therefore of the highest moral value. Indeed, Heloise Robinson has recently suggested pregnant women should be seen as having a higher moral status than other people:

> There is no other human being like a pregnant human being. While no one would suggest that pregnant women are not persons, our enquiry should not stop there. We must also ask whether, because of their unique state and because of the potential status of the fetus, we should in fact recognise that they can reach a second threshold of personhood, where, as a consequence, during the period of pregnancy they would have a temporary superior moral status, and an equal moral status to each other.[46]

We certainly need to protect wanted pregnancies through the criminal and tort law from unwanted termination, and to recognise the goodness of them. By contrast, unwanted

[43] C Mackenzie, 'Abortion and Embodiment' (1992) 70 *Australian Journal of Philosophy* 136, 155.
[44] See Herring, 'Ethics of Care' (n 29).
[45] ibid.
[46] H Robinson, 'Pregnancy and Superior Moral Status: A Proposal for Two Thresholds of Personhood' [2023] *Journal of Medical Ethics* doi: 10.1136/jme-2022-108799.

pregnancies lack moral value as these involve coerced care, which may well impede other wanted caring relationships.[47] As Bryon Stoyles puts it:

> Relational accounts of fetal value allow that pregnancies have whatever meaning and value they are given *by the pregnant woman*. Thus, relational accounts allow that pregnancy can have little or no positive value and also that pregnancy can have great value.[48]

This can lead to an argument that unwanted pregnancies lack moral value. As I have argued elsewhere:

> unwanted pregnancies are not marked by mutual care, and so lack moral value. The law has no interest in enabling these relationships to continue, and indeed cannot compel people to continue them when they involve the kind of bodily interference involved in pregnancy and childbirth. A coerced relationship is the opposite of a caring one. In no other context does the law compel one party to give up bodily integrity to save another, even to the slightest degree, let alone to the extent required in pregnancy. The law must enable unwanted pregnancies to be terminated, so that caring responsibilities may be fulfilled.[49]

These kinds of relational models provide a far more promising and effective way of responding to pregnancy: that rather than responding to 'the status of the fetus', we respond to the pregnancy relationship.

B. Miscarriage

Taking a relational approach helps to provide a far more effective legal response to the issue of miscarriage. That sensitive topic provides a particularly important example for this chapter because, in miscarriage, we see birth and death coinciding. Amber Griffioen suggests that, at a modest, estimate pregnancy loss between fertilisation and term runs at between 40–60 per cent.[50] As she goes on to note, it is striking how little academic literature there is on the topic, whether one looks to law, philosophy or even a subject like theology. Miscarriage can be a profoundly sad experience. Jessie Bendavid found a 'significant minority' of those suffering miscarriage suffer 'intense and sustained grief, depression and anxiety symptoms'.[51] However, it receives little, if any, recognition in the law. Indeed, there is little public or social acknowledgement of the issue, save in online forums.[52] Because the law is focussed on the status of the individual fetus, it is unable to distinguish between a miscarriage, a pregnancy ended by an assault and a termination.[53]

[47] ibid.

[48] BJ Stoyles, 'The Value of Pregnancy and the Meaning of Pregnancy Loss' (2015) 46 *Journal of Social Philosophy* 91, 93.

[49] Herring, 'Ethics of Care' (n 29) 23–24.

[50] A Griffioen, 'Toward a Philosophical Theology of Pregnancy Loss' in M Slawkowski-Rode (ed), *The Meaning of Mourning: Perspectives on Death, Loss, and Grief* (London, Lexington Books, 2023) 57.

[51] J Bendavid, 'Psychological Outcomes of Those Experiencing Early Pregnancy Loss' (PhD thesis, University of Melbourne 2019) 2.

[52] See H Keane, 'Foetal Personhood and Representations of the Absent Child in Pregnancy Loss Memorialization' (2009) 10 *Feminist Theory* 153.

[53] See V Browne, *Pregnancy Without Birth: A Feminist Philosophy of Miscarriage* (London, Bloomsbury, 2023) ch 5.

The status of the fetus, seen as an individual entity, is the same in all three cases. It is striking that it is not possible to obtain a death certificate in the case of a miscarriage,[54] nor is English criminal law able to see more than a case of an assault on the woman in a case terminating a pregnancy.[55] This is entirely understandable given the individualistic approach taken by the law. Recognising fetal legal status in any context is feared to immediately threaten important rights to abortion.[56]

The silence around miscarriage can be put down to several things. First, there is still a sense of guilt that surrounds miscarriage.[57] There is enormous pressure around the 'cult of motherhood' where mothers are expected to do everything to promote their children's well-being. The expectations around pregnant women are so great that it is impossible to be the 'perfect pregnant woman', meaning that, where there is a miscarriage, the mother is likely to blame herself for not living up to the ideal.[58] These feelings of guilt may be enhanced by the feeling that miscarriage is not something to be discussed in public.

Second, feminist commentators have noticed a reluctance for public acknowledgement around female bodies, especially linked to what is regarded as 'human messiness'. Like mensuration, the mixture of blood, sex and feminine leakiness is uncomfortable for the male imagination.[59] This is linked to the broader reluctance to talk openly about death and the physicality of birth.

Third, the links between abortion and miscarriage appear to have caused a reluctance of even feminists to write on the issue. Linda Layne claims that feminist commentators 'abandoned their sisters in hours of need' and contributed to their pain by 'retaining a studied silence' on pregnancy loss.[60] In part, there is a difficulty because the response to miscarriage seems tied into the debates over abortion. If we see miscarriage as a tragedy and something to be mourned, it is said to be difficult at the same time to promote rights to abortion. As Layne puts it '[t]he fear … is that if one were to acknowledge that there was something of value lost, something worth grieving in a miscarriage, one would automatically accede the inherent personhood of embryos and fetuses'.[61] However, this concern can be overcome. As argued above, the relational model of pregnancy sees a fundamental difference between a wanted and unwanted pregnancy, seeing the first as

[54] Although following the review required by the Civil Partnerships, Marriages and Deaths (Registration etc) Act 2019 (UK) s 3(1) a registration of a pregnancy loss can be requested. A death certificate can be offered in a case of a still birth: see Department of Health & Social Care, 'Government Response to the Independent Pregnancy Loss Review: Care and Support When Baby Loss Occurs Before 24 Weeks' Gestation' (22 July 2023) www.gov.uk/government/publications/government-response-to-the-independent-pregnancy-loss-review/government-response-to-the-independent-pregnancy-loss-review-care-and-support-when-baby-loss-occurs-before-24-weeks-gestation.

[55] See J Herring, 'The Termination of Pregnancy and the Criminal Law' in A Reed et al (eds), *Homicide in Criminal Law: A Research Companion* (Abingdon, Routledge, 2019).

[56] Of course, this does not necessarily follow and a strong case for abortion rights can be made even on the premise that a fetus has full moral status.

[57] See Keane (n 52).

[58] See A Mullin, 'Early Pregnancy Losses: Multiple Meanings and Moral Considerations' (2015) 46 *Journal of Social Philosophy* 27.

[59] See M Shildrick, *Leaky Bodies and Boundaries: Feminism, Postmodernism and (Bio)ethics* (Abingdon, Routledge, 1997).

[60] L Layne, *Motherhood Lost: A Feminist Account of Pregnancy Loss in America* (New York, Psychology Press, 2003) 239.

[61] ibid 240.

deserving of full moral and legal protection while the latter justifying a termination. Under such a view, it may be possible to explain that it is entirely understandable that a wanted termination can be seen as the appropriate, even required response, while a miscarriage is a tragedy.

C. The Legal and Moral Significance of Birth

The relational approach helps explains why it is that birth is so significant in legal and moral terms. The problem in terms of the individualised understanding of the self is that to many commentators there is little distinction between the nature of the fetus just before birth and just after. Charles Foster argues:

> Autonomy bestows its decisive favours on the adult woman rather than the 24-week fetus she carries, on the ground, apparently, that the fetus is on one side of the woman's vagina rather than the other. The mere geographical situation of the fetus means that it has no autonomy rights at all. A journey of a few centimetres would stamp it with the awesome imprimatur of autonomy and so invest it with the draconian protection of the English law.[62]

Others disagree and attempt to identify biological changes in the birthing process to the body of the fetus that occur on birth.[63] But the important thing that happens on birth is not that it marks a fundamental change in the nature of the fetus, but that it fundamentally changes the relationship between the woman and the fetus and the potential relationships of others with the fetus/baby.[64] Others can now interact with and care for the baby, without having to operate through the mother's body.

As this discussion has shown, the law has struggled to find the language to describe the significance of pregnancy and birth and to find legal rights that respond appropriately to it. In particular the law has struggled to find a way of distinguishing between wanted and unwanted pregnancies, in particular failing to respond effectively to unwanted miscarriages. The discussion has shown how the law's focus on individual selves and rights has failed to capture the inherently relational nature of pregnancy and birth. We now turn to the other end of the life course, death.

IV. Death as Relational

Defining 'death' is controversial and problematic.[65] The issue raises fundamental questions about our humanity. What is it to be a person? What are the essential elements of life? There are usually no difficulties in deciding whether a person is dead, even if there is disagreement over when death occurred.

[62] C Foster, 'Medical Law Too Often Doffs its Cap to the Doctor's White Coat' *The Times* (21 May 2009) www.thetimes.co.uk/article/medical-law-too-often-doffs-its-cap-to-the-doctors-white-coat-z63b5xtgx93.

[63] See, eg, AK Burin, 'Beyond Pragmatism: Defending the "Bright Line" of Birth' (2014) 22 *Medical Law Review* 494.

[64] See Herring, 'Ethics of Care' (n 29).

[65] See P-L Chau and J Herring, *Emergent Medicine and the Law* (Cham, Springer, 2021) ch 7.

The medical and philosophical literature on the definition of death is extensive and there is a growing body of case law on the issue.[66] English law has taken the clear view that brain stem death constitutes legal death. In *Airedale NHS Trust v Bland* Lord Keith explained: 'In the eyes of the medical world and of the law a person is not clinically dead so long as the brain stem retains its function'.[67] Lord Goff applied that to the case at hand which involved a patient in a persistent vegetative state (as it was known then), in this way:

> I start with the simple fact that, in law, Anthony is still alive. It is true that his condition is such that it can be described as a living death; but he is nevertheless still alive. This is because, as a result of developments in modern medical technology, doctors no longer associate death exclusively with breathing and heartbeat, but it has come to be accepted that death occurs when the brain, and in particular the brain stem, has been destroyed.[68]

The case is not a straightforward adoption of brain stem death as the legal test, but rather of the courts taking the view that the law should adopt the definition of death accepted by the medical profession; and that, as the medical profession in England and Wales used brain stem death as the test, the courts would adopt that. In *Re A (A Child)*, a more recent case, the fact the family had a different understanding of death was not a reason to depart from brain stem death.[69] In England and Wales, the Academy of Medical Royal Colleges' *A Code of Practice for the Diagnosis of Brain Stem Death* sets out in detail the definition of 'brain stem death'.[70] This outlines three requirements that must be met before a doctor makes a diagnosis of brain death, as follows:

(a) It must be concluded that the coma is not the result of reversible causes, such as drug overdose.
(b) It must be demonstrated that the several components of the brain stem have all been permanently destroyed. Significantly, this includes the respiratory centre.
(c) It must be proved that the patient is unable to breathe spontaneously.[71]

The issue is controversial in the medical ethics literature. Supporters of brain stem death[72] claim that a person whose brain stem is dead has ceased to live in anything but a mechanical way. Without brain stem activity the body is no longer an integrated whole.[73] It is also suggested that when the brain stem has gone, all that gives life value has been lost.[74] Although there may be some technical biological sense in which a body with no brain stem activity is alive, all of the facilities that give life its meaning and

[66] See, eg, PG Nowak, 'Death as the Cessation of an Organism and the Moral Status Alternative' (2023) 48 *Journal of Medicine and Philosophy* 504; JL Bernat, 'Refinements in The Organism as a Whole Rationale For Brain Death' (2019) 86 *Linacre Quarterly* 347; D Lamb, *Death, Brain Death and Ethics* (London, Croom Helm, 1985); P Lee, 'Total Brain Death and the Integration of the Body Required of a Human Being' (2016) 41 *Journal of Medicine and Philosophy* 300; J Lizza, 'Defining Death: Beyond Biology' (2018) 55 *Diametros* 1.

[67] *Airedale NHS Trust v Bland* [1993] UKHL 17, [1993] AC 789, 856.

[68] ibid 863.

[69] *Re A (A Child)* [2015] EWHC 443 (Fam). See also *Re M (Declaration of Death of Child)* [2020] EWCA Civ 164, [2020] 4 WLR 52.

[70] Academy of Medical Royal Colleges, *A Code of Practice for the Diagnosis of Brain Stem Death* (2008).

[71] ibid 17–20.

[72] See, eg, C Pallis and D Harley, *ABC of Brain Stem Death*, 2nd edn (London, BMJ Books, 1996).

[73] See M Schechtman, *Staying Alive: Personal Identity, Practical Concerns, and the Unity of a Life* (Oxford, Oxford University Press, 2014).

[74] See Pallis and Harley (n 72).

preciousness have gone.[75] Critics of brain stem death claim that it elevates the brain to being the essential organ of the person.[76] The body is made up of much more than the brain, opponents point out. Glannon argues:

> We are not just our brains but subjects whose ordered and disordered states of mind are the products of continuous interaction between and among the brain, body, and the social and natural world. The brain is not the sole cause of the mind but a relational organ that shapes and is shaped by the mind in mediating interaction between the embodied subject and the world.[77]

There are plenty of alternatives to brain stem death and it is not appropriate to go through them all here.[78] One alternative, which has received much attention, is that death should be defined as the moment at which a patient's heart stopped pumping and breathing ceased. However, medical advances have made this definition of death problematic. It is now clear that the stopping of the heart does not lead to an end of brain activity. One prominent supporter of the loss of cardiac function is the Danish Council of Ethics, which preferred it to brain death.[79] The Council took the view that the definition of death is not a technical question, but must be decided in terms of how the community as a whole understands death. It argued that the person in the street would view the stopping of the beating heart as the criterion for death, because the heart is widely seen as a symbol of life. So, even if the notion of the beating heart as the key to life is not logically or philosophically justifiable, it is intuitively felt to be the essential mark of life.

Yet much of the debate around the correct definition of death and the approach taken by the courts is marked by two assumptions. The first is that death occurs at a single moment and the second is that death is defined in terms of the loss of certain individual capacities. Both of these assumptions can be challenged. They suffer from the same essential difficulty as we encountered in seeking to define birth, in that they posit the human in terms of an isolated self-contained being. It fails to recognise that death is a process and that a key aspect of it is the relational context within which the individual is held. If our selves are seen as relational, death occurs when we are 'let go' by others; when our community no longer recognises us as an alive member.[80]

Fairly obviously, the debates around the definition of death reflect debates around the nature of personhood. For those for whom consciousness is key, the loss of a person's ability to have agency may be a marker of death. For those who see personhood as being about a human organism, the ending of the organism in biological terms may be the correct approach.[81] However, for those who understand humans in essentially relational terms, a rather different picture emerges. As that perspective on death has received less attention in the literature, I wish to develop it a bit more here.

[75] See P Lee and G Grisez, 'Total Brain Death: A Reply to Alan Shewmon' (2012) 26 *Bioethics* 275.
[76] See W Glannon, 'Our Brains Are Not Us' (2009) 23 *Bioethics* 321.
[77] ibid 329.
[78] See Chau and Herring, *Emergent Medicine and the Law* (n 65).
[79] Discussed in D Lamb, 'Wanting it Both Ways' (1990) 16 *Journal of Medical Ethics* 8.
[80] See J Ohs, A Trees and C Gibson, 'Holding On and Letting Go: Making Sense of End-of-Life Care Decisions in Families' (2015) 80 *Southern Communication Journal* 353.
[81] See MJ Walker, 'Narrative and Identity' in W Rogers et al (eds), *The Routledge Handbook of Feminist Bioethics* (New York, Routledge, 2022).

The argument of a relational self is that our identity, moral value, and recognition is found in and through our relationships. This means, in terms of death, that death occurs when we are no longer recognised as a person by those in relationship with us. It is the time when our bodies are treated as corpses and the person we were has gone (be that to nowhere or an afterlife).

A part of the relational self is a recognition that the body itself represents who we are to others and is used by us to engage with the world. But that means that the body receives social meanings and that social structures are inscribed to it.[82] It also means that death is a process. There is much evidence of the process of grief, which can start well before death, such as at the time of diagnosis. Shelley Bouchal et al refer to 'anticipatory mourning' at a terminal diagnosis as the family start the process of 'letting go' of their loved one.[83] They described how family members are, through the process, both holding on to their loved on, wanting to delay the departure, but also starting the process of letting go.

It is towards the end of life when relationships with others become key to one's identity, particularly if mental capacities fail. It is those with whom one is in a close relationship who can keep their identity together, by reminding the individual of their past, or making decisions that are in line with the values they lived by. Carers play a role towards the end of life in not just providing physical care, but ensuring the self is maintained. As Lindemann puts it:

> Once her family and the other people who cared for her engaged in the narrative work of constructing her identity, the stories by which we represented her will survive as long as any of us remember her. Indeed, they'll outlive even those of us who knew her personally, as long as they are handed down to those who come after us.[84]

It would be wrong, however, to see the law as utterly failing to take into account relational values. I will give three examples.

A. Bland

The first is well illustrated by the case of *Bland*, referred to earlier. That well-known case involved a young man in a persistent vegetative state. The judgment particularly focused on whether a withdrawal of treatment constituted a breach of duty of care. The details of the reasoning are complex, and have received much attention. I wish to focus on the outcome of the decision. Lord Goff put it this way:

> The correct formulation of the question is of particular importance in a case such as the present, where the patient is totally unconscious and where there is no hope whatsoever of any amelioration of his condition. In circumstances such as these, it may be difficult to say that it is in his best interests that the treatment should be ended. But if the question is asked,

[82] See A Halsema, 'Becoming an Embodied Social Self Capable of Relating to Norms: Ricoeur's Narrative Identity Reconsidered in the Light of Enactivism' (2020) 28(1) *Journal of French and Francophone Philosophy* 121.

[83] S Bouchal et al, 'Holding On and Letting Go: Families' Experiences of Anticipatory Mourning in Terminal Cancer' (2015) 72 *OMEGA* 42.

[84] Lindemann (n 1) 29.

> as in my opinion it should be, whether it is in his best interests that treatment which has the effect of artificially prolonging his life should be continued, that question can sensibly be answered to the effect that his best interests no longer require that it should be.[85]

This conclusion is expressed with subtlety. It means that while it was declared not to be in Tony Bland's best interests to receive the life sustaining treatment, their Lordships were careful to be clear they were not saying the life sustaining treatment was against his best interests. In other words, their Lordships were declaring the treatment neutral. This had the benefit of permitting the doctor, in consultation with the family to withdraw that treatment, even though it led to his death. However, the judgment would also have permitted the doctors, in consultation with the family, to keep the treatment going. Such an outcome would not have been possible had their Lordships declared the treatment was harming him. In effect, therefore, the judgment is passing the decision on to the doctors and families. In the absence of considerations around the rationing of health care resources, one might imagine that families will play a key role here. Where the family still want to interact with their relative and regard them as alive, the law permits that to occur. Where to the family the relative has passed on, then the patient can be permitted to die. This is very much in line with the approach advocated above.

B. Best Interests and End of Life Cases Involving Children

Second, we can see relational values being acknowledged in some of the cases involving very sick children.[86] For example, in *An NHS Trust v MB*, Holman J sided with the parents in not authorising withdrawal of life-sustaining treatment.[87] Of particular significance was that the child appeared to have very limited awareness and to be suffering relatively little in his greatly impaired sate. The life-sustaining treatment was justified by the benefits the boy received – namely, that he '[continues] to have a relationship of value to him with his family, and does continue to gain other pleasures from touch, sight and sound'.[88] The judge was clear that this was not a case where the law was giving weight to 'parental rights', but rather, that it was recognising that the mother's relationship with the child was central to his well-being.[89] Within that relationship, the boy had a quality of life worth preserving. We might imagine in a different relational context that a child with a similar medical condition might be found to lack any quality of life.

A similar point can be found in cases where the success of a treatment depends on the family providing post-operative care and support. This seemed a key feature in the English case of *Re T (A Minor) (Wardship: Medical Treatment)*, in which a child had a life-threatening liver condition.[90] The medical experts urged a liver transplant, without which the child would not live long beyond two and a half years, whereas with a liver

[85] *Bland* (n 67) 868.
[86] See J Herring, 'Disputes over Medical Treatment for Children' in J Dwyer (ed), *The Oxford Handbook of Children and the Law* (New York, Oxford University Press, 2020).
[87] *An NHS Trust v MB (A Child Represented by CAFCASS as Guardian Ad Litem)* [2006] EWHC 507 (Fam).
[88] ibid [101].
[89] ibid [106].
[90] *Re T (A Minor) (Wardship: Medical Treatment)* [1997] 1 WLR 242 (CA).

transplant the prognosis was fairly good. The parents refused to consent and the court refused to authorise the transplant. Although the case can be seen as a betrayal of children's rights, it can be justified on the basis that the treatment only had a good chance of success if those caring for the child were able to provide a supportive background to it.

Indeed, relational values can also appear even in cases where the decision is that withdrawal of treatment from the child is best. A good example case is *NHS Trust v Baby X*, involving a young boy profoundly brain damaged and kept alive by ventilation and nasal gastric tube feeding.[91] Hospital staff deemed it best to withdraw ventilation, but the parents objected. The parents thought that signs of improvement could be ascertained, and their religious faith prevented them consenting to a procedure that would lead to the child's death. The court sided with the doctors, but at the heart of the judgment Hedley J placed weight on the value of a 'good death', contrasting 'death in the arms and presence of parents and a death wired up to machinery and so isolated from all human contact in the course of futile treatment'.[92] The parent–child relationship played a key role in the welfare assessment, even though the outcome was not that desired by the parents.

Such cases may offer hope for the cases where doctors and parents disagree over very sick children, such as the controversies around the Charlie Gard case.[93] The solution is to bring together the expertise of doctors and parents. At least in cases of serious medical conditions, parents have a significant interest in whether the child receives the treatment. They have an interest as persons possessing parental responsibilities, as caregivers who have invested their lives (emotionally and practically) in the child and in his or her upbringing, and as persons whose own personal lives are bound up with the child's life and so can be impacted greatly by the decision ultimately made. In one of the best discussions on this issue, Jo Bridgeman writes:

> [R]ather than attempt to articulate justice and provide explanations for forced treatment in terms of the rights of the abstract autonomous individual of liberal legal theory or the paternalistic overriding of those rights, it would be instructive to listen to the parents of sick children, health care professionals and lawyers acting in partnership in order to secure the well-being of the child. If the "different voice" can be heard in what they say, decisions relating to the medical treatment of children may be more convincingly explained in terms of the responsibility of caring than presently achieved with expressions of autonomy. What we hear may enable us to develop, out of the vague best interests test, an ethic of care model for health care decisions in relation to children which explains why, because we care, sometimes medical treatment may be imposed upon them despite their wishes to the contrary.[94]

Encouraging this dialogue will enable doctors to combine their particular skills and knowledge with parents' knowledge of the individual child, as well as to respect the values of the child's family on issues over which there is no community consensus.

[91] *NHS Trust v Baby X* [2012] EWHC 2188 (Fam).

[92] ibid [25].

[93] See discussions in I Goold, J Herring and C Auckland (eds), *Parental Rights, Best Interests and Significant Harms: Medical Decision-Making on Behalf of Children Post-Great Ormond Street Hospital v Gard* (Oxford, Hart Publishing, 2019).

[94] J Bridgeman, '"Because We Care?" The Medical Treatment of Children' in S Sheldon and M Thomson (eds), *Feminist Perspectives on Health Care Law* (London, Cavendish Publishing, 1998) 113–14.

In this view, it is not possible to produce a single clear rule to apply in all cases so that parents always win or doctors always win. Rather, the solution is to be fashioned from the parent–child relationships themselves because, whatever else happens in these medical decisions, the child and his or her caregivers will need to continue in their relationships together and those relationships are worth more than any abstract legal rights. Health care professionals and public authorities should work with parents, to join together their respective skills to promote the best results for children. In the vast majority of cases, parents and medical professionals do cooperate well. Parents provide an invaluable source of information about the children, their relationships, and their quirks and individualised needs. Professionals recognise that forcing parents to accept treatment that they strongly oppose is likely to adversely impact the child's emotional well-being. Whether parents are preparing a child who is terrified before an operation, encouraging the child through months of recuperation and therapy, or holding a dying child, they see that a child's welfare is tied up with the interests of his or her parents and caregivers. It is thus wrong to view these cases as raising a simple tension between parental power and child welfare. The lives and loves of parents and children are entwined in complex ways.

C. Relational Death as Dignifying

COVID-19 has raised the issue of isolation at death. If we see death in relational terms, 'letting go' is an important aspect of human dignity. As Parks and Howard write, 'as we have seen during this pandemic, dying in nursing homes has become a lonely, fraught affair. Being isolated from loved ones has become standard procedure in nursing homes in order to protect all residents from a possible deadly infection'.[95] While this chapter cannot resolve the weighing up of the competing interests that they identify, it does highlight the particular harm of the lonely death. As those authors go on to write:

> [j]ust as relationships are an essential part of having a meaningful life for most people, so too are they necessary for a meaningful death.
>
> In an ideal world, everyone would die a death that they would consider good. A 'good death' – one in which a person died where they wanted, when they wanted, surrounded by who they wanted – is likely not possible for everyone living through Covid-19, but we can do more to ensure that people die in ways that are in keeping with their express wishes.[96]

As Lindemann put it, '[p]erhaps it's when we are dying that we need most to be held – even coercively held – in our identities, that others may ratify the goodness of our lives and being, and keep us in that goodness'.[97]

Perhaps one of the lessons of COVID is that we need to recognise the relational significance of death. It is not just a 'medical event'. A dignified death, usually, involves a relational experience. Depriving a dying person of others to hold on to and then let go

[95] Parks and Howard (n 9) 593.
[96] ibid 594.
[97] Lindemann (n 1) 193.

of them is to deprive them of what, for many people, is a central aspect of death. More than that, it is a failure of society to recognise our relational obligations to our fellow members.

V. Conclusion

Rainer Maria Rilke writes

> We need, in love, to practice only this: letting each other go.
>
> For holding on comes easily; we do not need to learn it.[98]

This chapter has explored birth and death as central moments in life. For both, the law struggles to find the language to describe or the categories to use for these moments. This is because the law tends to focus on individual concepts of the self and of legal rights. Yet the moments of birth and death are relational. The law cannot capture the profoundly interconnected relationship with its individualised understanding of the legal person or the rights that flow from that. Similarly, in death, the law struggles to find in the definition of death tests that reflect the relational nature of the letting go that is death.

This is not to say the law takes no account of relational values. We have seen in decisions around best interests in life or death cases that relational values are sometimes acknowledged. And the law is right to place enormous weight on the moment of birth, although the explanation for why that is important is in terms of the profound shift in the relational context, rather than the state of the fetus.

Life and death, however, are just the most striking examples of our relational natures. It is not just at birth or death that a relational self needs to be used to reimagine legal response. As Lindemann writes:

> Healthy specimens of our kind are inducted into personhood through the same social interactions by which we acquire our linguistic, rational, and moral agency. It's of the utmost importance that this be done, as we would otherwise be damaged, stunted, misshapen, unable … to live a human life.[99]

Our lives from birth onwards are deeply relational and marked by care and innate vulnerability. The image of the autonomous, self-sufficient and independent self, promoted too often by the law, is a fiction throughout our lives. In birth and death we see ourselves as we truly are: vulnerable, interconnected, dependent and relational.

[98] RM Rilke, 'Requiem for a Friend', S Mitchell (trans), (1981) 82 *Paris Review* 2.
[99] Lindemann (n 1) 202.

3

The Margins of Private Law: SB-8 and the Private Enforcement of Abortion Law

JESSE WALL

I. The Margins of Life and the Margins of Private Law

This chapter is about both private law at the margins of life and private law at the margins of private law. In the foreground is a response to a legislative attempt to relocate abortion law from the public law hemisphere into the private law hemisphere of a legal system. This chapter seeks to find a way to affirm the intuition that the law that governs the access to abortion services belongs to the public hemisphere – the criminal, administrative and constitutional law – of the legal system. The initial catalyst for this inquiry is the Texas state legislation that enables private individuals to bring a civil proceeding against physicians who perform an abortion, or any other person, who 'knowingly engages' in 'conduct that aids or abets the performance or inducement of an abortion', that contravenes the 'heartbeat rule'.[1] Constitutional changes, which now permit state officials to enforce the 'heartbeat rule',[2] lessen the need for the civil action. Nonetheless, this (momentary) privatisation of abortion law nonetheless brings to the fore questions about how and why we allocate disputes and controversies to either the public law or private law hemispheres of a legal system.

Hence, however we might respond to this new civil action engages a background inquiry into how we understand these two hemispheres of the legal system. And the scholarship on this is fractured. For critical scholars the distinction between the public and private hemispheres 'either does not exist or necessarily serves pernicious ends'.[3] Private law, for them, is just another thinly veiled instrument of public policy.[4] For economists of law, the distinction can be reduced to a procedural question that can be answered in terms of economic efficiency. According to them, we can employ the public sphere, and 'utilize public officials', either 'to decrease enforcement costs rather than

[1] Texas Heartbeat Act, ch 62, sec 3, § 171.208, 2021 Tex Gen Laws 125. This law is often referred to as 'SB-8'.

[2] *Dobbs v Jackson Women's Health Organization* 597 US 215 (2022).

[3] R West, 'The New Legal Criticism' (2017) 117 *Columbia Law Review* 144, 146.

[4] See D Kennedy, 'The Stages of the Decline of the Public/Private Distinction' (1982) 130 *University of Pennsylvania Law Review* 1349 and LM Seidman, 'Critical Constitutionalism Now' (2006) 75 *Fordham Law Review* 575, 578.

to escalate conflicts with individual defendants'[5] or where 'no private plaintiffs stand ready and available'.[6] Contrary to both these reductionist claims, formal scholars have sought to 'reclaim significant autonomy for private law and legal doctrine in both institutional and substantive terms'.[7] Hence, as Barker explains, private law is distinctly the law that governs interactions between private individuals, and the 'rights and remedies are structured in private law as interactions between the doer and sufferer of a particular injustice'.[8]

The problem, that Gardner observed in *From Personal Life to Private Law*, is that '[t]heoretical work on private law, as on many other issues in moral, political, and legal philosophy, tends to be excessively polarized'.[9] As he explains further:

> Depressed by utilitarianism, people are naturally tempted to become not just non-utilitarians but anti-utilitarians, siding against the utilitarians on anything and everything. Shocked by an economic analysis, people are naturally tempted to rest everything on the one thing which, to their eyes, the economists missed. Appalled by one kind of reductive thinking, people are inevitably tempted by reductive thinking of some diametrically opposed kind. But most of the truth, here as elsewhere, is not diametrically opposed to anything. Life is full of tragedies. But having to choose between hyper-relationalism and hypo-relationalism in how we think about private law, or about personal life, is not one of them.[10]

Following this cue, I aim to affirm here our shared intuition that the law that governs access to abortion services belongs to the 'public hemisphere' without this explanation becoming polarised. The explanation that I offer here looks beyond claims about relationality, accountability, public and private morality, and principles of justice, and considers the distinction between the public and private sphere in terms of *tasks*. I will claim here that private law has the modest task of protecting what each person has, whilst public law has the immodest task of limiting what each person (and the state) can do. We should therefore expect a *public law* restriction to access of abortion services, since it is a restriction of what each person can do with regards to their own body. Our concerns about relationality, accountability, public and private morality and principles of justice, then stem from this explanation.

II. Five Objections

The catalyst for this inquiry is an unease with recent abortion law reform in Texas. Let us start by considering how we might want to object to it. The Texas Legislature enacted two significant changes, the first being prohibiting the termination of a pregnancy once embryotic cardiac activity can be detected (typically after six weeks gestational age).

[5] RA Epstein, 'The Tort/Crime Distinction: A Generation Later' (1996) 76 *Boston University Law Review* 1, 8.

[6] ibid.

[7] K Barker, 'Private Law: Key Encounters with Public Law' in K Barker and D Jensen (eds), *Private Law: Key Encounters with Public Law* (Cambridge, Cambridge University Press, 2013) 12.

[8] ibid 13.

[9] J Gardner, *From Personal Life to Private Law* (Oxford, Oxford University Press, 2018) 57.

[10] ibid.

This is the 'fetal heartbeat rule'. The second change is the creation of a civil action for performing, or aiding or abetting, an unlawful abortion. It is this second development that will concern us here. The civil action was created prior to the United States Supreme Court overruling *Roe v Wade* and *Planned Parenthood v Casey* in *Dobbs v Jackson Women's Health Organization*.[11] At the time, the enactment of the civil action was an attempt by the legislature to 'privatise' a branch of the criminal law in order to by-pass public law standards that would otherwise apply (and now, no longer apply).

Specifically, the new action under 'SB-8' enables any person ('other than an officer or employee of a state or local governmental entity in this state') to bring a civil proceed ing against any person who performs an abortion that contravenes the 'heartbeat rule',[12] or any other person who 'knowingly engages' (or even 'intends to engage') in 'conduct that aids or abets the performance or inducement of an abortion' that contravenes the 'heartbeat rule'.[13] If the civil claim is successful, then the 'defendant' is required to pay damages of $10,000 or more for each abortion (along with costs and attorney's fees) to the private individuals who commenced the proceeding.[14] The objective behind SB-8 is clear: since the 'heartbeat rule' was inconsistent with the constitutional guarantees that limit a state's power to interfere with a person's right to personal privacy, the civil action attempts to restrict access to abortion services in a manner that infringes constitutional guarantees whilst attempting to insulate the state from judicial review by a federal court.

This attempt to by-pass public law standards and constitutional guarantees through the creation of a (nonetheless court-enforced) civil action leaves plenty for public lawyers to discuss. Private lawyers might otherwise feel that they have little to say. After all, it is the privatisation of public law that is the story here, and that should concern public lawyers. Yet, the privatisation of public law should also concern private lawyers. What needs to be explained, from a private law perspective, is why the conflict between fetal interests and reproductive autonomy cannot be properly addressed through the civil action under SB-8, specifically. And why, more generally, the conflict cannot be properly addressed through the private law. In formulating the specific explanation, we might start with some initial concerns:

(a) *The absence of relationality*. If private law 'governs our interpersonal relationships as free and equal persons'[15] then SB-8 pulls together private persons – such as a physician and an individual bystander – who have had no prior interaction or no interpersonal relationship into a civil procedure;
(b) *'[T]he radically discretionary authority that the private law plaintiff enjoys over the court, and through the court, over the defendant'*.[16] Under SB-8, an individual bystander can exercise broad prosecutorial discretion without being burdened by the public law standards that would otherwise apply to public officials;
(c) *The privatisation of a public morality*. If fetal interests and the right to reproductive autonomy are 'a matter of public interest in the sense that it properly concerns all

[11] *Dobbs* (n 2); *Roe v Wade* 410 US 113 (1973); *Planned Parenthood v Casey* 505 US 833 (1992).
[12] Texas Heartbeat Act, sec 3, § 171.208(a)(1).
[13] ibid sec 3, § 171.208(a)(2).
[14] Ibid sec 3, § 171.208(b)(2).
[15] H Dagan and A Dorfman, 'Just Relationships' (2016) 116 *Columbia Law Review* 1395, 1397.
[16] Gardner (n 9) 205.

members of the polity'[17] then SB-8 shifts those broad 'public law' concerns into a field of narrower, distinctly private law, values that are limited to a concern for freedom and equality; or

(d) *The attempt to punish wrongdoing rather than 'rectif[ying] both the normative gain and the normative loss'*[18] *through the award of damages.* If the purpose of the damages award ($10,000 or more for each unlawful abortion) under SB-8 is to deter and punish, then it is unclear why the third-party complainant – who has incurred no harm or suffered no loss – ought to financially benefit from the claim.

Yet, none of these concerns isolate the impropriety of SB-8. To be clear, they are all valid concerns that stem from an explanation for why abortion law ought to be public law, but they do not isolate (what I take to be) the fundamental distinction between the public law and private law spheres. What is complicated about this inquiry is that any disagreement here is disagreement about the explanatory priority of these concerns. For instance, we might disagree about whether one feature, such as 'relationality', explains the distinctiveness of private law, or whether that 'relationality' is only an implication of another feature (such as, civil process, private morality, corrective justice) where that latter feature *is* distinctive about private law. The implication may be a sound one, but only because it follows from something logically prior in the explanation of the distinction. It is my contention here (and more crudely elsewhere)[19] that the above features are mere implications of a fundamental distinction.

The fundamental distinction that I seek to endorse here is a distinction between:

(e) the tasks of public law and private law. The public and private hemispheres of the legal system perform the same general job in a different way; private law has the modest task of protecting what each person has whilst public law has the immodest task of limiting what each person can do. Hence, the problem with SB-8 is not that it limits what a person can do, but that it enables a private individual to be that limit.

An implication immediately falls out of this distinction: 'respecting what another person has' (being duty-bound) is not the same as 'being limited to what we can do' (being prohibited). I will explain this distinction when we return to my contention about *the task of private law*. But before we can do so, we need to first resolve our initial concerns about relationality, procedural powers (and accountability), public morality and principles of justice.

III. Relationality

SB-8 imposes a wide range of duties. It is not just physicians who may be the subject of a civil proceeding, but anyone else who 'knowingly engages in conduct that aids or abets

[17] RA Duff and SE Marshall, 'Public and Private Wrongs' in J Chalmers, F Leverick and L Farmer (eds), *Essays in Criminal Law in Honour of Sir Gerald Gordon* (Edinburgh, Edinburgh University Press, 2010) 71.

[18] EJ Weinrib, *The Idea of Private Law*, rev edn (Oxford, Oxford University Press, 2012) 136.

[19] J Wall, 'Public Wrongs and Private Wrongs' (2018) 31 *Canadian Journal of Law & Jurisprudence* 177.

the performance or inducement of an abortion' (regardless of whether the person knew the abortion was unlawful).[20] The aiding explicitly extends to 'reimbursing the costs of an abortion through insurance' and may even extend (given the broad and inclusive language) to other third parties, such as a clergyman who counsels women, or a friend who provides transport to an abortion clinic.[21] The claimant, who may initiate proceedings, is most likely to have no relationship with, or have had no interaction with the physician, the pregnant person, the fetus, the insurance company, the clergyman or the friend. In this sense, the claimant is a bystander or a third party.

In comparison, we are encouraged to think about private law in terms of relationality and interactions. 'At the heart of private law' we are told by Gold, 'is a conception of relational duties and rights. A relational duty is a duty owed by an individual to persons or classes of persons, in contrast to a general duty to simply act in a certain way'.[22] 'Private law addresses', according to Dagan and Dorfman:

> our interpersonal interactions by marshalling rights and obligations that take a relational form. … It addresses, in other words, the rights and duties they bear in relation to one another as well as the frameworks of interpersonal interaction they sustain.[23]

Finally, 'fair and coherent reasons for liability' are, according to Weinrib:

> correlative in structure in that they treat each party's position as the mirror image of the other's. This correlativity reflects the defining structural feature of liability itself: that liability of a particular defendant is always a liability to a particular plaintiff. Correlatively structured reasons focus not on either party separately from the other but on the relationship between them as doer and sufferer of the same injustice.[24]

Hence, we may formulate our concern with SB-8 in terms of relationality: there is no 'relational duty' owed by the physician (or the pregnant person, the insurance company, the clergyman or the driver) to the claimant; there are no 'interpersonal interactions' to marshal rights obligations around; the physician is not the doer, and the bystander-complainant is not the sufferer, of 'the same injustice'. We can also note, for now, that the absence of relationality is a feature of abortion law generally: the conflict is between fetal interests and a person's rights to reproductive autonomy, but the legal proceeding inevitably draws a third party into the conflict. How SB-8 differs is that it draws in a private individual, rather than a public official, as the third party (we will consider this distinction in the next section).

As I will explain in this section, the absence of relationality should not be our central concern with SB-8. Not because there will always be the absence of relationality, but because private law – contrary to the above 'hyper-relationalism' – is only 'loosely relational'.[25] Moreover, as I will eventually explain in this chapter, the loose relationality

[20] Texas Heartbeat Act, sec 3, § 171.208(a)(2).

[21] ibid. See IG Cohen, EY Adashi MD and LO Gostin, 'The Supreme Court, the Texas Abortion Law (SB8), and the Beginning of the End of *Roe v Wade*?' (2021) 326(15) *Journal of the American Medical Association* 1473.

[22] AS Gold, 'A Moral Rights Theory of Private Law' (2011) 52 *William & Mary Law Review* 1873, 1886.

[23] Dagan and Dorfman (n 15) 1410.

[24] EJ Weinrib, 'Private Law and Public Right' (2011) 61 *University of Toronto Law Journal* 191, 192.

[25] Gardner (n 9) 50.

of private law follows from, rather than constructs, the distinctiveness of the private law hemisphere.

In saying that private law is only 'loosely relational' I do not deny that 'strictly relational' duties sometimes arise in private law. They are, however, the exception and not the rule. For instance, consider how a medical professional owes a range of duties, some strictly relational, some loosely relational. All medical professionals who perform or facilitate the termination of a pregnancy will owe duties to provide services only in a particular way, only in particular circumstances and only after following a particular process. The reason for some of those duties will be grounded in the special relationship between themselves, a medical professional and the pregnant person, as a patient. For instance, the medical professional will owe duties of confidentiality because there is value in maintaining relationships of free and full disclosure of information. We have special reasons to sustain this particular '[framework] of interpersonal interaction'.[26] The duty imposed on the medical professional is a strictly relational duty since it exists because of 'some special relationship with the person to whom the duty is owed'.[27]

In comparison, the reason for some other duties will be grounded in the interests of the pregnant person (B), such as the duty to obtain informed consent and the duty to take reasonable care. These duties exist 'by reason of the threat that [the physician's] actions pose to some or all of the value in her life'.[28] A physician owes a duty of care when terminating a pregnancy, performing a sterilisation procedure, storing gametes or any other intervention that may affect her fertility, because the person has an interest in – or right to – control over their own reproductive body. The duty is imposed on the physician solely because the physician's actions pose a threat to reproductive autonomy. These are all loosely relational; 'relational' only in the way that the torts of trespass, invasion of privacy and defamation are relational, because one person's actions pose some threat to a value in someone else's life.

Except – the hyper-relational-theorists would interrupt – in each of those cases, the duty owed correlates with a *right* to reproductive control. In this way, relationality re-emerges on the basis that 'rights and their correlative duties provide the content for private law's correlatively structured reasoning' since '[b]y their very nature right and duty are correlative concepts'.[29] Now, rights (as distinct from interests) matter. There are important doctrinal features of how private law *rights* attract particular methods of protection – some being rights *in rem*, some imposing strict duties, some being actionable *per se*, and so on.[30] However, analysis is required to justify this form of robust protection, and this should not be shortcut by the assertion of 'rights' in the place of 'interests'. Nor should the existence of robust private law rights be taken to demonstrate that private law *is about* private law rights.

What we are interested in, here, is the imposition of the duty. Whether or not the duty is correlative with a right, *the reason for why* the duty is imposed, remains the

[26] Dagan and Dorfman (n 15) 1410.
[27] Gardner (n 9) 23.
[28] ibid 49.
[29] Weinrib (n 24) 192.
[30] See J Wall, *Being and Owning: The Body, Bodily Material, and the Law* (Oxford, Oxford University Press, 2015) 143–56.

same; because each person has a (sufficiently important) interest in making choices about her reproductive body. Hence, if we are interested in the imposition of duties, then the absence of a right should not concern us. If 'a duty counts as owed to another in virtue of the reasons for its existence, no more and no less',[31] then I can owe duties in the absence of rights-holders: I can owe duties to future generations to preserve the environment, I can owe duties to yet-to-be-born children or grandchildren to test for inheritable genetic conditions and (at the other margin of life) it is plausible for me to owe duties to respect the privacy and bodily integrity (and so on) of a deceased person. The existence of the duty does not, itself, compel relationality between rights-holder and duty-bearer. The duty, rather, is merely predicated upon sufficient reasons for its existence.

With that in mind, let us return to our specific concern here with SB-8. Here we have a duty on a physician that serves to protect fetal interests. It is not merely a duty without a correlative right, it is a duty-*bearer* (the physician) without a correlative rights-*holder* (the fetus). I say that, initially, as a matter of posited law: according to the 'born alive rule', the fetus has no enforceable rights before birth. Legal personhood, and all the rights associated with it, supervene on a child once the child is 'fully and completely born when it is completely delivered from the body of its mother'.[32] However, denying the fetus legal *personhood* should not be conflated with denying the fetus legal *status*. As Lord Mustill explained in *Attorney-General's Reference (No 3 of 1994)*:

> This seems to me an entire non sequitur, for it omits the possibility that the foetus does not … have any relevant type of personality but is an organism sui generis lacking at this stage the entire range of characteristics both of the mother to which it is physically linked and of the complete human being which it will later become.[33]

In other words, the 'born alive rule' does not reduce the fetus to the mother (thereby denying independent legal status) and nor does recognising independent legal status imply personhood. A fetus may have, in law, independent interests. It is possible, in our legal analysis, to consider the interests of the fetus as an 'organism *sui generis*'. It is also possible, I suggest, to do so in our ethical analysis. That is, we can accept that '[t]he human fetus is distinctly unlike rocks, trees, and insects in ways that render ascriptions of personhood *more* intelligible with respect to them'[34] without having to accept that the 'the biological continuity of fetuses with later humans' gives us 'enough to consider whether the moral status we accord to developed human beings extends back to human beings *pre*-birth'.[35] A fetus may have a moral and legal interests that are untethered to the question of moral and legal personhood.[36] *Life is full of tragedies*, we might say (following Gardner), *but having to choose between hyper-personhood and hypo-personhood, is not one of them.*

[31] Gardner (n 9) 56.

[32] *R v Hutty* [1953] VLR 338, 339; affirmed in *R v Iby* [2005] NSWCCA 178, (2005) 63 NSWLR 278; see K Savell, 'Is the "Born Alive" Rule Outdated and Indefensible?' (2006) 28 *Sydney Law Review* 62.

[33] *Attorney-General's Reference (No 3 of 1994)* [1998] AC 245 (HL) 255.

[34] K Greasley, *Arguments about Abortion: Personhood, Morality, and Law* (Oxford, Oxford University Press, 2017) 22.

[35] ibid.

[36] R Dworkin, *Life's Dominion: An Argument about Abortion and Euthanasia* (London, Harper Collins, 1993) 10; see J Wall, 'Abortion for Hedgehogs' (2020) 11 *Jurisprudence* 483.

In all jurisdictions that restrict access to abortion services, duties are imposed that are grounded in the interests of the fetus. These are general duties 'to simply act in a certain way'[37] that are owed 'in virtue of the reasons for its existence'.[38] The temptation is to say that such duties cannot be private law duties because private law duties are relational duties. The point of the discussion so far is that we ought to resist the temptation. There is nothing bound-up in the idea of a duty that requires a correlative rights-holder, and even private law duties are only relational in the sense that the duties relate to – serve to protect – someone else's interests. It is coherent (so far) to impose private law duties that serve fetal interests.

IV. Accountability

I have so far argued that if we are interested in the imposition of duties, then the absence of a right should not concern us. It should not concern us – that is – until we want to hold a person responsible for their breach of the duty (their 'wrongdoing'). When it comes to the notions of accountability or responsibility we need to recognise a different kind of right: the procedural right to hold another to account for their breach. As Duff explains, this is because, if we want to hold a person (A) responsible for their wrongdoing (X), then we must '[specify] … to whom A is responsible for X'.[39] If we are to hold person (A) responsible, then A must have the ability to respond, and another person (B) must have 'the right or standing to call [A] to account'.[40] We might then view the division between the public and private hemispheres of the legal system in terms of whether a private individual or a public official has the procedural right to hold another person responsible.

The contrast here does not merely concern the identity of the procedural right-holder, but the powers of the procedural right-holder. Herein lies an important contrast. Private individuals are both unconstrained and unsupported. A private individual has the broad discretion whether to exercise their procedural right to hold another to account (for their breach of duty) or not, a private individual may exercise their procedural right for good reasons, vindictive reasons or for no reason at all, and hence, a private individual may exercise their procedural rights erratically, unreasonably or not at all. At the same time, private individuals require the court's assistance if they are to exercise any investigative or forensic powers, and they must rely on their own resources to fund the exercise of holding another person to account. Public officials, in contrast, are constrained and supported. There are preconditions that may need to be satisfied before they can hold another person to account; they are required to act on a specified set of reasons when deciding whether to exercise the procedural right. Public officials are empowered to exercise standalone investigative and fact-finding powers and are publicly funded to commence proceedings in order to hold individuals to account for

[37] Gold (n 22) 1886.

[38] Gardner (n 9) 56.

[39] RA Duff, *Answering for Crime: Responsibility and Liability in the Criminal Law* (Oxford, Hart Publishing, 2007) 25.

[40] ibid.

their wrongdoing. Note that none of these features are strictly necessary. We might find strict procedural limitations in a private law proceeding (in family law, for instance), or privately funded organisations exercising powers of prosecution (in animal welfare law, for instance). Nonetheless, these features – of constraint/discretion and support/independence – tend to calcify around these two poles of either a private individual or public official.

Given this loose distinction between the procedural powers of public official and private individuals, what might then concern us about SB-8 is not just how the responsibility for holding people to account (for aiding or abetting abortions that are contrary to 'the heartbeat rule') is handed over to private individuals, but also how private individuals can now exercise 'radically discretionary authority'.[41] There are no limits on how the procedural right may be exercised in an arbitrary, unreasonable or even malicious, manner. In a different context, we might also be concerned about the lack of investigatory or financial support being afforded to the private individual or organisation being required to hold people to account for their wrongdoing.

Moreover, we need not look far for support for this type of proceduralist concern with SB-8. Scholars of different stripes try to explain the distinction between the public law and private law hemispheres in terms of the choice between the (unconstrained and unsupported) private individual and the (constrained and supported) public official. It should not surprise us that for economists of law, this is a choice about efficiency. If '[t]here is work to be done and it ought to be done in the best possible way', then the choice between private or public agents is a 'pragmatic' one that 'depends on a comparison between the expected efficacy' of these possible agents 'in performing the job'.[42]

What might surprise rather, is how the economists of law are not alone in viewing the choice between private and private agents as a 'pragmatic one'. Edwards and Simester, for instance, argue that:

> Wrongdoers are publicly responsible when public officials are well placed to get answers from those wrongdoers on behalf of beneficiaries – those whose interests generate the duty the wrongdoer has breached. In such cases, officials have a right to call such wrongdoers to answer for their wrongs.[43]

They note that the public official's right to call suspected wrongdoers to answer only arises where beneficiaries (or victims) are 'poorly placed to get the answers owed' and 'public officials are often better placed to get answers on their behalf'.[44] If 'putting officials in control of proceedings can help to solve problems of duplicated effort, unreliable detection, intimidation and manipulation' then public officials ought to have the procedural right.[45] This is an assessment that turns on *epistemic* (rather than economic) efficiency, and as Edwards and Simester note, it is an assessment that 'depends heavily on empirical facts'.[46]

[41] Gardner (n 9) 205.
[42] A Harel, 'Public and Private Law' in MD Dubber and T Hörnle (eds), *The Oxford Handbook of Criminal Law* (Oxford, Oxford University Press, 2014) 1051.
[43] J Edwards and A Simester, 'What's Public About Crime?' (2017) 37 *OJLS* 105, 132.
[44] ibid 125.
[45] ibid 126.
[46] ibid.

Now, if we are to impose duties that protect fetal interests, and hold others to account for the breach of those duties, then we require someone to hold the duty-bearer/wrongdoer to account. Typically, when it comes to abortion law, a public authority stands in that position. Yet, the implication so far is that there may be nothing in the idea of a duty, or the notion of accountability, that prevents private individuals from standing in that position – provided that there is a reason for them to do so, even if it is only a contingent empirical reason.

We could then, with relative ease, work through the pragmatic and empirical considerations that can explain why a civil claimant should not have the procedural right to claim against those who aid or abet the procurement of an unlawful abortion. Even if we limit ourselves to Edwards and Simester's empirical facts, we can note: individuals risk duplicating their efforts to bring proceedings; without any investigatory powers individuals are poorly placed to get answers and will identify and detect the wrongdoing in an unreliable way; and an individual may be intimidated or manipulated from bringing a claim.

There are, however, principles behind these pragmatic considerations, in the same way that there are always values that sit behind any concern for efficiency. For economists of law, it is the economic efficiency of allocated resources relative to an outcome. Whilst public officials may be a great drain on resources, economists of law explain that we 'utilize public officials' either 'to decrease enforcement costs rather than to escalate conflicts with individual defendants' or where 'no private plaintiffs stand ready and available' (and, I might add, incentivised) to pursue the wrongdoing.[47] There are other ways in which the law can be efficient: it can be epistemically (in)efficient – public officials can be more (or less) accurate in their fact-finding; it can be reconciliatorily (in)efficient – public officials may be more (or less) efficient at inflaming or extinguishing the underlying resentment; it can be rule-of-law efficient – public officials can dispassionately ensure consistent prosecution (without a personal or partisan agenda). As Gardner explains:

> What the law should be efficient at, the moral critic should say, is not, or not only, increasing wealth or allocating resources but (also) doing justice, preventing wrongs, protecting rights, mitigating insecurity, enabling recourse, guaranteeing freedom, aiding reconciliation, or … you can insert any imaginable good here.[48]

Public officials will be 'efficient' or 'inefficient' depending upon what we are interested in them being efficient at. What is interesting about how we 'utilise public officials' is how we are concerned about different 'goods' or 'values' when it comes to utilising public officials. We are sometimes entirely at ease with one party being coerced into an out-of-court settlement whilst, in other contexts, we insist on a very visible and transparent form of 'public' accountability. We are sometimes entirely at ease with financial incentives motivating the legal action whilst, in other contexts, we want dispassionate and consistent prosecution. We are sometimes at ease with public resources and standalone

[47] Epstein (n 5) 8.

[48] J Gardner, 'Tort Law and its Theory' in J Tasioulas (ed), *The Cambridge Companion to the Philosophy of Law* (Cambridge, Cambridge University Press, 2020) 369.

investigatory powers being used to pursue a wrongdoer, whilst, in other contexts, we expect privately funded claims that leave any procedural help to be judicially mediated.

Hence, in some contexts it is the (efficient) pursuit of a value (say, the rule of law) at the expense of the efficient pursuit of another value (say, rights-enforcement). These ostensibly 'pragmatic considerations' appear to be giving effect to some background values. If the choice between private individuals and public officials 'depends on a comparison between the expected efficacy' of these possible agents 'in performing the job', then we need clarity as to what the 'job' is. It may be that there are different 'jobs', or different ways of performing 'the job', that each engage different values. Nonetheless, the onus then is on the 'moral critic' or 'non-pragmatist' to find the principle that can explain why a private individual or public official ought to have the procedural right. Let us now see if we can discharge the burden of proof.

V. Public Morality

One principled reason for why we might want public officials, rather than private individuals, to hold another person to account for their wrongdoing (their breach of a duty) is because the wrong infringes a particular set of 'public values'. On this view, the public and private hemispheres of the legal system are animated by a different set of substantive values. In terms of the public sphere, a group can (according to Marshall and Duff):

> '[S]hare' the wrongs done to its individual members, insofar as it defines and identifies itself as a community united by mutual concern, by genuinely shared (as distinct from contingently coincident) values and interests, and by the shared recognition that its members' goods (and their identity) are bound up with their membership of the community.[49]

Understanding the public sphere as being animated by 'values of mutual concern' then might provide 'an appropriate perspective from which we can understand the point and significance of a "criminal" rather than a "civil" process'.[50] As a community united in shared and mutual concern, we 'owe it to the victim to take seriously the wrong she has suffered', and 'we also owe it to the wrongdoer … to respond … to her wrongdoing' in order to censure the wrong.[51] Public officials discharge the community's responsibility 'to take her wrong as also [a public] wrong' and the criminal law aims to address and remedy the wrong 'in terms of the wrongdoer's relationship to the community as well as to the individual victim'.[52]

In comparison, the private law hemisphere might then concern a narrower set of values, such as 'the liberal state's promise to respect the freedom of individuals'.[53] Private law adheres to the promise of respect by 'construct[ing] a framework of opportunities

[49] SE Marshall and RA Duff, 'Criminalization and Sharing Wrongs' (1998) 11 *Canadian Journal of Law & Jurisprudence* 7, 20.
[50] ibid.
[51] ibid 16.
[52] ibid 20.
[53] LF O'Mahony, 'Property Outsiders and the Hidden Politics of Doctrinalism' (2014) 67 *Current Legal Problems* 409, 423.

for individuals in cooperation with others to become authors of their own lives'.[54] It 'serves as guarantor of this equal freedom provided that it both articulates the appropriate standards of conduct and, should those standards be violated, it makes it as if the wrong had never happened'.[55] Hence, by imposing primary duties, coupled with duties of reparation, private law then 'stands on its own distinctive ground'[56] by seeking to give effect to a narrow set of values that are necessary to the freedom and autonomy of the individual, and avoids being 'just another means to serve our public goals'.[57]

On this understanding, the right to reproductive autonomy is a private law right,[58] one that speaks to the freedom and autonomy of persons to make their own procreative choices. And private law actions – such as, deceit,[59] negligence[60] and bailment[61] – protect (with mixed success) this right. The interests of the fetus will be protected, parasitically, when fetal interests align with the exercise of the right to reproductive autonomy. Otherwise, on this understanding, protection of fetal interests (where they do not align with the right to reproductive control) must come from a place of 'shared and mutual concern', where the fetus is a beneficiary of the state's protection.

It follows, on this values-based account, that limiting access to the termination of pregnancies represents a 'shared a mutual concern' for the interests of the fetus, and hence, belongs to the public morality of the public sphere. The impropriety of SB-8, on this account, lies in the privatisation of public morality, by transplanting a shared and mutual concern for the interests of the fetus (when it arises) into the narrow confines of freedom and equality of persons. This forces (on this values-based account) a reconfiguration in one of two ways: either a fetus has personhood (and rights to freedom and equality) by stealth (which is no surprise, given the broader political context), or a civil action is repurposed to give effect to values of shared and mutual concern.

The first reconfiguration takes us back to questions of personhood (which are touched on above but will not be resolved here). Contrary to the values-based distinction, I suggest that the second reconfiguration should not worry us. This is because the principled distinction between public (officials/law/hemispheres) and private (individuals/law/hemispheres) does not concern a distinct set of values. The criminal law and private law value the same things – they protect the same bundle of goods. The interests and values that the civil law is concerned with overlap with those that the criminal law is concerned with. For example, both the civil and criminal law protect a person's interest in having the exclusive use and control of their property. Both branches of the law also protect a person's interest in determining who (if anyone at all) may interact with their body and under what circumstances. Many of these 'traditional crimes against the

[54] H Collins, 'Utility and Rights in Common Law Reasoning: Rebalancing Private Law through Constititutionalization' (2007) 30 *Dalhousie Law Journal* 1, 4–5, as quoted in O'Mahony (n 53) 423.

[55] A Ripstein, 'As If it Had Never Happened' (2007) 48 *William & Mary Law Review* 1957, 1969.

[56] Dagan and Dorfman (n 15) 1442.

[57] ibid 1410, as quoted in J Gardner, 'Dagan and Dorfman on the Value of Private Law' (2017) 117 *Columbia Law Review* 179, 180.

[58] See A Broadmore, *The Private Law Right to Reproductive Control* (PhD Thesis, University of Auckland, 2023).

[59] *PP v DD* [2017] ONCA 180; *Magill v Magill* [2006] HCA 51, (2006) 226 CLR 551.

[60] *ACB v Thomson Medical Pte Ltd* [2017] SGCA 20, [2017] 1 SLR 918; *McFarlane v Tayside Health Board* [2000] 2 AC 59 (HL); *Cattanach v Melchior* [2003] HCA 38, (2003) 215 CLR 1.

[61] *Yearworth v North Bristol NHS Trust* [2009] EWCA Civ 37, [2010] QB 1.

person and property' each 'have a civil law analogue'.[62] As Lamond explains, '[t]he same interest underwrites both the civil claim and the criminal wrong'.[63]

To begin to separate the public and private spheres we need to consider the different ways in which these values can be threatened by the conduct of others. According to the Marshall and Duff account, conduct that is *somehow inconsistent* with shared interests and values represents wrongs that properly concern all members of the polity and are therefore proscribed as criminal wrongs. The implication is that potentially any conduct (that is inconsistent with a community's shared interests and values) could amount to a criminal wrong. Yet, to the extent that we have a shared and mutual concern for bodily integrity, reproductive control and privacy, there are a range of instances where we delegate to tort law the task of protecting these values, and other instances where we rely upon the criminal law. The same values, therefore, animate both spheres of the legal system and the puzzle remains unresolved: that SB-8 is – for some reason – an unwelcome addition to the private law sphere.

Here is the beginning of the way out: as we have seen, the public and private law spheres do not differ in terms of the set of interests that they protect, but they instead differ in terms of *how they go about* protecting the (same set) of interests. 'The starting position of the common law' Stevens explains, is the 'premium placed upon our freedom to choose how we live our lives'.[64] This freedom is not, of course, the only value that the law (in general) ought to serve, but, as we shall see, '[t]he value of freedom affects the means by which the other values' are pursued.[65] Freedom to choose how we live our lives is a value that is threatened by two sets of actors: other individuals and the state. We can now begin to find our fault-line. Recall how private law seems to concern the liberal state's promise to respect freedom by 'articulat[ing] the appropriate standards of conduct and, should those standards be violated, it mak[ing] it as if the wrong had never happened'.[66] It performs the 'garden-variety' job of 'helping people to avoid and mitigate their wrongs against other people, thereby protecting the rights of those other people'.[67] To the extent that we have an interest in the use and control of our property, in undertaking voluntary obligations, an interest in our privacy or reputation, financial security and the size of our family, private law will 'articulate standards of conduct' that help people avoid harming these interests (and require reparation where they do).

In doing so, it will give legal effect to values beyond the narrow confines of freedom and autonomy simply because there are values beyond those narrow confines. Rather than recognising additional values, private law scholars instead argue over how broadly or narrowly the values of 'freedom' and 'autonomy' can be construed to incorporate a 'plurality' of values. For instance, in reaction to the 'shallow libertarian conception of individual independence from the state', we might want to promote a 'substantive freedom' that seeks to secure for individuals 'the material wherewithal to truly guide their own lives on the basis of their chosen conception of the good'.[68] And, in reaction to the

[62] G Lamond, 'What is a Crime?' (2007) 27 *OJLS* 609, 630.
[63] ibid.
[64] R Stevens, *Torts and Rights* (Oxford, Oxford University Press, 2007) 9.
[65] Gardner (n 57) 195.
[66] Ripstein (n 55) 1969.
[67] Gardner (n 57) 201.
[68] West (n 3) 151; see Dagan and Dorfman (n 15) 1399–400.

shallow libertarian independence that is 'exhausted by the requirement that no one gets to tell anyone else what purposes to pursue',[69] we might want to endorse a 'perfectionist autonomy' that requires 'an adequate range of options' for an individual to pursue.[70]

Nonetheless, private law is preoccupied with a set of autonomy- and freedom-oriented values because it has the primary job of protecting what people have and how they choose to live their lives, from the threat that other people pose to that freedom. However, we need to be careful with this conclusion. The claim here is that the task of private law is to protect what people have and that this task *will typically* engage a narrow set of values. This does *not* mean that the task of private law *is to* exclusively engage those values.

That is the private law half of the story. To complete the story, and grasp how public law goes about protecting the (same set) of interests in a fundamentally different way, we will need to turn to consider the remedial responses of the public law and private law hemispheres.

VI. Principles of Justice

Let us return again to SB-8. The civil action awards a minimum sum of damages of $10,000. Conventional sums are not alien to private law. But conventional or lump sums are awarded in order to compensate the plaintiff for a loss that they suffered. The third party complainant under SB-8 may have an interest in how access to abortion services is limited, but suffers no 'loss' when an unlawful abortion is performed. In this way, the damages award is untethered from the position of the third-party complainant, and cannot be understood as reparatory, where the reparation 'rectifies both the normative gain and the normative loss in a single bipolar operation'.[71]

It is hard to construe the aim or purpose of the damages award to be anything other than punitive. The purpose of the damages award is to deter people from aiding or abetting an unlawful abortion, punish those who do, or both. It is then easy to associate punishment with the state (and its public officials) and object to SB-8 on the grounds that a private individual should not be the recipient of a punitive award, nor have the procedural right to instigate a punitive response from the law.

This objection is promising, but we need to be careful that it is not merely an objection by definitional fiat. We could object to SB-8 on the grounds that punishment is (by definition) something that can only be enacted by the state, that any punitive laws therefore belong in the public sphere, and SB-8 cannot be properly considered a civil action unless its aims are reparative and not punitive. We need to be wary, however, of the 'definitional full stop'.[72] For this objection to work we need an explanation for why

[69] H Dagan, *Reconstructing American Legal Realism & Rethinking Private Law Theory* (New York, Oxford University Press, 2013) 172–73 fn 44, citing A Ripstein, *Force and Freedom: Kant's Legal and Political Philosophy* (Cambridge, Harvard University Press, 2009) 14, 34, 45.

[70] Dagan (n 69) 172–73, citing J Raz, *The Morality of Freedom* (Oxford, Clarendon Press, 1986) 162.

[71] Weinrib (n 18) 136.

[72] See, for instance, HLA Hart in *Punishment and Responsibility* (New York, Oxford University Press, 1968) 4–6, in response to AM Quinton's 'On Punishment' (1954) 14 *Analysis* 133.

the state (and only the state) should be able to punish. To help with this question, we can start with an adjacent one: *what* does the state punish?

Lamond furnishes us with an answer to the adjacent question. Since punishment 'is the deliberate imposition of a burdensome liability on an individual for some blameworthy conduct in order to censure that conduct', the idea of punishment 'presupposes blameworthy conduct'.[73] For Lamond, the blameworthy conduct that attracts a punitive response is conduct 'that manifests a *disrespect* for the interest or value that has been violated' by demonstrating an unwillingness to be guided by the appropriate interest or value.[74] The suggestion here is that (in principle) 'any serious violation of a value that the state is responsible for supporting is a candidate for criminal punishment'.[75] Criminal punishment and civil reparation do not differ in terms of the values that they protect but the different categories of conduct that threaten the (same underlying) values. For paradigmatic crimes or fault-based offences, that may be conduct that is antithetical to that value, and for regulatory crimes or strict liability offences, the conduct 'demonstrates a disrespect' for 'schemes of conduct that have the effect of co-ordinating risk reduction or the promotion of certain goods'.[76]

Nonetheless, even if we conceptualise criminal wrongdoing as conduct that manifests disrespect for a value that the state is responsible for supporting, it remains unexplained why the state ought to have a monopoly on the punitive response to such conduct. The answer to our main question lies in the reasons that a punishment conveys. Punishment aims to guide (ie deter) those away from the prohibited conduct (who are unguided by the value itself) or to blame those who were unwilling to be guided (by the value itself). Its aim is to change the way people would otherwise choose to live their lives; to guide people who would be otherwise unguided by a value; or to require people to accept the burdens imposed on them because of their unwillingness to be guided. When the law promotes certain values, requires respect for certain values and punishes a person's unwillingness to be guided by those values, the law limits the freedom to choose how to live our own lives. This may be for good reasons, in protection of important values (or it may be for reasons and values we, ourselves, do not endorse). In either case, the criminal law has the distinct task of curtailing the freedom to choose how to live our own lives.

In comparison, consider the reasons that the duty of reparation conveys. There are, of course, normative consequences that follow from a breach of a private law duty. To respect that 'every person has a right to be secure from harm to person or possessions' is to accept 'that an obligation of reparation is incumbent on a person responsible for an infringement' of these rights, 'regardless of his being morally at fault or blameworthy in the matter'.[77] Norms of corrective justice therefore impose an obligation to repair the losses that follow from the breach of the primary obligation. The reasons to perform the

[73] Lamond (n 62) 621.

[74] ibid.

[75] ibid 626.

[76] ibid 630; see also A Brudner, *Punishment and Freedom: A Liberal Theory of Penal Justice* (Oxford, Oxford University Press, 2009) 176.

[77] DN MacCormick, 'The Obligation of Reparation' (1977–78) 78 *Proceedings of the Aristotelian Society* 175, 183.

primary obligation continue to apply to the obligation-bearer and the secondary obligation to repair represents the 'best still-available' way of conforming to such reasons.[78] Hence, the 'existence of an obligation of reparation is not necessarily conditional upon fault or blameworthiness'.[79] Whereas, we have seen how the 'imposition of a burdensome liability … presupposes blameworthy conduct'.[80] I labour this contrast because I promised to make good on the following claim, that: 'respecting what another person has (being duty-bound) is not the same as being limited to what we can do (being prohibited)'.

The point here is that there are two distinct tasks that each impact upon individual freedom in different ways. We have reasons to primarily respect (and secondarily repair or restore) what another person has (or had) because of how our actions can impinge upon their freedom to choose how they live their lives through the things they are entitled to. And we have reasons to abstain from conduct that manifests a disrespect for certain values, despite how the prohibition limits how we may live our lives.

The simple point that I add to this observation is that we do not permit one individual to curtail the freedoms of another person. That immodest task we assign to the state. We do, however, permit one individual to protect what they have by imposing duties on another person. Note here that the law, in both spheres, will be performing the same general task of helping 'people to do the things that they ought to be doing anyway, quite apart from the law'.[81] In performing the same general task, the law will be protecting the same values, and in particular, protecting the freedom to choose how to live our own lives. The hemispheres nonetheless differ in terms of the 'acceptable ways of bringing those values into people's lives'.[82] If we value fetal life (at some gestational stage), then it is acceptable to place limits on the termination of pregnancies, provided that we find the 'acceptable ways of bringing those values into people's lives'. Finding these 'acceptable ways' may require dispassionate, procedurally constrained and publicly funded public officials exercising the right to hold a person to account for the breach of their duties. Here, we can see a procedural implication of the fundamental distinction between the tasks of public law and private law. We will now turn to conclude by auditing the full set of implications of this distinction.

VII. Private Law Reasons to Expect Public Law

This chapter has three main aims. The first aim is to find a way to affirm the intuition that the law that governs access to abortion services belongs to the 'public hemisphere' – the criminal, administrative and constitutional law – of the legal system. The second aim is to explain the inappropriateness of the civil action under SB-8 in a way that resists the polarisation that can be found in formal and reductionist theories of private law.

[78] J Gardner, 'What is Tort Law For? Part 1. The Place of Corrective Justice' (2011) 30 *Law and Philosophy* 1, 34.
[79] MacCormick (n 77) 176.
[80] Lamond (n 62) 621.
[81] Gardner (n 57) 197.
[82] ibid 195.

The third aim is to explain the inappropriateness of SB-8 by isolating a fundamental objection, which the other objections stem from. Allow me to finish by unpacking how my account of the tasks of public and private law explains the inappropriateness of the civil action under SB-8, in a way that is logically prior to our concerns about relationality, procedural powers and accountability, public morality and principles of justice.

With regards to relationality, I have contended here that the private law hemisphere is not defined by the relationality or correlativity between private persons; it is instead defined by the modest task of protecting what each person has through the imposition of duties. Given this task (of protecting what each person has), *it follows* that private law will be focused on the interactions and relationships between private persons. The fundamental problem with SB-8 is not that there is no relationality between medical professional/defendant and bystander/claimant; the problem is that SB-8 is not concerned with protecting what each person has, but with curtailing what each person can do.

When it comes to accountability, whilst the private law hemisphere could be defined by the discretionary procedural powers that an individual can exercise, we can now appreciate that such procedural rights follow the private law task; there is an acceptable manner in which one person may claim against another person for a loss that they suffered – it may be (and most likely is) financially incentivised, it may be radically discretionary, it may be out-of-court, and gagged, and so on. There is also an acceptable manner in which a person's freedom or liberty can be curtailed – with state-sponsored fact-finding, consistent and impartial prosecution, in open and public proceedings, and so on. Hence, the further problem is that SB-8 curtails what each person can do through an unacceptable process.

As far as public morality is concerned, there is a reason why the private law hemisphere is preoccupied with a narrower set of values or interests (than the public law hemisphere). The values are narrower because the task of protecting what one person has against the conduct of another person *typically* (but not necessarily) only engages the freedom and equality of two actors (the claimant and defendant). The public hemisphere, in comparison, is concerned with conduct that manifests disrespect for an open-ended list of values that the state is responsible for promoting. The problem with SB-8 is not that it is trying to pursue distinctly public law values (such as the protection of fetal interests) through a private law mechanism. Unless we are willing to posit fetal personhood (again, touched upon here and not resolved), the broader point is that the conflict between fetal interests and reproductive autonomy does not concern 'standards of fair interaction'. Instead, the nature of the conflict necessitates one value (fetal interests) at the expense of another value (reproductive choice). Hence, the fundamental problem with SB-8 is that it curtails a freedom through a mechanism designed to maximise it.

In terms of principles of justice, the punitive response of the criminal law is the most immediate implication of the freedom-curtailing task of the criminal law; in order to prohibit conduct, the remedial response is to punish it. The problem with SB-8 is not that a third-party complainant financially benefits from the punitive damages award for each unlawful abortion that was aided or abetted; the problem with SB-8 is that the purpose behind the punitive-yet-civil-damages-award is that it is a civil claim that curtails what a person can do with their own body.

There is, therefore, something fundamentally wrong with SB-8: it performs a task that is entirely foreign to private law itself. The task of private law is to protect what each person has. Not just their property or contractual rights, but their rights to privacy, reputation, bodily integrity and reproductive autonomy. Protecting 'what each person has' tends to require others to repair 'what each person had', it tends to engage a narrow set of values that gravitate around the choices of each person, we tend to leave each person to their own devices to protect 'what each person has', and protecting 'what each person has' tends to impose duties on others to respect (and repair) what each person has (or had). SB-8 limits what a person can do. And if the law is to limit what a person can do, we have good reasons – from private law theory – to expect something very different from the law. In short, we have private law reasons to expect public law.

4

Deceit and the Creation of Life

ANNA BROADMORE*

I. Introduction

The creation of life is an intensely intimate experience, particularly when it occurs in the bedroom, rather than the fertility clinic. We hold tightly to the mantle of privacy that exists over our sexual intimacies and resist external scrutiny of the same. However, when one partner deceives the other into procreation by lying about, or sabotaging contraceptive measures, the life of the dupe is fundamentally disrupted. The loss of reproductive control which results raises questions about how far the courts should intrude into the bedroom and impose civil liabilities for deceitful conduct in intimate relationships.

Much of the judicial attention into disrupted reproductive choices has involved medical negligence, where concerns around privacy interests do not loom so large. Scenarios include a medical practitioner who carelessly muddles up gametes in IVF treatment[1] or negligently performs a sterilisation operation, leading to the birth of an unwanted child.[2] The decisions in this context reveal incremental moves towards recognising injury to reproductive autonomy as an actionable form of damage in negligence. This acknowledges the autonomy interests of the parents that are transgressed as a result of the negligent act, while avoiding labelling a healthy child itself as damage.[3]

Less attention has been given to the legal position when one partner deceives another about contraception or sterility, resulting in the dupe taking a reproductive risk of which they were unaware and consequently impregnating – or being

* I would like to thank Kit Barker and Jesse Wall for their very helpful comments on drafts of this chapter. The views expressed here are my own.

[1] See *ACB v Thomson Medical Pte Ltd* [2017] SGCA 20, [2017] 1 SLR 918, where negligent provision of IVF treatment led to a healthy child being born to ACB who was conceived with the sperm of an unknown donor instead of that of her husband.

[2] See, eg, *Rees v Darlington Memorial Hospital NHS Trust* [2003] UKHL 52, [2004] 1 AC 309.

[3] In *Rees*, ibid, at [123] Lord Millett supported the award of a conventional sum of £15,000 for 'the denial of an important aspect of their personal autonomy, viz the right to limit the size of their family'. In *ACB* (n 1) the Court recognised a new form of actionable damage, being a loss of genetic affinity, noting that the disruption of ACB's reproductive plans had frustrated her decisional autonomy and her ability to make free choices about her reproductive life. See also Todd, ch 5 of this volume.

impregnated by – their sexual partner without their consent.[4] In this context of reproductive deceit, it is conceptually helpful to identify the two different interests engaged in sexual relations, being our interest in bodily integrity and our interest in reproductive control, respectively. As in the medical negligence cases, in cases of reproductive deceit the autonomy interest of the dupe in reproductive control is transgressed when they find themselves thrust into parenthood by a deceitful partner. However, beyond compensating a woman for the interference with her bodily integrity when the deceit leads to pregnancy and a personal injury,[5] there is currently judicial reluctance to provide any remedy.[6] Difficulties facing the claimant include identifying a remedial path within existing torts on which to pin liability and justifying judicial interference with the independence of each of the parties in a personal relationship. Even if these obstacles can be navigated, reconciling litigation within the family circle with the best interests of the child is difficult.

The purpose of this chapter is to demonstrate why judicial intervention in cases of reproductive deceit would be internally consistent with existing private law intervention into sexual relationships. It proceeds in five stages. First, the value of reproductive control is identified and compared to other interests that receive direct protection in private law. Second, the interest is extracted and distinguished from the interest in bodily integrity, and a remedial path to compensation identified through the tort of deceit. The third stage addresses the mantle of privacy and considers the circumstances in which courts are prepared to lift the mantle in order to remediate a wrong which occurs within our private lives. Fourth, the spectrum of conduct amounting to deceit is examined, and consideration given to whether private law should respond differently to different conduct falling within that spectrum. The final stage shifts attention to the interests of the child and considers whether these should trump remediation of the wrong that led to the child's creation.

II. Why Should Private Law Care About Reproductive Control?

Our personal lives are full of disruptions and upsets which are not remediable in private law. Our friends stop calling us, our flatmates never clean up after themselves and our partners are unfaithful. Each of these scenarios may cause us distress, and yet private law does not care. In contrast, if we are injured by the negligent driving of our spouse,[7]

[4] There are a number of decisions from the United States which are detailed in AM Payne, 'Sexual Partner's Tort Liability to Other Partner for Fraudulent Misrepresentation Regarding Sterility or Use of Birth Control Resulting in Pregnancy' (1992) 2 *American Law Reports 5th* 301. In Canada, the most significant decision is that of the Ontario Court of Appeal in *PP v DD* [2017] ONCA 180.

[5] See *Barbara A v John G* 145 Cal App 3d 369, 193 Cal Rptr 422 (Ct App 1983), where an ectopic pregnancy resulted from the deceit, necessitating an operation which rendered the claimant sterile. The claim for the personal injury succeeded. In contrast, in *CAM v RAW* 237 NJ 532, 568 A 2d 556 (1990) the mother's claim for, inter alia, pain and suffering in pregnancy and childbirth, was denied.

[6] See, eg, *PP v DD* (n 4); *Wallis v Smith* 130 NM 214, 22 P 3d 682 (Ct App 2001); *Stephen K v Roni L* 105 Cal App 3d 640, 164 Cal Rptr 618 (Ct App 1980).

[7] *Greatorex v Greatorex* [2000] EWHC 223 (QB), [2000] 1 WLR 1970 [59] (obiter).

infected with a venereal disease following false representations of a partner[8] or our flatmate puts up a hidden camera in the bathroom and records us taking a shower,[9] private law does care. These actions involve an interference with our body, or our privacy, which are both core interests now protected in private law.

Given the spectrum of life-disruptions with which private law either will – or will not – engage, the first issue we need to examine is whether our interest in controlling whether (and with whom) to try to have a child is an interest that private law should care about. This involves looking beneath the surface of private law to identify the substance of those interests which receive direct protection in private law, and which can explain and justify it. We can then identify whether our interest in reproductive control shares substantive coherence with those protected interests in terms of the values that inform it.

On one, persuasive view, the core rights that are protected in private law are justified by the idea of equal freedom, understood as 'each person's ability to set and pursue his or her own purposes, consistent with the freedom of others to do the same'.[10] The idea of equal freedom is animated further by Robert Stevens:

> [I]n a world of absolute liberties, each of us would be free to stab one another in the neck, to steal a farmer's crops and to shout 'Fire!' in crowded theatres. Freedom for the pike is death for the minnow, but we are all of us both pikes and minnows. In order for each of us to be able to choose how to live our own lives, it is necessary that we have rights against others that they refrain from interfering with this freedom. We have a right to be secure from interference in order that we may be independent of others. The correlative general duties are ones to refrain from behaving in certain ways. This results in a system of equal freedom for all.[11]

The basic rights we have at common law protect the means that we have available to us to 'set and pursue our own purposes' and determine the shape of our lives.[12] These include rights to property, bodily integrity, reputation and rights to privacy. Each of these are 'things' that we have, and we can use them to pursue our purposes in life. They are weighted in autonomy. If they are intruded upon, or injured or damaged, then the ends that we may pursue are diminished, either temporarily or permanently. The injured leg cannot be skied on while it heals, the damaged car cannot be driven, the destroyed reputation affects our job prospects. When this diminishment has been caused by the negligent or intentional act of another, private law may step in to restore the balance.

Comparing reproductive control to the other interests that private law currently cares about, reproductive control consists in our ability to decide whether – and with whom – to try to have a child. Underlying reproductive control is our status interest as a parent or a non-parent.[13] Our parental status has a profound impact

[8] *Kathleen K v Robert B* 150 Cal App 3d 992, 198 Cal Rptr 273 (Ct App 1984).

[9] *C v Holland* [2012] NZHC 2155, [2012] 3 NZLR 672.

[10] A Ripstein, 'Beyond the Harm Principle' (2006) 34 *Philosophy & Public Affairs* 215, 231. See also EJ Weinrib, *The Idea of Private Law* (Oxford, Oxford University Press, 2012), EJ Weinrib, *Corrective Justice* (Oxford, Oxford University Press, 2012).

[11] R Stevens, 'Damages for Wrongdoing in the Absence of Loss' in JNE Varuhas and NA Moreham (eds), *Remedies for Breach of Privacy* (Oxford, Hart Publishing, 2018) 104 (citation omitted).

[12] A Ripstein, *Private Wrongs* (Cambridge, Harvard University Press, 2016) 8.

[13] The interest in reproductive control is more nuanced than this and can capture existing parental status to *x* number of children (*McFarlane v Tayside Health Board* [2000] 2 AC 59 (HL)), and genetic affinity with children (*ACB* (n 1)) but for the purposes of deceit, the binary comparison between parent/non-parent is sufficient.

on our identity, in determining our inclusion or exclusion from social groups, our responsibilities and our economic interests. Our parental status is determined by our reproductive choices which can result in the creation, or avoidance, of lifelong relationships and responsibilities. The reproductive choices we make are influenced by whether we seek the emotional, moral, financial and legal responsibilities that come with parenthood, and by our desires about who we might wish to parent with.[14] These choices fundamentally shape our lives. The relationships and responsibilities that come with a decision to be a parent will be part of our lives forever. Consequently, if private law cares about those things we have that we can use to decide the shape of our lives – the means that we use to fashion our own destiny[15] – then reproductive control demonstrably fits within these parameters. Preserving our choice around whether and with whom to become a parent protects for us our agency around one of the most significant decisions anyone can make in determining the shape of their life. The injured leg will heal, the car will be repaired, but unplanned children will – save tragedy – outlive us.

Of course, not all disruptions to life can be protected in a system of equal freedom. A system of equal freedom only protects what you already have independently of others, not what you desire to acquire. All that is required is that we each stay out of a space in which we are not welcome. This explains why private law does not engage with my personal disputes when my partner is unfaithful, my flatmate does not do the dishes or my friends do not call me back. Their means are theirs, and there is no obligation for anyone else to use their means in the way that most suits my wishes.[16] This would affect their independence. In contrast, actions which injure my body, or invade my privacy, are actions which go beyond simply not providing an ideal context for my exercise of my means: they diminish the possible use I can make of those means and therefore set back my independence.[17] For this reason, sanctions which restore the diminished means can be justified within a system which protects equal freedom.

Now I raise this here, because, if recognition of reproductive control as a protected interest within the common law is to be justified by its fit with Kantian equal freedom, which provides a compelling explanation of much of private law, then we need to satisfy ourselves that reproductive control has the right shape. This requires demonstrating that our reproductive choices can be protected from the interference of others, and that the exercise of our reproductive choices will not deprive others of their own. In this context, we need to consider directly the reproductive choice to procreate: this necessarily requires the cooperation of two parties. If you desire to procreate, you cannot obtain what you desire unless someone of the opposite sex consents to procreate with you, or to provide you with the necessary reproductive materials. However, this need for a symbiotic goal does not disqualify reproductive control from protection within

[14] N Priaulx, 'Rethinking Progenitive Conflict: Why Reproductive Autonomy *Matters*' (2008) 16 *Medical Law Review* 169, 176.

[15] See J Raz, *The Morality of Freedom* (Oxford, Clarendon Press, 1986) 369.

[16] A Ripstein, *Force and Freedom: Kant's Legal and Political Philosophy* (Cambridge, Harvard University Press, 2009) 51.

[17] Ripstein (n 12) 83.

a system of equal freedom, but simply requires that each party consent to that goal. Ripstein observes that:

> Voluntary cooperation enables people to use their powers together to pursue purposes they share. It can be made to look as though potential cooperators are always subject to each other's choice: unless you agree to cooperate with me, I can't use my powers in the way I want to. But this is an example of our respective independence. Cooperation only contrasts with domination when it is voluntary on both sides. You get to decide whether to cooperate with me because you get to decide how your powers will be used. I can no more demand that you make your powers available to accommodate my preferred use of mine than you can make that demand of me. Each of us is sovereign over our powers, and the power to decide who to cooperate with is a basic expression of that sovereignty.[18]

Recognising reproductive control as an interest capable of receiving the direct protection of the common law would simply recognise that the consent of both parties is required to procreate, just as the protection given to bodily integrity imposes the requirement that both parties consent before bodies are engaged in sexual relations themselves. The requirement of consent is a manifestation of the protection given to the interest in a system structured around equal freedom.

So, we see, then, that our interest in reproductive control – in being able to decide whether and with whom to try to procreate – is an interest that has substantive coherence with other core interests currently protected as rights within the common law. Our reproductive control allows us to pursue our own purposes and shape our own lives, and it can be protected within a framework of mutual independence. A system of private law that is designed to promote equal freedom can justify giving similar protection to reproductive control as it gives to other core interests.

The next step is to identify the remedial path that can be used by a party who has been deceived by their sexual partner into procreation. There exists judicial confusion on this issue, which can be cleared away once reproductive control is pulled out into the light and identified as an independent interest.

III. A Remedial Path for Intentional Interference with Reproductive Control in a Personal Relationship

A review of the case law involving intentional interference with reproductive control in a personal relationship reveals claims pleaded across various torts, including battery, deceit and intentional infliction of emotional distress. The cases have been pleaded either in opposition to claims for child support, whereby the duped father resists having to pay support due to alleged false statements around contraception,[19] or as claims by the father for damages so far in excess of the agreed support that they amount to the same thing.[20] These claims are contrary to child protection statutes. All have been unsuccessful.

[18] Ripstein (n 16) 47.
[19] *Douglas R v Suzanne M* 127 Misc 2d 745, 487 NYS 2d 244 (Sup Ct 1985); *Stephen K* (n 6); *Wallis* (n 6).
[20] See *PP v DD* (n 4) in which damages of $4 million were sought.

Putting issues around child support to one side for now, we can unravel how identifying our interest in reproductive control as an independent interest might clarify an available remedial path in a manner that is both consistent with the existing law governing claims for emotional harm, and which avoids missteps into battery.

To animate the quandary, let us consider the Canadian decision *PP v DD*.[21] This involved a man who was deceived to forego contraceptive precautions by DD's false assurances that she was taking the contraceptive pill. She fell pregnant and had a healthy child. *PP* asserted that he was happy to pay child support but claimed damages of $4 million for battery and deceit. Both claims were unsuccessful.

Focussing first on battery, the tort protects bodily integrity, and only bodily integrity. In the context of sexual activity, our interest in bodily integrity protects, for each of us, the ability to choose with whom we engage in sexual activity, and what sort of sexual activity to participate in. When a claimant who has been duped into procreative sex brings a claim in battery, the court's inquiry is focussed on whether the claimant's consent to the sexual interaction is vitiated by the false statements around sterility/contraception, and whether these statements change the nature and quality of the act consented to, such that there is no uniting of wills and the sexual activity is an unconsented-to interference with the claimant's body.[22]

When it is a woman who makes false statements concerning contraceptive measures, it is difficult to see how this affects the experience of the man's body during the sexual relations. In *PP v DD*, PP consented to the sexual nature of the act, and he consented to the act with DD. In terms of the engagement of his body, there *was* a uniting of wills. Where the wills deviated was with regard to the purpose of the sexual relations: PP consented to recreational sex, not to procreative sex, or to the consequences of that procreative sex for the rest of his life. The grievance did not concern his body experiencing something to which he did not agree. Rather, it related to the loss of reproductive control: the misinformation deprived him of the ability to decide on the reproductive risk that he was taking and resulted in a child and a lifelong tether to a duplicitous partner. Unsurprisingly, the claim in battery was unsuccessful.

Pulling reproductive control out into the light as a separate interest enables us to clearly see why battery is an inappropriate remedial path in this context. *Two* interests are engaged in sexual relations: bodily integrity and reproductive control. Consenting to sex does not involve consenting to procreation. The entire contraceptive industry is built on creating a boundary between the two, enabling parties to consent to sexual relations while keeping the gate to reproduction firmly closed. Battery, however, only looks at whether the lies told around contraception change the experience of the body to something different to what was agreed to. For the man relying on a woman's false assertions that she is taking the contraceptive pill, the experience of his body aligns with his consent. Of course, it might be different for a woman who is duped about contraception or sterility. Here, the grievance may genuinely be that she has ended up with unconsented-to reproductive materials inside her body.[23] Whether or not a pregnancy

[21] ibid.

[22] ibid [73].

[23] See R Williams, 'A Further Case on Obtaining Sex by Deception' (2021) 137 *LQR* 183, critiquing *R v Lawrance (Jason)* [2020] EWCA Crim 971, [2020] 1 WLR 5025, in which Lawrence advised his sexual

results, battery could be pursued as a private wrong to her body. However, the focus of the battery claim would still be on the short-term impact on her body, rather than the long-term impact on the life that is captured by her interest in reproductive control.

Given the unsuitability of battery, the tort of deceit is more promising. The modern conception of deceit as developed by Jason Neyers is that, far from being an economic tort, it 'protects all of our rights (to things, to money, to contracts, to our bodies) from non-consensual dispossession as a result of another's fraud'.[24] Larry Alexander and Emily Sherwin have observed that:

> [C]ourts do not regularly protect a free-standing autonomy-based right not to be deceived. Instead, they prohibit deception as a means of causing harm to independently recognized interests, such as the interests in bodily integrity, property, physical liberty and reputation.[25]

These observations reveal that, like negligence, deceit does not protect just one right. Rather, deceit is a horizonal tort which protects all our rights. It does this by recognising a broad range of actionable 'damage'. In this regard, Ripstein observes 'at issue is not … being lied to, but being deprived of what you have through deceit'.[26] What we have is a power of control in respect of each of our rights, and it is deprivation of this power which illuminates deceit. While a lie alone is not actionable, a lie which deprives us of a power of control in respect of one of our rights, and thereby results in damage to the interest at the heart of a right, *is* actionable.

Now, in *PP v DD*, the claim in deceit also failed. The Ontario Court of Appeal highlighted the absence of any actionable damage, noting that the plaintiff had not suffered any physical injury or emotional harm that was pathological in nature. The 'damage' was summarised as consisting of the plaintiff's 'emotional upset, broken dreams, possible disruption to his lifestyle and career and a potential reduction in future earnings, all of which are said to flow from the birth of a child he did not want'.[27] The lower Superior Court decision had also rejected the claim, noting that the torts of intentional infliction of emotional distress[28] and negligence are the conventional legal tools of private law to redress misconduct causing emotional harm.[29] Both require a recognisable psychiatric condition to anchor the claim as damage, and the Court considered that allowing a claim for mere distress in through the doors of deceit would circumvent the established boundaries around claims for emotional harm.[30]

partner on two occasions that he had had a vasectomy, only to advise later 'I have a confession. I'm still fertile. Sorry'. It was held that his lie about fertility was not capable in law of negating consent under the Sexual Offences Act 2003 (UK) s 74.

[24] JW Neyers, 'Form and Substance in the Tort of Deceit' in A Robertson and J Goudkamp (eds), *Form and Substance in the Law of Obligations* (Oxford, Hart Publishing, 2019) 325.

[25] L Alexander and E Sherwin, 'Deception in Morality and Law' (2003) 22 *Law and Philosophy* 393, 432.

[26] Ripstein (n 12) 50 fn 32.

[27] *PP v DD* (n 4) [46].

[28] In the UK, this is generally known as the tort in *Wilkinson v Downton*, although the Supreme Court in *O (A Child) v Rhodes* [2015] UKSC 32, [2016] AC 219 [73], [81] (Baroness Hale and Lord Toulson JSC, Lords Clarke and Wilson JJSC agreeing) referred to it as the tort of wilful infringement of the claimant's right to personal safety.

[29] *PP v DD* [2016] ONSC 258 [58].

[30] ibid [71], [73]. However, in Canada, post *Saadati v Moorhead* [2017] SCC 28, [2017] 1 SCR 543, the threshold for compensable mental injury is not linked to the medical profession's diagnostic tools, but must nevertheless be serious and prolonged, and above the ordinary annoyances, anxieties and fears that come with living in civil society.

However, once reproductive control is identified as an independently recognised interest[31] similar to bodily integrity, property, physical liberty and reputation, this creates the conceptual space in which to anchor a claim in deceit to the loss of reproductive control suffered by the dupe when a child results. It is the violation of reproductive control that is the actionable damage, not the emotional harm. The violation of reproductive control sets back the dupe's independence and puts the metaphorical peg in the ground, which the court can then use to ground recovery of the non-pecuniary harm suffered.[32] Non-pathological emotional harm has always been compensable in tort law provided it flows from harm to an independently recognised interest: one only need look to interferences with bodily integrity[33] and privacy[34] for illustrations of this. When these interests are interfered with, courts are able to remedy the consequential pecuniary and non-pecuniary losses which flow. Non-pecuniary losses which are not pathological in nature, but which are caused by interference with other independently protected interests, are recoverable.

In this way, allowing a claim in deceit for false statements leading to a loss of reproductive control would not circumvent established boundaries around recovery for emotional harm. This is because – in contrast to the torts of intentional infliction of emotional distress and negligence causing pure psychiatric harm, both of which require pathological emotional harm – a claim in deceit would be anchored to the violation of an independently recognised interest, being our interest in reproductive control.

Now that we have cleared the mechanical issues out of the way, by identifying how recognition of an independent interest in reproductive control can be justified within a system of equal freedom and open up a remedial path for reproductive deceit, we can turn to thornier matters.

In cases of reproductive deceit, courts have expressed concerns that intervention into promises made between sexual partners would involve unwarranted intrusion into the private sphere. The Court in the Californian decision of *Stephen K v Roni L* expressed the concern that the dispute involved 'nothing more than asking the court to supervise the promises made between two consenting adults as to the circumstances of their private sexual conduct. To do so would encourage unwarranted governmental intrusion into matters affecting the individual's right to privacy'.[35]

The second issue that causes difficulties arises from the spectrum of conduct amounting to deceit: while a case involving sabotage of one party's contraceptive measures involves a deprivation of reproductive control, in the more common cases involving a false statement as to sterility or contraceptive precaution, the dupe is never prevented from taking his or her own precautions. Again, in *Stephen K v Roni L* the Court observed: 'As to Stephen's claim that he was tricked into fathering a child he did

[31] Protecting our parental status – see the discussion above at n 13 and accompanying text.

[32] The metaphor of actionable damage being a 'peg' which allows the court to assess factual pecuniary and non-pecuniary losses is Eric Descheemaeker's: see E Descheemaeker, 'Unravelling Harms in Tort Law' (2016) 132 *LQR* 595, 597.

[33] See the Judicial Council, *Guidelines for the Assessment of General Damages in Personal Injury Cases*, 16th edn (Oxford, Oxford University Press, 2022).

[34] *Campbell v MGN Ltd* [2004] UKHL 22, [2004] 2 AC 457.

[35] *Stephen K* (n 6) [2].

not want, no good reason appears why he himself could not have taken any precautionary measures'.[36]

Each of these concerns can be examined through the lens of equal freedom. Using this framework, we can identify whether either concern justifies withholding a remedy in a claim of reproductive deceit.

IV. Should Private Law Enter the Bedroom to Remediate Reproductive Deceit?

When the law intrudes into communications made within a personal relationship, this violates the freedom which is preserved within that private sphere. Our sexual lives are the most private space of all. We do not expect to have them scrutinised or regulated by anyone else. Consequently, there is a discernible judicial reluctance to intrude into our private lives, and an awareness that 'there must remain a realm of private morality and immorality which is, in brief and crude terms, not the law's business'.[37] There are also significant difficulties around proving who said what, and did what, in the bedroom. This creates judicial hesitation towards intervening in cases of reproductive deceit.[38] It does not mean, however, that the deceiver is granted a total immunity.

Much of the academic and philosophical attention concerning judicial or state intrusion into sexual pursuits has addressed the question whether the law should step in to criminalise the behaviour of consenting adults in the bedroom which is immoral according to societal standards: for example, sadomasochistic activities.[39] However, in the context of reproductive deceit, the focus is different because there is a grievance between the parties involved. Rather than regulating intimate behaviour that the affected participants are mutually exercising their freedom to enjoy, the court is being asked to sanction behaviour which has caused one party distress and disrupted their life plans. This is not a case of the judiciary regulating sexual liberty, but one in which it is asked to recognise and protect the interest that one has in controlling one's reproductive choices. Consequently, the question the court must address is whether the violation of the dupe's reproductive control justifies legal intervention which will violate the realm of privacy. Should the courts supervise statements made concerning sterility or contraception in the course of private sexual conduct?

We can illuminate the limits of judicial intervention by identifying the cases in which courts have lifted the mantle of privacy in order to sanction behaviour in the bedroom – and cases where they have not – and by scrutinising the boundary between the two types of case through the ideal of equal freedom.

[36] ibid [3].

[37] Home Office, *Report of the Committee on Homosexual Offences and Prostitution* (Cmnd 247, 1957) para 61.

[38] *Stephen K* (n 6) [2].

[39] See *R v Brown* [1994] 1 AC 212 (HL); *Laskey v UK* (1997) 24 EHRR 39 and, for an illuminating discussion, J Herring, '*R v Brown* (1993)' in P Handler, H Mares and I Williams (eds), *Landmark Cases in Criminal Law* (Oxford, Hart Publishing, 2017). See also Mill's Harm Principle: JS Mill, *On Liberty* (New Haven, Yale University Press, 2003), and the Hart/Devlin debate: HLA Hart, *Law, Liberty and Morality* (Oxford, Oxford University Press, 1963); P Devlin, *The Enforcement of Morals* (Oxford, Oxford University Press, 1965).

The Australian decision *Magill v Magill*[40] involved a claim in deceit brought by a husband against his wife for misleading him into believing that all three children to which she had given birth during their marriage were his, when in fact two of them were the result of an extra-marital affair. To bring a claim in deceit, Mr Magill needed to hang his claim on a misrepresentation, and the misrepresentation relied on concerned the wife's *failure* to disclose her sexual infidelity. Absent a finding that his wife had an obligation to disclose her infidelity, there was no misrepresentation to anchor the claim. Thus, the Court was obliged to consider whether or not a spouse is obligated to disclose infidelity. The majority held:

> There is currently no recognised legal or equitable obligation, or duty of care, on a spouse to disclose an extra-marital sexual relationship to the other spouse during the course of a marriage. There is a mantle of privacy over such conduct which protects it from scrutiny by the law.[41]

Without a duty to disclose infidelity, there was no misrepresentation, and in the absence of a misrepresentation, Mr Magill's claim in deceit could not progress.[42] Viewing the claim through the lens of equal freedom explains the Court's decision: there was no duty on Mrs Magill to disclose her infidelity because it did not affect Mr Magill's own independence. Mr Magill's means remained intact to use towards his desired ends, notwithstanding his wife's infidelity. If one spouse decides to be unfaithful, this does not impact on the other spouse's ability to lead their own life in their own way. Their interests are intact – their body is uninjured, their property is undamaged, their reputation unsullied. While the infidelity means that Mr Magill's familial life is not as ideal a context in which Mr Magill can exercise his means as compared to a relationship of loyalty, no one has a duty to live their life in the way that best suits another's wishes. Critically, actions taken by Mr Magill unaware of his wife's infidelity did not diminish his means in the way actions taken unaware of a sexual partner's undisclosed venereal disease might. The mantle of privacy recognised in the common law protects our ability to be whoever we wish to be *provided* we do not interfere with the independence of others. Private law in common law jurisdictions does not normally require us to be good:[43] rather, it requires us to respect the freedom of others.

Of course, the decision does not imply that the courts would never entertain false claims of *paternity* in the tort of deceit. In principle, a false claim of paternity might result in a diminishing of means, and therefore an interference with another's independence when a dupe spends money, in accordance with legal and moral obligations, raising a dependent child on the false belief that the child is his,[44] although there are often

[40] *Magill v Magill* [2006] HCA 51, (2006) 226 CLR 551.

[41] ibid [130] (Gummow, Kirby and Crennan JJ) (citation omitted).

[42] Even had a positive misrepresentation been proven, reliance and damage were both stumbling blocks. As child support payments were not part of the claim, it was not clear what legally recognised right Mr Magill has been dispossessed of.

[43] Of course, there are some exceptions to this, including the positive obligations to rescue in civilian jurisdictions, and exceptional instances in which positive obligations to protect, absent an undertaking to act, are recognised in common law jurisdictions.

[44] See *P v B (Paternity: Damages for Deceit)* [2001] 1 FLR 1041 (QB), in which Stanley Burnton J was open to a claim in deceit in domestic relations in similar circumstances. This was only a preliminary hearing.

complications in these claims,[45] not the least of which is that sums paid in support of the child are usually recoverable through statutory schemes, so that there is no resulting pecuniary loss.[46] Deceit claims are anchored in damage and damage is the violation of one of our legally protected interests which protect our independence. If our protected means are not diminished by conduct occurring within a personal relationship, the courts will not intervene.

So, we see, then, that in a system of equal freedom, there is no legally protected interest in the fidelity of one's sexual partners, just as there is no legally protected interest in the loyalty of one's friends. To suggest otherwise would be to impose intolerable, autonomy-diminishing duties on one's friends and lovers, merely to provide one with the context most favourable to one's own ends. This is contrary to a system of equal freedom.[47] Our own independence gives us the freedom to behave morally or immorally, with devotion or disloyalty, faithfulness or infidelity, provided this behaviour does not interfere with the independence of another party. In the absence of interference with another's freedom, the judiciary will not enter the private sphere to remediate a lovers' quarrel.

On the other side of the boundary line exist cases in which courts do intervene in private sexual conduct. These involve actions which violate the claimant's rights and *diminish* their means. The Californian decision of *Kathleen K v Robert B*[48] recognised a duty to disclose genital herpes to one's sexual partner. The intrusion into the private sphere is explained by the ideal of equal freedom: the disease put the partner's bodily integrity at risk, our bodies are one of the means we have which we can use towards our ends. If our bodies are harmed, our ability to live an independent life is diminished. Similarly, in the Californian case of *Barbara A v John G*[49] the Court allowed a woman's claim for personal injury suffered when her partner's lies regarding sterility resulted in her falling pregnant, with the complication of an ectopic pregnancy which rendered her sterile and destroyed her reproductive possibilities. Sexual conduct that causes personal injury is justiciable in private law because it interferes with the victim's independence by

Issues concerning whether the payments made in support of the child would be recoverable, or whether the claim for general damages for indignity, mental suffering, and humiliation could be paid, were not adjudicated. Of course, money might be spent on a marriage in the absence of knowledge of infidelity and perhaps an argument could be raised around this expenditure being a diminishment of means. However, there is an element of choice around expenditure on one's partner that is absent when one is maintaining a dependent child in the false belief of paternity to which legal obligations attach.

[45] See *FRB v DCA* [2019] EWHC 2816 (Fam), [2020] 2 WLR 671. The Court acknowledged that the tort of deceit can exist between husband and wife on intimate matters. However, the deceit claim was caught up in the relationship property claim and was struck out as being incompatible with the proceedings under the Matrimonial Causes Act 1973 (UK), whereby the wife's conduct would be taken into account. The husband sought as damages the difference between the financial award he would now be required to make, and that he would have been required to make at the time of the child's birth had he been advised on the paternity at that stage.

[46] However, consider the case of the grandparent who, on being told his son and his partner cannot pay for the education of their child, agrees to pay for the education on the faith of a knowingly false representation by either of them that his son is the child's father. An action in deceit here could hang on the pecuniary loss caused – the dispossession of money. See *Magill* (n 40) [227] (Heydon J).

[47] Ripstein (n 16) 48.

[48] (n 8); see also *Long v Adams* 175 Ga App 538, 681 SE 2d 725 (Ct App 1985).

[49] (n 5).

reducing the possible use they may make of their body.[50] Our body is one of the primary means we have with which to pursue our purposes. When injured, the possible use that might be made of one's body is diminished. The private sphere cannot be used as a shield behind which one party can act to diminish the independence of another without civil recourse.

Each of these cases simply demonstrates that one of the things private law cares about is our ability to use our means towards our own ends, consistent with the entitlement of others to do the same.[51] If, within the private sphere, actions cause harm to another's means in a way which interferes with their independence, then the law will be motivated to intrude into the private sphere to restore the balance. This intrusion is justified within a system of equal freedom.

In the first part of this chapter, reproductive control was demonstrated to have a weight and shape that is similar to other interests which receive the direct protection of private law. It is fundamental to our ability to shape our own lives and can be protected within a system of mutual independence. When false statements are made in a sexual relationship regarding contraception or sterility, and reliance on the statements leads to the birth of an unplanned child, the dupe's life is permanently disrupted. The deceit results in a diminution of the dupe's independence by the imposition of unwanted, but lifelong relationships and responsibilities. Plans to refrain from having children at all, or to wait until one meets the right person with whom one desires to have a child, are forever thwarted. If we view the willingness of the court to lift the mantle of privacy through the lens of equal freedom, then the same rationale that justifies the court's intrusion into a sexual relationship to remediate the harm caused in cases of personal injury applies to a scenario of reproductive deceit. Unlike many personal injuries which will heal, or have intermittent flare-ups, responsibility for – and connection to – a child is consistent and lifelong. When we view the impact of an unwanted child on the independence of the parent and compare this to the impact of a personal injury on the independence of the victim, the lens of equal freedom allows us to see that judicial intervention in cases like *PP v DD* and *Stephen K v Roni L* would not be an 'unwarranted governmental intrusion' but, instead, would be internally consistent with the existing pattern of private law intervention into sexual relationships. The law would not be intruding inappropriately into the exercise of sexual liberty but would rather be stepping in to protect the separate interest in reproductive control, in the same way it steps in when bodily integrity requires protection.

V. The Tension between the Liberty of Each Party and the Spectrum of Deceit

In a situation of contraceptive sabotage – for example, where a dupe relies on a condom, unaware that his partner has sabotaged it with a pin,[52] or a woman relies on contraceptive

[50] Ripstein (n 12) 83.
[51] ibid 7–8.
[52] See *R v Hutchinson* [2014] SCC 19, [2014] 1 SCR 346 for a criminal claim involving a man deliberately sabotaging a condom with a pin.

pills, unaware that her partner has replaced them with sugar pills – the deceiver deprives the dupe of their own precautionary measures. When a pregnancy results, civil remediation is consistent with a system of equal freedom which protects, for each of us, the ability to use our own means towards our own ends, because one party has deprived another of their means of reproductive control without their permission.

The trickier scenario is the more common one arising in the case law, where the claimant relies on their sexual partner's false assertion of infertility, or unseen contraceptive measures, before engaging in sexual relations without taking their own precautions, *even though they could have done so*. When a child results and the dupe seeks remediation, the question has arisen as to why the deceiver should be liable when the dupe chose to relinquish their own responsibility for reproductive control in a situation where the equilibrium of power between the parties did not necessitate this.

Equal freedom just protects for each of us the means that we can use towards our ends, consistent with the entitlement of others to the same. It does not protect for anyone a favourable context in which to pursue their purposes. When a lie is told, the context in which we act becomes less favourable to our purposes, but a lie alone does not deprive us of a right.[53] So, the question that requires examination is this: is private law intervention into a reproductive deceit, which never actually prevented the dupe from taking their own contraceptive precautions, consistent with the idea of equal freedom?

This issue can be resolved by viewing the four elements of an action in deceit with the idea of mutual independence in mind:

> First, there must be a representation of fact made by words, or, it may be, by conduct. … Secondly, the representation must be made with a knowledge that it is false. … Thirdly, it must be made with the intention that it should be acted upon by the plaintiff, or by a class of persons which will include the plaintiff, in the manner which resulted in damage to him … Fourthly, it must be proved that the plaintiff has acted upon the false statement and has sustained damage by so doing.[54]

When lies are told about contraception, the deceiver is acting intentionally to get the dupe to use their means towards the deceiver's ends. First, there is a representation that contraceptive measures are in place which, secondly, the deceiver knows to be false. Thirdly, the deceiver makes the statement with the intention that the dupe's independence will be undermined, by giving the dupe false information on which to reach a decision. While the dupe is never deprived of the liberty to take reproductive precautions, they are deprived of both the ability to decide the reproductive risk they are running, and their freedom to decide whether, and with whom, to try to have a child. Critically, however, the lie only becomes actionable when it is relied on and the fourth element is met, with the dupe proving that damage has been suffered as a result of acting upon the false statement. It is this requirement of damage which makes an action in deceit consistent with a system of equal freedom. Exploring the idea of damage

[53] Ripstein (n 12) 50 fn 32; and contra, see R Stevens, *Torts and Rights* (Oxford, Oxford University Press, 2017) 8.

[54] *Bradford Third Equitable Benefit Building Society v Borders* [1941] 2 All ER 205 (HL) 211 (Viscount Maugham).

in deceit, Neyers observes that deceit, similarly to the tort of negligence, can 'protect a multitude of rights from damage'[55] and further:

> [T]he damage requirement of the tort of deceit is not to be understood as pecuniary loss or a simple interference with autonomy but rather as the claimant's non-consensual dispossession of his or her rights in consequence of the defendant's fraud. Thus, the damage which is the gist of the tort of deceit occurs at the moment when the representee acts on the representation and thereby gives up control of a right or otherwise dispossesses him or herself of it. Once there has been a dispossession, the cause of action is complete.[56]

When a deceiver lies about contraceptive measures, they are manipulating the dupe into acting against their own interests and using the dupe's means to advance ends that the dupe has not set for themselves, usurping the dupe's powers by making the dupe's choice subject to the deceiver's.[57] The deceit is actionable when the dupe is dispossessed of their power to make their own choices around their parental status, and a child results. While the dupe may, in hindsight, have been a fool, contributory negligence is not a defence to a claim in deceit.[58] It is no answer to a deceit claim to say that the dupe should have been more paranoid and suspicious about the promises made by the deceiver. Language is the means by which we interact in the world. We use it to unite our wills, to expand the possibilities available to us by consenting.[59] If we cannot interact and make choices on the presumption that others are telling us the truth, then we lose the ability to unite our wills, because every statement made must be heard as possibly meaning the opposite:[60] the sexual partner who hears the words 'I am taking contraception' must understand those words as also meaning 'I am not taking contraception'; the sexual partner who hears the words 'I do not have herpes' must understand those words as also meaning 'I have herpes'. A reduction in, or avoidance of, liability on the basis that the dupe could have taken their own precautions places the damage suffered at the dupe's feet for being foolish enough to trust an intimate partner. This is not how deceit operates even in an arms-length commercial context where parties are not in a relationship of trust and confidence.[61] In an intimate relationship, trust and confidence are paramount.

Consequently, while in some cases there may be simple steps that a dupe could take to look after their own interests, this is true in virtually every case of actionable deceit and yet the failure to take such steps does not defeat the claim. Guns can be examined by an independent dealer before purchase;[62] property records can be obtained and scrutinised before one moves out of a rent-controlled apartment;[63] accounts can be examined before a business is purchased.[64] The failure to be paranoid and take these steps does not defeat the dupe's claim because it is only through being able safely to rely upon the

[55] Neyers (n 24) 325.
[56] ibid 325–26 (citation omitted).
[57] Ripstein (n 10) 234.
[58] *Dobell v Stevens* (1825) 3 B&C 623; 107 ER 824; *Redgrave v Hurd* (1881) 20 Ch D 1.
[59] Ripstein (n 16) 109.
[60] J Weinrib, 'The Juridical Significance of Kant's Supposed Right to Lie' (2008) 13(1) *Kantian Review* 141, 152–53.
[61] See the cases referred to above at n 58.
[62] *Langridge v Levy* (1837) 2 M&W 519; 150 ER 863.
[63] *Mafo v Adams* [1970] 1 QB 548 (CA).
[64] *Redgrave* (n 58).

assumption that a person means what they say that language can be of any use to any of us, or that our wills can be united. As Jacob Weinrib observes,

> [T]he liar does wrong by using language, the means through which wills are united and rights proceed, in a manner that is inconsistent with its publicity. Deception is incompatible with a united will and with the rights that proceed from the united will because a will cannot be united if the parties within the will are entitled to deceive each other by expressing one thing and meaning another.[65]

Further, to reduce or avoid liability in deceit because of the gullibility of the dupe would allow the deceiver to have their cake and eat it: the deceiver cannot, at one and the same time, deliberately act in a way that induces the dupe to act against the dupe's interests, and then claim the benefit of the dupe's trusting nature in their own defence.[66] John Murphy, while highly critical of the blanket inability to plead contributory negligence in deceit, concedes that it is plausible to reject the defence in relation to foolhardy acts of the claimant that were specifically induced by the defendant's false statement,[67] and it is precisely these acts that are under the microscope in claims of reproductive deceit.

Of course, whenever a claim in deceit is made out in this context, the deceiver's liberty of expression is sacrificed to the right of the dupe, which is violated by reliance on the lie. However, in a system of equal freedom, one liberty can be favoured over another. Ripstein observes:

> Once freedom is understood in terms of people's respective independence, one person's freedom need not conflict with another's. Each person is free to use his or her own powers to set and pursue his or her own purposes, consistent with the freedom of others to use their powers to set their purposes. A system of equal freedom demands that no one use his or her own powers in a way that will deprive others of theirs, or use another person's powers without his or her permission.[68]

This last sentence illuminates the occasions when one liberty can be favoured over another. You cannot use your powers in a way that will deprive others of theirs. Whenever a claim in deceit is made out, the liberty of expression is sacrificed to the right of the dupe that was violated by reliance on the lie. This is a justifiable restriction on the conduct of the deceiver because their lie involves them using their powers of speech to compel another to use their means in a way they have not agreed to, using their own powers in a way to deprive another of theirs.

Importantly, allowing a claim in deceit in this context does not impose a duty on one partner to take contraceptive measures to facilitate their sexual partner's reproductive choice, but requires only honesty that would enable the partner to be able to decline to pursue purposes they have not set. It recognises the wrong done when one intentionally acts to deceive another into relinquishing their reproductive choice. As Ripstein observes, 'Getting other people to do things by deceiving them is necessarily inconsistent with separate persons pursuing their separate purposes'.[69]

[65] Weinrib (n 60) 152–53.
[66] J Murphy, 'Misleading Appearances in the Tort of Deceit' (2016) 75 *CLJ* 301, 329.
[67] ibid.
[68] Ripstein (n 10) 231.
[69] Ripstein (n 12) 50 fn 32.

Nor does allowing a claim in deceit necessarily open the door to a claim for negligence in the taking of contraceptives in a personal relationship.[70] If A and B are in a sexual relationship, and A is, in good faith, taking contraceptive measures to the knowledge of B, and B decides they need take no measures themselves, that is B's choice. It is plausible that in certain contexts ('don't worry, I am taking the contraceptive pill') the law could consider that A has assumed responsibility for contraception, but it does not necessarily follow that a duty of care would be imposed in such circumstances. Whether a duty of care follows from an assumption of responsibility is an enquiry which is informed by policy considerations[71] and is also responsive to the different interests engaged. In a situation where there is an equilibrium of power such as a good faith sexual relationship, burdening one party with a duty of care regarding contraception would put B in charge of what A could do with their body, imposing a duty on A to medicate their body in a certain way, and it would fall foul of the ideal of equal freedom. Courts are unlikely to impose a duty of care in these circumstances.

VI. The Best Interests of the Child

This discussion has illustrated that, once reproductive control is pulled out into the light and recognised as an independent, legally protected interest, it can be channelled into the existing action in deceit, so as to provide a remedy for the loss of such control that is doctrinally coherent with the existing law. However, there is still an innocent child at the centre of the deceit. Concerns around the impact upon the best interests of that child of one parent litigating against the other for the life disruption suffered have usually put the final nail in the coffin in claims of reproductive deceit. This nail is rather more stubborn to remove than the others we have considered, although perhaps there is some movement to be had if we reframe the problem.

Part of the solution involves identifying the dupe's reproductive control as an independent interest. This creates the space to pivot away from regarding the child itself as damage. The concern to avoid classifying the child in this way is currently being navigated in medical negligence cases, which recognise the way in which the reproductive decisions we make shape the fabric of our lives, and which directly compensate the disruption of the parents' autonomy interest.[72] A similar path can be followed in reproductive deceit.

However, in contrast to cases of medical negligence, cases of reproductive deceit raise two, additional concerns about the best interests of the child which relate to the undesirability of litigation within the family circle, and the payment of compensation by one parent to another.

The first concern is probably misplaced, since it is the initial deceit that causes dysfunction between the parents, not the availability of a legal remedy. Indeed, some kind of acknowledgement of the wrong and compensation may bring closure and help

[70] This concern was raised in *PP v DD* (n 4) at [65].
[71] See D Nolan, 'Assumption of Responsibility: Four Questions' (2019) 72 *Current Legal Problems* 123, 134.
[72] See Todd, ch 5 of this volume.

the parents move forward without ongoing resentment before the child is of sufficient age even to be aware of the circumstances of the conception. Nor need the child ever find out, given the routine suppression of names in such proceedings. To the extent that more harmonious relations result from a judicial acknowledgment of the wrong, this can only benefit the child. In any event, if the child is going to find out about the deceit involved in their conception, the harbinger of that news is more likely to be their duped and resentful parent, than the court's grant of a remedy.

Turning to the second concern, the general approach taken by courts is that allowing recovery by one parent against the other is contrary to the spirit and purpose of child protection legislation, according to which parents are equally responsible for maintaining a child.[73] Consequently, while judicial recognition of a loss of reproductive control as actionable damage in deceit would theoretically bring all direct pecuniary and non-pecuniary losses associated with the unplanned child within the scope of compensable losses, the maintenance costs are out of reach in a deceit-between-parents case where the child support is mandated and set through legislation.

There is more wriggle room with non-pecuniary losses. In this context, when it is the woman who is the dupe and who ends up pregnant and with the responsibility for raising a child, the concerns that an order for compensation would not be in the best interests of the child recede. Say, for example, the father is an immoral man who deceitfully impregnated his partner, and pays the minimum child support required, but otherwise has no connection with the child. The mother's claim for damages against him for the non-pecuniary losses suffered by the disruption to her life are likely to also be in the best interests of the child, as it will increase the coffers from which the child is raised. To deny a remedy in this context on the basis of the child's best interests seems counter to those very interests.

The more problematic case is where it is the father who is the dupe. Where the deceitful mother is the primary caregiver of the child conceived after deceiving the father out of taking his own contraceptive measures, the father's claim for compensation for non-pecuniary losses caused by the deceit might prima facie conflict with the best interests of that child. This is because success in the claim will take money out of the purse from which the child is raised (pooled with child support) and place it back in the father's pocket. The situation is difficult. Of course, it is no defence to any other private law claim raised against a tortfeasor that the tortfeasor has a child who would be adversely affected by a damages award, and the weight of the interest in reproductive control suggests the position should be no different in these difficult claims in deceit. The difference in this situation is that the claimant is the child's parent and – in contrast to other claimants – should also have the best interests of the child as a priority. However, as raised above, the absence of compensation may lead to a resentful father. Recognition and settlement of the wrong is likely to be the best route to reconciliation of the family circle, which itself is in the best interests of the child. Further, there can be no presumption regarding how the claimant's money is spent that can defeat a claim for deceitful interference with a right. A court 'does not look beyond the judgment to the spending of the damages'.[74]

[73] *PP v DD* (n 4) [63].

[74] *H West & Son Ltd v Shephard* [1964] AC 326 (HL) 364.

Perhaps the deceitful mother spends all her spare cash on shoes, bags, and champagne. Perhaps the duped father will spend the compensation taking the child on an enriching holiday that he could not otherwise afford, or paying for music lessons to which the mother refuses to contribute. Perhaps the deceiver is rich, and the dupe poor. The availability of an action cannot depend on a pre-conceived answer to these questions. Justice is more likely to be achieved if compensation is awarded at a level that acknowledges the wrong but does not defeat the essence of the child maintenance order.

Where the evidence validates the claim in deceit and reveals the domination of one partner's reproductive choice over the other's, it is important to isolate the wrong from preconceived notions that claims are being brought to evade child support obligations. The award would be directed at compensating the injury to reproductive control, not the existence of the child. Further, the injury to reproductive control occurs at the time when the child is conceived and born without the consent of the dupe. Once parenthood is imposed on the dupe, the rewards obtained from any relationship between the dupe and the child offset the ongoing interference with autonomy. For this reason, judicial concerns that the compensation payable would increase the more a parent engages with the child are unfounded.[75]

Child support legislation exists to protect the maintenance interests of the child. Outside that, if private law is to provide robust protection to our interest in reproductive control, then there should be a private law response in scenarios of reproductive deceit.

VII. Concluding Words

No parent is fully aware of the way their life will change when a baby arrives, but those who desire to have children seek the lifelong relationships and responsibilities that come with parenting, and are often joyous with it. In the scenarios considered in this chapter, the situation is rather different. One parent has been duped into procreation. They do not desire either the relationship, or the responsibilities that come with parenthood, but have had them imposed upon them, together with a lifelong tether to the duplicitous partner. Understanding the significance that our reproductive choices have on the shape of our life, and contextualising this within other interests protected in private law, provides clear grounds for protection of that interest in a system that promotes equal freedom. Of course, within our private lives and family circles, there are added complications around judicial intervention. The modest aim of this chapter has been to unpack some of these complications and demonstrate how recognition of reproductive control as an interest worthy of independent protection, together with the idea of equal freedom, can help overcome the obstacles in a manner which is internally consistent with the common law. If it is desirable to live in a world where sexual partners are obliged to consider their partner's interest in reproductive control in making statements around contraception or sterility, there is clearly a good argument that reproductive deceit should no longer go unrecognised in private law.

[75] *PP v DD* (n 4) [63].

5

Human Existence as Actionable Damage?

STEPHEN TODD*

I. Introduction

In developments starting in the 1980s, a series of decisions in common law courts in different countries sought to resolve the question whether the parent or parents of an unplanned child could recover damages from a medical professional whose conduct had resulted in the child's conception, either by negligently performing a sterilisation operation on the mother or father, or by giving negligent advice about the efficacy of the operation. A particular difficulty emerged in cases in which the child was born with a disability, prompting questions as to whether, or how, a distinction might be drawn between a claim in respect of an unplanned child who was 'healthy', and one who was disabled. In a variation on this theme, similar claims were made by parents in respect of conduct (or advice given) by a medical professional concerning an existing pregnancy, usually where the mother was misinformed that the fetus was healthy and she consequently decided not to seek a termination. Running in parallel with these developments were a small number of claims by disabled children themselves, who sought damages in respect of their disabilities where their mothers had been misled in this way. More recent developments have concerned negligence in the execution of in vitro fertilisation (IVF) procedures, where culpable mistakes have been made in fertilising human eggs or implanting embryos. These have resulted in new and controversial claims being brought by parents, who sue on account of certain unwanted genetic characteristics of their children.

These claims have been described in the courts as, respectively, claims for 'wrongful conception', 'wrongful birth', 'wrongful life' and 'wrongful fertilisation'. But critics say that such expressions do not reflect the true nature of, and motivations behind, these claims, that they are emotive and that they implicitly denigrate life.[1] Alternative expressions used in this chapter include 'unplanned' or 'unwanted birth' (as regards claims by parents) and 'disabled life' (as regards claims by the children), although these may not

* I would like to thank Kit Barker very much for his many penetrating comments on a draft of this chapter. The opinions expressed in it about a number of controversial issues of course are mine.

[1] H Teff, 'The Action for Wrongful Life in England and the United States' (1985) 34 *ICLQ* 423, 427–28.

capture entirely accurately the nature of every claim. None of the various expressions are intended to carry any denigratory implications. Again, references to a 'healthy' child are always intended to mean, simply, a child who does not have any disability or other potentially actionable condition.

The common, and unique, character of all these claims is that, in one way or another, they treat the existence of a human being, or some feature of that existence, either as damage in itself, or as the cause of some other type of damage. For this reason, they raise some fundamental questions of policy. Claims by parents require a court to determine whether it is acceptable to treat the existence of an unplanned child, and the expenses involved in bringing him or her up, as an actionable type of harm. The same question arises where the child is planned but has unwanted characteristics, including a disability. If it is improper to treat the child's existence itself as damage, a second question is whether there may nonetheless be a right of action in these cases in respect of some other form of harm which is not open to the same criticism. Claims by children raise an equally fundamental, and controversial, question. Can a child born with a disability ever maintain an action where, but for the defendant's negligence, he or she would not exist?

II. Unplanned Conception or Birth

As recently stated in the United Kingdom Supreme Court, the first question to be asked in determining liability in negligence is whether the plaintiff has suffered an actionable form of harm.[2] All of the 'failed sterilisation' cases involve allegations that the negligence of a doctor (or other health care professional) caused a child to come into existence; that proper care would have prevented the birth; and that, by reason of the birth and existence of the child, the parents suffered loss.[3] Accordingly, each case required the court to determine whether (and if so, to what extent) the expense associated with the unplanned or unwanted existence of a human being ought to be recognised as amounting to actionable damage. The House of Lords and the United Kingdom Supreme Court, on the one hand, and the High Court of Australia, on the other, have taken opposing views in answering this question.

A. Special Rules: *McFarlane v Tayside*, *Parkinson v St James* and *Khan v Meadows*

In *McFarlane v Tayside Health Board*,[4] the pursuers were a married couple with four children who did not wish to have any more. The defendant surgeon carried out a vasectomy

[2] *Khan v Meadows* [2021] UKSC 21, [2022] AC 852 [28].

[3] The cases usually involve claims by the mother alone, or by the mother and father jointly. Complications can arise in the case of a claim by the father alone or possibly by another person having care of a child. For discussion of this question, which is outside the scope of this article, see *Parkinson v St James and Seacroft University Hospital NHS Trust* [2001] EWCA Civ 530, [2002] QB 266 [93]; *Whitehead v Searle* [2008] EWCA Civ 285, [2009] 1 WLR 549 [51], [62]–[68].

[4] *McFarlane v Tayside Health Board* [2000] 2 AC 59 (HL); T Weir 'The Unwanted Child' (2000) 59 *CLJ* 238; M Jones 'Bringing Up Baby' (2001) 9 *Tort Law Review* 14.

operation on the husband, and afterwards informed the couple that contraceptive measures were no longer necessary. They acted on that advice, which was incorrect, and the wife became pregnant and gave birth to a healthy daughter. The pursuers then sought damages from the Health Board for the loss caused by the birth of the child and the costs of bringing her up.

Their Lordships rejected an argument that the wife's failure to undergo an abortion – or arrange an adoption on discovering her pregnancy – was a new act, breaking the chain of causation between the surgeon's negligence and the birth. By a majority,[5] they granted her general damages for the pain, suffering and inconvenience of the pregnancy and childbirth, together with associated expenses. By contrast, however, they unanimously rejected the parents' claim for the costs of bringing up their child. The policy considerations underlying this aspect of the decision included an unwillingness to regard a normal, healthy child as a financial liability, or as more trouble and expense than it was worth; a recognition that the potentially counterbalancing rewards of parenthood are unquantifiable; and a view that making an award for such a loss against the UK National Health Service would be a misallocation of public resources. The underlying ethos of the decision was perhaps best captured by Lord Millett, who observed that the birth of a child was in truth a mixed blessing, but that society had to regard it, on balance, as beneficial. The advantages and disadvantages of parenthood were inextricably bound together, and it would be subversive of the mores of society for parents to enjoy the advantages, but transfer the responsibilities to others.[6]

There are frequent references in *McFarlane* to the legal principles to be applied in the case of an unplanned, 'healthy' child. Their Lordships did not decide whether a claim might lie where the unplanned child suffers from a disability. This question was considered in *Parkinson v St James and Seacroft University Hospital NHS Trust*.[7] The claimant, a mother of four children living with her husband, underwent a negligently performed sterilisation operation. She later conceived and gave birth to a fifth, severely disabled, child after her marriage had broken down. It was held that she was entitled to recover the costs of providing for the child's special needs and care relating to his disability, but, applying *McFarlane*, not his basic maintenance costs. In Hale LJ's opinion, the extra expenses attributable to the child's disability fell outside the *McFarlane* bar, on the basis that they simply acknowledged that he cost more. Awarding them still treated a disabled child as having exactly the same worth as a non-disabled child, with the same dignity and status. And statutory definitions in welfare legislation identifying those whose special needs required special services could be used in identifying a qualifying disability. Brooke LJ, taking a slightly different approach on this last point,

[5] Lords Slynn, Steyn, Hope and Clyde (Lord Millett dissenting on this point).

[6] Three of the judgments in *McFarlane* mentioned, without discussion, the question whether the same policies applied in the case of actions for breach of contract. In *B v IVF Hammersmith* [2018] EWCA Civ 2803, [2019] 2 WLR 1094 Nicola Davies LJ recognised that, where a breach of contract resulting in the birth of an unplanned child arose in the absence of a liquidated damages clause in the contract, the resulting obligation to pay damages was a secondary obligation arising by implication of the common law. But where there was nothing in the contract which modified the approach of the common law, which necessarily included legal policy, there was no legal basis upon which to differ in terms of the recovery of the claimed loss as between contract and tort.

[7] *Parkinson* (n 3); O Quick, 'Damages for Wrongful Conception' (2002) 10 *Tort Law Review* 5. See also *Groom v Selby* [2001] EWCA Civ 1522, [2002] Lloyd's Rep Med 1.

said that the disability would need to be 'significant' and that the decision as to whether or not it qualified would be made on a case-by-case basis. The expression would include disabilities of the mind, but not minor defects or inconveniences.

The question whether a parent can recover damages in respect of the birth of a disabled child arose again in *Khan v Meadows*.[8] The claimant attended her general medical practice in order to determine whether she was a carrier of the haemophilia gene. The defendant, Dr Khan, arranged for blood tests, but these could not confirm whether or not she was a carrier of the gene, and she should have been referred to a haematologist for genetic testing. Dr Khan then advised the claimant that her results were normal, leading her to believe that any child she might have would not have haemophilia. She later became pregnant and gave birth to a son, who both suffered from haemophilia and was diagnosed as autistic. Dr Khan conceded her liability to compensate the claimant for the additional costs associated with the child's haemophilia, but contested her responsibility for those associated with his autism.

The UK Supreme Court held that the defendant was responsible only for the costs associated with the haemophilia, and that the autism costs were outside the scope of the defendant's duty. Dr Khan's advisory duty concerned the specific risk of the child having haemophilia, and did not extend to unrelated risks (such as autism) which might arise in any pregnancy.[9] *Khan* was not a failed sterilisation case, but notably, in reaching its decision, the Court discussed and approved the decision of the Court of Appeal in *Parkinson*.

B. Ordinary Principle: *Cattanach v Melchior*

Developments in Australia contrast markedly with those in the United Kingdom. In *Cattanach v Melchior*,[10] the defendant obstetrician negligently gave inadequate advice to the plaintiffs, a husband and wife, concerning the success of a tubal ligation operation that he had performed on the wife. The plaintiffs were led to believe that the wife could not conceive, a consequence being the unplanned conception and birth of their third child. The High Court of Australia, in a 4-to-3 majority decision,[11] was not persuaded that there were any policy considerations precluding recovery, declined to follow *McFarlane*, and upheld the trial judge's decision to award damages for the cost of raising the child.

The majority view was that the defendant could be held liable on the application of ordinary negligence principles. McHugh and Gummow JJ said that no novel head of damages was involved. The loss that the plaintiffs claimed was not the coming into existence of the parent-child relationship itself, but simply the economic expenditure

[8] (n 2).

[9] On the scope of the duty question, see *Todd on Torts*, 9th edn (Thomson Reuters New Zealand Ltd, 2023) [4.2.4], [19.3].

[10] *Cattanach v Melchior* [2003] HCA 38, (2003) 215 CLR 1; J Seymour, '*Cattanach v Melchior*: Legal Principles and Public Policy' (2003) 11 *Torts Law Journal* 208; K Weston-Scheuber, 'Victory for Reluctant Parents: *Cattanach v Melchior*' (2003) 26 *University of New South Wales Law Journal* 717; P Cane, 'The Doctor, the Stork and the Court: A Modern Morality Play' (2004) 120 *LQR* 23.

[11] McHugh, Gummow, Kirby and Callinan JJ (Gleeson CJ, Hayne and Heydon JJ dissenting).

that they had incurred, or would incur in the future. If this was causally connected to the negligence and reasonably foreseeable, then it ought to be recoverable. Kirby J maintained that, in the real world, cases of this kind were about money, not love or the preservation of the family unit. The notion that, in every case, the birth of a child was a 'blessing' represented a fiction that the law should not accept in the absence of objective evidence bearing it out. In any event, the parents' claim was simply for economic loss consequential upon physical injury to the mother. To deny such recovery was to provide a zone of legal immunity to medical practitioners engaged in sterilisation procedures that was unprincipled and inconsistent with established legal doctrine. Furthermore, the emotional benefits of parenthood were different in quality from the costs incurred in child-raising and should be ignored in calculating damages.

The decision in *Cattanach* avoids any need to make special provision for claims by the parents of disabled children. In the view of the majority, the ordinary rules governing liability and the recoverability and quantum of the damage claimed will apply. Yet political reaction to *Cattanach* was negative, and in three Australian states legislation was quickly introduced to reverse it.[12] An important reason, no doubt, was the desire not to place an extra financial burden on public health services. However, let us put aside any such pragmatic difficulties in funding medical services and turn to the principle of the matter.

C. An Evaluation

The very special nature of the damage which is alleged to be actionable – financial loss by way of expenditure on a child who, but for the defendant's negligence, would not exist – suggests that the majority approach in *Cattanach* is not a policy-free application of ordinary principle. As Cane has remarked, the view that 'legal principle' can tell us whether Dr Cattanach should have been held responsible for the cost of rearing the unplanned child might justly be called a fairy tale.[13] Even if the loss is characterised as consequential upon physical damage to the mother (which seems doubtful), claims of this kind have unique features and require the courts to make judgements on matters involving controversial questions of moral and philosophical principle. And while the issues involved are certainly contestable, and many commentators are highly critical of *McFarlane*,[14] its core arguments are ultimately persuasive and should prevail.

The fundamental contention – made very clearly by Lord Millett in *McFarlane* – is that the birth of a healthy child should not in law be treated as 'harm', or a 'loss' because it is morally offensive to regard a normal healthy baby as more trouble than it is worth. This leads us to consider whether we ought to characterise all money expended on a child as a 'loss'. Why separate the expense incurred by the parents in providing for their

[12] Civil Liability Act 2003 (Qld) ss 49A, 49B; Civil Liability Act 2002 (NSW) s 71; Civil Liability Act 1936 (SA) s 67.

[13] Cane (n 10) 26.

[14] See, for example, L Hoyano, 'Misconceptions about Wrongful Conception' (2002) 65 *MLR* 883; M Fordham, 'Blessing or Burden? Recent Developments in Actions for Wrongful Conception and Wrongful Birth in the UK and Australia' [2004] *Singapore Journal of Legal Studies* 462.

child from the emotional benefit to the parents in providing for his or her happiness, self-esteem and security and in showing that he or she is a loved and wanted member of the family? We should at least recognise that the answer involves an evaluative choice between recognising the claimant parents' subjective rejection of the benefits to them in having a child, and laying down a principle affirming and promoting the inestimable value of children as a matter of social policy. It is not a matter merely of quantifying a loss.

If, contrary to this view, we accept that parents *have* suffered a loss in paying for their child, we need to determine which expenses ought to be included and which excluded, and whether there should be an offsetting of any prospective financial benefits. In his dissenting judgment in *Cattanach*, Gleeson CJ asked some pertinent questions. Why not include wedding expenses, or costs of tertiary education? Why distinguish between child-rearing costs and the adverse effects on the career prospects of the parents? Why exclude the natural and moral obligations owed by children to parents, and the financial consequences in later years that these may entail? Certainly, if the action is allowed there must be *some* limit on what can and cannot be claimed. So, a partial answer to his Honour's questions might be to limit the damages to, say, the upbringing expenses that are reasonably ascertainable and objectively necessary. But solutions of this kind do not deal with the possible financial advantages to the parents of having children and explain why these must be ignored. As for the disadvantages, many of the expenses involved – like private school fees, presents and holidays – are perfectly reasonable, but not 'necessary'. A court seeking to compensate only for strictly necessary expenses is not quantifying a loss, but is choosing to award a lesser sum, precisely because the award of a proper compensatory sum is unpalatable, or even offensive.

Two related and fundamental propositions which encapsulate the objections to the parents' claim were identified and applied in the decision of the Court of Appeal of Singapore in *ACB v Thomson Medical Pte Ltd*.[15] This was a claim by a husband and wife in respect of negligence by their IVF provider in using an embryo created from an unknown man's sperm rather than that of the husband. The plaintiffs' claim raised novel issues, which are considered below,[16] but we will consider here the claim for the upkeep costs of the child. Phang Boon Leong JA, delivering the judgment of the Court, said that the success of the claim necessarily depended on recognising the obligations of parenthood as actionable damage, yet the duty to maintain a child was a duty lying at the very heart of parenthood and the expenses which were incurred in its discharge were not capable of characterisation as a loss. The obligations of parenthood were *fundamental, indivisible and incapable of sounding in damages*. No parent could claim a legal entitlement to be free from the responsibilities of parenthood, whether financial or otherwise. Further, to recognise the upkeep claim would be fundamentally inconsistent with the nature of the parent-child relationship and would place the mother in a position where her personal interests as a litigant would conflict with her duties as a parent. Parents would have to prove that their children represented a net loss to them. The very nature of such an exercise would encourage the exaggeration of any infirmities and the

[15] *ACB v Thomson Medical Pte Ltd* [2017] SGCA 20, [2017] 1 SLR 918.
[16] See section III.B.

diminution of such benefits as might exist in their children, in order that the account might be made as favourable to the parents possible. Such conduct was fundamentally at odds with the overarching duty that parents have to provide for, care for and love their children. So the public interest lay in the adoption of a bright-line rule that absolutely precluded parents from being placed in a position where their personal interests might conflict with their parental duties.[17]

Let us consider now the position where the child is born with a disability. In *Khan v Meadows* it was accepted by all members of the United Kingdom Supreme Court that the claimant could recover damages for the expenses associated with the child's haemophilia, relying on *Parkinson* as a key authority.[18] Lord Hodge and Lord Sales said that the object of the service undertaken in *Parkinson* was to prevent the birth of *any* child, and were satisfied that the economic costs of caring for a disabled child were of a nature that was 'clearly actionable'.[19] Lord Burrows thought that a remedy in respect of the haemophilia was an uncontroversial aspect of the law applicable to the facts, and also that the authority of *Parkinson* had been confirmed by the House of Lords in *Rees v Darlington Memorial Hospital NHS Trust*.[20] Lord Leggatt said that it was not in dispute that the expense of caring for a child born with a disorder, if it resulted from negligent advice, was a kind of expense for which damages could in principle be claimed, again citing *Parkinson* and *Rees*.[21]

In fact, however, it is clear that *Rees* did not determine this question. On the contrary, it puts the view taken in *Khan* in considerable doubt. *Rees* concerned a claim by a *mother* with a disability, not her child, and the decision of their Lordships is notable for having introduced the idea of a claim by the mother for loss of autonomy.[22] Only the minority judges in *Rees* – Lords Steyn, Hope and Hutton – supported *Parkinson*, on the basis that the same or a similar principle should apply to the mother's claim.[23] By contrast, three of those in the majority – Lords Bingham, Nicholls and Scott – rejected it, preferring to make an award for loss of autonomy without differentiation between cases in which the child or parent was disabled.[24] Lord Millett had serious doubts about *Parkinson*, but in the end left the question open.[25]

Accordingly, while *Rees* did not finally determine the fate of *Parkinson*, there was no majority view in its favour. Lord Bingham recognised that it was anomalous that the defendant's liability in *Parkinson* should be related to a disability which the doctor's negligence did not cause, and not to the birth, which it did.[26] Suppose, indeed, that a child is born healthy and suffers a disabling injury after birth. *Parkinson* held that the risk that a child might be born with a disability was small but nonetheless foreseeable, and one might think that accidents after birth are also foreseeable. But an argument

[17] *ACB* (n 15) [87]–[105].
[18] *Khan* (n 2) [63] (Lords Hodge and Sales), [73(iv)] (Lord Burrows), [86] (Lord Leggatt).
[19] ibid [63], [67]. The decision of the Court of Appeal in *Groom* (n 7), was approved on the same basis.
[20] *Rees v Darlington Memorial Hospital NHS Trust* [2003] UKHL 52, [2004] 1 AC 309.
[21] *Khan* (n 2) [86].
[22] See below section III.A.
[23] *Rees* (n 20) [35] (Lord Steyn), [57] (Lord Hope), [91] (Lord Hutton).
[24] ibid [9] (Lord Bingham), [18] (Lord Nicholls), [147] (Lord Scott).
[25] ibid [112].
[26] ibid [9].

that a defendant caused the plaintiff to exist and thus to encounter the accident (and that he or she therefore should be liable for it) can only be characterised as bizarre. It is not clear why there should be a difference in the case of negligence prior to conception. Certainly, in cases such as *Parkinson*, where the defendant's negligence causes a child to be born and the child has a disability unrelated to that negligence, the damages still represent the costs of bringing up a child, albeit a child with a disability. And notwithstanding the arguments of Hale LJ in *Parkinson*, the courts can be seen as drawing an invidious distinction between the 'value' or 'worth' of healthy and disabled children. As Lord Millett remarked in *Rees*, a disabled child is not 'worth' less than a healthy one. The blessings of his or her birth are no less incalculable. Society must, equally, regard the balance as beneficial.[27]

Lord Millett went on to say that the law does not develop by strict logic, and most people would instinctively feel that there was a difference, even if they had difficulty in articulating it. But even accepting *Parkinson*, his Lordship recognised that it would be necessary to limit the compensation to the *additional* costs attributable to the child's disability, and thought that this might prove difficult to achieve without introducing nice distinctions and unacceptable refinements of a kind likely to bring the law into disrepute. Indeed, their Lordships in *Khan* did not seek to draw this distinction, simply referring to the costs of caring for, or bringing up, the disabled child. Seemingly, this includes 'ordinary' upbringing costs.

The objections to awarding the costs of bringing up a child are compelling. However, the question remains whether a duty nonetheless ought to be recognised in the circumstances in *Khan*, which is not, after all, a sterilisation case. Dr Khan did not simply cause the child to be born, but also caused him to be born *with haemophilia*. In fact, this is not a relevant distinction and the principle is the same wherever a court needs to determine whether to award the costs involved in raising a disabled child. It is not enough to say that, in *Khan*, the defendant assumed responsibility for advising the plaintiff about the risk of the child being born with haemophilia. It might equally be said that in *McFarlane* the defendant assumed responsibility to prevent a pregnancy, yet the parents' claim for the costs of upbringing was defeated by overriding concerns of public policy. The objections to awarding the costs of having a child apply whether or not the child is disabled.

However, this is not to say that a claim by the parents should fail in total, particularly, as we shall see, where they have a disabled child. *McFarlane* does not bar actions which do not treat the cost of the child as itself constituting damage. The mother's claim for the injury of pregnancy and childbirth, allowed by the House of Lords, was a straightforward claim for physical damage and associated economic costs, and can be recognised and understood in that light. And a possible remedy in any failed sterilisation case (and other, analogous cases) is to make an award in respect of the parents' loss of reproductive autonomy as a free-standing head of claim. As we shall see, a child's disability could be a highly significant factor in determining the level of an award for harm of this type; and if the defendant *caused the disability*, the child arguably may have an action in his or her own right.

[27] ibid [112].

III. Interference with Autonomy

A. An Unconventional Award: *Rees v Darlington Memorial Hospital NHS Trust*

In *Rees v Darlington Memorial Hospital NHS Trust*[28] the House of Lords followed and applied *McFarlane*, yet recognised a right of action by an unwilling mother in respect of the interference with her autonomy caused by the birth of her child. This decision points to a way forward which is coherent in principle, and which avoids the policy objections identified in *McFarlane*. Critically, a claim in respect of the upbringing of a child, whether healthy or disabled, is a claim to recover *the financial costs of maintaining the child*. A claim by a parent in respect of the impact on her or his autonomy of having the child is not a claim for those costs.

Ms Rees had undergone a sterilisation operation because she suffered from a severe visual handicap which she feared would prevent her from properly looking after a child. Having later conceived and given birth, she sought damages to recover the costs of providing for the child. Ordinary costs being precluded by *McFarlane*, the question was whether the mother's special difficulties could be taken into account. The Court of Appeal,[29] in a majority decision, held that, just as the parent of a child with significant disability was entitled to compensation for providing for the child's special needs associated with his disability, so too was a disabled parent entitled to the extra costs of discharging her responsibility towards a healthy child. In the House of Lords, the minority took this view,[30] while the majority allowed the appeal, but also introduced what Lords Bingham and Nicholls called a 'gloss' on the holding in *McFarlane*. Lord Bingham accepted and supported a rule of legal policy which precluded recovery of the full cost of raising an unplanned child, yet questioned the fairness of a rule which denied the wronged parent any recompense at all beyond the immediate expenses of pregnancy and birth. The real loss was that the parent – particularly the mother – had been denied the opportunity to live her life in the way that she wished and planned.[31] His Lordship accordingly supported the suggestion favoured by Lord Millett in *McFarlane* that there should be a conventional award to mark the plaintiff's injury and lost autonomy. This sum, fixed at £15,000, would be in addition to any award for pregnancy and birth and would be applied without differentiation to all cases, including those in which either the child, or the parent, was disabled. However, as we have seen, the question whether the extra costs of raising a child where it is disabled might also be recoverable was not determined.

A claim for loss of autonomy following an unwanted birth is conceptually quite different from a claim for the costs of bringing up a child. The same objections of principle do not apply, and the focus is on the impact of the child on the lives of the parents,

[28] *Rees* (n 20); P Cane, 'Another Failed Sterilisation' (2004) 120 *LQR* 189; A Redain, 'Unconventional Justice in the House of Lords' (2004) 63 *CLJ* 19.

[29] *Rees v Darlington Memorial Hospital NHS Trust* [2002] EWCA Civ 88, [2003] QB 20.

[30] *Rees* (n 20) (Lords Steyn, Hope and Hutton).

[31] ibid [8].

rather than on the unwanted expenditure on the child. However, a significant question that their Lordships did not clearly decide is whether the lump sum award was intended to be vindicatory (publicly marking the wrong done to the parents), or compensatory of a real loss, or both.[32] Lord Bingham said that the conventional award would not be – and would not be intended to be – compensatory and would not be the product of calculation. Its object was to afford some measure of recognition of the wrong done. Lord Nicholls explained that the award was intended to recognise that, in respect of the birth, the parent had suffered a legal wrong which had a far-reaching effect on the lives of the parent and her family. Lord Millett, elaborating on his view in *McFarlane*, said that the right to limit the size of one's family was an important human right and a proper subject for compensation. He also explained that, while he had formerly contemplated a variable award, he was persuaded that it ought to be purely conventional, not susceptible of increase or decrease by reference to the circumstances of the case. Finally, Lord Scott said that the plaintiff was entitled to the benefit of the doctor's obligation to carry out the operation with due care, and that it was open to the court to put a monetary value on that expected benefit.[33]

While there was no clear consensus, the views of Lords Nicholls, Millett and Scott broadly contemplated the award having both a vindicatory and a compensatory purpose. This is perfectly acceptable in theory and, indeed, desirable in practice. The primary purpose of a claim in negligence is compensatory and, as recently reasserted in *Khan*, negligence is actionable only on proof of damage, but that does not exclude a vindicatory function. Torts which are actionable per se, by contrast, seek to vindicate the right by giving damages for wrongful interference with the protected interest, but compensation for consequential loss can naturally be awarded as well. Whether or when an award of vindicatory damages standing alone ought to be made is controversial, but a compensatory award with a vindicatory purpose is not.[34]

B. Unwanted Fertilisation

Negligent conduct or advice concerning the conception of a child can take many forms apart from those already mentioned. In particular, negligence by a fertility body in providing IVF services may result in a child being born who lacks any genetic connection with one or both of the putative parents. An egregious instance comes from the United States. An Asian couple (AP and YZ) were suing a fertility clinic after an IVF mix-up which led to the woman being implanted with the wrong embryo. As a result, AP gave birth to twin boys who did not appear to be of Asian descent, and genetic testing showed that the boys were unrelated either to the couple or, indeed, to each other. In subsequent custody proceedings, AP and YZ were required to relinquish custody of

[32] K Barker, 'Private and Public: The Meaning of Vindication in Torts and Private Law' in S Pitel, J Neyers and E Chamberlain (eds), *Tort Law: Challenging Orthodoxy* (Oxford, Hart Publishing, 2013) suggests that there is no single, institutional conception in the law of what it means to vindicate rights: at 59.

[33] *Rees* (n 20) [8], [17], [123], [148] respectively.

[34] See *R (Lumba) v Secretary of State for the Home Department* [2011] UKSC 12, [2012] 1 AC 245, especially at [97]–[101].

each boy to his biological parents. The fertility clinic had not advised them about what had happened to their own embryos, which they suspected had been lost or destroyed. Their claim against the clinic alleged, inter alia, medical malpractice, negligence, reckless and wanton misconduct, deceit and fraudulent concealment.[35] It may be that established tort remedies could provide a sufficient remedy in this case, but sometimes, certainly, they will not.

A leading discussion is that of the Singapore Court of Appeal in *ACB v Thomson Medical Pte Ltd*.[36] Here, as we have seen, the defendant fertility clinic used the wrong sperm in the course of the plaintiff's IVF treatment, causing her to give birth to a child who was not biologically related to her husband. Phang Boon Leong JA rejected the plaintiff's claim for the cost of raising the child,[37] and was not disposed to recognise loss of autonomy as a recoverable head of damage in its own right either,[38] but nevertheless did recognise autonomy as *an important background consideration*. The appellant's loss could not be understood without a more developed and substantive (as well as nuanced) notion of 'autonomy' that took into account existing family-building practices, kinship arrangements and the socially constituted value of genetic relatedness. The true loss which she had suffered in this case – which should be considered a distinct and recognisable head of damage – was a loss of genetic affinity.

His Honour recognised that the desire for genetic affinity was complex and multifaceted. It was, at its core, a desire for identity bounded in consanguinity. The ordinary human experience was that parents and children were bound by ties of blood and shared physical traits. This fact of biological experience – heredity – carried deep socio-cultural significance. It was affinity which distinguished familial ties from ties of friendship. Persons who *consciously chose* to undergo IVF did so because of a deep desire to experience, as far as possible, the ordinary experience and incidents of parenthood. And when, as in the present case, a person had been denied this experience due to the negligence of others then she had lost something of profound significance and had suffered a serious wrong. The appellant's interest in maintaining the integrity of her reproductive plans in this very specific sense – where she had made a conscious decision to have a child *with her husband* to maintain an intergenerational genetic link and to preserve 'affinity' – was one which the law should recognise and protect.[39]

How, then, should the damages to compensate for such loss be quantified? Phang Boon Leong JA said that in deciding on an appropriate award it was vital to take into account the unique types of harm suffered by a person when his or her reproductive plans were disrupted. These types of harm would vary depending on the particular reasons why fertility treatment was sought, the precise manner in which the negligence took place, and the personal circumstances of the plaintiff (such as the presence of other

[35] Rachel Montgomery, 'Couple Sues IVF Clinic After Embryo Mix-Up' (*Bionews* 1006, 15 July 2019) www.bionews.org.uk/page_143806; and see Hannah Flynn, 'Israeli Woman Carrying Unrelated Fetus Following IVF Mix-Up' (*Bionews* 1160, 26 September 2022) www.progress.org.uk/israeli-woman-carrying-unrelated-fetus-following-ivf-mix-up/.

[36] *ACB* (n 15).

[37] See text to nn 15–17.

[38] See text to n 47.

[39] *ACB* (n 15) [125]–[136].

children, or the familial or cultural histories particular to him or her). Accordingly, the court should benchmark the eventual award as a percentage of the financial costs of raising the child. Although this was not an appropriate case in which to award upkeep costs as such, the financial costs of raising the child were not wholly irrelevant as, absent such costs, there would be no other criterion or standard by which to assess the quantum of damages. Whilst it was perhaps not theoretically elegant, this approach was practical, and it prevented the court from having to pluck a figure out of thin air, so to speak. Applying this approach, his Honour concluded that the appellant should be awarded 30 per cent of the costs, which was an amount that properly reflected the seriousness of the appellant's loss and was just, equitable and proportionate in the circumstances of the case.[40]

C. Interference with Reproductive Autonomy

We have seen that there are persuasive policy concerns against awarding damages for the costs of bringing up children, whether healthy or disabled, but that claims for interfering with parents' autonomy concerning their sterilisation, or with their wishes concerning their genetic connection with a planned child are not open to similar objection. We need to consider now how these latter developments might be rationalised, as coming under the umbrella of a wider principle of law that protects a person from interference with his or her reproductive autonomy. Let us note, first, that the common law recognises a person's autonomy as worthy of recognition and protection in civil proceedings in a number of ways. A form of negative protection is found in the general rule that there is no general duty to take action to prevent harm being suffered by another person,[41] which brings into account core issues relating to the desirability of maintaining, within reasonable limits, the freedom and autonomy of individuals to act as they wish.[42] Furthermore, the courts sometimes recognise that autonomy is, or can be, a value protected by an award of damages under an existing cause of action. For example, a claimant who became infertile as a result of the defendant's negligent delay in diagnosing her with cancer of the cervix recovered damages which included the expense of pursuing a commercial surrogacy agreement in California, their aim being to restore her personal autonomy in being able to found a family.[43] Again, the courts often have emphasised a patient's right of autonomy in giving effect to a doctor's duty to obtain the patient's informed consent to treatment.[44] Protection from interference with personal autonomy also can provide a rationale for torts other than negligence and underlie any

[40] ibid [145]–[150].

[41] *Home Office v Dorset Yacht Co Ltd* [1970] AC 1004 (HL) 1060; *Poole BC v GN* [2019] UKSC 25, sub nom *N v Poole BC* [2020] AC 780, 824 [28].

[42] See, eg, *Stuart v Kirkland-Veenstra* [2009] HCA 15, (2009) 237 CLR 215 [88]–[98].

[43] *XX v Whittington Hospital NHS Trust* [2018] EWCA Civ 2832, [2019] 3 WLR 107 [71]. In *Whittington Hospital NHS Trust v XX* [2020] UKSC 14, [2021] AC 275 the Supreme Court dismissed the defendant's appeal and affirmed that no question of illegality was involved. While statute rendered commercial surrogacy unlawful in the UK, it did not purport to legislate for any other country, or prohibit the claimant from doing what she proposed.

[44] See *Montgomery v Lanarkshire Health Board* [2015] UKSC 11, [2015] AC 430 [108] (Lady Hale).

award of damages. A clear example is found in the widespread recognition of a remedy for the misuse of private information, by the developing tort of invasion of privacy.[45]

These examples do not consider whether, or how far, loss of autonomy standing alone can give rise to a right of action. Certainly, the Court of Appeal in England in *Shaw v Kovac*[46] rejected the notion of injury to autonomy as a new and separate head of loss in a personal injury claim. Davis LJ downplayed *Rees*, saying that the approach adopted by the majority was 'striking' and noting that three of the seven judges dissented and regarded the conventional award as wholly contrary to principle. Again, in *ACB*, Phang Boon Leong JA rejected the notion of autonomy (without more) as an actionable injury in its own right. There was: (a) a conceptual objection, in that it was too nebulous and contested a concept; (b) a coherence objection, in that there might be no objective detriment in the case, for example, of a paternalistic act; and (c) an over-inclusiveness objection, in that any form of damage could, with some ingenuity, be reconceptualised in terms of an injury to autonomy. So his Honour preferred to recognise only the loss of genetic affinity that was suffered in that case specifically as the actionable damage.[47]

Notwithstanding these views, there are good arguments in favour of recognising parents' lost autonomy as the foundation for their claim.[48] The conceptual difficulty stems from the need to recognise lost autonomy as damage in its own right, as opposed to damage consequential upon personal injury or some other recognisable head of loss. But the House of Lords did precisely this in *Rees*. The award was not consequential upon personal injury suffered by the plaintiff, or upon the invasion of some other protectable interest. The lost autonomy was the damage *in and of itself*. Further, the objections outlined in *ACB* disappear once we confine the scope of recovery to lost *reproductive* autonomy. This is not a nebulous concept, but one with reasonably identifiable boundaries involving objectively ascertainable detriment. Nor is its recognition paternalistic, or over-inclusive. Rather, there is a right of action only in cases where a person has been deprived of the opportunity to decide whether, or in what circumstances, to have a child or, as we shall see, to decide certain of the child's critical characteristics. Decisions of this kind are, for most people, among the most important of their lives, and it is strongly arguable that wrongful interferences with their exercise should be redressable by the victims. Such interferences normally have the consequence of permanently altering their family circumstances to an unwanted state of affairs.

While the principle adopted in *Rees* is eminently supportable, the award of a single conventional sum can be criticised as likely to be inadequate in some cases, in failing to reflect the true value of a parent's lost autonomy. Furthermore, if we accept the award

[45] See, in particular, *Campbell v MGN Ltd* [2004] UKHL 22, [2004] 2 AC 457; *Hosking v Runting* [2004] NZCA 34, [2005] 1 NZLR 1.

[46] *Shaw v Kovac* [2017] EWCA Civ 1028, [2017] 1 WLR 4773.

[47] *ACB* (n 15) [109]–[124].

[48] The argument being summarised here is developed in S Todd, 'Common Law Protection for Injury to a Person's Reproductive Autonomy' (2019) 135 *LQR* 635. A Mulligan, 'A Vindicatory Approach to Tortious Liability for Mistakes in Assisted Human Reproduction' (2020) 40 *Legal Studies* 55 favours a new cause of action, actionable per se, to which she gives the working title of 'interference with reproductive endeavours'. The gist of the action would not be damage, but the importance of the underlying right. However, it is arguable that an action in negligence is the better solution, and, importantly, existing authority supports it and no new tort is needed. For another view, see C Auckland and I Goold, 'Offsetting Damages in Wrongful Conception and Birth Cases: A Way Through the Post-*McFarlane* Mire' (2022) 138 *LQR* 407.

as compensatory, albeit with a vindicatory purpose, a fixed sum also abandons ordinary principle in quantifying damages, by ignoring the circumstances of the particular plaintiff and the particular types of harm that he or she has suffered. A better approach would be for a court to make an award of general damages for non-pecuniary loss, which takes into account the full extent of the loss of autonomy in issue. The award should not include the expense to the parent of having an unplanned child, or one that is different to that which was planned and wanted, since this would fall foul of the policy upheld in *McFarlane*. But causing an unwilling parent to need to cope with an unplanned child constitutes a clear invasion of the parent's reproductive autonomy, and if the child is disabled, the effect of the invasion upon the parent is undoubtedly magnified. Even if the defendant did not cause the disability, as in cases such as *Parkinson*, defining the damage in this way means that the defendant has to take the plaintiff as found, bringing up an unplanned child with a disability. In such a case, the exceptional demands on the parent's time and resources in looking after the child, as opposed to the costs of upbringing, could be taken into account. Other personal circumstances also could be relevant, such as special difficulties facing a single mother with little family support. Further relevant factors might include impairment of the parent's career satisfaction, or other significant personal aspirations, and any associated mental distress.

What other forms of interference with reproductive autonomy might be similarly actionable? One instance could be the loss of genetic affinity experienced by the parents in *ACB*, notwithstanding the rejection of this solution in the case itself, for it seems both unnecessary and inconvenient to delimit a new head of actionable damage in such a narrow way.[49] Certainly there would be no such loss in the case of other mishaps involving IVF providers where it was always planned to use donor sperm or a donor embryo. An instance could be where a child is born with a disability inherited from an improperly vetted sperm donor.[50] Another possibility, posing obvious scope for controversy, is where the child is of a different race than that which the parents wanted and had specified for a sperm donor.[51] Or a child may be of the 'wrong' sex, as where a female couple who were assured that they would have a girl sued their fertility clinic after the mother gave birth to a boy.[52] Again, the child may have other features or characteristics unwanted by the parents, or even lack a wanted disabling feature already possessed by the prospective parents.[53] It is manifest that errors in IVF treatment can produce many new and difficult questions.

[49] Quantifying the damage as 30 per cent of the costs of bringing up an unplanned child also may be criticised as random and as inconsistent with the refusal of the court to accept the costs of bringing up the child as actionable damage.

[50] See Laura Riggell, 'Mother Takes Legal Action Against Sperm Bank for her Child's Dwarfism' (*Bionews* 1022, 4 November 2019) www.progress.org.uk/mother-takes-legal-action-against-sperm-bank-for-her-childs-dwarfism/.

[51] See *A (A Minor) v A Health and Social Services Trust* [2010] NIQB 108, on appeal *A v A Health and Social Services Trust* [2011] NICA 28, where the claim was made by *twin children* who were born following such a mistake; see below n 86. In *ACB* (n 15) at [133] Phang Boon Leong JA recognised that race as a social concept could lie at the root of real and significant harms, including unkind questions as to a wife's fidelity and the paternity of children. See generally D Valentine, 'The Wrongs of "Wrongful Birth": Disability, Race, and Reproductive Justice', in JM Reynolds and C Wieseler (eds), *The Disability Bioethics Reader* (Routledge, online, 2022).

[52] See Helen Robertson, 'Couple Who Wanted a Girl Sue IVF Clinic for Transferring Male Embryo' (*Bionews* 1139, 4 April 2022) www.progress.org.uk/couple-who-wanted-a-girl-sue-ivf-clinic-for-transferring-male-embryo/.

[53] M Spriggs, 'Lesbian Couple Create a Child who is Deaf Like Them' (2002) 28 *Journal of Medical Ethics* 283.

We can also contemplate other forms of interference with reproductive autonomy not involving conduct or advice concerning sterilisation or IVF procedures. One could be where a maternity hospital misidentifies two new-born babies, so that the parents take home the wrong child.[54] Or, moving out of a medical context, one sexual partner might sue the other for misrepresenting that he or she was sterile or was using contraception.[55] There might equally be an actionable head of damage where a person has been deprived of the opportunity of becoming a parent. Examples could be a claim by a cancer survivor who had frozen his sperm prior to chemotherapy treatment against a hospital for allowing the sample to thaw,[56] or for losing it.[57]

While the invasion of a person's reproductive autonomy could provide the foundation for a potential action in these and other cases, the limits to the action would need to be determined. Sometimes, claims such as these would be rejected. For example, there are good reasons of policy against awarding damages for losing an opportunity to choose the sex of a child, the objections being bound up with the fear of disturbing the gender balance in society. Again, negligence by a fertility clinic concerning parents' mere cosmetic choices for a child would be unlikely to qualify as actionable damage. There also may be limits on what precisely a fertility clinic is permitted to screen for, in carrying out fertility treatment, pursuant to any applicable statutory regime.[58] Speaking broadly, questions such as these are capable of resolution, by taking due account of relevant considerations of policy in determining the ambit of the action.[59]

IV. Disabled Life

A. Claim by the Child: *Harriton v Stephens* and *Waller v James*

We have examined the question of civil liability where a person is suing in respect of loss attributable in some way to *another person's* existence. We turn now to where a plaintiff

[54] See 'Switched Before Birth: Couple Files Lawsuit Over Devastating IVF Mishap; 'It Was Truly My Hell' *CBS News Chicago* (9 November 2021) www.chicago.cbslocal.com/2021/11/09/ivf-mixup-daphna-cardinale-lawsuit-babies-switched-before-birth/.

[55] See, eg, *PP v DD* [2017] ONCA 180, an action by a father against a mother who had conceived a child after untruthfully saying she was taking contraceptive precautions, which failed on the application of the *McFarlane* principle. This issue is discussed in detail in Anna Broadmore's contribution to this collection (see ch 4).

[56] *Yearworth v North Bristol NHS Trust* [2009] EWCA Civ 37, [2010] QB 1.

[57] See B Soury, 'NZ Fertility Clinic Loses Cancer Survivor's Sperm' (*Bionews* 1191, 30 May 2023) www.progress.org.uk/new-zealand-fertility-clinic-loses-cancer-survivors-sperm/.

[58] See, eg, the Human Fertilisation and Embryology Act 1990 (UK) sch 2, which does not permit screening in order, inter alia, to establish the sex of an embryo, save where there is a particular risk that any resulting child will have, or develop, a gender-related serious physical or mental disability or illness.

[59] A liquidated damages clause in a contract which makes provision for a payment by the party in breach in the event of the birth of a child or, it may be, the birth of a child with unwanted characteristics, may operate as normal. Liquidated damages clauses may only be struck down if they constitute a penalty, as to which see *Cavendish Square Holding BV v Makdessi* [2015] UKSC 67, [2016] AC 1172; *Paciocco v Australia and New Zealand Banking Group Ltd* [2016] HCA 28, (2016)258 CLR 525; *127 Hobson Street Ltd v Honey Bees Preschool Ltd* [2020] NZSC 53, [2020] 1 NZLR 179, or are otherwise unlawful, as to which see *Patel v Mirza* [2016] UKSC 42, [2017] AC 467; *Henderson v Dorset Healthcare University NHS Foundation Trust* [2020] UKSC 43, [2021] AC 573.

is suing in respect of some feature of his or her *own* existence and where, but for the defendant's conduct, the plaintiff would never have been born. Such claims are often described as involving 'wrongful life' and pose their own, unique problems.

A common example is a claim by a child who is born with a disability of some kind, alleging negligence by the medical advisers of his or her mother (or father) in failing to diagnose the disability, or warn about its risk. In *Harriton v Stephens*,[60] the plaintiff's mother contracted rubella whilst pregnant, and as a consequence of the infection the plaintiff was born suffering from severe congenital disabilities. She sued her mother's doctor, who had failed to diagnose the rubella, alleging that she had suffered damage in living her profoundly disabled life. The claim failed in the High Court of Australia, where Crennan J delivered the leading judgment.[61] Her Honour was satisfied that the damage claimed was not amenable to determination by the application of ordinary legal method, for, had the respondent not been negligent, the appellant would not be living at all. Damages were ordinarily measured using the compensatory principle, but a comparison between a life with disabilities and non-existence was impossible. Relevant concerns of policy also indicated that the claim should be rejected. First, there would be a conflict between the interests of the mother and those of the child and, indeed, the prospect of an action by a child against his or her own mother. Secondly, it was repugnant to devalue the life of a disabled person by suggesting that such a person would have been better off not to have been born into a life with disabilities. Thirdly, there was a lack of certainty about the degree of disability that could potentially give rise to a claim. Fourthly, to allow a disabled person to claim his or her own existence as actionable damage would be inconsistent with statutes prohibiting differential treatment of the disabled, and with the law's sanction of those who take a life. Accordingly, the claim could not be reconciled with values expressed generally in the common law and statute. Life with disabilities, like life without them, was simply not actionable.[62]

Kirby J was the single dissentient. He considered it to be arguable that a life of severe and unremitting suffering was worse than non-existence and that, in principle, damages for such suffering should be recoverable in an action brought by, or for, the child. Awarding damages would enable the child to lead a more dignified existence; the action would be unlikely to provoke familial discord; admitting a claim against a healthcare professional would not necessarily mean admitting a claim against a mother; the availability of a remedy for the parents was irrelevant; and likely advances in genetic science, making it impossible to know the consequences of accommodating the claim, were not a reason for putting the common law into deep freeze.[63]

Waller v James[64] is a second decision of the High Court delivered on the same day as *Harriton*. The plaintiff was born with anti-thrombin 3 deficiency, a serious genetic

[60] *Harriton v Stephens* [2006] HCA 15, (2006) 226 CLR 52; A Grey, '*Harriton v Stephens*: Life, Logic and Legal Fictions' (2006) 28 *Sydney Law Review* 545; K Warner, 'Wrongful Life Goes Down Under' (2007) 123 *LQR* 209; H Teff, 'Condoning Wrongful Suffering' (2007) 15 *Tort Law Review* 7.

[61] Gleeson CJ, Gummow and Heydon JJ agreeing, Hayne and Callinan JJ concurring, Kirby J dissenting.

[62] *Harriton* (n 60) [242]–[277]. For a similar decision in England, see *McKay v Essex Area Health Authority* [1982] QB 1166 (CA); and see *Whitehead* (n 3). In Singapore see *JU v See Tho Kai Yin* [2005] SGHC 140, [2005] 4 SLR(R) 96, also rejecting the claim on the ground of public policy.

[63] *Harriton* (n 60) [95]–[155].

[64] *Waller v James* [2006] HCA 16, (2006) 226 CLR 136.

deficiency inherited from his father, following IVF procedures conducted by the defendant gynaecologist. He suffered a stroke shortly after his birth. The plaintiff alleged that the defendant had negligently failed to warn his parents about the deficiency, but, as in *Harriton*, the claim failed. Had the defendant given a warning, the plaintiff would never have been born, and any child born without the deficiency would have been a different person.

The reasoning in *Harriton* and *Waller* reflects the debate in many decisions overseas, particularly those in the United States. The two most common reasons why 'wrongful life' claims have failed are because courts have held that life itself cannot be a legal injury, and because courts are unable to measure compensation that involves comparing the harm of living in a disabled state with never living at all. The minority of cases that allow such claims are based on the defendant's responsibility for having created an impaired life. They are premised not on the concept that non-life is preferable to an impaired life, but on the policy that law should respond to the call of the living for help in bearing the burden of their affliction.[65]

While wrongful life claims have almost invariably been rejected in the courts, many commentators have criticised these decisions, advocating the imposition of a legal duty of care to prevent 'life with disabilities' or 'suffering as a life in being', and seeing no insuperable arguments of principle standing in the way of treating these as compensable heads of loss.[66] So let us examine the arguments against recovery and consider whether there are any circumstances in which they might be overcome.

The objections to recognising an action at common law are arguably unavoidable where the defendant's negligence causes a child *who is already doomed to disability* to be born. There is no satisfactory solution to the underlying conceptual problem of comparing life and non-existence. How can we say anything about 'the utter void of non-existence'?[67] Similarly, how can we say anything about whether non-existence is 'better' than an existence with disabilities? The problem here is fundamental, affecting the very foundations of our concept of damage.[68] As two commentators have maintained, in the absence of any justifiable methodology for making a comparison with non-existence, the safest path is a policy which chooses life.[69]

The absence of any way of determining that the child has suffered damage underlies the core objection to imposing a duty to avoid the child being born, or as Crennan J expresses it, to recognising 'a right of a foetus to be aborted, or an interest of a foetus in its own termination'.[70] How do we conduct such an inquiry? Whether the fetus should be aborted must be determined by the mother (or the parents) who, even if fully informed,

[65] See, eg, *Procanik v Cillo* 97 NJ 339, 478 A 2d 755 (1984). In Israel, see *Zeitzoff v Katz* [1986] 40(2) PD 85 (SC).

[66] E Ellis and B McGivern, 'The Wrongfulness or Rightfulness of Actions for Wrongful Life' (2007) 15 *Tort Law Review* 135; M Fordham, 'A Life Less Ordinary – The Rejection of Actions for Wrongful Life' (2007) 15 *Torts Law Journal* 123; R Scott, 'Reconsidering "Wrongful Life" in England after Thirty Years: Legislative Mistakes and Unjustifiable Anomalies' (2013) 72 *CLJ* 115.

[67] *Gleitman v Cosgrove* 49 NJ 22, 227 A 2d 689 (1967).

[68] C Stolker, 'Wrongful Life: The Limits of Liability and Beyond' (1994) 43 *ICLQ* 521.

[69] P Dimopoulos and M Bagaric, 'The Moral Status of Wrongful Life Claims' (2003) 32 *Common Law World Review* 35.

[70] *Harriton* (n 60) [245].

are likely to make the decision based on her (or their) own interests. It is difficult to see how the decision can be made on the basis of *the child's* interests. And how can it be determined whether a disability is sufficiently serious that non-existence is preferable? The quality of and level of satisfaction with life of even seriously disabled people is infinitely variable and may be unknowable. And where should the line be drawn? A whole spectrum of claims would have to be admitted as potentially actionable. Indeed, admitting the wrongful life action has been broadly condemned on the basis that it requires courts to draw lines among different types of impairments, reinforcing the medical model of disability and creating deep divisions among individuals with disabilities. It has been strongly maintained that the negative historical consequences of such 'benevolence', however well intended, are legion.[71] And the action certainly can be seen as demeaning to disabled people. Critics of the *Perruche* decision in France, where the Cour de Cassation admitted the claim,[72] took it to suggest that their lives amounted to damage and were not worth living.[73] The legislature subsequently intervened and denied legal redress to anyone claiming to be harmed solely by being born.[74]

In summary, the courts cannot give compensation for being in this world with whatever disadvantages that may entail. The negligence of the defendant has conferred on the plaintiff the benefit of being alive, and this cannot be the subject of legal action.

B. Conduct Causing Both Injury and Birth

Let us consider now the position in law where a defendant causes *both injury and birth*. This can happen in a medical context where, for example, a fertility drug leads to a multiple pregnancy and the premature birth of children with disabilities associated with their prematurity,[75] or, in a private context, where a man with a sexually transmissible disease has sexual intercourse resulting in the birth of a child with a disability caused by that disease. Indeed, the Law Commission of England and Wales in its *Report on Injuries to Unborn Children*[76] asked whether a child born with a disability ought to have an action against a man suffering from syphilis who had intercourse with a woman without telling her that he was infected, and considered that there should be compensation, not for the fact of being born, but for causing the disability.

A number of decisions in Canada have wrestled with cases of this kind. In *Cherry v Borsman*[77] the defendant surgeon attempted to carry out an abortion, but negligently

[71] W Hensell, 'The Disabling Impact of Wrongful Birth and Wrongful Life Actions' (2005) 40 *Harvard Civil Rights-Civil Liberties Law Review* 141.

[72] *Perruche*, Cass ass plén, 17 Novembre 2000, n°99.701, n°457P; P Lewis, 'The Necessary Implications of Wrongful Life Claims: Lessons from France' (2002) 12 *European Journal of Health Law* 135 explains the decision and its consequences.

[73] Association des Paralysées de France, 'Questions éthiques posées par l'affaire Nicolas Perruche' *Laennec*, 2001-06, v49, n°2, 3; 'Les parents des handicapés dénoncent l'arrêt Perruche' *Libération*, 2 Décembre 2000; A Pereira, C Prieur, 'Cent familles dénoncent l'arrêt Perruche et poursuivent l'Etat; Elles condamnent les dérives eugénistes' *Le Monde*, 4 Décembre 2000.

[74] Loi no 2002-303 du 4 mars 2002 relative aux droits des malades et à la qualité du système de santé, Art I.

[75] *Florence v Benzaquen* [2020] ONSC 1534.

[76] (Law Com No 60, 1974) para 88.

[77] *Cherry v Borsman* (1992) 99 DLR (4th) 487 (BCCA).

failed to do so and succeeded only in injuring the fetus. The subsequently born child sued in respect of injuries sustained in the procedure, and the defendant argued that he owed no duty to protect the fetus because that was inconsistent with his duty to the mother to terminate her pregnancy. But the court held, in convoluted reasoning, that the surgeon owed a duty of care to the mother to perform his task properly, and was liable for any damage caused to the fetus by his failing to meet his duty to the mother. The result was that the court allowed a claim for injuries which resulted from the very procedure which, but for the negligence, would have ended the pregnancy and would have prevented the infant plaintiff from being born.

However, later claims have failed on the basis of the conflicting duties that would be owed to the mother and to the child. For example, in *Paxton v Ramji*[78] a mother's medication for acne caused severe disabilities in her subsequently conceived child. Feldman JA noted that, on the one hand, the duty on the doctor was to ensure the child was not conceived, making her claim one for wrongful life. On the other hand, the doctor's duty was to refuse to prescribe the medication to a woman of child-bearing potential, and, if this duty was discharged, the child would have been born healthy. Her Honour preferred not to decide the case by categorising the claim as one or the other, holding instead that the doctor owed no duty of care to the child because of the conflicting duties which were owed to the patient.

If we accept the 'conflicting duties' argument, perhaps a claim can nonetheless succeed where a defendant causes both disability and birth and there is no such potential conflict. Indeed, the Law Commission considered that its example of a father causing syphilis in his child was not properly called a 'wrongful life' action.[79] Yet, obviously, without the sexual intercourse, the child would not have been born. The question is whether we can find a convincing explanation in favour of allowing the claim.

A possible argument might go something like this. Where there is no conflict with the interests of the mother, there remains a wrong committed vis-à-vis the child. A child cannot normally succeed in an action where proof of damage depends on establishing that his or her existence with disabilities is 'worse' than not existing at all: there is no basis for making any comparison between them. But a defendant who can be shown to have caused a disability equally cannot *defend* an action on that basis either: he or she cannot establish that the child is *not* damaged by the disability. As it is the child bringing the action, the burden is on him or her to adduce proof of damage, but this may be done in the ordinary way. Let us take the Law Commission's example of a man who has caused a new-born child to suffer from syphilis. Clearly, if he deliberately or negligently infected the mother, he has caused her damage, and the same applies if he has infected the child. Likewise, if medication causes conception and injures the child in circumstances where there is no competing interest of the mother, the injury may be actionable.

How might the preceding argument apply to the facts in *Khan*? The defendant's negligent advice was a cause of the plaintiff conceiving and giving birth, *and was also*

[78] *Paxton v Ramji* (2009) 299 DLR (4th) 614 (Ont CA). For earlier decisions, see *Lacroix v Dominique* (2001) 202 DLR (4th) 121 (Man CA); *Bovingdon v Hergott* (2008) 290 DLR (4th) 126 (Ont CA).

[79] See text to n 76.

a cause of her son being born with haemophilia. The scope of the defendant's duty was specifically directed to the risk of haemophilia, as opposed to any risk of other potentially disabling conditions, and can be seen as being owed to the child. So, on this view, a claim by the child himself could succeed.

The argument recognises where the loss truly lies and gives the child a remedy specifically related to his or her disability and its associated costs, rather than the consequences of living. It also is consistent with the view expressed by Lord Scott in *Rees*, who contemplated a remedy, albeit for the parent, in a case in which the very purpose of a sterilisation operation had been to protect against the fear of some inherited disability.[80] Giving a remedy in these circumstances also avoids the further, associated, objections to a wrongful life action. The measure of the damages relates solely to the disability and not the child's life itself. The courts are not required to make an impossible comparison between life with disabilities and non-existence. Nor is it demeaning to the child to make such an award. The claim is not in respect of his or her life, and is treated in the same way as any other personal injury claim.[81]

The preceding argument operates to draw the line at pre-conception negligence. It could therefore apply in the circumstances in *Waller*, but not those in *Harriton*, where the defendant's post-conception negligence did not cause the disabling condition, but only caused the birth. This is an appropriate boundary point, as can be seen from statutory reforms overseas. The statutory overruling of *Perruche* in France has denied redress to anyone harmed *solely* by being born, leaving room for claims where the birth is not the sole cause of the disability. In the UK, the Congenital Disabilities (Civil Liability) Act 1976 has been interpreted so as to achieve a similar result. The Act relevantly provides that where a child is born disabled as the result of an 'occurrence' before its birth that affected either parent of the child in his or her ability to have a normal, healthy child, and a person (other than the child's own mother) is, under the relevant section, answerable to the child in respect of the occurrence, the child's disabilities are to be regarded as damage resulting from the wrongful act of that person, and actionable at the suit of the child.[82] In *Toombes v Mitchell*,[83] the claimant was born with a congenital developmental defect which she alleged to have resulted from her mother taking insufficient folic acid during pregnancy. She brought a claim against the defendant, her mother's doctor, alleging that he had failed to advise her of the potential benefits of taking folic acid before conception. Lambert J held that the circumstances surrounding an act of sexual intercourse were capable of being an 'occurrence' for the purposes of the statute, and that the claimant's mother's alleged reliance upon the defendant's negligent advice was such an occurrence. The elements of the statutory cause of action were made out, and the claimant had a lawful claim for damages.[84]

[80] *Rees* (n 20) [147].

[81] In *TBS v Metropolitan Police Commissioner* [2017] EWHC 30 (QB) the court refused to strike out a claim for mental injury suffered by the claimant on discovering that the defendant, his father, was an undercover police officer who had formed a liaison with his mother by pretending to share her politically activist views. So here the defendant's pre-conception conduct caused the birth and also the injury later suffered by the child.

[82] Congenital Disabilities (Civil Liability) Act 1976 (UK) ss 1(1), 1(2)(a).

[83] *Toombes v Mitchell* [2020] EWHC 3506 (QB), [2021] QB 622.

[84] The claim succeeded at the subsequent trial: *Toombes v Mitchell* [2021] EWHC 3234 (QB).

Lambert J recognised that her decision was consistent with the Law Commission's general view that liability for pre-natal injuries should, where possible, be equated with ordinary claims for damages for personal injuries, and that the principles governing liability should be the same as for personal injuries inflicted after birth. It was also consistent with the view that there should be recovery where negligence actually caused the intercourse resulting in the conception of a disabled child. The fact that the claimant never had a chance of being born other than disabled was no bar. The Act drew a distinction between pre-conception and post-conception occurrences, and for good reason. A negligent failure to prevent the birth of an already conceived child engaged a range of social and moral policy issues, not least the imposition upon the medical profession of a duty to advise abortion in possibly dubious circumstances. But claims based upon a wrongful act before conception, which led to the intercourse and conception, raised no such difficulties.

V. Conclusions

In *Rees*, Lord Bingham began his judgment by considering *McFarlane*, saying that an orthodox application of familiar and conventional principles of the law of tort would have pointed towards giving full damages against the tortfeasor for the costs of rearing the unplanned child.[85] Many critics of the decision consider that their Lordships should have decided precisely that. In fact, however, and to the contrary, the policy position underlying *McFarlane* – a refusal to treat the costs of an unplanned child as actionable damage – is compelling. That policy should cover all unplanned children, including those who are disabled, and the decision of the United Kingdom Supreme Court in *Khan* is open to criticism by reason of its failure to address the implications of *McFarlane* to the facts in issue.

In *Rees* itself, their Lordships introduced the novel idea of making an award of damages specifically for the loss of autonomy suffered by a parent bearing the responsibility of bringing up an unplanned child. This solution does not treat the existence of a child as damage in itself, but puts the focus on the impact of having the child on the parent's life. It has obvious implications where the child is born with a disability. The decision in *Parkinson*, giving damages for 'disability expenses' is hard to reconcile with *McFarlane*, and inconsistent with ordinary principle in making a defendant liable for harm that he or she did not cause. But by building upon the decision in *Rees*, while abandoning a fixed sum by way of damages, a court could specifically deny recovery of upbringing expenses while making an award for loss of reproductive autonomy that recognised the life-changing impact on a particular parent of having a disabled child. In this respect a court could take the plaintiff as found, as the victim of a failed sterilisation who has given birth to a child who unfortunately is disabled.

A rule of this kind could be developed and refined. It certainly could extend beyond cases involving failed sterilisations, or negligent or deceptive conduct leading to the conception of a child.

[85] *Rees* (n 20) [3]–[4].

On the above analysis, there can be no recovery for expenses incurred specifically as a cost of the child. However, it is open to the courts to recognise a remedy for the child himself or herself in some circumstances. Where the defendant has caused the child both to be born and to have a disability, it is possible to point to the disability alone as damage. Ordinary personal injury claims involving disability can be used by way of support, and the defendant should not be able to contend that the child would not otherwise exist in order to establish that no damage has been suffered. Special policy implications involved in possible claims by disabled children against a parent for conceiving them, or allowing them to be born, could be excepted from any general rule. This analysis leads to a satisfactory result: the parent and the child both get damages for their own losses – the parent for his or her loss of autonomy, and the child for his or her disability. A court would need to take care to avoid any duplication in the awards, but this should be achievable without too much difficulty.

The child's remedy would not cover undesired characteristics of the child not amounting to a disability, which might perhaps be the subject of complaint by the parent, but which could not be treated as damage by the child.[86] Nor could the rule extend to complaint about social or financial disadvantages to the child stemming from the circumstances of his or her conception.[87]

We have seen that it is possible to make provision by statute for claims by children who only exist by reason of some form of medical negligence, or other wrongdoing. But looking to legislatures to act may involve a long wait. In the absence of statutory reform, a satisfactory solution to the profound difficulties raised by 'birth torts' litigation is within the reach of the common law courts.

[86] See *A (A Minor) v A Health and Social Services Trust* (n 51), where Girvan LJ said that it would be perverse and objectionable to suggest that children born with a different skin colour to their parents were in some way damaged, disabled or injured; S Sheldon, 'Only Skin Deep? The Harm of Being Born a Different Colour to One's Parents' (2011) 19 *Medical Law Review* 657.

[87] See, eg, *Zepeda v Zepeda* 41 Ill App 2d 240, 190 NE 2d 849 (Ct App 1963) (disadvantages of illegitimacy).

6

The Rights of the Dead

ANDREW FELL*

I. Introduction

I suspect that many people would regard the claim that the dead have rights as patently false. When I asked my grandmother for her views, she responded that 'when you're dead, you're dead', and suggested that I write about something else. This intuition certainly has legal support. According to one judge, 'the dead have no rights and can suffer no wrongs. The living alone can be the subject of legal protection'.[1] The infamous common law rule, *actio personalis moritur cum persona*, provides that a personal action dies with the person, whether that person is the plaintiff or defendant.[2] Although, on its face, the rule only applies to actions that arise during a person's life and subsist at their death, it has been understood as preventing actions from arising after their death as well.[3] The rule was abolished by legislation nearly a century ago in its application to (most) actions that subsist at the person's death,[4] leaving whatever effect it might have on post-death actions untouched. The conventional view seems to be that the dead have no continuing rights, and that any apparent wrong to a deceased person is really to their living relatives (for the emotional distress they suffer), if there is any wrong at all.[5]

In this chapter, I argue that the dead do in fact have rights, and more specifically, legal rights recognised in (Anglo-Australian) private law. Of course, this depends entirely on what we mean by 'rights', which I will clarify in section II. The term is often (but not always) used to refer to interests that justify imposing duties on others, or to indicate that a duty protects the interests of a particular person. This, however, gives rise to the fundamental question of whether it is even possible for the dead to have 'interests',

* I am thankful to Kit Barker, Kate Falconer, Mark Lunney, Bill MacNeil and Graeme Orr for their helpful comments.

[1] *R v Ensor* (1887) 3 TLR 366, 367 (Stephen J).

[2] For the history of the rule, see PH Winfield, 'Death as Affecting Liability in Tort' (1929) 29 *Columbia Law Review* 239.

[3] See, eg, *Krahe v TCN Channel Nine Pty Ltd* (1986) 4 NSWLR 536, 541.

[4] Law Reform (Miscellaneous Provisions) Act 1934 (UK) s 1. Actions for defamation are the main exception, which are still subject to the common law rule and are therefore extinguished. As Lunney details in ch 9 of this volume, similar legislation was adopted in all Australian jurisdictions.

[5] See, eg, H Conway, *The Law and the Dead* (London, Routledge, 2016) 79–86.

on which there is a substantial philosophical literature. I will argue in section III that the dead can indeed have interests, and in section IV, I identify the extent to which such interests are (or should be) recognised in private law. I argue that private law recognises the interests of the dead in a variety of contexts. Although there are some notable exceptions, in particular the law of defamation, this is somewhat anomalous and at least open to question. On the whole, private law is surprisingly accommodating of the interests of the dead.

II. Rights and Interests

The word 'right' is used in a variety of ways. In one sense, it identifies the person to whom a duty is owed: a person has a 'right' when a duty is owed *to them*.[6] Hohfeld referred to such rights as 'claims'.[7] This definition does not itself determine who particular duties are owed to, and is compatible with a range of views on that issue. On the will theory, a duty is owed to a person when they have a power to waive or enforce the duty.[8] On the interest theory, a duty is owed to a person when it protects their interests, regardless of whether they have any waiver or enforcement powers.[9]

In a second sense, a 'right' can also refer to one kind of *justification* for a duty. In Raz's view, for example, a person has a right when some interest of theirs is a sufficient reason for holding some other person to be under a duty.[10] Webb gives as examples of rights in this second category a person's 'rights to life, to freedom of expression, to bodily security and to privacy', which operate as reasons for imposing particular duties rather than as statements of a conclusion that duties are owed to the person.[11] A third sense appears in the phrase 'right of action', which refers to a power to enforce the duty in court. These last two senses clearly resemble the will and interest theories, but they are nevertheless distinct, since they do not depend on any view about who the relevant duties are owed to.

Can the dead have rights of these kinds? On a strict interpretation of the will theory, according to which the right holder must *personally* exercise the power of enforcement or waiver, it would make little sense for the dead to have rights in the first sense, since a deceased person clearly cannot exercise those powers personally. However, many commentators reject the will theory due to its supposedly implausible implications, which include denying that duties can be owed to children, animals, and others with limited capacity.[12] Some commentators instead adopt a modified version of the will theory, according to which it is sufficient that the relevant powers are exercisable by the

[6] WN Hohfeld, 'Some Fundamental Legal Conceptions as Applied in Judicial Reasoning (1913) 23 *Yale Law Journal* 16, 32.
[7] ibid.
[8] See HLA Hart, 'Are there Any Natural Rights?' (1955) 64 *Philosophical Review* 175, 180.
[9] VAJ Kurki, 'Rights, Harming and Wronging: A Restatement of the Interest Theory' (2018) 38 *OJLS* 430.
[10] J Raz, *The Morality of Freedom* (Oxford, Clarendon Press, 1986) 166.
[11] C Webb, 'Three Concepts of Rights, Two of Property' (2018) 38 *OJLS* 246, 252–55.
[12] See M Kramer, 'Do Animals and Dead People Have Legal Rights?' (2001) 14 *Canadian Journal of Law and Jurisprudence* 29, 30–31. The theory does not necessarily deny that duties should nevertheless be imposed for the protection of such entities.

person *or on their behalf.*[13] This would be compatible with the possibility of the dead having rights, if the relevant powers were exercisable by their personal representative. The concept of a 'right of action' could conceivably be understood in a similar way.[14]

The interest theory also allows for post-death rights.[15] On that theory, the identity of the person who has the power to enforce a particular duty gives no necessary insight into who the duty is owed to; the only question is whose interests it protects. If the duty protects the interests of a deceased person, then the duty is owed to that person, who could therefore be described as having a corresponding right.[16] If those interests were the justification for the duty, the deceased person could also be described as having a right in the second (justificatory) sense.

There are therefore a number of senses in which it is possible, at least conceptually, for the dead to have rights. In this chapter, I will mainly focus on whether the dead have rights in the second sense, or in other words, whether they have interests that private law should protect by imposing duties on others. Whether we should treat these duties as owed *to* the deceased person is only really a matter of how we should describe the law rather than its appropriate content. In any event, on both the interest theory and some versions of the will theory, describing the duties as being owed to deceased persons would be perfectly acceptable, and present no conceptual difficulty.

III. Are Posthumous Rights Possible?

The discussion in the previous section indicates that whether the dead can have 'rights' hinges (to a large extent) on whether they can have interests for those rights to protect. This question has been debated for millennia.[17] As these debates show, the conclusion that the dead have interests depends on a wide range of contestable moral premises. These premises should nevertheless all be accepted, in my view.

At the most general level, a person's 'interests' refer to what is 'good' for them. If something is good for the person, it is in their interests. If it is bad for them, it sets their interests back, or harms them. There are two main reasons why the dead might not have interests, which are often referred to as the 'existence requirement' and the 'experience requirement'.[18] The existence requirement provides that, for a person to have interests (and for those interests to be affected) at a particular time, the person must exist at that time. This would rule out the possibility of the dead having interests, at

[13] See HLA Hart, *Essays on Bentham: Jurisprudence and Political Philosophy* (Oxford, Clarendon Press, 1982) 184 fn 86.

[14] Although there may be some value in retaining a concept for identifying the person who can actually exercise the power.

[15] J Bowen, 'The Interest Theory of Rights at the Margins: Posthumous Rights' in M McBride and VAJ Kurki (eds), *Without Trimmings: The Legal, Moral and Political Philosophy of Matthew Kramer* (Oxford, Oxford University Press, 2022).

[16] However, even on the interest theory, it has been suggested that there is a separate requirement that the putative right holder is the kind of entity that is *capable* of holding rights: see Kramer (n 12). I will leave this requirement to one side, since deceased persons would likely satisfy it (as Kramer also concludes), if the arguments in this chapter are accepted.

[17] For a survey of the classical literature, see RA Belliotti, *Posthumous Harm: Why the Dead Are Still Vulnerable* (Plymouth, Lexington Books, 2012) ch 1.

[18] ibid 10–16, 22–23.

least when combined with the 'annihilation thesis', which provides that a person ceases to 'exist' when they die. The experience requirement provides that, for a person to have an interest in something (and for that interest to be affected), it must affect the person's subjective experiences in some way. This would also rule out the dead having interests, since they cannot (I will assume) have subjective experiences.

In my view, both of these requirements should be rejected. I will consider the experience requirement first, since it is more vulnerable, and many philosophers have rejected it.[19] The requirement really boils down to a particular conception of what interests people have, including living people. There are three dominant theories about what interests people have, which are referred to as *hedonistic*, *desire-fulfilment* and *objective list* theories respectively.[20] According to hedonism, a person has an interest in having (or not having) certain subjective experiences (eg pleasure, pain). On desire-fulfilment theories, a person has an interest in their wants or desires being fulfilled. Conversely, their interests are set back when their desires are frustrated. On objective list theories, certain things (eg friendship, learning) are good or bad for a person regardless of the person's attitudes towards them. There can obviously be different views about what things are objectively good or bad.

Hedonism clearly entails the existence requirement (since only a living person can experience pleasure and pain), so it is not surprising that many philosophers have identified its inconsistency with the possibility of posthumous interests.[21] The conclusion that posthumous interests are possible therefore depends on rejecting hedonism as an exhaustive statement of what interests people have, which many philosophers do anyway. They instead hold the view that something can be in a person's interests even if it has no effect on their subjective experiences.[22] The most well-known argument for this view is Nozick's 'experience machine' thought experiment, which posits the existence of a machine that can make a person think that they are having certain experiences, such as writing a book or making a friend, despite the fact (of which the person is unaware) that they are actually 'floating in a tank, with electrodes attached to [their] brain'.[23] Most people would likely regard a life in which they are plugged into the machine as worse than a 'real' life that is otherwise the same as the one they would experience in the machine. The best explanation for this is that something can be good or bad for a person, whether or not it affects their subjective state of mind.[24]

Many other examples have been used to make the same point.[25] A common one is a person whose spouse cheats on them without their knowledge, which most people would regard as bad for the person. The same could be said of a person whose colleagues ridicule them behind their back. If this kind of 'unfelt harm' is possible, it is a short

[19] See E Lin, 'The Experience Requirement on Well-being' (2021) 178 *Philosophical Studies* 867.

[20] Following D Parfit, *Reasons and Persons* (Oxford, Clarendon Press, 1984) 493.

[21] B Bradley, *Well-Being and Death* (Oxford, Oxford University Press, 2009) ch 1; JS Taylor, *Death, Posthumous Harm, and Bioethics* (New York, Routledge, 2012) chs 3–4.

[22] See D Boonin, *Dead Wrong: The Ethics of Posthumous Harm* (Oxford, Oxford University Press, 2019) ch 2.

[23] R Nozick, *Anarchy, State and Utopia* (New York, Basic Books, 1974) 42–43.

[24] E Lin, 'How to Use the Experience Machine' (2016) 28 *Utilitas* 314.

[25] Boonin (n 22) 16–21.

step to the conclusion that the experience requirement is unsound, and that it therefore provides no argument against the possibility of posthumous interests.

The existence requirement is a more difficult obstacle. This requirement reflects the view that, even if something can affect a *living* person's interests without affecting their subjective experiences, this cannot be true of a dead person, since dead people do not exist, and nothing can be good or bad for non-existent entities. This is the generally referred to as the 'problem of the subject' – the problem of identifying the subject of posthumous harm. As mentioned earlier, once a person dies, there is clearly a sense in which they no longer 'exist'. Their physical body might still exist (at least temporarily), and they might still 'exist' in the memorics of those who survive them, or in the legacy of their effect on the world, but the person themselves does not.

There are several possible solutions to this problem, some more convincing than others.[26] The most prominent solution is to treat the effect on the person's interests as occurring during their lifetime, in which case the living person is really the subject of (what at first appears to be) posthumous harm. While this solution is perfectly consistent with the existence requirement, it appears to involve a problematic kind of 'backwards causation', in that events after a person's death are treated as capable of harming the person during their lifetime, that is, before the events even occur. The most well-known attempt to dispel the appearance of backwards causation is Pitcher's,[27] whose solution was later adopted by Feinberg,[28] which has (perhaps unfairly) led to it being described as the 'Feinberg–Pitcher solution'.

In short, Pitcher argues that a person is harmed during their lifetime by the fact that a harmful event *is going to happen* after their death. He gives the example of a parent whose child is going to die at a young age, and suggests that the parent is harmed by this fact, even before the child dies, and before the parent knows this is going to happen. While this conclusion might seem counterintuitive, he defends it using the different example (current at the time) of a catastrophic event that destroys the world in the presidential term after Reagan's. Even before the event occurs (and before anyone knows it will occur), it is already true to say that Reagan is the penultimate president of the US. There is no backwards causation; what is true all along is simply made apparent by later events. In the same way, when a person is harmed by a later event, the event merely makes it apparent that the person was in a harmed state all along, the harm consisting in the fact that the event was going to happen.

Pitcher's argument that a person is harmed during their lifetime by post-mortem events has come in for (justified) challenge. As Taylor points out, the property of being 'penultimate' is a different kind of property than being harmed (or benefited), so it does not necessarily follow from Pitcher's example that a person can be harmed before the events that cause the harm.[29] The fact that a person *will be* harmed in the future is arguably not itself a distinct kind of harm, contrary to Pitcher's claim.[30]

[26] Various solutions are outlined in D Sperling, *Posthumous Interests: Legal and Ethical Perspectives* (Cambridge, Cambridge University Press, 2008) 25–34; Belliotti (n 17) ch 4; Taylor (n 21) ch 2; Boonin (n 22) 117–21.

[27] G Pitcher, 'The Misfortunes of the Dead' (1984) 21 *American Philosophical Quarterly* 183.

[28] J Feinberg, *The Moral Limits of the Criminal Law*, vol 1 (New York, Oxford University Press, 1984) 89–91.

[29] Taylor (n 21) 14.

[30] Belliotti (n 17) 60. Cf Boonin (n 22) 151–54.

Some philosophers have nevertheless endorsed a solution like Pitcher's for certain kinds of interests, such as the achievement of goals and desires. Suppose that a person spends their life attempting to develop a cure for some illness and that, although they make some progress, they are not successful during their lifetime. If, however, their work is taken up by others after their death and eventually plays a significant role in developing the cure, these later events are arguably relevant in evaluating the person's actions during their lifetime. It was good for the person to perform work during their life that played a role in achieving the goal.[31] In a similar way, others have suggested that it is good for a person to hold desires during their lifetime that end up being satisfied, even if this occurs after their death.[32] While this kind of argument might work for goals and desires, it does not work for interests that do not depend on future events in the same way.

In my view, a better solution, which allows for the recognition of a wider range of interests, is simply to abandon the existence requirement. This solution has some support in the literature. Boonin briefly mentions it but does not defend or reject it.[33] A similar solution has been positively accepted by Belliotti, in something of a surprise twist, in the final sentence of his book.[34] In one respect, however, Belliotti does not go quite as far as rejecting the requirement entirely. Although he argues that a person's interests can continue to exist after their death, these interests, do not exist as 'free-floating metaphysical constructs' but instead are held 'in trust' for the deceased by surviving proxies or guardians.[35] The premise of this argument is still that interests must be held by some existing person. In my view, this requirement is unnecessary. The notion of 'having' or 'holding' an interest is merely a metaphor to refer to certain states or events being good for a person. It does not involve anyone actually having or holding anything. To suggest that the one person can hold interests on trust for another somewhat reifies the metaphor.

The main reason for abandoning the existence requirement, and instead holding that a person's interests can continue to exist and be affected after their death, is that it is the simplest way of accounting for our intuitions about how we should treat the dead. Most cultures have some conception of a proper funeral or burial, and of the proper

[31] S Luper, 'Retroactive Harms and Wrongs' in B Bradley, F Feldman and J Johansson (eds), *The Oxford Handbook of Philosophy of Death* (New York, Oxford University Press, 2012); S Luper, 'The Moral Standing of the Dead' (2018) 373 *Philosophical Transactions of the Royal Society B* 20170270. See also S Keller, 'Posthumous Harm' in S Luper (ed), *The Cambridge Companion to Life and Death* (Cambridge, Cambridge University Press, 2014).

[32] Luper, 'Retroactive Harms' (n 31) 327–32; Boonin (n 22) ch 4. This argument depends on the view that the benefit or harm of a desire occurs at the time of the desire. However, there is a reasonable argument that, for future-oriented desires, the benefit or harm occurs at the time of the events that satisfy or frustrate the desire: see E Lin, 'Asymmetrism about Desire Satisfaction and Time' in M Timmins (ed), *Oxford Studies in Normative Ethics: Volume 7* (Oxford, Oxford University Press, 2017). This might be after the person's death. If so, the benefit or harm would be ruled out by the existence requirement, which both Luper and Boonin accept, which means that their argument is unsuccessful.

[33] Boonin (n 22) 116–17. If anything, he appears favourably disposed to it, and does not argue for it only because 'I do not want my response to the no subject objection to depend on' it.

[34] Belliotti (n 17) 174, accepting the 'modified strong thesis of posthumous harms', which he describes at 171–73.

[35] ibid 171. A similar view is put forward in K Falconer, 'Reconceptualising the Law of the Dead by Expanding the Interests of the Living' (2019) 45 *Monash University Law Review* 757.

treatment of the deceased's body, among other things.[36] A common feature of these practices is that they involve treating the deceased with dignity and respect. We would readily accept that we treat living people with dignity and respect primarily because that is how they deserve to be treated, and because it is good *for them personally* to be treated that way. The simplest explanation of why we treat deceased persons in the same way is therefore the same; we regard it as being in their interests.

Now, the obvious response to this argument is that we cannot explain our treatment of the dead in this way, because the dead cannot have interests, because they do not exist. If this response is correct, though, it would follow that our practices relating to the dead must be irrational, unless some other explanation can be given for them that does not depend on the dead having interests. Clearly, any explanation that avoids having to treat our intuitions and practices as irrational is preferable to that extent. The most plausible alternative explanation is that those practices are really for the benefit of the living. It is certainly plausible that they do benefit living people in various ways, such as by enabling them to create or preserve a positive memory of the deceased, to grieve, or perhaps even to avoid having to accept that the deceased is really gone. There are several reasons, however, why this should be rejected as the sole explanation for such practices.[37] One is that it is likely not the explanation that those involved in the practices would give for their own conduct. Indeed, they would likely be insulted by the suggestion that it is. They would instead explain their conduct as being for the benefit of the deceased. Of course, they may be wrong about their true subconscious motivations, as people often are, but this is arguably not the case here. It seems odd to suggest, for example, that someone meticulously preparing a eulogy for their beloved parent, spouse, child, and so on is really doing it for themselves. Second, to the extent that the explanation for these practices is that the living *want* the deceased to be treated in a certain way, and would be distressed if the deceased were treated otherwise (for example, if their body was interfered with), these desires would be irrational unless the living have some reason to care how the deceased is treated. It is not clear what this reason would be if the deceased themselves has no interest in the matter. Finally, some people have no friends, family members or others who would benefit from these practices being carried out, and yet in such cases most people would likely still think the practices would be justified. Indeed, there is something particularly poignant about the thought of the deceased being treated with dignity in such cases.

The more plausible explanation for these practices is therefore that they are for the benefit of the deceased, and are inconsistent with the existence requirement. It follows that we should reject the existence requirement, unless there is some other reason why the dead having interests would be impossible or problematic. One possible argument is that it is impossible as a matter of logic: how can *a person* have interests if *that person* does not exist? There is no reason, however, why we cannot say that the interests are those of a person *who existed in the past*. There is no logical difficulty in the proposition

[36] See, eg, CM Parkes, P Laungani and W Young (eds), *Death and Bereavement Across Cultures*, 2nd edn (London, Routledge, 2015), H Selin and RM Rakoff (eds), *Death Across Cultures: Death and Dying in Non-Western Cultures* (Cham, Springer, 2019). While some of these might reflect a belief in an afterlife of some kind, not all of them do.

[37] D Herzog, *Defaming the Dead* (New Haven, Yale University Press, 2017) 22–26.

that the interests of a person who existed in the past can be furthered or set back now, unless we also assume that the person must exist now for their interests to be furthered or set back now, which would beg the precise question in issue. The existence requirement cannot be derived solely from logic, since it is really a moral claim about how we should act and why. It therefore depends just as much on moral premises and argument as the claim that the dead can have interests.

The existence requirement also cannot be derived solely from physical facts about deceased persons, since this would involve an 'is–ought' fallacy. If anything, describing the requirement in terms of physical facts reduces its plausibility; whether electrical impulses occur in a person's brain should not determine whether they are of any moral concern, or worthy of moral protection. The fact that the existence of posthumous interests cannot be *proved* by physical facts is also irrelevant, since this is equally true of the interests of living persons. Further, something being good or bad for someone has no physical effect on them, so there is no need for the person to exist in order to experience some physical effect as a condition of having interests.

Another possible reason why accepting that the dead can have interests might be thought to be theoretically problematic is that it necessarily involves accepting the further proposition that their quality of life, wellbeing or welfare can be changed by post-death events, which seems implausible, given that these properties are only possessed by living entities.[38] This thought is encouraged by the fact that those properties are often used interchangeably to refer to a person's interests.[39] However, it is possible to treat them as distinct. Having a good life can be understood as merely one good thing for a person;[40] even if post-death events cannot retrospectively render a person's otherwise good life a bad one,[41] those events can nevertheless be bad for the person in other ways. Similarly, the fact that deceased persons do not possess interests such as wellbeing or welfare would also not necessarily prevent the person from having other interests that can be furthered or set back post-death.

It might also be thought that, if we were to accept that deceased persons can have interests, this would require us to accept that they have the *full range* of interests possessed by living persons. This is not the case. At the very least, a dead person cannot feel pleasure or pain, and therefore has no interests in experiencing (or not experiencing) them.[42] They also cannot develop new goals or desires. Further, even if we accept that dead people have interests, it does not follow that they have a moral or legal right to their protection, since those interests (like the interests of the living) might not be

[38] See Luper, 'Retroactive Harms' (n 31) 320: 'It is not plausible to attribute a welfare level to a subject a time when that subject does not exist'.

[39] See, eg, Parfit (n 20) 493: 'What would be best for someone, or would be most in this person's interests, or would make this person's life go, for him, as well as possible? Answers to this question I call *theories about self-interest*'. See also Keller (n 31) 182: 'A discussion of harms and benefits is, for philosophers, a discussion about "welfare." A person's welfare is the measure of how well things go for her. Your welfare can be identified with your "well-being" and with your "best interests" – something that advances your welfare is something that serves your best interests – and we can also say that something that advances your welfare makes you better off rather than worse off, makes your life go better rather than worse, and is good for you, rather than bad for you'. Interestingly, both Parfit and Keller nevertheless accept the possibility of posthumous harm.

[40] Boonin suggests that a person's life going less well for them is '*one way* in which things can go worse' for them: (n 22) 52 (emphasis added).

[41] Cf B Kultgen, 'Posthumous Repugnancy' (2022) 22 *Journal of Ethics and Social Philosophy* 317.

[42] Keller (n 31) 195.

sufficiently strong, and must be weighed against other private and public interests. Rejecting the existence requirement also does not require us to accept that we should care about the interests of all non-existent people (whatever that would even involve), including those for whom there is no possibility that they will ever exist.[43] It is entirely plausible to say that a person must exist *at some point*, in either the past, present or future, to have interests.[44] The point is only that a person's interests can still exist after they die.

This all leaves the question of what interests the dead *do* have. It is not possible to give a complete account here, only to make some preliminary suggestions. The earlier discussion indicates at least two possible sources of post-death interests. One is the goals and desires that the person formed during their lifetime, to the extent that they can still be furthered or frustrated. A second is the person's dignity. Although the concept of dignity is difficult to define,[45] several commentators have relied on it in arguing for the recognition of post-death legal rights.[46] As the next section demonstrates, both of these interests have been referred to in a number of private law contexts.

IV. Posthumous Rights in Private Law

Whether or not these arguments are accepted, the extent to which posthumous rights are recognised in private law is a separate question. As mentioned earlier, on one view, this question is easily answered: the dead have no rights, and that is that. Any protection that private law appears to give to the interests of the dead is really for the benefit of the living. In this section, I argue against this view. Private law directly protects some of a person's most basic interests, so it is one area of law where we might expect the interests of the dead to surface, which I suggest they do. The law is not always uniform or consistent in recognising them, either within or across jurisdictions, which is not surprising, given the substantial philosophical disagreement about whether such interests are even possible. The issue of whether the dead possess certain interests also gives rise to difficult questions about the scope and content of those interests at a deeper level. Nevertheless, it is arguable that private law does recognise a number of interests that continue post-death.

A. Property

In common law systems, the owner of property generally has the power (subject to various limits) to decide who will receive it after they die,[47] just as they have the power

[43] On the other hand, the extent to which we should care about the interests of possible future people whose existence is prevented by the very acts that protect their interests is a more difficult question: see D Boonin, *The Non-Identity Problem and the Ethics of Future People* (Oxford, Oxford University Press, 2014). This issue is discussed further in ch 1 of this volume.

[44] See also Belliotti (n 17) 172.

[45] The concept of dignity is examined in more detail in ch 1 of this volume.

[46] KR Smolensky, 'Rights of the Dead' (2009) 37 *Hofstra Law Review* 763; Herzog (n 37) chs 5–6.

[47] *Ilott v Mitson (No 2)* [2017] UKSC 17, [2018] AC 545 [1]. See also Vines, ch 11 this volume.

to transfer it *inter vivos*. While this is often taken for granted, in a sense it is puzzling. The deceased clearly can no longer use the property themselves, so why does their right to the property not simply end and the property become *bona vacantia*? The interests of the intended beneficiaries are not a sufficient explanation, since there would usually be others who could benefit equally (if not more) from the property, particularly where it is just money. It is not necessarily possible to point to any special entitlement of the beneficiaries based on some relationship with the deceased, since the deceased is generally free to leave the property to whomever, or for whatever valid purpose, they want.[48] Appealing to some public interest in enforcing wills (promoting optimal distributions, providing comfort to the living) seems somewhat artificial.[49]

The simplest explanation is that the purpose of enforcing wills is to benefit (that is, further the interests of) the deceased,[50] in that it fulfils the deceased's desires or wishes. Property rights allow the owner to benefit from the property for some period of time, either by using or expending it themselves or by transferring it to someone else. Although this time period is sometimes limited to the owner's lifetime, in many cases it is not. In such cases, although the deceased can no longer personally use or expend the property, it is still possible to fulfil their desire that it be given to a particular person (or that it be used for a particular purpose) and therefore still possible to benefit the deceased in that way.

In some cases, the law enables the deceased to control the property for an extended period of time after their death, not merely in its immediate aftermath. For example, they are permitted to impose conditions on the recipient, or declare that the property be held on trust. In jurisdictions where the rule against perpetuities still applies, the duration for which the owner's desires will be given effect is nevertheless limited, but not always by much.[51] Charitable trusts are (for the most part) an exception to the rule altogether,[52] potentially enabling the owner to control the use of the property indefinitely. In facilitating their desires to this extent, there is a plausible argument that the law not only recognises the interests of deceased owners, but goes well beyond what is reasonable to protect them.[53]

B. Contracts

As a starting point, contractual rights are not extinguished on the promisee's death. The most obvious example of this is a debt, which is still payable to the promisee's estate at

[48] Subject to family provision legislation: eg Succession Act 1981 (Qld) s 41.

[49] Herzog (n 37) 59–61.

[50] See *Grey v Harrison* [1997] 2 VR 359, 366 (Calloway JA): '[I]t is one of the freedoms that shape our society, and an important human right, that a person should be free to dispose of his or her property as he or she thinks fit'.

[51] For an overview of the current state of the rule against perpetuities in several jurisdictions, see AC Evans, 'The Rule Against Perpetuities: How We Got Here and Future Directions' (2017) 46 *Australian Tax Review* 71.

[52] *Monds v Stackhouse* [1948] HCA 47, (1948) 77 CLR 232, 243: '[W]here there is a good charitable gift the money may be held in perpetuity for charitable purposes, but the gift itself must satisfy, in relation to the time of its inception, the rule against perpetuities'.

[53] RD Madoff, *Immortality and the Law: The Rising Power of the American Dead* (New Haven, Yale University Press, 2010) chs 2–3; B Lam, 'The Invisible Hand from the Grave' (2019) 15 *Journal of Ethics and Social Philosophy* 197.

the time it falls due.[54] If a particular contractual right ceases on death, this is an exception and not the rule.

The main reason why a contractual right might cease on death is the doctrine of frustration, which provides that a contract will be terminated 'when the parties enter into it on the common assumption that some particular thing or state of affairs essential to its performance will continue to exist or be available, neither party undertaking responsibility in that regard, and that common assumption proves to be mistaken'.[55] In *Hall v Wright*, Crompton J suggested that

> where a contract depends on personal skill, and the act of God renders it impossible, as for instance, in the case of a painter employed to paint a picture who is struck blind, it may be that the performance might be excused, and his death might also have the same effect.[56]

Although this passage refers to the death or incapacity of the promisor, a similar principle applies to the promisee. For example, where a contract stipulates for the provision of nursing care to the promisee for a fixed period of time, and the promisee dies before the time period expires, the contract is frustrated,[57] since the assumption underlying such a contract is clearly that the promisee will be alive to receive the care.

On this reasoning, however, not all contracts will be frustrated by the promisee's death. Indeed, a pre-paid funeral plan, under which a person contracts during their lifetime to have a funeral provided for them after their death, is premised on the promisee not being alive at the time of performance. Far from triggering the extinction of the contract, in this instance death actually enlivens the promisor's contractual obligation. Even where a contract is frustrated by the promisee's death, this is merely because in the particular case the parties happened to make an assumption about whether the promisee will be alive at the relevant time, and not because the doctrine of frustration regards their death as itself having any inherent significance.

C. Intellectual Property

Intellectual property rights also survive their owner's death. Indeed, the duration of copyright in particular is explicitly defined as running for the life of the author (generally the original owner) and for some period after, typically 70 years.[58] Although copyright cannot be used by a deceased owner personally, the deceased can assign it in their will, and the same is true of patents and trademarks.[59] In the US, several states have also recognised (either by statute or at common law) that the so-called 'right of publicity', which allows a person to commercially exploit their name, image and so on,[60] continues

[54] Indeed, the executor has a duty to take reasonable steps to 'get in' the debt: *National Trustees Executors and Agency Co of Australasia Ltd v Dwyer* [1940] HCA 5, (1940) 63 CLR 1.

[55] *Codelfa Constructions Pty Ltd v State Rail Authority (NSW)* [1982] HCA 24, (1982) 149 CLR 337, 357.

[56] *Hall v Wright* (1858) El Bl & El 746, 749; 120 ER 688, 690.

[57] *Lobb v Vasey Housing Auxiliary (War Widows Guild)* [1963] VR 239, 245–46.

[58] Copyright Act 1968 (Cth) ss 33, 35.

[59] Patents Act 1990 (Cth) s 13(2); Trademarks Act 1995 (Cth) s 106.

[60] See *Haelan Laboratories Inc v Topps Chewing Gum Inc* 202 F 2d 866, 868 (2nd Cir 1953).

for some period after their death and can be assigned by will.[61] No similar right exists in the UK or Australia.[62]

The fact that intellectual property rights are not extinguished on the owner's death is initially puzzling for the same reason as for other property rights. Again, however, the power to assign them can be understood as being for the benefit of the deceased. This is not necessarily to say that intellectual property rights are solely designed to further the owner's private interests. On one view, their purpose is instrumental, in that they provide an incentive to create certain kinds of works, which is in the public interest, by giving the author an exclusive right to commercially exploit the work, and a power to assign that right.[63] Nevertheless, this does not change the fact that the power to assign intellectual property rights does further the interests of deceased owners.

D. Moral Rights

An even stronger example is the so-called 'moral rights' of authors of copyright works. These rights are distinct from the copyright in the work, which is often referred to as the 'economic rights' to distinguish it from the moral rights.[64] While the precise content of these moral rights differs between jurisdictions, there are generally three. In Australia (which closely follows the *Berne Convention*),[65] these are the right to be identified as the author of the work when it is reproduced, published and so on,[66] the right that authorship of the work not be falsely attributed[67] and the right for the work not to be subject to 'derogatory treatment',[68] which refers to treatment of the work (mutilation, distortion or alteration of the work, for example) that is 'prejudicial to the author's honour or reputation'.[69] This last right is referred to as the 'right of integrity'.

These moral rights generally have the same duration as the copyright in the work,[70] which as mentioned earlier is typically 70 years from the author's death. A crucial difference, however, is that moral rights cannot be assigned,[71] and, after the author's death, are exercisable on the author's behalf by their personal representative.[72] The possible remedies

[61] See Madoff (n 53) 135.

[62] See J Eaton and O Oroeye, 'Image Rights and the Law in Australia and a Comparison with the United States' (2018) 40 *European Intellectual Property Review* 186.

[63] P Drahos, *A Philosophy of Intellectual Property* (Canberra, ANU Press, 2016) ch 6.

[64] See Berne Convention for the Protection of Literary and Artistic Works (Paris, 9 September 1886) art 6*bis*.

[65] ibid.

[66] Copyright Act 1968 (Cth) s 193.

[67] ibid s 195AC.

[68] ibid s 195AI.

[69] ibid ss 195AJ–195AL.

[70] ibid s 195AM.

[71] ibid s 195AN(3).

[72] ibid s 195AN(1). For a helpful discussion of several obstacles to enforcing the post-mortem right of integrity (and possible solutions), see J McCutcheon, 'The Honour of the Dead: The Moral Right of Integrity Post-Mortem' (2014) 42 *Federal Law Review* 485. The position is slightly different in the UK. Although moral rights cannot be assigned, some can pass by will to a person nominated by the author: Copyrights, Designs and Patents Act 1988 (UK) ss 94, 95(1). The combination of these rules suggests that the nominated person does not hold the rights for their own benefit.

for their enforcement include an injunction, damages or an order that the defendant make a public apology.[73] The latter remedy, combined with the non-assignability of the rights, and the fact that they are only conferred on individuals (and not artificial persons),[74] strongly indicate that their purpose is to protect some non-pecuniary interest of individual authors. Their honour and reputation are the most likely candidates. These interests are explicitly protected by the right of integrity, and may be considered by the court in deciding the appropriate relief for any of the moral rights.[75] The moral rights relating to attribution can also be understood as protecting these interests, since their purpose is to preserve the author's reputation as the author of the work.

McCutcheon argues that an author's interest in their honour and reputation cannot be the justification for post-mortem moral rights, since the dead do not themselves have interests that are capable of being harmed.[76] She instead identifies the public interest in cultural heritage (preserving the work in the form intended by the author) as the rationale for post-mortem moral rights.[77] However, my arguments in section III suggest that the dead are capable of having interests. Furthermore, as McCutcheon herself acknowledges, the public interest rationale cannot explain various features of moral rights in their current form, in particular (in the case of the right of integrity) the need to show prejudice to the author's honour or reputation.[78] There is therefore a strong case for understanding the persistence of moral rights as recognising the private interests of the dead in their honour and reputation.

E. Defamation

The persistence of moral rights stands in stark contrast to the position with respect to defamation. At common law, a defamatory statement about a person who is dead at the time of publication is not actionable, and the same rule is now reflected in statute in Australia.[79] Not only this, existing causes of action for defamation that arise during the plaintiff's lifetime are extinguished by their death, in contrast to nearly all other causes of action.[80]

The apparent clarity and incontrovertibility of the current position is not reflected in its history. Originally, there was no similar rule for criminal libel.[81] As late as 1887, in the context of criminal libel, Stephen J remarked that 'the authorities upon the subject

[73] Copyright Act 1968 (Cth) s 195AZA(1).

[74] ibid s 190.

[75] ibid s 195AZA(2)(b).

[76] J McCutcheon, 'Dead Loss: Damages for Posthumous Breach of the Moral Right of Integrity' (2014) 40 *Melbourne University Law Review* 240, 248–51. McCutcheon also argues that 'honour' (in the context of the particular provision) is something that is only subjectively experienced and therefore cannot be possessed by the dead: at 269–70.

[77] ibid 251–53.

[78] ibid 281.

[79] See, eg, Defamation Act 2005 (Qld) s 10.

[80] See, eg, Law Reform (Miscellaneous Provisions) Act 1934 (UK) s 1.

[81] Although this is no longer the case in some jurisdictions: see, eg, Criminal Code 1899 (Qld) s 365(1). On the development of a tort of defamation separate from the criminal and ecclesiastical jurisdictions, see J Baker, *An Introduction to English Legal History*, 5th edn (Oxford, Oxford University Press, 2019) ch 25.

are few',[82] and identified only two as relevant, both of which held that libelling the dead could be an offence. The first was the *De Libellis Famosis* case.[83] There, the Star Chamber held that 'although the [subject of the libel] be dead at the time of the making of the libel, yet it is punishable; for … it stirs up others of the same family, blood, or society, to revenge, and to break the peace'.[84] This argument appeals to the interests of the living, but it does not necessarily deny the interests of the dead. The other authority identified by Stephen J was *R v Topham*,[85] in which Lord Kenyon held that libelling the dead,

> whether soon or late after the death of the party, if it be done with a malevolent purpose, to vilify the memory of the deceased, and with a view to injure his posterity … then it is done with a design to break the peace, and then it becomes illegal.[86]

On this argument, the defendant must intend to injure the deceased's living relatives (posterity) *and* vilify their memory, which can be interpreted as recognising the deceased's interests as well. Stephen J followed the approach in *Topham* but gave a somewhat different justification for it: 'the dead have no rights and can suffer no wrongs. The living alone can be the subject of legal protection'.[87] This does not follow from the authorities on which he relied.

Authority with respect to the tort of defamation is also surprisingly thin. In *Krahe v TCN Channel Nine Pty Ltd*, Hunt J stated in obiter dicta that 'where a statement is published which is defamatory of a dead person', although the person's family members can sue for any implicit defamatory imputation about themselves, 'there is no cause of action given to [the family members] to sue on [the dead person's] behalf'.[88] No authority was given for this proposition, other than the *actio personalis moritur cum persona* maxim, mentioned earlier. It is not entirely clear whether the maxim supports this conclusion. On its face, it only applies to actions subsisting at the plaintiff's death, although it is certainly arguable that it applies *a fortiori* to actions arising after death. More significantly, however, the maxim was never intended to apply to *all* rights, only those that are 'so annexed to the persons of the parties, that it shall die with the persons; [otherwise] if he to whom [a] promise is made dies, his executors should not have any action, which no man will affirm'.[89] As this indicates, the rule does not apply (and perhaps never applied) to breaches of contract.[90] While on some statements it applies to all torts,[91] other statements limit it to torts causing personal injury.[92] It was applied to a defamation action in at least one case, although (again) without reference to authority

[82] *Ensor* (n 1) 367.
[83] *De Libellis Famosis* (1606) 5 Co Rep 125; 77 ER 250.
[84] ibid 251.
[85] *R v Topham* (1791) 4 TR 126, 130; 100 ER 931.
[86] ibid 933.
[87] *Ensor* (n 1) 367.
[88] *Krahe* (n 3) 541.
[89] *Pinchon's Case* (1611) 9 Co Rep 86, 89a; 77 ER 859, 863.
[90] *Woolworths Ltd v Crotty* [1942] HCA 35, (1942) 66 CLR 603, 613–15 (Latham CJ).
[91] *Ryan v Davies Bros Ltd* [1921] HCA 53, (1921) 29 CLR 527, 533; *WorkCover Queensland v Amaca Pty Ltd* [2010] HCA 34, (2010) 241 CLR 420 [34]. See also *Hambly v Trott* (1776) 1 Cowp 371, 374–75; 98 ER 1136, 1138.
[92] *Rose v Ford* [1937] AC 826 (HL) 833; *Woolworths* (n 90) 612.

or detailed consideration of the issue.[93] Although the legislation that abolished the *actio personalis* rule included an exception for defamation actions, this did not reflect a considered judgement that defamation actions should not survive post-death. It was intended merely to sidestep the issue, the main purpose of the legislation being to deal with the application of the *actio personalis* rule to road accidents.[94]

In any event, if the question is whether the law should be reformed, the *actio personalis* rule is not a real barrier, since courts have noted its lack of any apparent logic or rationality.[95] What arguments might there be for extending the tort of defamation post-death? One is that statements about the deceased can cause emotional distress to their living relatives.[96] The most obvious problem with this argument is that there is generally no free-standing duty to avoid causing emotional distress (as distinct from recognisable psychiatric illness) to others. Moreover, at least part of the reason why the relatives would suffer distress, and what makes their distress legitimate, is that they would regard the statements as harming the deceased. Surely, if the relatives believed that the deceased could not be harmed, they could rest easily and happily ignore anything said about the deceased? Any distress they suffer would likely be grounded (at least in most cases) in the belief that it is bad *for the deceased* to have defamatory statements made about them, perhaps more so after their death. Otherwise, why would they care? Finally, as mentioned earlier, some deceased persons do not have friends or relatives who would be distressed by the statements, yet it is arguably still wrongful to make such statements.[97] This all indicates that it is really the deceased's interests that support the claim.

The deceased's interests are therefore a better justification for allowing actions for post-death defamatory statements, although there are several possible counterarguments. One (which appealed to Stephen J) is that the dead do not have interests. I argued against this view earlier, and the law rejects it in other contexts. Another argument is that, even if the dead can have interests, their reputation is not one of them. This argument does not sit well with the moral rights mentioned above, which continue to protect the author's honour and reputation post-death. Of course, one might respond that the law of moral rights is wrong to do this. The dead clearly have a reputation (since it is possible for the living to remember and hold views about them), but whether that reputation should be protected depends on the reasons why reputation is important in the first place, and whether those reasons continue to apply post-death.

What even is 'reputation'? In *Sim v Stretch*, Lord Atkin suggested that a statement is defamatory if 'the words tend to lower the plaintiff in the estimation of right-thinking members of society generally'.[98] Along similar lines, the majority of the High Court in *Radio 2UE Sydney Pty Ltd v Chesterton* suggested that 'a person's reputation may … be said to be injured when the esteem in which that person is held by the community

[93] *Hatchard v Mege* (1887) 18 QBD 771, 774, 777.

[94] Lord Chancellor's Department, *Report of the Committee on Defamation* (Cmnd 5909, 1975) paras 399–400.

[95] *Ryan* (n 91) 533: '[T]he maxim is not, as has been said, a very rational part of the law'; *Rose* (n 92) 841: '[N]o one has claimed that it is logical'.

[96] *Report of the Committee on Defamation* (n 94) para 420.

[97] Herzog (n 37) 3–11.

[98] *Sim v Stretch* [1936] 1 All ER 1237 (HL) 1240.

is diminished in some respect'.[99] These statements reflect the view that 'an individual's reputation is a social judgment of the person based upon facts which are considered relevant by a community'.[100]

Herzog identifies three reasons why a person might have an interest in their reputation, or in other words, why they might be harmed by defamatory statements about them.[101] The first is that defamatory statements might be upsetting to them, or injure their subjective feelings of self-worth or belonging, which depend on how they are viewed by others. The second is that defamatory statements about a person can affect how others treat them. The third is that defamatory statements about a person are 'intrinsically' bad for them, since they are a depredation of their 'dignified personhood'.[102] The point seems to be that harm to reputation is (or involves) a kind of unfelt or unexperienced harm, similar to being ridiculed behind your back.

While the dead cannot suffer harm of either the first or second kind, Herzog argues that the third kind of harm is still possible.[103] Extending the tort of defamation to statements about the dead could therefore be justified as protecting them from the third kind of harm, if indeed it were a harm, which I suggest it is. It matters how a person lived their life and what kind of person they were, and it is important that, as a matter of respect for the person, this is properly reflected in how we represent their life, especially post-death.[104] As Herzog colourfully puts it, given the choice, most people (including those with no friends or family who would be distressed by the statements) would choose not being defamed after their death over the French fries during their life being marginally better. This choice would be irrational if their post-death reputation did not matter at all.[105]

The value of post-death reputation is recognised in other contexts, such as the enforcement of moral rights, but also in broader social practices such as the granting of posthumous pardons and awards.[106] It is also recognised in other jurisdictions and cultures. In the well-known *Mephisto* judgment, for example, the Federal Constitutional Court of Germany held that its constitutional guarantee of human dignity protects a person's reputation after their death:

> [i]t would be inconsistent with the constitutional mandate of the inviolability of human dignity, which underlies all basic rights, if a person could be belittled and denigrated after his death. Accordingly an individual's death does not put an end to the state's duty under Art 1 GG [*Grundgesetz*, or Basic Law] to protect him from assaults on his human dignity.[107]

[99] *Radio 2UE Sydney Pty Ltd v Chesterton* [2009] HCA 16, (2009) 238 CLR 460 [3].

[100] L McNamara, *Reputation and Defamation* (Oxford, Oxford University Press, 2007) 21.

[101] Herzog (n 37) 245–47.

[102] See also J Waldron, *The Harm in Hate Speech* (Cambridge, Harvard University Press, 2012).

[103] Herzog (n 37) 250–52. Herzog also argues that they can suffer the second kind of harm to a limited extent.

[104] ibid 264: 'Surely the dead's intrinsic interest in reputation is especially poignant. Your reputation after death is a final setting of accounts, unlike your reputation while alive, ordinarily in flux as you continue to act. When that account is damaged by defamation, it's all too likely to stay that way. "This will always be there"'.

[105] ibid 11–12.

[106] ibid 243–44. See also F Tomasini, *Remembering and Disremembering the Dead: Posthumous Punishment, Harm and Redemption over Time* (London, Palgrave Macmillan, 2017) chs 3–4; Belliotti (n 17) 33; Boonin (n 22) 193–94.

[107] (1971) BVerfGE 30, 170.

Another interesting example is *Ellis v R*,[108] where the Supreme Court of New Zealand relied on *tikanga* Maori principles in allowing Ellis's appeal against his conviction to continue after his death. Those principles recognise that a person's *mana*, which is affected by their reputation (among other things), is not extinguished by death.

The view that the defamation of a deceased person should be actionable has been accepted in law reform reports across several common law jurisdictions.[109] Indeed, this was the recommendation of the report that led to the Australian uniform legislation,[110] although in the end the legislation expressly denied actions for defaming the dead. No reason was given for this other than its consistency with the existing statute and common law,[111] which, as the earlier discussion indicates, is not an entirely secure footing. To some extent, the rule has bootstrapped itself into existence.

Interestingly, most of these reports nevertheless recommend that such an action should only be available for defamatory statements made during some limited period after the person's death, generally three to five years, and that the available remedies not include damages (and be limited to a declaration, injunction etc).[112] The basis for excluding damages is not entirely clear. It likely reflects the view that damages are supposed to benefit the defamed person and not the beneficiaries of their estate.[113] As McCutcheon points out in the context of moral rights, this argument somewhat ignores the fact that damages equally form part of a living plaintiff's estate,[114] which the plaintiff can then choose to leave to others instead of expending it themselves. As mentioned earlier, allowing a person to give their property to others is one way of benefiting them, and awarding damages would fulfil this purpose even if the defamed person is dead.

A stronger reason for limiting damages would be that certain heads of loss do not arise if the defamed person is dead, but this does not support a total bar on damages. Compensatory damages for defamation have several purposes, including consoling the victim for their distress and hurt, repairing the harm to their reputation, and 'vindicating' their reputation, in addition to compensating economic loss.[115] While a dead person cannot experience hurt or distress, and therefore should not receive damages for such loss, the other heads are unaffected by the fact that the person is dead. An award of damages, albeit reduced, may therefore be justified.

The proposed time limit is also questionable. Its purported justification is that the available evidence about a person diminishes over time, making it too difficult to establish a truth defence.[116] This is said to be most significant in the context of historical writing, which is in the public interest, but which would be chilled by the possibility of liability for defamation. There is no doubt a public interest in the accurate recording of history, but it

[108] *Ellis v R* [2022] 1 NZLR 239.

[109] See Australian Government Attorney-General's Department, *Revised Outline of a Possible National Defamation Law* (Report, 2004) 12–13.

[110] ibid 13.

[111] See, eg, Explanatory Notes to the Defamation Act 2005 (Qld) 6. The explanatory memoranda in other States and territories are in identical terms.

[112] *Revised Outline* (n 108) 13.

[113] As Lunney demonstrates in ch 9 of this volume, this argument was prominent in the debates over the survival of actions legislation, in particular regarding damages for loss of expectation of life.

[114] McCutcheon, 'Dead Loss' (n 76) 263–64.

[115] *Carson v John Fairfax & Sons Ltd* [1993] HCA 31, (1993) 178 CLR 44, 60–61.

[116] *Revised Outline* (n 109) 13.

is not clear that a time limit on (or blanket denial of) actions for post-death defamation is the best solution. Several law reform reports have expressed doubt about whether liability for defaming the dead would have any real effect on historical writing.[117] Moreover, if truth is the end goal, perhaps writers should be circumspect in making factual claims that cannot be sufficiently proved? As long ago as *R v Topham*, Lord Kenyon's solution to this precise issue was to require statements to be made 'fairly and honestly' to avoid liability.[118] In today's terms, sufficient protection would arguably be provided by the combined effect of the peer review and honest opinion defences, supplemented where necessary by the public interest and fair report defences.[119] These defences satisfy the relevant public interest concerns without sacrificing the reputations of the dead.

F. Breach of Confidence and Privacy

There is a strong argument that equitable rights with respect to confidential information continue post-death, although the issue is complicated by the fact that such rights protect several different kinds of information. It is clear that trade secrets are capable of being assigned by will,[120] which implies that the right to protect them is not extinguished on death. The right closely resembles an intellectual property right, and provides primarily economic benefits, so this is not surprising. The justification for the right's continuing existence and assignability is arguably the same as that of intellectual property rights.

There is somewhat less authority on whether the right to protect personal or private information persists after death, although a line of cases dating back to the eighteenth century indicates that it does. In *Duke of Queensberry v Shebbeare*,[121] the Earl of Clarendon had given an unpublished book manuscript to his son, who gave it to the defendant for the defendant's personal use. The defendant later attempted to publish it after the Earl's death. The Earl's administrator obtained an injunction restraining the publication. In *Thompson v Stanhope*,[122] the executor of the Earl of Chesterfield obtained a similar remedy preventing the publication of letters that the Earl had written to his son. In *Phillip v Pennell*, Kekewich J referred to 'the right established by law of the writer of a letter during his life-time, and of his legal personal representatives after his death, to prevent the publication of letters written by him'.[123] Although the basis for this right is sometimes said to be a common law property right of authors,[124] Ashburner argues that its basis is really the equitable doctrine of breach of confidence.[125]

[117] ibid.

[118] *Topham* (n 85) 933.

[119] Defamation Act 2005 (Qld) ss 29, 29A, 30A, 31.

[120] *Morison v Moat* (1851) 9 Hare 241; 68 ER 492; *Smith Kline and French Laboratories (Australia) Ltd v Secretary to the Department of Community Services & Health* (1990) 22 FCR 73, 121; *Farah Constructions Pty Ltd v Say-Dee Investments Ltd* [2007] HCA 22, (2007) 230 CLR 89 [118]. For detailed discussion, see *Mid City Skin Cancer and Laser Centre Pty Ltd v Zahedi-Anarak* [2006] NSWSC 844, (2006) 67 NSWLR 569; *TS & B Retail Systems Pty Ltd v 3Fold Resources Pty Ltd (No 3)* [2007] FCA 151, (2007) 159 FCR 444 [74]–[77].

[121] *Duke of Queensberry v Shebbeare* (1758) 2 Eden 329; 28 ER 924.

[122] *Thompson v Stanhope* (1774) Amb 737; 27 ER 476.

[123] *Philip v Pennell* [1907] 2 Ch 577, 584.

[124] ibid 585.

[125] W Ashburner, *Principles of Equity* (London, Butterworth, 1902) 515–16.

Today, many cases involving unpublished manuscripts would be decided on the basis of copyright law, given that publication of the work is no longer required for copyright to subsist in it.[126] In Australia, the bequest of an unpublished manuscript is taken (unless a contrary intention appears) to include the copyright in the work,[127] which gives the beneficiary the right to publish it.[128] The point for present purposes, though, is that the right to protect confidential personal information can continue after death. The same conclusion would apply to the English tort of misuse of private information, given its shared historical roots with breach of confidence.[129]

Privacy legislation also provides some, albeit limited, protection to information about deceased persons. In Australia, although the Freedom of Information Act 1982 (Cth) s 41(1) and Archives Act 1983 (Cth) s 33(1)(g) both explicitly deny access to information that would unreasonably disclose personal information about a deceased person, it is generally understood (although not authoritatively decided) that the Privacy Act 1988 (Cth) (which contains some private remedies)[130] only applies to information about living persons.[131] The Australian Law Reform Commission has recommended on several occasions that it be extended to information about deceased persons, at least for some limited period after their death.[132] In doing so, it referred to privacy legislation in several States and territories that protects the information of deceased persons,[133] and to the fact that equitable rights of confidence persist post-death.[134] The Commission's main arguments for extending the Privacy Act were that the mishandling of the information of deceased persons can cause distress to their living friends or relatives, and the fact that individuals would be hesitant to share personal information during their life, even for their own benefit, if they thought it could be disclosed after their death.[135] Neither argument appeals to the deceased's interest in privacy directly, but neither makes sense without it. Why would a person want to avoid their information being disclosed after their death, or would their friends or relatives be distressed by its disclosure, if its disclosure does not harm the deceased at all?

In contrast, in later recommending the creation of a private cause of action for invasion of privacy, the Commission recommended that it should *not* survive the plaintiff (or defendant's) death.[136] This presumably also implies that an action would not be

[126] Copyright Act 1968 (Cth) s 32(1).

[127] ibid s 198.

[128] ibid s 31(1).

[129] See *Campbell v MGN Ltd* [2004] UKHL 22, [2004] 2 AC 457 [11]–[14].

[130] Privacy Act 1988 (Cth) s 52(1)(b); N Witzleb, 'Determinations under the *Privacy Act 1988* (Cth) as a Privacy Remedy' in JNE Varuhas and NA Moreham (eds), *Remedies for Breach of Privacy* (London, Hart Publishing, 2018).

[131] Office of the Privacy Commissioner, *Getting in on the Act: The Review of the Private Sector Provisions of the Privacy Act 1988* (Report, 2005) 281–82. The recent review of the Privacy Act by the Commonwealth Attorney-General's Department mentioned this issue, but made no specific recommendations: see *Privacy Act Review* (Report, 2022) 41–42.

[132] Australian Law Reform Commission, *Essentially Yours: The Protection of Human Genetic Information in Australia* (Report No 96, March 2003) vol 1, paras [7.84]–[7.91]; Australian Law Reform Commission, *For Your Information: Australian Privacy Law and Practice* (Report No 108, May 2008) vol 1, ch 8.

[133] *For Your Information* (n 132) paras [8.15]–[8.17].

[134] ibid paras [8.18]–[8.19].

[135] ibid para [8.44].

[136] Australian Law Reform Commission, *Serious Invasions of Privacy in the Digital Era* (Report No 123, 2014) 172–76.

available for invading the privacy of an already-deceased person, which is consistent with the position in the US.[137] In support of this, the Commission relied heavily on the *actio personalis* rule and its continuing application to actions for defamation, and also argued that any damages would be a windfall to the beneficiaries of the deceased's estate.[138] My earlier discussion of these arguments applies equally here.

The Commission noted that equitable rights with respect to confidential information (which may be a closer analogy than defamation) can persist after the right holder's death, but distinguished them on the basis that such rights are quasi-proprietary and often protect commercial information.[139] These arguments are also not entirely convincing. In discussing the nature of the action for breach of confidence, Deane J pointed out that 'its rational basis does not lie in proprietary right'.[140] Finn describes the issue of whether confidential information is property as 'perhaps the most sterile of the debates which have arisen around the subject'.[141] Further, as mentioned earlier, such equitable rights arguably do protect personal information post-death, not merely commercial information.

The Commission also argued that the purpose of privacy actions is to remedy the emotional distress to the person whose privacy is invaded,[142] which rules out an action for deceased persons, who cannot suffer emotional distress. This conception of privacy actions is overly constrained. In *Gulati v MGN Ltd*, the England and Wales Court of Appeal held that the purpose of damages in misuse of private information cases is to compensate not merely for emotional distress, but also for the misuse of the information itself, because the claimant is deprived of their right to control its use.[143] Although the claimant cannot control information personally after their death, their personal representative can exercise control on the claimant's behalf. In any event, Moreham identifies the harm to the claimant's dignity as an additional basis for this head of loss, which applies even where the claimant is unconscious or lacks legal capacity,[144] and which could similarly extend to deceased claimants. There is therefore an argument that invading the privacy of deceased persons is a private wrong, for which compensatory damages should be available.

G. Trespass to the Person

The final set of rights that I will consider are those relating to interference with the person, which underlie the torts of battery, assault and false imprisonment. It is possible

[137] See Madoff (n 53) 124: '[I]t is a settled principle of American law that the right of privacy (like the claim for defamation) does not continue after death'.

[138] *Serious Invasions of Privacy* (n 136) 172–73.

[139] ibid 173.

[140] *Mooregate Tobacco Co Ltd v Philip Morris Ltd (No 2)* [1984] HCA 73, (1984) 156 CLR 414, 438.

[141] See P Finn, *Fiduciary Obligations* (Annandale, Federation Press, 2016) 142–43.

[142] *Serious Invasions of Privacy* (n 136) 172.

[143] *Gulati v MGN Ltd* [2015] EWCA Civ 1291, [2017] QB 149 [45].

[144] NA Moreham, 'Compensating for Loss of Dignity and Autonomy' in JNE Varuhas and NA Moreham (eds), *Remedies for Breach of Privacy* (London, Hart Publishing, 2018) 136.

to rule out any right of a deceased person not to be assaulted, in the sense of being subjected to a reasonable apprehension of an imminent battery.[145] The right protects the person against a specific kind of 'emotional disturbance',[146] which cannot occur if the person is dead. A right not to be falsely imprisoned also seems unlikely, given that its purpose is to protect the person's freedom of movement or liberty,[147] which deceased persons cannot enjoy.

In contrast, although some commentators suggest otherwise,[148] it is arguable that the so-called 'principle of bodily inviolability' continues after a person's death. This principle refers to 'the right in an individual to choose what occurs with respect to his or her own person', and which entails that 'prima facie, any physical contact … is unlawful' (constituting the tort of battery).[149] This right is not absolute, of course. The personal representative of a deceased person has a duty at common law to dispose of the body and a corresponding right to possession for this purpose,[150] which will necessarily permit various kinds of physical contact with the body. However, apart from this or other specific authorisation, the principle of inviolability remains. This is most evident in cases relating to the removal of sperm from a person after their death, the premise of which is that interference with the body is prima facie unlawful. As Chesterman J put it in *Re Gray*,

> the principle clearly established, that the … right to possession of the body [is] only for the purposes of ensuring prompt and decent disposal has, I think, the corollary that there is a duty not to interfere with the body or … to violate it.[151]

The 'duty' referred to here is a civil rather than criminal law duty, the latter being distinguished in the following paragraph.[152] Hargrave J later endorsed *Re Gray* on this point in *AB v Attorney-General (Vic)*, adding that 'policy and logic dictate that the inviolability principle should extend to a corpse in the absence of a statute regulating the extent to which violation is permitted'.[153]

Several later cases have departed from aspects of *Re Gray*, but none have challenged the fundamental point that the common law prohibits interference with the body of the deceased. Although Atkinson J in *Re Denman* regarded removing sperm from a body as 'not unlawful', this likely refers only to it not being prohibited by statute, since the issue was whether the court could order the removal in its inherent jurisdiction.[154]

[145] *ACN 087 528 774 Pty Ltd (formerly Connex Trains Melbourne Pty Ltd) v Chetcuti* [2008] VSCA 274, (2008) 21 VR 559 [16].
[146] See JG Fleming, *The Law of Torts*, 9th edn (Sydney, LBC Information Services, 1998) 31.
[147] See *Lewis v Australian Capital Territory* [2020] HCA 26, (2020) 271 CLR 192 [14], [25], [45].
[148] See, eg, RN Nwabueze, 'Cadavers, Body Parts and the Remedial Problem' in I Goold et al (eds), *Persons, Parts and Property: How Should We Regulate Human Tissue in the 21st Century?* (London, Hart Publishing, 2014) 165.
[149] *Secretary, Department of Health and Community Services v JWB (Marion's Case)* [1992] HCA 15, (1992) 175 CLR 218, 233.
[150] *Williams v Williams* (1882) 20 Ch D 659, 664–65.
[151] *Re Gray* [2000] QSC 390, [2001] 2 Qd R 35 [20].
[152] ibid [21].
[153] *AB v Attorney-General (Vic)* [2005] VSC 180, (2005) 12 VR 485 [136]. See also *Re Cresswell* [2018] QSC 142, [2019] 1 Qd R 403 [161]: '[M]y analysis of the authorities does not support the existence of any common law principle pursuant to which sperm may be ordered to be removed from a deceased absent legislation'.
[154] *Re Denman* [2004] QSC 70, [2004] 2 Qd R 595, 597–98.

Several later cases have specifically authorised the removal of sperm on the basis of the court's inherent jurisdiction to protect the subject matter of the proceedings.[155] The premise of this argument is that, without authorisation, interference with the body is not permitted.

The post-death application of the inviolability principle recognises that a person has an interest in how their body is treated after they die. As Fleming argued, when applied to living persons, the principle affords protection 'not only against bodily harm but also against any interference with his person which is offensive to a reasonable sense of honour and dignity'.[156] Although a deceased person has no interest in avoiding bodily harm as such, preserving their honour or dignity provides a continuing basis for applying the principle.[157] The principle is also reflected in various other rules, such as the statutory provisions prohibiting post-mortem examinations or the removal of tissue (outside of a coronial setting) where the deceased expressed an objection to them during their lifetime,[158] or a person's right that their remains not be disturbed after their burial.[159]

There is some authority indicating that interfering with a dead body is not tortious, but it is not directly on point. In *Re Organ Retention Group Litigation*, the court refused to recognise the novel tort of wrongful interference with a body.[160] However, the claimant had framed the tort in proprietary terms as an interference with their right to possession of the body.[161] The claimant also argued that the tort prohibited the retention of organs that were lawfully removed from the body during a lawful autopsy for the purpose of subsequent examination (as part of the autopsy process), and the court's rejection of the tort was inherently bound up with its rejection of this particular argument. It therefore has limited precedential value with respect to whether the tort of battery prohibits unauthorised contact with the body of a deceased person. The right to possession is solely for the purpose of disposal, so it is arguable that it does not support or entail any general right of non-interference. This says nothing, though, about whether the deceased themselves has a right to bodily inviolability enforceable by their estate through the tort of battery. The cases discussed earlier indicate that there is indeed such a right. There are, of course, difficult questions about its precise extent,[162] but this is a separate issue. The existence of difficult cases is no reason to deny the existence of the right where its application is clear.

[155] *Re H, AE* [2012] SASC 146, (2012) 113 SASR 560 [48]–[49].
[156] Fleming (n 146) 29.
[157] Herzog (n 37) ch 5.
[158] See, eg, Transplant and Anatomy Act 1979 (Qld) ss 22, 23, 26, 27.
[159] *Beard v Baulkham Hills Shire Council* (1986) 7 NSWLR 273, 278 (Young J).
[160] *Re Organ Retention Group Litigation* [2004] EWHC 644 (QB), [2005] QB 506 [161].
[161] ibid [128]–[130].
[162] For example, Hardcastle argues that it does not apply to organs and material that have been removed from the body: R Hardcastle, *Law and the Human Body: Property Rights, Ownership and Control* (Oxford, Hart Publishing, 2007) 185–86.

V. Conclusion

The calls for increased protection for the dead are generally quiet, not least because the dead cannot take to the streets themselves. Even for those who share the intuition that we should treat the dead with dignity and respect, and preserve what mattered to them during their life, the philosophical and legal hurdles might seem too high. I have made some attempt to overcome them in this chapter. I have argued that the interests of the dead continue to make moral claims on the living. And in various contexts, private law can be understood as offering its protection for those interests, although in some cases it is notably absent. I am sure that some readers will remain unconvinced. I hope to have shown at least that there is more to the issue than one might think.

7

With this Ring I Thee Slay: The Death of Coverture

DANAYA WRIGHT

I. Introduction

Since at least the fourteenth century in England, a woman who married experienced a form of legal death under the doctrine of coverture. The classic definition of coverture was provided by William Blackstone in 1767 when he explained that,

> [b]y marriage, the husband and wife are one person in law: that is, the very being or legal existence of the woman is suspended during the marriage, or at least is incorporated and consolidated into that of the husband; under whose wing, protection, and *cover*, she performs every thing; and is therefore called in our law-French a *feme-covert* … and her condition during her marriage is called her *coverture* … For this reason, a man cannot grant anything to his wife, or enter into covenant with her: for the grant would be to suppose her separate existence; and to covenant with her, would be only to covenant with himself.[1]

As a result of coverture, a married woman lost all legal agency.[2] She was often classified with infants, imbeciles and lunatics in terms of her legal status, but in fact her legal rights were even more limited as she was denied ownership of most of her property, while infants or lunatics could own property even if they were unable to manage it.[3]

[1] W Blackstone, *Commentaries on the Laws of England*, vol 1 (Chicago, University of Chicago Press facsimile, 1979, originally published 1765) 430–31. Carolyn Steedman explains that Blackstone's version of coverture was relatively unknown at the time he wrote, as magistrates and justices of the peace routinely dealt with legal disputes involving married women without using the term or affirming the strict form of legal death Blackstone posited: 'Blackstone and Women' in A Page and W Prest (eds), *Blackstone and His Critics* (Oxford, Hart Publishing, 2018).

[2] A married woman did have a remainder interest in real property she brought to her marriage in the event she survived her husband, but if he had sold the property during the marriage and purchased other property, real or personal, she lost her remainder interest: J Baker, *An Introduction to English Legal History*, 4th edn (London, Butterworths, 2002) 484–87.

[3] Women lost title to all personal property upon marriage, and lost control over real property during their coverture. They also had no claim to real or personal property acquired during the marriage, even if it was acquired with the proceeds from the sale of a wife's real estate. Infants and lunatics, however, were not limited in their ownership of any kind of property (unless of course they were married women) although they had guardians or trustees to manage their property: ibid.

Worse, infants or lunatics had guardians who operated under a fiduciary standard in managing their affairs, while a wife had only her husband to protect her and he had no fiduciary duty whatsoever toward her person or her property.[4]

Blackstone's image of the husband providing cover and protection for the wife, like a mother bird providing for her nestlings, is quite compelling.[5] Yet for many women, coverture was anything but benign – it was often suffocating and deadly. And Blackstone's claim that the law of coverture shows that women are the *favourites* of the English law can hardly be taken seriously.[6] Comparing the benign image of the mother bird to the realities of women's legal death calls for a closer examination of Blackstone's defence of women's legal status and its true effects on those who experienced it.

Blackstone's metaphor of the wing is an unusual choice given the many metaphoric and literal meanings of the term coverture he could have used, which simply translated means the state of being covered. In addition to a protective wing, a cover can be a lid, such as the lid of a coffin; it can be a material covering, such as a shroud or a winding sheet; it can be a disguise, such as a hijab or veil that allows people to pass undercover; it can be a narrative that explains certain outcomes, such as a cover story or an alibi; it can be a barrier to prevent speech or action, such as a gag or a straitjacket; it can be a shield to keep dirty secrets buried, such as a manhole cover. Lawmakers, who were entirely men, not surprisingly embraced the benign meaning of coverture as shelter rather than the smothering pillow Othello used to kill Desdemona. Like a cover story, coverture provided an excuse for women's oppression and legal death, the appropriation of their labour and the theft of their intellects.

In this chapter I explore the similarities between death and coverture through four effects: the silencing, binding, entombing and disembodiment that married women experienced when their husbands did not adhere to the Blackstonian ideal of the protective wing. By examining the imagery of death through the writings of women experiencing the bleak effects of coverture, and the situations of nineteenth-century wives caught up in the legal system, we get a far more benighted view of women's legal status than that offered by Blackstone.

II. The Legal Death of Coverture

As Blackstone explained, in exchange for a legal right to financial support, a wife gave up her property and autonomy to her husband when she consented to marry. A married woman could not own personal property during her marriage, could not manage real property brought to her marriage, nor could she enter into contracts, sue or be sued,

[4] Husbands had no fiduciary duty even though the husband's relationship was called a guardianship. As John Baker explained, 'Like wardship in chivalry, … the guardianship of a wife by her husband was not subject to judicial review': ibid 484.

[5] The wing metaphor was perhaps more acceptable than the thirteenth century's version by Bracton that the wife was 'under her husband's rod': Bracton, *On the Law and Customs of England*, vol 4 (Cambridge, Belknap, 1968, trans, revisions, notes by S Thorne, originally published c 1235) 287.

[6] Blackstone wrote that 'These are the chief legal effects of marriage during the coverture; upon which we may observe, that even the disabilities which the wife lies under are for the most part intended for her protection and benefit: so great a favourite is the female sex of the laws of England': (n 1) I-433.

make a will, open a bank account or hire a lawyer.[7] In practice, however, many wives did precisely those things. Abigail Adams wrote a will.[8] Caroline Norton had accounts at her bankers where she deposited the earnings from her literary writings.[9] Emily Westmeath signed a contract with her husband and trustees to provide a settlement for her daughter.[10] Elizabeth Packard had a lawyer defend her in court against her husband's allegation of insanity under a *habeas corpus* petition.[11] Yet despite these actions, all of these women did so in a state of legal uncertainty, and either with the permission of their husbands or, as they learned to their dismay, against the wishes of their husbands whose superior legal rights often nullified their actions.

A small percentage of elite women had limited options to protect their property, options that did not exist for their working- or middling-class sisters. If their fathers or brothers had the foresight, they might establish separate trusts prior to their marriages that would grant the woman limited access to wealth through male trustees within their own families.[12] In the absence of a separate trust, married women could not carry on their independent businesses or purchase necessaries without doing so on their husbands' account or without a male friend acting on their behalf.[13] And if their husbands decided not to pay their wives' debts, creditors often had a very difficult time recovering from either party, as the wife had no legal agency to enter into credit relations, and a husband could claim that his wife had acted without his permission in racking up debts, thus escaping their financial responsibilities and reducing the likelihood that credit would be extended for a wife's needs.[14]

As marriages broke down, some couples entered into private separation agreements with trustees and guarantors who had the legal capacity to sue on behalf of the wife if the husband failed to uphold his agreement to pay maintenance or provide pin money.[15] But these deeds were vulnerable to manipulation by husbands or their lawyers as both Emily Westmeath and Caroline Norton learned. And under the control of the long-serving Lord Eldon, the Court of Chancery would not enforce many non-economic terms of private separation agreements, such as terms regarding custody of children or promises not to sue for restitution of conjugal rights.[16]

[7] Baker (n 2) 483–89.

[8] Will of Abigail Adams, 18 January 1816. From founders.archives.gov/documents/Adams/99-03-02-3025.

[9] C Norton, *Letter to the Queen on Lord Chancellor Cranworth's Marriage and Divorce Bill*, 3rd edn (London, Longman Brown, 1855) 82.

[10] L Stone, *Broken Lives: Separation and Divorce in England, 1660–1857* (Oxford, Oxford University Press, 1993) 291.

[11] E Packard, *Marital Power Exemplified* (Chicago, Clark & Co, 1870) 88.

[12] Mary Beard argued in the 1940s that married women were not as badly off as Blackstone's description of coverture might suggest because he was referring only to legal and not equitable rights. See M Beard, *Women as Force in History* (New York, MacMillan, 1946). Much work since, however, has shown the narrow class of women who could protect their property through separate trusts in equity. And even if they had separate trusts, their ability to exercise full control would be limited to whether the male trustees approved or not: see S Staves, *Married Women's Separate Property in England, 1660–1833* (Cambridge, Harvard University Press, 1990).

[13] Baker (n 2) 487–89.

[14] ibid.

[15] Staves (n 12) 162–95. This happened to Caroline Norton whose husband refused to pay her maintenance and then was able to shirk paying her creditors: see Norton (n 9) 86–89.

[16] *Lord St John v Lady St John* (1805) 11 Ves Jr 525; 32 ER 1192; *Westmeath v Westmeath* (1821) Jac Rep 126; 37 ER 797; *Westmeath v Westmeath* (1827) 2 Hagg Ecc (Supp) 61; 162 ER 987.

Until 1858, a wife could not obtain a divorce with the right to remarry except through a Private Act of Parliament, and only upon a showing of adultery aggravated by bigamy or incest. Over the previous 250 years, only four wives received a Parliamentary divorce and were returned to *feme sole* status. A wife could obtain a divorce *a mensa et thoro* from the ecclesiastical court which allowed her to live on her own, with a right to alimony, but the ecclesiastical courts had no authority to enforce the alimony order.[17] An alimony order also gave her no control over marital assets or property she might have brought to the marriage; it simply imposed an obligation on her husband to honour his legal obligation of support. Although the law changed somewhat in 1858 with the creation of the civil Divorce Court, the standard for divorce remained just as difficult for wives until well into the twentieth century and it is hard to speak of meaningful change for the majority of wives until the end of the twentieth century.[18] Getting husbands to pay support could be quite a challenge even while husbands were readily allowed to enforce legal rights to their wives' property and labour.

The plight of Elizabeth Kimbell is illustrative of the divergence between the legal logic and the lived experiences of many wives under coverture. Elizabeth lived with her husband Thomas for eight years after their marriage in 1840 during which they carried on a jewellery business. But in 1848 Thomas turned her out of the house and began cohabiting with a woman named Catherine Grace. Elizabeth brought suit in the London Consistory Court for restitution of conjugal rights in which she obtained a decree ordering him to take her home. But Thomas refused to oust Catherine Grace or support his legal wife. Elizabeth then sued to enforce the decree and Thomas was sentenced to imprisonment in 1850. Shortly before going to prison, he made over all his interest in the house and business to Catherine Grace, including any property Elizabeth brought to the marriage. He even put Catherine Grace's name over the door of their shop. After cooling his heels in prison for four months, Thomas was released on undertaking to obey the decree of the court. Forced to live up to his legal obligation to support his wife in exchange for the property she brought to the marriage, he took a single unfurnished room for Elizabeth and then returned home to resume cohabitation with Catherine Grace. Elizabeth subsequently sued for a divorce *a mensa et thoro* in the Consistory Court on the basis of his adultery, which she received in 1855, but no alimony order was made since he had relinquished title of his property to his unmarried *feme sole* mistress. Seven years later, after she had supported herself and acquired furniture for two rooms, Elizabeth sought a protective order for property under section 21 of the 1857 Divorce Act[19] on the grounds that her husband had deserted her and she needed to be restored to *feme sole* status so he could not seize the property she had acquired since he stopped supporting her.[20] But the property order was denied because Thomas had not met the legal grounds of desertion since he had provided her all that he was legally obligated to

[17] Staves (n 12) 18.

[18] Although the grounds for divorce were equalised in 1923, allowing wives to obtain a full divorce with a right to remarry on the grounds of a husband's adultery, it was 1937 before a divorce would be allowed for any grounds other than adultery, such as cruelty or desertion.

[19] Matrimonial Causes Act 1857 (20 & 21 Vict c 85).

[20] See pleadings in Supreme Court of Judicature, 'Divorce Court File: K24. Appellant: Elizabeth Kimbell wife of Thomas Kimbell. Type: Wife's petition for protection of earnings [Prot]' (Reference: J 77/31/K24, The National Archives, Kew, 1862).

provide: rent on her unfurnished room. Only if he had denied her all financial support and was out of the jurisdiction would she be entitled to a return to *feme sole* status to enable her to have independent financial control over her life or her earnings. Unable to obtain a divorce and unwanted at home, Elizabeth was trapped.[21]

Elizabeth's story is not unusual, although few deserted wives had the financial wherewithal to sue their husbands in multiple courts as she did. After doing everything she could to make her husband comply with his legal obligation of support, and after having lost all the property she brought to the marriage and the equity they had acquired in jointly building their business, Elizabeth could get nothing from her husband except the rent for a single unfurnished room and, after nearly 15 years of legal struggles, she could not protect her earnings if he asserted the rights given him by the law of coverture. Even if a protective order had been granted, Elizabeth would have received nothing from her marriage, and only the right to begin anew without the threat of her husband's appropriation of future property. On the other hand, Thomas was able to retain all of Elizabeth's property, including the proceeds from her labour during the eight years they cohabited and worked together, he avoided virtually all obligations to his legal wife, and he could shield himself from future obligations by transferring his property to his mistress who was not legally incapacitated because she did not do the respectable thing and marry.[22] It was simple for a husband, who chose not to offer the protective wing to his wife, to avoid his legal obligations; it was virtually impossible for a wife to demand that protection.

The laws of coverture began to change after 1858 when wives who received a divorce *a vinculo*, judicial separation or annulment, as well as wives who could prove desertion, were returned to *feme sole* status. In 1870, married women received limited control over their wages and small inheritances, and in 1882 they received rights to property they brought to the marriage, earned, or inherited during the marriage.[23] Yet wives would not have equal rights to custody and education of their children, to control over marital property earned during the marriage or the right to determine their own domicile until late in the twentieth century. No-fault divorce was also a late comer to the law. In the nineteenth century, wives like Elizabeth Kimball had very few legal options.

Coverture was both a legal reality and a social construct about the appropriate roles of men and women. Male power lay in controlling the marital property, the family's domicile and the labour and expectations of dependants. Women who suffered legal death upon marriage learned quickly that they had given up their legal autonomy, property and rights for a protective wing that was insecure and vulnerable to the husband's whim. The legal right to support, for which she had traded all her rights, was a cover

[21] Perhaps Elizabeth could have sought a judicial separation in the new divorce court on the grounds of Thomas' adultery, but since they were already living apart under the ecclesiastical divorce *a mensa et thoro*, it is unclear what grounds she would have, which means she was limited to the financial remedies of the earlier ecclesiastical divorce, which did not entail a return to feme sole status.

[22] Ironically, by giving his property to Catherine Grace to avoid Elizabeth getting any, he made himself vulnerable to the former's demands. He could not later decide he wanted control back. A feme sole who controlled property could not be forced to give it up unless she made the supreme mistake of marrying, a fate foreclosed to Catherine Grace since Thomas was already married to Elizabeth.

[23] See Married Women's Property Act 1870 (33 & 34 Vict c 93); Married Women's Property Act 1882 (45 & 46 Vict c 75).

that frequently disappeared, was torn, and was protective only if a husband willingly chose to extend it.

In 1735, 30 years before Blackstone's *Commentaries*, Sarah Chapone published her pamphlet entitled *The Hardships of the English Laws in Relation to Wives*, pointing out the injustices of a law that gave all power to the husband and none to the wife to demand her husband's protection and support. Chapone warned unmarried women to understand the consequences of marriage, else they risked becoming legally dead. Calling it the law of 'annihilation', she powerfully connected the legal death of coverture with the very literal deaths that women experienced when the law failed to police the salutary bargain a wife made when she gave up her property and her autonomy in exchange for a husband's protective wing.

> But if after all, these Representations should not be thought worthy the Consideration of the Legislature, or if they should be considered, and we should yet fail of obtaining any Relief; either because the Legislature cannot find proper Means, or wants the Inclination to give it; there is still one Part of my Sex, who may receive some Advantage from them; namely, the Unmarried, to whom I now Address myself, entreating them to consider the Hazards they run, when they venture an Alliance with the other Sex, who were designed by Nature for their *Counter-parts*, but who have taken upon themselves to be the *whole*, insomuch that they have voted us *Dead in Law*, except in criminal Causes. They do us indeed the Favour to consider us as real Persons, when they think fit to *burn* or *hang* us: This is *incorporating* with a Vengeance! *They swallowed us up quick, when they were so wrathfully displeased at us!*
>
> But God be thanked, I have an Husband who lets me be *alive*, and gives me leave to be *some Body*, and to tell other People what I think they are.
>
> I am persuaded there are many Wives in *England*, who by the Favour of their Husbands, are still in a State of *Existence:* And am also sensible, that some Wives have so little Apprehension of this Law of *Annihilation*, that they are in Fact the *freer* Agents of the two. But at Present I am not enquiring into Facts, I am reporting what I take to be Law, in Order to have the Hardships of it known at least, that if they can't be amended, they may be avoided, by making Women more cautious, how they deliver themselves into the Hands of a Man, *lest he bring them to nothing.*[24]

Chapone's exhortation fell on deaf ears as it was nearly 200 years before many of the legal incapacities of coverture she critiqued were finally lifted. In the interval, many women criticised coverture as being not a life-giving or protected status, but a deadly one.

III. The Many Deaths of Coverture

A. Silence in the Courtroom: The Suppression of Women's Voices

Although women were often depicted as chattering gossips, their voices were notably silenced once they became *femes covert*. In court they could not testify in cases of alleged adultery, could not bring libel suits in their own names and were prevented

[24] S Chapone, *The Hardships of the English Laws in Relation to Wives* (London, Bowyer, 1735) 51–52 (emphasis in original).

from speaking under the doctrine of spousal immunity.[25] Because they could not enter into contracts or be sued, they could not speak in court as legally autonomous persons. Especially in disputes against their husbands, they often could not testify nor defend themselves.[26] The silencing of their voices left them vulnerable to being defined by others, especially their husbands.

The debilitating effect of this exclusion was made very public in the life of Caroline Norton. Caroline was the middle daughter of Thomas Sheridan, the son of the Irish playwright and Whig politician, Richard Brinsley Sheridan. Caroline, born in 1808, and her two sisters lost their father during childhood, which left the family nearly penniless. But through an arrangement by Prince Frederick, the Duke of York, the dependent family lived at Hampton Court Palace in a *grace and favour* apartment for many years. The three sisters, often referred to as the three 'Graces', were able to frequent fashionable society and Caroline's two sisters, Helen and Georgiana, both married into the peerage. Caroline's marital adventure was far less fortunate. She married George Norton, a barrister and MP for Guildford and the younger brother of the third Baron Grantley. It was a bad match. Norton was jealous and possessive, given to drink, unsuccessful as a barrister and completely overshadowed by his brilliant and beautiful wife.[27] Almost immediately after their marriage in 1827 he pressured her to use her social connections to find him a position in government. In 1831 she eventually landed him a post as a police magistrate through her friendship with William Lamb, 2nd Viscount Melbourne, who was Home Secretary at the time. But the job was not prestigious or lucrative enough for George who berated her for having brought no wealth to the marriage and who beat her when he was drunk.

As their marriage quickly deteriorated, George demanded of Caroline that she use her influence to further his career by encouraging her friendship with Lord Melbourne who became Prime Minister in 1834, and again from 1835–41. In 1836, when Caroline was not only unsuccessful at securing him a more lucrative position, but also left him because of his violence and drunkenness, George sued Lord Melbourne for criminal conversation, demanding £10,000. After a nine-day politically tinged trial, the jury returned a verdict of not guilty, but Melbourne was nonetheless encouraged to relinquish his friendship with Caroline, especially as the elder statesman was taking on an outsize role mentoring the new young Queen Victoria.[28] The evidence of adultery was so lacking that the jury arrived at its verdict without requiring evidence from any of Lord Melbourne's witnesses and without leaving the jury box.[29]

[25] Until 1853 wives were deemed incompetent to give evidence for or against a husband, but that changed with the passage of the Evidence Amendment Act 1853 which provided that a spouse was competent but could not be compelled to testify against a spouse: (16 & 17 Vict c 83).

[26] They could bring charges of abuse against husbands, but most often there needed corroboration before judges would take a wife's word in court. In civil suits against their husbands, they could not speak: E Coke, *Commentaries Upon Littleton*, 18th edn (London, Clarke, Pheney & Brooke, 1823) 6b, 243.

[27] George Meredith's novel *Diana of the Crossways* (published in 1885) was based on Caroline Norton's life, involving a brilliant and artistic woman tethered to a weak-minded, jealous, and overbearing brute of a husband. See also J Perkin, *Women and Marriage in Nineteenth-Century England* (Chicago, Lyceum Books, 1989); A Chedzoy, *A Scandalous Woman: The Story of Caroline Norton* (London, Allison & Busby, 1992).

[28] See D Cecil, *Melbourne* (New York, Random House, 1979).

[29] Norton (n 9) 67.

Two aspects of the trial were particularly upsetting to Caroline. First, George had accused his own wife of committing adultery and, although the claim was for damages as a result of debauching his wife, George's allegations and the law of coverture gave no agency and no voice to Caroline. She was not permitted to act as a witness nor give testimony in court. The criminal conversation tort was premised on a husband's proprietary interest in his wife's body and his sexual access to her. The suit was, although far more salacious, not juridically different from a case of trespass to chattel. And the chattel never had a voice in court. Second, she could not escape having her intimate behaviour reduced to a political battle between her Tory husband and his backers and the Whig Prime Minister. Thirty years earlier Emily Westmeath's husband had threatened to sue another Prime Minister, the Duke of Wellington, in criminal conversation, egged on by the Duke's political rivals.[30] Although politics and sex scandals may go hand-in-hand, the law of coverture that silenced the wife in court made it painfully clear that a man's proprietary rights in his wife's sexuality had economic and political value precisely because the wife had no voice to defend herself.

In the 1850s, as Parliament was debating the Divorce Act that would create a civil divorce and matrimonial causes court, the embarrassing criminal conversation action was discussed. As illustrated in *Norton v Melbourne*, it relied on testimony of servants who were often paid to perjure themselves in the name of vindicating a husband's proprietary rights in his wife's chastity. It was the silencing more than the monetising that bothered Caroline, however. Even after the jury vindicated her, she had no venue to speak her experiences. She could not speak in court to defend herself, she could not sue her husband for defaming her, and she was pressured by Lord Melbourne to remain silent to protect his political career. For nearly 20 years she remained quiet. It was not until 1855, after Melbourne's death, that she published her critique of the case in a lengthy pamphlet entitled *A Letter to the Queen on Lord Chancellor Cranworth's Marriage and Divorce Bill*.

In her pamphlet, Caroline critiqued the law of criminal conversation for silencing the wife and providing her no forum to speak her truth.

> After the action against Lord Melbourne (in which, according to the preposterous English code, I could have *no personal defence*, nor any means of showing how I had been treated as a wife): I consulted counsel whether *I* could not now divorce my husband: whether a divorce 'by reason of cruelty' might not be pleaded for me; and I laid before my lawyers the many instances of violence, injustice, and ill-usage, of which the trial was but the crowning example. … I was an ENGLISH WIFE, and for me there was no possibility of redress. The answer was always the same. The LAW 'Have I no remedy?' – 'No remedy in LAW. The LAW can do nothing for you: your case is one of singular, of incredible hardship; but there is no possible way in which the LAW could assist you.'[31]

Ironically, Caroline's refusal to be silent by publishing a critique of the law of child custody in 1836 led to additional silencing in court. The publisher of the *British and Foreign Quarterly Review* had claimed that Caroline was the author of a radical article entitled 'On the Grievances of Woman'. The publication also called her a 'she-devil' and

[30] Stone (n 10) 310.
[31] Norton (n 9) 70.

a 'she-beast'.[32] But when she asked her solicitor if she could sue the publication in libel, she was informed that

> being a married woman, I could not prosecute of myself; that my husband must prosecute: my husband – who had assailed me with every libel in his power! There could be no prosecution: and I was left to study the grotesque anomaly in law of having my defence made *necessary*, – and made *impossible*, – by the same person.[33]

The law of coverture treated a wife's reputation as it did her chastity, as a proprietary right belonging to the husband. Thus, a wife who was libelled could not defend herself or sue for damages without being represented by her husband. And if the husband encouraged the libel, she had no recourse in a court of law. The law that silenced a woman to protect a man's speech is hard to square with Blackstone's claim that women are the favourites of the law.

Moreover, women whose husbands legally injured them, or refused to defend them, were not the only wives silenced in court. Married women could not sue for assaults committed against them because only their husbands 'spoke' for them. Sarah Arlett was physically injured by Thomas Witley, a tailor of Wardrobe Place, but she was unable to commence proceedings to recover for her injuries because her husband, Benjamin, had deserted her 12 years earlier.[34] Similarly, Elizabeth Holland sought a property order to enable her to sue George Johnson and George Payne for their assaults upon her after her husband Alfred had deserted five years earlier.[35] Married women who lived without the protection of their husbands were particularly vulnerable to violence by other men who knew they could not bring civil suit to defend their rights in any court.

Thanks in part to the writings of Caroline Norton, the 1857 Divorce Act granted Sarah Arlett and Elizabeth Holland a court where they could voice their complaints. Each were returned to *feme sole* status so they could sue on their own behalf for their physical injuries. But until such a remedy existed, only a husband could sue for his wife's bodily harm and, not surprisingly, if he was uninterested in his wife's wellbeing, he would not defend her. Not all courts were entirely barred to wives, as they often sued articles of the peace against violent husbands or they could seek relief in the ecclesiastical courts if their husbands were profligate or cruel.[36] But these remedies were often wholly inadequate, as Elizabeth Kimbell learned. Coverture made it very difficult for average women to use the law to enforce any of their rights against husbands who did not willingly choose to extend a protective wing.

The silencing of married women in courts of law was a direct result of the logic of coverture which assumed that a husband could and would adequately represent his wife in legal matters. Where their interests aligned, coverture worked. But when they did

[32] ibid 77.

[33] ibid.

[34] The Supreme Court of Judicature, 'Divorce Court File: A26. Appellant: Sarah Arlett, wife of Benjamin Arlett. Type: Wife's petition for protection of earnings [Prot]' (Reference: J77/1/A26, The National Archives, Kew 1860).

[35] Supreme Court of Judicature, 'Divorce Court File: H58. Appellant: Elizabeth Holland. Respondent: Alfred Garner Holland. Type: Wife's petition [wx].' (Reference: J77/24/H58, The National Archives Kew, 1859).

[36] See E Foyster, *Marital Violence: An English Family History, 1660–1857* (Cambridge, Cambridge University Press, 2005).

not align, wives had no voice to speak their experiences. And lacking any fiduciary duty toward a wife's property or physical well-being, and often having interests adverse to hers, husbands had no obligation to protect their wives' interests. They often refused to extend that protective wing in order to exploit their own power. The silence imposed on wives interred them in a legal tomb.

B. The Ties that Bind: The Winding Sheet of Marriage

Nineteenth-century Anglican marriage vows, unlike the vows of Catholics, Quakers or Jews, stated that the wife and husband promise 'to have and to hold, in sickness and in health', til death do them part. The term 'to hold' invokes an image of wrapping one's arms around another, holding onto them, protecting and also constraining them. Under the unequal laws of coverture, however, the marriage bond is easily seen as a bond on the wife and not the husband. The ties that bind the wife to the husband, the bond of holy matrimony and the bounden obligation of the wife to serve her husband reinforce the marital relationship as one of servitude. She is expected to love, honour and obey her husband. She is expected to labour to provide a comfortable home and to forsake all others. Her failure to do so can make her liable to divorce. He is expected to endow her with his worldly goods and forsake all others, but his failure to do so has no consequences. He is not bound.

Caroline Norton invoked a whimsical image of the different bonds of husband and wife:

> Marriage is, according to the great law authorities in and out of Parliament, not a religious bond, but a civil contract. The religious vow, taken by the man in marriage, is merely to give him civil rights over the woman 'sworn in' as his special wife. She is bound to afford him every assistance; to be 'true till death'; to be obedient to his will; and to 'condone' his guilty pleasures – and *he* is bound to nothing at all, except a nominal union, much resembling in its principle that singular invention, the Russian 'Drosky', in which we see one horse harnessed within shafts, and drawing the weight of the carriage, and the other caracoling and frisking in the most light agreeable and ornamental manner by its side, but bearing no part of the restraint imposed.[37]

To Caroline, the wife is bound to the husband and her labour serves him; the husband dictates the terms of the wife's servitude and is her master, bound to no duties.

Like the bonds of a parent over a child or a master over a servant, a husband's control entitled him to the wages of his wife; he could enter into a contract with her employer for her labour and collect her wages directly. Wives worked for their husbands, either directly or indirectly. As Norton explained:

> An English wife cannot legally claim her own earnings. Whether wages for manual labour, or payment for intellectual exertion, whether she weed potatoes, or keep a school, her salary is *the husband's*; and he could compel a second payment, and treat the first as void, if paid to the wife without his sanction.[38]

[37] Norton (n 9) 46–47.
[38] ibid 9.

Just as a wife could not bind herself to labour for another, she could not bind the family's financial resources. Her signature meant nothing, whether between herself and her husband, or between herself and creditors. Coverture kept married women interred in a private sphere where they lacked economic agency. If they bought food, they either paid cash or purchased on their husband's credit. If they had a marital spat, their husbands could advertise that they would no longer cover their wives' debts. A creditor who extended credit to such a wife did so at his peril.[39] Since husbands took control over a wife's personal property, she had no resources to pledge credit, and unless her husband gave her cash to purchase necessaries, she might starve. The benign wing of the protective bird could provide no relief for a married woman with no ability to enter into any financial transactions – her word was not her bond, and her bond was legally null.[40]

Caroline Norton discovered her economic handicap when her mother died, leaving her a small annuity, carefully settled out of George's reach. George had already appropriated all personal property she brought to the marriage and all property she acquired or purchased with money from her writings, and he took the interest off the portion bequeathed to her by her father. Then, he discontinued the allowance he had agreed to pay her in a private separation agreement on the grounds that she no longer needed the money since she had her mother's annuity. Not only was she unable to make him pay her what he had agreed to pay her, her creditors could not collect against him either.[41] George refused to pay her debts claiming that they were unenforceable because they were taken by a wife who had no legal existence. Frustrated at her financial helplessness, she complained:

> In consequence of this rule of my 'non-existence,' Mr Thrupp, and the group of creditors, can claim payment from *no one*. They cannot sue the 'non-existent' married woman; the husband cannot *contract* with the 'non-existent' married woman; and the 'non-existent' married woman cannot be compelled to pay, if she refuses to discharge the debt.[42]

She went on:

> I am *not* divorced, and I cannot divorce my husband; yet I can establish no legal claim upon him, nor upon any living human being! My reputation, my property, my happiness, are irrevocably in the power of this slanderer on false grounds; this rapacious defender of his right to evade written bonds. I cannot release myself. I exist and I suffer; but the law denies my existence.[43]

Caroline discovered that she was bound with legal incapacities that thwarted her economic decisions. She could not control her own earnings or her legacies unless the latter were settled out of his reach, but if they were available for her then his obligation of support ended because she had independent resources. If she was extended credit on the basis of the husband's agreed-upon support, neither she nor her husband would be bound to repay, thus guaranteeing no creditor would be willing to provide goods or services on credit to a separated wife.

[39] Baker (n 2) 488.
[40] ibid 487–89.
[41] *Thrupp v Norton* (1853) 6 Cty Cts Chron 113.
[42] Norton (n 9) 87.
[43] ibid 96.

Sarah Chapone recognised the financial constraints of coverture that required desperate married women to transact their necessary business in a grey economy, which opened them up to further exploitation either by husbands, friends or creditors.

> The last Resource in such a Case is, to transact her Business in another's Name. But it is very difficult to find a Friend generous enough to involve himself in the intricate Affairs of an helpless undone Woman, who may be commanded from the Place and Employment, at the Pleasure of her Lord and Master, against whose Injunctions she can make no Appeal. The most that her Friends can do, is to afford her a small Pittance by Stealth in the Nature of an Alms, by which she may be sometimes relieved, but never provided for, unless they were in Condition to settle an Estate in Trustees Hands for her Use, which (considering the Power the Husband has over her Person) he may soon convert to his own. Hence it appears, that Wives have no Property neither in their intellectual, or personal Abilities, nor in their Fortunes.[44]

Working wives were also in a bind when they were able to acquire enough money to squirrel it away. George went to Caroline's bankers and withdrew all of her savings since the bankers could not resist the legal claims of a husband. He also successfully seized her earnings from her publishers, leaving her dependent on friends and family, or on informal credit for her support. Sarah Gulliver invested her savings in a friend's name fearing her husband Joseph would seize it, but the friend betrayed her confidence and appropriated the whole of the money to his own use.[45] She had no legal remedy against him for theft because her husband had deserted her and the courthouse door was barred to a married woman.

The excuse often given for failing to reform the laws of coverture was that 'it is much better one or two women should suffer unjustly, than that the authority of husbands should be doubted'.[46] Yet for women whose husbands were not abusive cads like George Norton, but were merely hapless labourers who left their wives and children to escape creditors, coverture condemned them to a state of legal non-existence that made it very difficult to support themselves and their children. Because wives were expected to remain in the domestic sphere and not participate in the economic or political world, those who had no choice but to labour for their own support did so in a straitjacket. Mary Byrne was a successful Dublin hotel owner prior to her marriage to Bernard, one of her employees. Immediately upon the marriage he stopped working and in a little over a year had spent all her savings and her earnings, leaving her unable to pay her creditors. After he had run through her money and left her, it took her over three years to repay her debts from before her marriage.[47] Like Mary, I suspect Caroline Norton would have happily paid off her debts and engaged in paid work if she could be free of George's malicious interference.

[44] Chapone (n 24) 10–11.

[45] Supreme Court of Judicature, 'Divorce Court File: H58. Appellant: Elizabeth Holland. Respondent: Alfred Garner Holland. Type: Wife's petition [wx].' (Reference: J 77/24/H58, The National Archives Kew 1859).

[46] Norton (n 9) 105.

[47] Supreme Court of Judicature, 'Divorce Court File: B233. Appellant: Mary Byrne wife of Bernard Byrne. Type: Wife's petition for protection of earnings [Prot].' (Reference: J77/7/B233, The National Archives Kew, 1865).

To be bound was to be an object of property, not a subject in control. Norton argued that wives were not like other objects of property, but her argument belies the truth of a wife's legal situation.

> A man does not purchase a wife as he would buy a fine blood-mare, or a hound, to continue a race of animals and then be got rid of, her offspring remaining his undoubted and undisputed property. He chooses a companion; a thinking, acting, reflecting being; one, who, if a mother, is the mother of immortal souls, and accountable to God for the trust. That man may afterwards repent the choice he made and become discontented with it, but his discontent does not transform the woman into a cipher or a slave: it does not reverse and alter every right and purpose of her existence: it does not, or rather it *ought not*, to change her from a wife and mother into a thing as helpless, useless, and blighted, as a scathed tree. She can make no other choice; she can form no other tie; it is a sin if she even allow her secret heart to wander to another object; SHE belongs (parted though she be) to *him* and to his children: – Do neither then belong to *her*?[48]

To answer, no – nothing belonged to her; she had no property to pledge and no authority to bind her labour. Such was the winding sheet of marriage. The unbound husband could appropriate his wife's labour and property, leaving her no remedy against him because the law made him her master; the deserting husband could seize his wife's property and leave her incapacitated, still bound but to no one.

C. The Home as Sepulchre: Immured in the Domestic Sphere

Many wives faced physical interment when they married, as their husbands dictated their domicile, locked them in attics or confined them to asylums. Certainly, most wives were not literally imprisoned by their husbands, but the law permitted them to establish where their wives would live, and until the late nineteenth century husbands could commit their wives to asylums solely on their own word.[49] Elizabeth Ware Packard was an American wife who wrote about being physically confined by her husband in a private asylum.[50] Mary Wollstonecraft's unfinished novel *Maria: Or the Wrongs of Woman* takes place in an asylum where an innocent wife is committed by a husband seeking control over her property. And other women wrote of being interred in the home by husbands who often believed that their control over their wives' labour and domicile translated to control over their bodies and souls.[51]

Incarceration in a private asylum was a fate facing many wives whose husbands wanted them out of the way. Elizabeth Packard was just such a wife. Elizabeth was born in 1816 in Ware, Massachusetts and married the Calvinist minister Theophilus Packard

[48] C Norton, *Observations on the Natural Claim of the Mother to the Custody of her Children* (London, Ridgeway & Sons, 1837) 64–65.

[49] See, eg, Act of Feb 15 1851, § 10, 1851 Ill Laws 96, 98.

[50] B Sapinsley, *The Private War of Mrs Packard* (New York, Paragon House, 1991); L Carlisle, *Elizabeth Packard: A Noble Fight* (Champaign, University of Illinois Press, 2010).

[51] See E Foyster, 'At the Limits of Liberty: Married Women and Confinement in Eighteenth-Century England' (2002) 17 *Continuity and Change* 39.

at the insistence of her parents. They had six children and eventually settled in rural Illinois where her husband served as minister for the local congregation. In 1860, after disagreeing with her husband's religious views, Theophilus had Elizabeth committed to the Jacksonville Insane Asylum where she lived for three years before being released as incurable. She was deemed incurable because she absolutely refused to admit that she was anything but sane, or to alter her religious beliefs. While in the asylum, Packard wrote extensively, detailing the frustration of having everything one said be ignored or misinterpreted. Her insistence that she was not insane was given as evidence that she was; her insistence that she had a right to her own religious views and not to be dictated to by her minister husband was evidence that she was not in her right mind; her rejection of her husband's moral control over her soul was proof positive to the men in her congregation that she was hopelessly incurable. Though not silenced, her words were intentionally misinterpreted by a male audience as evidence of incapacity. For how could a mere woman have independent thoughts? How could a woman chafe under a law that so clearly showed what a favourite she is?

After being released from the asylum, Theophilus locked Elizabeth in their house as he made preparations to leave the state and take her and their children back to Massachusetts where he could find another asylum in which to confine his intransigent wife. But she was able to get a note down to passers-by on the street who alerted friends of her predicament. A *habeas corpus*[52] petition was filed which eventually turned into a five-day trial on the question of her sanity. When the jury came back with a verdict that Elizabeth was completely sane, she returned home to find that Theophilus had emptied their home, packed up the children and moved to Massachusetts. Unable to gain custody of her children or regain any of her property, Elizabeth began a one-woman lobbying tour of state legislatures to encourage better laws for the protection of wives who could be committed to asylums solely on the signatures of their husbands. Elizabeth's campaign resulted in important changes to child custody, married women's property, and confinement laws in numerous states in the US. In 1866, she published a book with the pithy title: *Marital Power Exemplified in Mrs Packard's Trial, and Self-Defence from the Charge of Insanity; or Three Years of Imprisonment for Religious Belief, by the Arbitrary Will of a Husband, with an Appeal to the Government to so Change the Laws as to Protect the Rights of Married Women.*

A householder who gave Elizabeth shelter after her husband deserted her recognised that a husband's control over a wife's domicile could be abused. He recounted to the Kankakee Gazette that

> [a]fter having aided her husband for twenty-one years, by her most indefatigable exertions, to secure for themselves a home, with all its clustering comforts, he, with no cause, except a difference in religious opinions, exiled her from her home, by forcing her into Jacksonville Insane Asylum, where he hoped to immure her for life, or until she would abandon what *he* calls her 'insane notions.'[53]

[52] P Halliday, *Habeas Corpus: From England to Empire* (Cambridge, Harvard University Press, 2010) describes using the great writ in family matters to remove wives from control of husbands starting in the late eighteenth century.

[53] Packard (n 11) 44.

Bertha Mason was immured for life at Thornfield Hall in Charlotte Bronte's novel *Jane Eyre*; Maria was immured for life in a private asylum in Wollstonecraft's novel *Maria*; and Georgina Weldon barely escaped being immured in a private asylum for refusing to consent to her husband's demands that she leave the house he decided he no longer wanted to provide to her.[54]

Even if not subjected to being confined in an asylum, wives could not choose where they would live. After Packard convinced the trustees of the asylum that she was actually sane they instructed the superintendent to release her, but she explained to them the true state of her situation.

> These intelligent men at once endorsed my statements, and became my friends. They offered me my liberty at once, and said that anything I wanted they stood ready to do for me. Mr. Brown, the Chairman, said he saw it was of no use for me to go to my husband; but said they would send me to my children if I wished to go, or to my father in Massachusetts, or they would board me up in Jacksonville. I thanked them for their kind and generous offers; 'but,' said I, 'it is of no use for me to accept of any one of them, for I am still Mr. Packard's wife, and there is no law in America to protect a wife from her husband. I am not safe from him outside these walls, on this continent, unless I flee to Canada; and there, I don't know as a fugitive wife is safe from her husband. The truth is, he is determined to keep me in an Asylum prison as long as I live, if it can be done; and since no law prevents his doing so, I see no way for me but to live and die in this prison.'[55]

She further complained that the confinement made her a prisoner in her own home,

> as there is no law in the State that will allow a married woman the right of a trial against the charge of insanity brought against her by her husband; and God only knows how many innocent wives and mothers my case represents, who have thus lost their liberty for life, by this arbitrary power, unchecked as it is by no law on the Statute book of Illinois.[56]

The private asylums, as described by Mary Wollstonecraft and Elizabeth Packard, proved an important resource to husbands who wanted their wives out of their way. Unscrupulous superintendents who benefitted by accepting wives who were not sufficiently docile at home, especially when their husbands wanted access over their wives' separate property, could often count on the fact that a husband's claim of his wife's insanity was nearly impossible to counter. Elizabeth Packard was lucky in being able to defend herself in court, although even there she was not permitted to testify on her own behalf. Even as the witnesses parsed her behaviour and her religious statements, she was forced into silence. Ironically, Packard was released not because she was actually sane, but because she had been admitted to a public asylum and was therefore being confined at cost to the state. The state asylum trustees had sufficient oversight and a fiduciary duty to the taxpayers to insist that the state's resources were being used properly. Private asylums that would take wives upon payment of room and board by husbands were much harder to supervise. It was Theophilus Packard's greed in wanting to palm off his support obligation onto the state that saved Elizabeth from being, truly, immured for life.

[54] L Lowe, *The Bastilles of England* (London, Crookenden & Co, 1883) 40–42.
[55] Packard (n 11) 7.
[56] ibid 11.

The family home could also become a prison, especially when a husband refused to provide coal for a fire or sufficient food to ward off starvation. In 1735, Sarah Chapone, told the familiar story of

> Mr. *Veezey*, tryed at the *Old Bailey*, where it was proved that he confined his wife for some Years in a Garret, without Fire, proper Cloathing, or any of the Comforts of Life; that he had frequently Horse-whipt her; that her Sufferings were so great and intolerable, that she destroyed her wretched Life by flinging herself out at the Window.
>
> But as there was Bread found in the Room, which, though hard and mouldy, was supposed sufficient to sustain Life; and as it was not thought that he pushed her out at the Window himself, he was acquitted, and that Complaint of her Sufferings served only to instruct Husbands in the full Extent of their despotick Power.[57]

Chapone concluded: 'it appears that Husbands have a more *Afflictive* Power than that of *Life* and *Death*'.[58] So long as a husband provided a roof over her head, whether in an unfurnished room, a private asylum or a gold garret, a wife had no legal grounds to leave. Being immured in an asylum or relegated to an unheated garret were the fate of many wives who had become inconvenient, either because they demanded support or they were conduits of property their husbands sought to control. And for many women who perished in prisons and asylums, the tomb was likely a blessing. Mrs Vezey and Wollstonecraft's Maria perished because the protective wing of their husbands was withdrawn or had become weapons. With no legal supervision, the protective wing became a tomb.

D. Disembodiment of Body and Soul

Wives experienced near complete loss of control over their voices, labour and domicile when they married. They also were unable to control their own bodies and intellects. Wives could not be raped, they could be physically chastised for disobeying their husbands and the products of their labour, both intellectual and reproductive, were denied them. Sara Butler, describing the conjugal debt that spouses owed each other, explained 'All of these legal and moral restrictions put married women in the uncomfortable situation of being, at best, co-owners of their own bodies, at worst, mere property belonging to their husbands.'[59] As in death, coverture gave wives little control over their corporeal or intellectual expression.

Matthew Hale explained that a husband could not be guilty of raping his wife. 'But the husband cannot be guilty of a rape committed by himself upon his lawful wife, for by their mutual matrimonial consent and contract the wife hath given up herself in this kind unto her husband which she cannot retract.'[60] Caroline Norton and Emily Westmeath

[57] Chapone (n 24) 8–9. See also the records of Mrs Vezey's case in The Old Bailey Proceedings Online, 'Trial of Corbet Vezey' (Reference: t17320114-12, Harvard University Library, 14 January 1732) www.oldbaileyonline.org/browse.jsp?id=t17320114-12-defend145&div=t17320114-12.

[58] Chapone (n 24) 9.

[59] S Butler, 'Whose Property? Women's Bodies and Marital Rape' (Medium, 29 September 2020) www.medium.com/the-sundial-acmrs/whose-property-womens-bodies-and-marital-rape-3fefdeb593ee.

[60] M Hale, *Pleas of the Crown*, vol 1 (London, Nutt & Gosling, 1736) 629.

learned the painful way that women's control over their own bodies was at the will of their husbands. A husband's control over his wife's body is one of the last vestiges of coverture to fall. The marital exemption from rape was recognised in England until 1991 when the exemption was finally abolished at common law in the case of *R v R*.[61] In the United States, the marital exemption was gradually abolished starting in the 1970s, but it still persists in differential standards of proof and levels of punishment.[62]

Some husbands used their rights over their wives' bodies and sexuality to pimp their wives, offering up their sexual services to admirers in the upper classes, or to men on the streets in the lower classes. George Norton told Caroline that he would be thankful if she would render whatever services were necessary to convince Lord Melbourne or others to give him a lucrative position in the government. Lord Westmeath and his mother suggested that Emily 'should make use of her prettiness' to attract the Duke of Wellington's interests.[63] Wollstonecraft's fictional Maria was also offered up by her husband to serve the sexual demands of an admirer.[64] With no control over their own bodies, most wives tolerated the sexual aggression of their husbands without expecting any relief from other men or a court of law. As Sarah Chapone wrote:

> By the very Nature of the Marriage Contract, the Husband and Wife acquire a Property in each others Person. Our Laws give the Husband the entire Disposal of the Wife's Person, but she does not seem to retain any Property in his; He may recover Damages of any Man who shall invade his Property in her, but she cannot recover Damage from a Woman, who shall invade her Property in him.[65]

Elizabeth Packard put her lack of control over her body to advantage when her husband had her committed to the Jacksonville Asylum. Knowing that she had no legal control over where she was being sent, she sat down and refused to walk to her destination.

> I told my husband I should not go voluntarily into the Asylum, and leave my six children and my precious babe of eighteen months, without some kind of trial; and that the law of force, brute force, would be the only power that should thus put me there. I then begged of him to handle me gently, if he was determined to force me, as I was easily hurt, and should make no physical resistance. I was soon in the hands of the sheriff, who forced me from my home by ordering two men to carry me to the wagon which took me to the depot.[66]

Elizabeth instructed her keepers how to carry her by interlocking their arms and creating a seat for her. Her resistance made visible to onlookers the extent of a husband's control.

But wives needed more than freedom from sexual assault; they also sought recognition that they had a claim to the product of their reproductive labour – their children. Yet under coverture, a wife had no control over her children. She was entitled only to 'reverence and respect'[67] according to Blackstone, a situation George Norton deftly

[61] *R v R* [1991] UKHL 12, [1992] 1 AC 599.
[62] JE Hasday, 'Contest and Consent: A Legal History of Marital Rape' (2000) 88 *California Law Review* 1373.
[63] Stone (n 10) 300.
[64] M Wollstonecraft, *Maria* (New York, Norton, 1975, originally published in 1798) 110–11.
[65] Chapone (n 24) 15–16.
[66] Packard (n 11) 4.
[67] Blackstone (n 1) 441.

exploited. Shortly after their separation, George absconded with their three sons and hid them in Scotland with relatives, prohibiting them from any contact with their mother. Caroline did not see her boys again until six years later when a riding accident caused the death of one of them and George relented to allow her supervised visitation with the other two after that. Caroline complained that control over the children encouraged a husband to become a tyrant and that the law treated the mother as incapable and inert.

> In the matter of marriage, a girl even of fifteen or sixteen is held to be a capable and responsible being, able to make a choice, to decide on her future destiny, and to bind herself by a voluntary oath to the husband she has chosen. Does she *cease* to be a capable and responsible being after her marriage, that in the matter of Maternal Right she is no more considered than a stock or a stone? Is she, whose responsibility in early youth was so great that the rashness of an hour could bind her for life, transformed in her maturer years into an automaton to be moved only at the will of others? Is she, who was so all-important as a bride, *nothing* as a mother?[68]

Complaining that the '[f]ather's right is absolute and paramount, and can no more be affected by the mother's claim, than if she had no existence',[69] Caroline also published pamphlets on the injustices of mothers having no rights to their children. Numerous Chancery cases supported Blackstone's rule that mothers were entitled only to reverence and respect.[70] And if a husband refused to grant her that small pittance, she had nothing. Although the law was amended in 1839 to allow a wife to *petition* for custody of her children, no Victorian wife was granted custody until 1849 if her husband challenged her.[71] Untold scores of wives lost custody of, or access to, their children by husbands who could use their power over children to force wives to relinquish property rights they might have. George Nugent withheld access to their children Rosa and William in order to influence a private property settlement between himself and his wife; Mary Eleanor Bowes, the Countess of Strathmore, was denied custody of her children by her second husband, Andrew Stoney Bowes, who tried to pressure her into relinquishing control over her vast fortune to him after she had safely settled it out of his control prior to their marriage.[72] Governess Nelly Weeton was denied access to her child by an abusive husband.[73] Custody disputes are often bitter, but the fact that wives had no legal rights to the custody or care of their children made them particularly vulnerable to peevish husbands who wanted access to their wives' property, to punish their wives for some affront, or control over the children in order to control their labour.

Many wives were further alienated from their bodies and their labour as they had no control over what happened to them physically, whether they were forced to endure sexual intercourse or were locked in insane asylums. Control over their bodies and the

[68] Norton (n 48) 63–64.

[69] Norton, *Separation of Mother and Child by the Law of "Custody of Infants" Considered* (London, Roake & Varty, 1838) 3.

[70] *DeManneville v DeManneville* (1804) 10 Ves 52; 32 ER 762; *Ex P Skinner* (1824) 9 Moore 278; *Greenhill v Greenhill* (1836) 1 Curt 462; 163 ER 162; *Re Agar-Ellis* (1883) 24 ChD 317.

[71] *Warde v Warde* (1849) 2 Ph 786; 41 ER 1147. See also DC Wright, 'The Crisis of Child Custody: A History of the Birth of Family Law in England' (2002) 11 *Columbia Journal of Gender & Law* 175.

[72] W Moore, *Wedlock: The True Story of the Disastrous Marriage and Remarkable Divorce of Mary Eleanor Bowes, Countess of Strathmore* (London, Crown Publishing, 2009).

[73] E Hall (ed), *Miss Weeton: Journal of a Governess*, vol 2 (New York, Augustus Kelley, 1969).

fruits of their labour lay entirely with their husbands who could claim damages from other men for interference with their proprietary rights in their wives' services. For Caroline Norton, that control extended even to her intellect and ideas. She complained that the legally 'existent' husband could subpoena her bankers and lay claim to her copyrights because 'the copyrights of my works are *his*, by law: my very soul and brains are not my own!'[74] From the labour over her children to labouring for wages and to her own copyrights, Caroline Norton found that her very essence was not her own. Just as the soul leaves the body at death, many wives felt disembodied during their marriages as they lost control over their bodies, their reproduction, their labour and even their intellectual ideas.

Mrs Packard recounted a conversation she had with the Mayor of Chicago when she sought his protection for her book manuscript, a product of her labour after Theophilus deserted her.

> I fear he may intercept the publication of my book; for you probably know, Sir, he can come either himself, or by proxy, and, with his Sheriff, can demand my manuscript of my printer, and the printer, nor you, Sir, have no legal power to defend it. He can demand it, and burn it, and I am helpless in legal self-defense. For, Sir, my identity was legally lost in his, when I married him, leaving me nothing and nobody in law; and besides, all I have is his in law, and of course no one can prosecute him for taking his own things – my manuscript is his, and entirely at his disposal. I have no right in law even to my own thoughts, either spoken or written – he has even claimed the right to superintend my written thought, as well as post office rights. I can not claim these rights – they are mine only as he grants me them as his gifts to me.[75]

Sarah Chapone also noted that a wife, while not denied her own intellectual abilities, could not exercise them.

> Her intellectual and personal Abilities seem to be her own, since no Pacts can transfer them to another, yet her Husband can prevent her Exertion of them, either for herself or Children, even when he won't do any thing for them himself.[76]

Lacking legal control over their bodies and their minds left wives alienated and helpless. Coverture transformed a free woman into a 'fine blood-mare or hound', a chattel whose bonds and legal incapacities rendered them silent, inert and legally dead.

IV. Conclusion

Under English law, a husband controlled his wife's domicile; he determined what food she was allowed; whether she could work or not; whether she would bear children; whether her body would be prostituted to support him; whether she would have any interaction with her children; whether she could express her opinions. Although most men did not silence and smother their wives to the extent done by George Norton and

[74] Norton (n 9) 82.
[75] Packard (n 11) 50.
[76] Chapone (n 24) 67–68.

Theophilus Packard, these legally extinct wives knew that even what breath they were able to breathe was a gift from their husbands that could be denied them at any time.

A few women, like Caroline Norton, Emily Westmeath, Sarah Chapone and Elizabeth Packard, fought back against the law that dealt them a legal death and, although not always successful, they generated public sympathy and awareness because they wrote about their wrongs. Even if the courts silenced them and so many other wives, their powerful rhetoric of death and annihilation helped bring about legal change. Although their copyrights, intellects and genius were not their own, the legal death they described could not be appropriated or denied. In contemplating the efforts afoot to reconcile English and Scottish marriage law, Caroline expressed her fear of exporting England's suffocating and silencing laws.

> I cannot prophesy whether Lord Cranworth's views, or those of Lords Eldon, Thurlow, and Rosslyn, would preponderate; whether, in the 'assimilation' that would take place, a better mercy to women would be borrowed from portions of the Scotch law, or the Desdemonas of Scotland be smothered by a jealous English legislation.[77]

In the end, the Scottish law prevailed and married women would no longer suffer the legal death these writers experienced as the legal constraints of coverture were gradually abolished over the next century and a half. But Blackstone's metaphor of the protective wing remains a paradox as the law of coverture refused to compel husbands to honour their bargain while it strictly enforced the wife's bargain. Men's refusal to hold other men to account reveals the law of coverture to be a sepulchre more than a benign protective wing.

[77] Norton (n 9) 144.

8

Suicide, Madness and the State: The Tale from Tort

KIT BARKER*

I. Introduction

Any book on life, death and the law must sadly make space for debates about suicide. To date, most of these have been public law ones about the proper role of the state in regulating individuals' decisions to end their lives. They have focused on the question whether citizens owe public duties *to the state* not to kill – or attempt to kill – themselves, or not to encourage, or help others to do so. As things currently stand, most[1] jurisdictions have now decriminalised both the act of suicide itself and attempts to commit it, and the focus of discussion has shifted to the propriety and design of laws which permit suitably qualified medical personnel to assist the ending of life with dignity. Citizens do not (as yet) have a right that the state provide them with the means to die, but they do have a legal liberty to take their own lethal measures, and an increasing number of jurisdictions grant immunities from prosecution to those assisting them on compassionate grounds, within strict parameters designed to ensure that the decision is competent, informed and free of external pressures or undue influence.[2]

The general shift has hence been from a stance of historic disapproval and prohibition to far greater toleration and respect for private choice in the modern day. The transition has nonetheless been neither consistent, nor easy. In England and Wales, Parliament is still struggling to pass voluntary assisted dying (VAD) laws despite the fact that they command overwhelming public support,[3] and the awkward gap is meanwhile

* My thanks to Andrew Fell, Iain Field, Mark Lunney, Jason Neyers and Warren Swain for helpful comments and references. All remaining errors are my own.

[1] It remains a crime in more than 20 countries: United for Global Mental Health, 'Suicide Decriminalisation' www.unitedgmh.org/knowledge-hub/suicide-decriminalisation.

[2] Six Australian states have adopted such laws: see, eg, Voluntary Assisted Dying Act 2022 (NSW). In the US in 2018, six states and the District of Columbia had legalised some form of physician-assisted suicide. A further 23 were considering legislation: H Chang, 'A Brief History of Anglo-Western Suicide: From Legal Wrong to Civil Right' (2018) 46 *Southern University Law Review* 150.

[3] The latest attempt was Baroness Meacher's private Assisted Dying Bill, which passed its second reading in the House of Lords in Oct 2021, but which ran out of time in February 2023. 84 per cent of the British public

having to be plugged by the state relying upon its discretion not to prosecute those who assist a suicide, in sympathetic cases. This not only leaves citizens unclear as to where exactly they stand, but the policy governing the exercise of the discretion ironically expressly excludes from leniency those (doctors) who are in the best position to ensure that people receive the help they need if they are successfully to choose a painless and dignified end.[4]

All of this is public law. The purpose of this chapter, by contrast, is to examine the relationship between the state and suicide through the lens of tort law. It asks when, if ever, the state owes a duty *to its citizens* to take reasonable care to prevent them foreseeably taking their own lives. This is a new question in the grander scale of things and is again not short on controversy, for several reasons. It posits a world in which the state owes a duty to the citizen to stop him or her engaging in an act which, until the latter part of the twentieth century, the citizen was under a public duty *to the state not to commit*. It also contradicts the well-established general rule in most common law jurisdictions that no one – whether private person or state agent – is liable for carelessly failing to prevent, as opposed to actively causing, another person's death – the so called 'omissions rule'. And it superficially frets against the sentiment now expressed in modern VAD laws that voluntary decisions about life and death are private choices into which the state should not poke its paternalistic nose.

Despite this, the state does now have duties to take reasonable care to prevent suicidal behaviour in some cases, and for good reason. This is a function both of the serious risk that the phenomenon poses to the most fundamental of human interests, and of the extensive array of powers that have been accorded to the welfare state for the explicit purpose of protecting vulnerable persons against self-harm. Defining the exact circumstances in which such duties arise, however, remains a challenge outside of certain, core cases in which the individual concerned is a patient in the public health system, a state employee, is held in actual state custody, or has relied upon some specific undertaking of protection given by a state agent. The legal criteria that courts use to determine the duty of care question broadly reflect the background normative concerns about foreseeable risk, control, state power, personal vulnerability and respect for decisional autonomy, but the precise meaning and scope of these concepts is unsettled. Moreover, there are signs, I suggest, that courts may now be placing so much emphasis on the (true) fact that suicide can be an autonomous act, as to overlook the

was cited as supporting reform during the debate: HC Deb 22 October 2021, vol 815, col 394. Previous polls suggested the figure to be higher than 90 per cent: Owen Bowcott, 'Legalise Assisted Dying for Terminally Ill, Say 90% of People in UK' *The Guardian* (4 March 2019) www.theguardian.com/society/2019/mar/03/legalise-assisted-dying-for-terminally-ill-say-90-per-cent-of-people-in-uk. A further petition prompted Parliamentary debate in Westminster on 29th April 2024. The Government again refused to sponsor legislation, but undertook to make time for further Private Members' Bills. A private Bill was introduced to the Scottish Parliament in March, 2024 by MSP Liam McArthur: Assisted Dying for Terminally Ill Adults (Scotland) Bill.

[4] Crown Prosecution Service, 'Policy for Prosecutors in Respect of Cases of Encouraging or Assisting Suicide' (February 2010, updated October 2014); R Heywood, 'The DPP's Prosecutorial Policy on Assisted Suicide' (2010) 21 *King's Law Journal* 425. Assisting suicide thus remains an offence under the Suicide Act 1961 (UK) s 2, although the Director of Public Prosecutions reported in 2014 that there has only ever been one prosecution: *R (Nicklinson) v Ministry of Justice* [2014] UKSC 38, [2015] AC 657 [48].

practical reality that, in the vast bulk of cases forming the focus of tort actions, those who take, or try to take, their own lives do so in circumstances that tend to undermine the freedom of their choice. This approach yields a distorted emphasis – it focuses on the exceptional instance in which suicide represents a rational personal decision to justify a general rule that the state need do nothing to use its powers to prevent a foreseeable risk that it may occur.

At the end of the day, the extent to which the state should bear civil responsibility for the consequences of suicide is a very difficult question. I make no contrary pretence. The same hesitations and controversies that beset the public law debate about VAD laws saturate the private law one. Courts' decisions reflect not just their understanding of the political limits of the state's public power and modern welfare role, but also their difficulties in understanding the exact relationship between suicide, mental illness and rational choice.

The chapter divides into four sections. Section II presents some of the confronting facts about suicide that make it a legitimate focus of serious state concern. Section III tracks changes in social attitudes towards the act in England from the mediaeval period to the present day. The thrust of this section is that any understanding of the modern duty of care question must be grounded in a deeper appreciation of the way in which social attitudes toward suicide have developed – and continue to change – over time. The extent of the state's tort liability for suicide is bound, I argue, to reflect the way in which the phenomenon is publicly understood; and the extent to which public attitudes toward it have been expressed and shaped over time through our public laws. It is hence only when the taking of one's own life is no longer socially reviled or publicly condemned that the prospect of the state being legally liable for failing to prevent it materialises as a realistic possibility. Equally, recent adjustments in our public laws, which frame suicide as a civil liberty and a facet of an individual's human right to privacy, are bound to influence judgements about the extent to which anyone else – state or private individual – should be responsible for having failed to mitigate its risk. The gradual recognition and expansion of state duties of care in respect of suicide is therefore a function of an important shift from condemnatory religious prejudices of the past to more tolerant, secular conceptions of the deed, as well as of the better understanding we now have of the relationship between suicide and mental illness, and of the emergence of the powerful protective philosophy of the welfare state. Section IV details the modern law on the state's duty of care, focusing on one, particularly difficult case, which tests the outer limits of its responsibility. This is the case in which a state agent carelessly fails to exercise public powers to take a potentially vulnerable person into protective custody as a precaution again suicide risk. The example is especially sensitive because the precautionary measures that might be taken in such an instance are potentially restrictive not just of a citizen's decision whether or not to die, but also of his or her physical liberty – an interest that tort law itself has always jealously protected. Despite these difficulties, I suggest that duties of care should be recognised in such instances where the risk to a particular individual is actually known, whilst acknowledging that the task of decision-makers in discharging this duty is such a difficult one as to justify according them a wide margin of appreciation for error. Section V states some brief conclusions.

II. Statistics and Risk Factors

Every modern discussion of suicide begins with a blood-chilling statement about its prevalence and the seriousness of the harms it can engender.[5] Unsuccessful attempts can result in horrific, long-term physical injuries; and the economic and psychological ripple-effects of a successful suicide on families and friends are clearly severe. Although global rates of suicide have decreased in the last 20 years,[6] it still accounts for more fatalities annually than malaria, HIV/AIDS, breast cancer, homicide or war.[7] In 2021, there were 5,583 suicide-related deaths in England and Wales alone, equating to about 11 deaths per 100,000 members of the population.[8] In Australia, the rates are a little higher generally and markedly so in the Northern Territory and amongst Aboriginal and Torres Strait Islander peoples.[9] Nearly three times as many Australians died by their own hand in 2021 as in road accidents.[10]

The phenomenon is also a frightening scourge upon our young. In the United Kingdom, it was the leading cause of death in persons aged 20–34 in each and every year between 2001 and 2018.[11] The position is similar in Australia, where self-harm constituted the primary cause of death in persons aged 15–44 in the 2018–20 period and accounted on average for nearly a quarter of all cases in that age-bracket.[12] It was also the leading cause of death in children (aged 5–17) in 2021.[13] Similarly disturbing figures are reported in the United States, where more than 40,000 people take their lives each year and the rate of increase since 1994 has bucked the downward world trend in an especially alarming fashion.[14]

[5] The lament of the 'suicide epidemic' has been sung since at least the eighteenth century: D Wright and J Weaver, 'Introduction' in J Weaver and D Wright (eds), *Histories of Suicide: International Perspectives on Self-Destruction in the Modern World* (Toronto, University of Toronto Press, 2009) 8.

[6] World Health Organisation, *Suicide Worldwide in 2019: Global Health Estimates* (Geneva, WHO, 2021) 11 (estimating a decrease of 36% between 2000 and 2019). The decline in rates in Australia since 1907 is mapped by the Australian Institute of Health and Welfare in 'Suicide & Self-Harm Monitoring' (25 October 2023) www.aihw.gov.au/suicide-self-harm-monitoring.

[7] The global estimate in 2019 was 703,000 deaths a year: *Suicide Worldwide* (n 6) 1.

[8] Office for National Statistics, 'Suicides in England and Wales: 2021 Registrations' (6 September 2022) www.ons.gov.uk/peoplepopulationandcommunity/birthsdeathsandmarriages/deaths/bulletins/suicidesintheunitedkingdom/2021registrations.

[9] The rate in the NT is about 18 per 100,000. It has increased significantly amongst Aboriginal and Torres Strait Islander People since 2012, despite reduction being a governmental priority: Australian Bureau of Statistics, 'Causes of Death, Australia, 2021' (19 October 2022) www.abs.gov.au/statistics/health/causes-death/causes-death-australia/latest-release#intentional-self-harm-deaths-suicide-in-australia ('*ABS 2021*'). The rate amongst First Nations people in NSW, QLD, NT, SA and WA in 2022 was 2.6 times that of non-indigenous people: Australian Institute of Health and Welfare, 'Suicide and Self-Harm Monitoring' www.aihw.gov.au/suicide-self-harm-monitoring/data/populations-age-groups/suicide-indigenous-australians.

[10] Department of Infrastructure, Transport, Regional Development and Communications, *Road Trauma Australia, 2021 Statistical Summary* (Statistical Report, 2022) iii: 1,123 road crash deaths, compared to 3,144 suicides reported in *ABS 2021* (n 9).

[11] Office for National Statistics, 'Leading Causes of Death, UK: 2001 to 2018' (27 March 2020) www.ons.gov.uk/peoplepopulationandcommunity/healthandsocialcare/causesofdeath/articles/leadingcausesofdeathuk/2001to2018 (note – the figure relates to suicide and 'injury or poisoning of undetermined intent').

[12] Australian Institute of Health and Welfare, 'Deaths in Australia' (11 July 2023) www.aihw.gov.au/reports/life-expectancy-death/deaths-in-australia/contents/leading-causes-of-death.

[13] *ABS 2021* (n 9). Over 50 per cent of these were aged 16 or 17.

[14] Chang (n 2) 193 (reporting a 24 per cent increase between 1994 and 2014, with suicide again featuring as the second leading cause of death in persons aged 15–34).

Importantly for arguments made later in this chapter, in 90 per cent of cases in the recent Australian study, suicide was associated with one or more recognised risk factors. These included mental or behavioural disorders in about 63 per cent of cases and other, psychosocial factors in two thirds.[15] Mood disorders (including depression) were the most common risk factor in every age-group, with the exception of the over-85s.[16] The range of psychosocial factors is very extensive[17] and whilst all such factors are just that – *factors*, not provably what tort lawyers would identify as 'necessary and sufficient *causes*' of a death – they are of key importance. Not only do they provide useful tools for formulating strategies around social and clinical intervention, but they also illustrate the extent to which reported suicidal behaviours are overwhelmingly associated with circumstances of diminished personal autonomy.

This is important, because the public law debates about assisted dying to which we alluded above have focused on the (true) fact that suicide can be a free, full and informed personal choice. Those debates are framed in a context in which a person's autonomy is assumed to be fully protected by guarantees in the state's regulatory apparatus. Tort law, by contrast, tends to deal with those unfortunate, quotidian cases in which something has gone horribly awry and a person's decisional autonomy is absent, or highly constrained by either internal or external factors. The cases concern psychiatric patients,[18] refugees (often children) held in remote places of detention,[19] prisoners in police custody, on remand, or with histories of depression and self-harm,[20] young people entering the

[15] *ABS 2021* (n 9). For an excellent overview of the various theories of suicide and discussion of some of the statistics (and the difficulties involved in interpreting them), see J Herring, *The Right to be Protected from Committing Suicide* (London, Bloomsbury, 2022) ch 3.

[16] *ABS 2021* (n 9).

[17] The five most common psychosocial factors identified in 2021 were (in order of frequency): a history of self-harm; partner relationship problems; separation or divorce; loss of a family member; and (increasing in frequency as one gets older) limitation of a person's activities due to a disability: Australian Institute of Health and Welfare, 'Psychosocial Risk Factors and Deaths by Suicide' (25 October 2023) www.aihw.gov.au/suicide-self-harm-monitoring/data/behaviours-risk-factors/psychosocial-risk-factors-suicide.

[18] *Paterson v Lanarkshire Health Board* [2023] CSOH 1, 2023 SLT 67; *Williams v Betsi Cadwaladr University Local Health Board* [2022] EWHC 455 (QB); *Smith v South Western Sydney Local Health Network* [2017] NSWCA 123; *Baker v Cambridgeshire and Peterborough NHS Foundation Trust* [2015] EWHC 609 (QB); *Rabone v Pennine Care NHS Foundation Trust* [2012] UKSC 2, [2012] 2 AC 72 (negligence claim settled); *Savage v South Essex Partnership NHS Foundation Trust* [2008] UKHL 74, [2009] AC 681 (claim for breach of Art 2 of the European Convention on Human Rights ('*ECHR*')); *Walker v Sydney West Area Health Service* [2007] NSWSC 526; *Warner v State of Queensland* [2006] NSWSC 593; *Brumen v State of Queensland* [1999] QSC 238; *Drake v Pontefract HA* [1998] Lloyd's Rep Med 425 (QB); *Walsh v Gwynedd Health Authority* (27 April 1998, unreported), CC; *Selfe v Ilford and District Hospital Management Committee* (1970) 114 SJ 935 (QB); *Thorne v Northern Group Hospital Management Committee* (1964) 108 SJ 484 (QB) (patient with mental illness).

[19] *FRX17 v Minister for Immigration and Border Protection* [2018] FCA 63; *AYX18 v Minister for Home Affairs* [2018] FCA 283; *BAG18 v Minister for Home Affairs* [2018] FCA 1060; *SBEG v Secretary, Department of Immigration and Citizenship (No 2)* [2012] FCA 569, (2012) 292 ALR 29.

[20] *Hanaghan v Chief Constable of Greater Manchester* (8 June 2009, unreported), CC (police detainee with history of self-harm, homelessness and drug abuse); *Butchart v Home Office* [2006] EWCA Civ 239, [2006] 1 WLR 1155 (prisoner with history of depression and suicidal ideation suffering psychiatric harm as a result of suicide of another prisoner – his cellmate); *Zinzuwadia v Home Office* [2000] Inquest LR 143 (QB); *Keenan v UK* (2001) 33 EHRR 913 (prisoner with prior history of paranoid schizophrenia and self-harm – claim for breach of Art 2 *ECHR*); *Reeves v Commissioner of Police of the Metropolis* [2000] 1 AC 360 (HL) (remand prisoner with prior history of suicide attempt); *Orange v Chief Constable of West Yorkshire* [2001] EWCA Civ 611, [2001] 3 WLR 736 (police detainee pending charge or release for drunk and disorderly behaviour, with

adult prison system for the first time,[21] war-veterans with histories of post-traumatic stress disorder and suicidal behaviour,[22] young mothers suffering from depression,[23] persons in fractured and violent domestic relationships,[24] Aboriginal detainees suffering from episodes of hallucination during phases of alcohol withdrawal,[25] hospital patients suffering depressive reactions as a result of believing they have cancer[26] and so on. The tale told by tort, in other words, is a dark one – a story not of enlightened choice made by persons seeking the ultimate expression of their agency and dignity in leaving the world on their own terms, but of vulnerable individuals whose options or capacities life has seriously limited and whose personal autonomy is dangerously compromised.

III. Social Attitudes – A Short English History

In determining whether, when and why the state owes a duty in tort law to take reasonable steps to prevent suicide, we must step back in history and understand the way in which the relationship between suicide, mental illness and public power has developed over time. The very idea of such a duty is likely to be anomalous in any society in which the act is condemned as a crime – *ex turpi causa non oritur actio*. It is only when social attitudes shift from condemnation to tolerance or empathy, that the possibility of state agents owing a duty of care in respect of suicide-related harm emerges as a realistic proposition. How and why, then, has this shift come about?

The exact answer to this question is complicated, because attitudes toward life and death are fluid and generalisations about the collective mind of any society are always subject to exceptions. If the tide of opinion is generally flowing one way, there are always eddies and countercurrents. Most modern histories of suicide[27] nonetheless suggest a swing from tolerant attitudes in England in the period up to the early fifth century CE, to a period of strong disapproval and state-backed sanction under Christian influence peaking in the seventeenth; thence back again to social tolerance in the eighteenth and

no prior history of depression or self-harm); *Kirkham v Chief Constable of Greater Manchester Police* [1990] 2 QB 283 (CA) (remand prisoner with history of alcoholism and suicidal behaviour). Remand prisoners are the highest-risk group, accounting for 45% of cases between 1972 and 1982, according to one English study: *Orange* (n 20) [30] (Latham LJ).

[21] *Douglas v Ministry of Justice* [2018] EWHC B2 (Costs), [2018] Inquest LR 71.

[22] *McColley v Commonwealth* [2014] ACTCA 21.

[23] *Sherratt v Chief Constable of Greater Manchester* [2018] EWHC 1746 (QB).

[24] *Batchelor v Tasmania* [2005] TASSC 11 (murder-suicide).

[25] *Quayle v New South Wales* (1995) Aust Torts Reports 81-367.

[26] *Hyde v Tameside Area Health Authority*, The Times, 16 April 1981 (CA).

[27] A leading account is M MacDonald and T Murphy, *Sleepless Souls: Suicide in Early Modern England* (Oxford, Clarendon Press, 1990). See also Chang (n 2); G Rosen, 'History' in S Perlin (ed), *A Handbook for the Study of Suicide* (Oxford, Oxford University Press, 1975); R Healy, 'Suicide in Early Modern and Modern Europe' (2006) 49 *The Historical Journal* 903; J Watt, 'Toward a History of Insanity in Europe' in J Watt (ed), *From Sin the Insanity: Suicide in Early Modern Europe* (New York, Cornell University Press, 2004); H Brody (ed), *Suicide and Euthanasia: Historical and Contemporary Themes* (Boston, Kluwer, 1989); Weaver and Wright (eds), *Histories of Suicide* (n 5); M MacDonald, 'The Inner Side of Wisdom: Suicide in Early Modern England' (1977) 7 *Psychological Medicine* 565; A Murray, *Suicide in the Middle Ages*, 3 vols (Oxford, Oxford University Press, 1998–2000); N St John-Stevas, *Life, Death and the Law: Law and Christian Morals in England and the United States* (Bloomington, Indiana University Press, 1961) ch 6; R Guernsey, *Suicide: History of the*

nineteenth centuries. This was capped off by official decriminalisation in the twentieth, and the advent of permissive state attitudes in modern VAD laws in the twenty-first. The following passages put some explanatory flesh on this otherwise skeletal account.

A. The Early Years – From Tolerance to Condemnation

Accounts of attitudes toward suicide in England in the pre-Augustine period are sketchy, but, to the extent that Roman influences were present in Britain at that time, they are likely to have been forgiving. Suicide was never a crime in ancient Rome and was socially revered in certain cases. Although the picture is not wholly black-and-white,[28] it was the tolerant, Stoic view that clearly prevailed at the time of the Empire.[29]

Pagan rituals for the desecration of the suicide's body developed in England in the early pre-Christian era, the practice being to bury the corpse, often at a crossroads, with a wooden stake driven through its heart to prevent the ghost from walking. Strong, religious condemnation then began to spread in the fifth century with the publication of St Augustine's *City of God* (426CE),[30] the Church's formal denunciation of the act at the Council of Arles (452CE) and its subsequent decision at the Council of Braga in 563CE to deny funeral rites to the deceased.[31] The refusal of such rites passed into ecclesiastical law in England in 673CE[32] and thence into secular law in the reign of King Edgar in 967CE,[33] but the idea that suicide was actually a crime (a felony upon oneself – *felo de se*) only materialised later for reasons that had little to do with moral or religious judgement and more to do with the Crown's rapacious appetite for revenue, on the one hand, and an associated trick (or error) of legal reasoning, on the other. The King had started to forfeit the personal property (and occasionally the land) of some suicides by the early thirteenth century[34] and, because forfeiture was at that time a consequence normally brought to bear only upon felons, suicide came in turn to be considered a felony by way of a form of backward, logical deduction.[35] With the benefit of hindsight, it is easy to recognise this as a fallacious syllogism: '(i) The property of felons is forfeit.

Penal Laws Relating to it in their Legal, Social, Moral, and Religious Aspects, in Ancient and Modern Times (New York, Strouse & Co, 1883); E Wicks, *Suicide and the Law* (Oxford, Bloomsbury, 2023), ch 2.

[28] Those taking their lives to evade the consequences of a criminal conviction had their property confiscated; those who hanged themselves were denied an honourable burial; and soldiers who attempted suicide to evade service were put to death. Later laws also punished slaves attempting suicide, on the basis of the financial harm this caused to their owners: Chang (n 2) 155–56, 159; St John-Stevas (n 27) 247.

[29] St John-Stevas (n 27) 247–48; McDonald and Murphy (n 27) 16–18; CA Ruff, 'The Complexity of Roman Suicide' (Master's thesis, University of Richmond, 1974).

[30] Augustine, *The City of God*, book 1, 16–27 (suicide violates the commandment 'thou shalt not kill').

[31] St John-Stevas (n 27) 248–49.

[32] ibid 233.

[33] See *The Canons of Edgar*, as cited in Guernsey (n 27) at 24.

[34] MacDonald and Murphy (n 27) 22. The practices are described by Bracton, although he was uncertain when they began and may, on some accounts, simply have been reproducing the Roman position. Felons evading punishment had both their lands (escheat) and goods forfeited, as did those who killed themselves 'without cause through anger or ill-will' (maliciously). Ordinary persons committing suicide 'from weariness of life or impatience of pain' forfeited only their goods. The insane and those who killed themselves by accident escaped penalty altogether: W Mikell, 'Is Suicide Murder?' (1903) 3 *Columbia Law Review* 379–81.

[35] T Plucknett, *A Concise History of* the *Common Law*, 5th edn (Boston, Little, Brown & Co, 1956) 445; J Barry, 'Suicide and the Law' (1965) 5 *Melbourne University Law Review* 1, 2–3; St John-Stevas (n 27) 234.

(ii) The property of suicides is forfeit. (iii) Therefore, suicides are felons'. However, by the fourteenth century, it had stuck. The chime of criminality also resonated with the Church's increasingly vocal condemnations at the time, encapsulated in St Thomas Aquinas' insistence in *Summa Theologica* (1266–73) that suicide is a wrong three times over – against nature, community and God.[36]

Despite this, MacDonald and Murphy make a convincing case that social attitudes toward suicide remained basically tolerant in England up until about 1500.[37] Verdicts of *felo de se* by coroners' juries were very rare up until this point. The real shift toward 'severe' treatments of the act occurred only in the subsequent period between about 1500 and 1660, when over 95 per cent of recorded suicides were convicted by juries as felons.[38] This dramatic increase in recorded felony verdicts was, they suggest, largely attributable to measures introduced by the Tudors to strengthen the enforcement of forfeiture laws (again, a way of boosting cashflow to the Crown), but is also likely to have been influenced by the intense religious fervour of the Reformation, which adopted and evangelised condemnatory Augustinian attitudes, framing suicide in the minds of jurors as the work of the devil himself.[39]

It was toward the end of this period, in 1563, that Judge Brown, in the course of investigating the death of Sir James Hale, famously reviled the act as a heinous offence against nature, God, and the King. The explicit and powerful synthesis of legal and religious censure in his thinking is striking, although one should note, as one reads it, that it contains a bizarre suggestion that it is worse in the eyes of God to kill oneself than another, which has never been a position entertained in our positive law:

> It is an offence against Nature, against God, against the King. (1.) Against Nature, because it is contrary to the rules of self-preservation, which is the principle of nature for everything living does, by instinct of nature, defend itself from destruction, and then to destroy oneself is contrary to nature and a thing most terrible. (2.) Against God, in that it is a breach of His commandment, 'Thou shalt not kill,' and to kill himself by which act he kills in presumption his own soul, is a greater offence than to kill another. (3.) Against the King, in that he has hereby lost one of his mystical members; also, he has offended the King in giving such an example to his subjects, and it belongs to the King, who has the government of the people to take care that no evil example be given them; and an evil example is an offence against him.[40]

By the end of this period, one therefore sees the emergence of a view that the life of a person belonged to a deity, to a sovereign, to his or her family, or to the community, but not really (or at least not foremost) to himself, or herself. To take one's life was to violate the rights and interests of *others* (including the interests of the state) and a sin, not the assertion of a legitimate human and civic liberty of one's *own*.

[36] *Summa Theologica* 2–2, q 64, art 5.

[37] MacDonald and Murphy (n 27) 22–23.

[38] ibid 16.

[39] ibid 24–29, ch 2. See further G Ferngren, 'The Ethics of Suicide in the Renaissance and Reformation' in Brody (n 27) 155, 162. Note, however, Ferngren's observation (at 167) that although Protestants considered suicide a terrible sin, they were ultimately 'somewhat more flexible' than Catholics, on account of the greater liberty they accorded to independent thought.

[40] *Hales v Petit* (1563) I Plow 253, 282; 75 ER 387, 400.

B. From Condemnation Back to Tolerance

The acme of intolerance for suicide occurred, on this account, in the sixteenth and early seventeenth centuries. Thereafter, from about 1660 onwards, verdicts of '*felo de se*' plummeted dramatically in number, with coroners' jurors increasingly entering verdicts of '*non compos mentis*' (literally 'having no control or mastery of the mind') instead. One set of records from Norwich shows a particularly dramatic increase in the use of the '*non compos*' verdict between 1670–1760, from 30 per cent to over 90 per cent.[41] By 1800, 97 per cent of recorded suicides were superficially being pitied by juries as lunatics, rather than 'punished' as felons.[42] The main reason for the reversal had little to do with any new, medicalised understanding of suicide amongst jurors, but resided in their rebellious disdain for the state's avaricious forfeiture practices, which had left so many unfortunate families not just grieving, but destitute. The '*non compos*' verdict was one tool that sympathetic jurors could use to avoid the normal, devastating consequences of a felony verdict for the suicide's family, forming part of a broader pattern of behaviour through which ordinary people conspired to protect themselves and others against state greed.[43]

Popular distaste for forfeiture laws was not the only reason for the shift toward more lenient treatments of suicide at this time. MacDonald and Murphy also credibly identify as important the abolition during the English Revolution of the Tudor enforcement machinery we mentioned above; increases in rates of literacy and education in the middle classes from which coroners' jurors were drawn; the resurrection of humanism and the rise of Enlightenment philosophy; the spread of sympathetic accounts of victims' plights in the expanding periodical press; and the developing reputation and influence of medical science, which increasingly presented alternative explanations for the act that were free of moral or religious judgement.[44] Collectively, these forces resulted in the eighteenth and nineteenth centuries in the act becoming gradually 'secularised' – loosened from the grip of traditional Christian intolerance and lay superstition. In 1823, George IV banned the old practices of corpse desecration at public crossroads in response to the new thinking.[45] This was followed in 1870 by the abolition of forfeiture[46] and then (in 1883) by repeal of the secular laws denying burial rites to the deceased.[47] Then, in 1897, Emile Durkheim's seminal sociological study, *Le Suicide*[48] burst upon the scene, presenting the act for the first time as a product not simply of either internal moral choices or mental morbidities, but of social forces and circumstances beyond an individual's control. The result was that, for all intents and purposes, state 'punishment'

[41] MacDonald and Murphy (n 27) 124, table 4.3.

[42] ibid 133.

[43] ibid 114–32; M MacDonald, 'The Medicalization of Suicide in England: Laymen, Physicians, and Cultural Change, 1500–1870' (1989) 67 *The Milbank Quarterly* 69, 75–77; Wright and Weaver, 'Introduction' (n 5) 11. Other devices including the reconstruction of suicides as accidents; the concealment or undervaluing of a suicide's personal property; and the bribery of coroners.

[44] MacDonald and Murphy (n 27) 5 and Part II.

[45] Burial of Suicides Act 1823 (4 Geo 4 c 53) (suicides to be buried in a churchyard, but at night and without religious rites).

[46] Forfeiture Act 1870 (33 & 34 Vict c 23).

[47] Interments (felo de se) Act 1882 (45 & 46 Vict c 19).

[48] E Durkheim, *Suicide, A Study in Sociology*, trans J Spaulding and G Simpson (London, Routledge, 1952).

of suicide ceased by the end of the nineteenth century in England, even though it was formally still a crime on the books.

The transition away from the perception of suicide as an offence against God and State was not smooth. Religious objections persisted long after coroners' jurors took their stand and the state withdrew its most despised sanctions. It was also, ironically, only shortly before the penalty of forfeiture for suicide was abolished in 1870, that *attempted* suicide was recognised as a crime at common law for the first time, in 1854.[49] Although this development was in one way just a logical extension of the earlier syllogism that had resulted in suicide itself becoming a felony (if suicide is a crime, then so too is attempting it), it was clearly out of kilter with the softening of social attitudes at the time, and with the rise of the new secular rationalism. It resulted in a horrific case in 1860 in which a man who had failed in an attempt to kill himself by slitting his own throat was promptly given medical treatment, so that he could be hanged.[50] It was another hundred years before the move was reversed in England and attempted suicide decriminalised alongside the principal offence, in 1961.[51]

The time-lag between the renaissance of more sympathetic attitudes and formal acts of state decriminalisation betrays both the sluggishness of the law to respond to changes in social morality, and the residual presence of currents counter to the general flow of public opinion. Even 20 years after English decriminalisation, in 1981, Lord Denning hence thought that a strong policy stance should be taken against granting tort compensation to persons injured whilst attempting suicide, or to their families upon their death, because, although such acts were no longer criminal, they were still contrary to ecclesiastical law and claims arising out of them were antisocial in imposing costs on the general community.[52] That view bucked the general judicial trend, which took decriminalisation in 1961 to represent a key turning-point in social attitudes.[53] In the same way, although suicide ceased to be a crime anywhere in Australia some time ago,[54] members of the public in most jurisdictions are still expressly authorised to use reasonable force to prevent a person attempting it, whether or not they understand that person to be engaged in a free expression of rational choice.[55] There is therefore both complexity and residual tension in public attitudes toward the phenomenon.

C. Medicalisation – Suicide and Mental Illness

The rising tendency of seventeenth- and eighteenth-century jurors to return verdicts of '*non compos mentis*' in cases of suicide, was, we have said, largely a product of hostility

[49] *R v Doody* (1854) 6 Cox Crim Cas 463.

[50] Chang (n 2) 166.

[51] Suicide Act 1961 (UK) s 1.

[52] *Hyde* (n 26).

[53] See, eg, *Reeves* (n 20) 292 (Lloyd LJ); 296 (Farquharson LJ).

[54] The last decriminalisation took place in the Northern Territory in 1996: Criminal Code Amendment Act 1996 (NT). It was a crime in Queensland until 1979 and in the ACT until 1990: Crimes (Amendment) Ordinance (No 2) 1990 (ACT) s 5.

[55] Crimes Act 1958 (Vic) s 436B; Crimes Act 1900 (NSW) s 574B; Criminal Law Consolidation Act 1932 (SA) s 13A; Crimes Act 1900 (ACT) s 18; Criminal Code Act 1983 (NT) s 27. Each provision was introduced when the principal offence of committing suicide was abolished.

to state avarice and other social factors, not medical judgement. Doctors had little to do with such verdicts at that time and their influence on the softening of public attitudes and changes in the substantive law came later and was less direct.[56] They were, as MacDonald puts it, 'riding in the caboose of change, not driving its engine'.[57] Doctors' interest in mental illness certainly grew from about 1580 onwards and associations between suicide and 'melancholy' became increasingly frequent amongst physicians and the educated elite in the sixteenth and seventeenth centuries,[58] but there nonetheless remained a good deal of confusion and difference of opinion about such matters. Some educated men simply folded the new science into their religion, attributing suicide to the 'disease' of melancholy, but considering the latter an instrument of the devil – the '*balneum diaboli*' (devil's bath) in which Satan encouraged his sinners to drown.[59]

In the eighteenth and nineteenth centuries, medical explanations for suicide became increasingly assertive and commonplace amongst a group of doctors specialising for the first time in the new science of mental illness ('alienists').[60] This hardening of views about the connection between suicide and mental illness in turn formed the basis upon which England enacted lunacy legislation providing for the institutional detention of persons perceived to be at risk of self-harm.[61] Even at this stage, however, contemporary medical voices disclaimed any *necessary* connection between suicide and insanity[62] – a position for which there was much historical evidence,[63] and which is clearly accepted in the modern day.

Nowadays, practitioners consider mental illness a risk factor, rather than a necessary or sufficient cause of suicidal behaviour. The statistics show that very few of those with severe mental illness commit suicide,[64] and certainly not all those who wish to take their own lives are mentally ill, but of those who do kill themselves, as many as 90 per cent are reported as having some form of mental disorder, most usually depression, or a substance-abuse problem.[65] The existence of any given condition is hard to use as a

[56] R Houston, 'The Medicalization of Suicide: Medicine and the Law in Scotland and England circa 1750–1850' in Weaver and Wright (eds), *Histories of Suicide* (n 5) 93 ('pure' medical interpretations of suicide were uncommon before about 1835).

[57] MacDonald (n 43) 85.

[58] MacDonald, 'The Inner Side of Wisdom' (n 27) 572–73.

[59] MacDonald (n 43) 72–74.

[60] Houston (n 56) 92–93. If the 'medicalization' of suicide began at this stage, its full 'psychiatrization' is a more 'contested twentieth century phenomenon' and has arguably only just begun in some societies: Wright and Weaver, 'Introduction' (n 5) 11.

[61] Wright and Weaver, 'Introduction' (n 5) 4. For the detail, see further A Shepherd and D Wright, 'Madness, Suicide and the Victorian Asylum: Attempted Self-Murder in the Age of Non-Restraint' (2002) 46 *Medical History* 175, 187–89.

[62] I Ray, *A Treatise on the Medical Jurisprudence of Insanity* (Boston, Charles C Little and James Brown, 1838) 383 cited in *Stuart v Kirkland-Veenstra* [2009] HCA 15, 237 CLR 215 [44] (French CJ); MacDonald, 'The Medicalization of Suicide' (n 43) 86 (citing the views of Henry Maudsley and Thomas Wakely).

[63] K Siena, 'Suicide as an Illness Strategy in the Long Eighteenth Century' in Weaver and Wright (eds), *Histories of Suicide* (n 5) (the taking of one's life in the eighteenth century was often a perfectly rational response to the horrors of sickness during this age).

[64] L Bràdvik, 'Suicide Risk and Mental Disorders' (2018) 15 *International Journal of Environmental Research and Public Health* art no 2028, 1 (citing estimates of between 5–8 per cent). See also S Pridmore, 'Mental Disorder and Suicide: A Faulty Connection' (2015) 49 *Australian and New Zealand Journal of Psychiatry* 18 (only 2 per cent of persons with mental disorders).

[65] ibid; M Henriksson et al, 'Mental Disorders and Comorbidity in Suicide' (1993) 150 *American Journal of Psychiatry* 935 (93 per cent of the random sample of 229 suicide victims had one or more mental disorders as

predictor of self-harm on its own, because risk is a function of both the stressor condition itself and a person's vulnerability or tendency (diathesis) to experience, or act on, suicidal ideation. It hence only ever forms part of a multi-factorial approach to risk-assessment and the experts continue to call for additional research to be done to further improve our understanding and predictive tools.[66]

The upshot is that attitudes have shifted, over the course of time, from the Tudor view that suicide is 'bad', to the view of some medical men in the nineteenth century that it is virtually always 'mad', to the modern view that it is neither bad, nor necessarily mad, but that it is in a high proportion of cases associated with definable risk factors, the precise operation and interaction of which is unknown, but which frequently tend – either in isolation or in combination – to undermine the autonomy of decisional choice.

D. Institutional Politics

The above history highlights the way in which attitudes toward suicide have been shaped in more recent times by better medical understanding. It also alerts us to the institutional politics framing societal views. Both the Church and the Crown clearly had powerful, vested interests historically in constructing social judgements about the deed and in acting punitively around it. Nowadays, the Church's interests are generally voiced in terms of sympathetic moral concern, not in terms of its righteous dominion over souls, and the state's interests are expressed in terms of its paternal commitment to preventing harm, rather than its financial stake in a deceased's assets. The state's approach has shifted not just in response to the new medical science, but as a consequence of the development of its powerful welfare role in the twentieth and twenty-first centuries.[67] With the political commitment to welfarism has naturally come a greater sense of its 'responsibility' for suicide, manifested in a raft of public powers designed to protect citizens against its risks. At the same time, however, the practical implementation of welfare policy is being impacted in both England and Australia by shortages in public resources and the rise of neo-liberal political models, according to which citizens are encouraged to rely more upon themselves and not to look to government for protection. The paternalistic outlook of modern welfarism is also under particular pressure in

defined by DSM-III-R. 59 per cent had a depressive co-morbidity). Some have recently criticised the 90 per cent statistic as politicised and implying a stronger causal connection between mental illness and self-harm than is supported by the evidence-base (pointing to the unreliability of post-death interview methods as diagnostic tools): H Hjelmeland and B Knizek, 'Suicide and Mental Disorders: A Discourse of Politics, Power, and Vested Interests' (2017) 41 *Death Studies* 481. A more recent, meta-analysis of studies based only on recorded diagnoses nonetheless affirms a strong association – persons having a mental disorder being eight to nine times as likely to commit suicide as those who do not: LS Too et al, 'The Association between Mental Disorders and Suicide: A Systematic Review and Meta-analysis of Record Linkage Studies' (2019) 259 *Journal of Affective Disorders* 302, 311.

[66] Bradvik (n 64) 3; Henriksson et al (n 65) 939 (stressing the need for further analysis of the impact of multiple co-morbidities). Some writers maintain that the connections made by modern psychiatry between mental illness and suicide are still too strong: H Maung, 'Mental Disorder and Suicide: What's the Connection?' (2022) 47 *The Journal of Medicine and Philosophy* 345.

[67] The welfare state is detectable in the poor laws of the sixteenth century, but most of its machinery is a twentieth-century product. See K Woodroofe, 'The Making of the Welfare State in England: A Summary of Its Origin and Development' (1968) 1 *Journal of Social History* 303, 324.

relation to suicide from human rights instruments that regard decisions about life and death as implicated not just by the importance of the right to life (on the one hand), but also by norms of personal privacy (on the other). The end result is that the balance between public protectionism and interventionism, on the one hand, and the values of privacy and personal decisional autonomy, on the other, is extremely delicately poised – perhaps more so than at any previous point in time.

All of this has complex implications for the modern law of tort, where the existence and incidence of positive state duties of care in respect of suicide reflects a difficult compromise between competing contemporary understandings of personal choice and state responsibility, and continuing uncertainties in the mind of both judges and legislators about the true nature of the relationship between suicide, mental illness and decisional autonomy.

IV. Positive Law – The State's Duty of Care

The question of when the state owes a duty to protect a citizen against suicide forms part of a much larger and very difficult question in tort law about its duty to use reasonable care in the exercise (or non-exercise) of its statutory functions and powers.[68] There are some subtle structural differences in the way that English and Australian courts tackle this question, but these have lessened in recent years and in the following account, I treat the basic approaches as being *methodologically* equivalent in their most important aspects, even if the two jurisdictions probably draw up the substantive boundaries of state responsibility in different ways.[69] The strategy in both countries is to recognise a small number of precedential categories in which duties to protect persons against self-harm are firmly established; and then, in new cases, to reason analogically and incrementally from those categories, referring to a variety of 'factors' or 'salient features' expressed in them to determine the answer to the duty question in the new instance.[70]

[68] See, generally, D Fairgrieve and D Squires, *The Negligence Liability of Public Authorities*, 2nd edn (Oxford, Oxford University Press, 2019); J Bell-James and K Barker, 'Public Authority Liability for Negligence in the Post-Ipp Era: Sceptical Reflections on the Policy Defence' (2016) 40 *Melbourne University Law Review* 1; S Tofaris and S Steel, 'Negligence Liability for Omissions and the Police' (2016) 75 *CLJ* 128; M Aronson, 'Government Liability in Negligence' (2008) 32 *Melbourne University Law Review* 44; D Nolan, 'The Liability of Public Authorities for Failing to Confer Benefits' (2011) 27 *LQR* 260; H Willberg, 'In Defence of the Omissions Rule in Public Authority Negligence Claims' (2011) 19 *Torts Law Journal* 159; C Harlow, *State Liability* (Oxford, Oxford University Press, 2004).

[69] Although the method is now similar (see the text to, and cases listed at n 70 below), a residual *substantive* difference is that English Courts now tend to equiparate state duties of intervention with those of private citizens, save where a statute expressly or impliedly provides for one. The result is that a high degree of emphasis is placed on the need to prove that a state agent 'assumed responsibility' to a particular citizen, before a positive protective duty will arise. See, eg, *Michael v Chief Constable of South Wales Police* [2015] UKSC 2, [2015] AC 1732; *Robinson v Chief Constable of West Yorkshire Police* [2018] UKSC 4, [2018] AC 736 [38], [89], [96], [115]; *Poole BC v GN* [2019] UKSC 25, sub nom *N v Poole BC* [2020] AC 780. By contrast, Australian courts are more open to idea that the state has special functions that private individuals do not, such that the 'rule of equality is not regarded as wholly applicable': *Stuart* (n 62) [129] (Crennan and Kiefel JJ).

[70] In England, see *Robinson* (n 69). In Australia, see *Crimmins v Stevedoring Industry Finance Committee* [1999] HCA 59, (1999) 200 CLR 1 [93] (McHugh J); *Graham Barclay Oysters Pty Ltd v Ryan* [2002] HCA 54, (2002) 211 CLR 540 [146], [149] (Gummow and Hayne JJ), [84] (McHugh J); *Stuart* (n 62) [114] (Gummow, Hayne and Heydon JJ), [137]–[138], [149] (Crennan and Kiefel JJ).

These 'factors' represent a blend of both moral and policy concerns and can vary in their relevance according to the facts.

A. Precedent Categories of Duty

The state is currently liable for the consequences of foreseeable suicidal behaviour in four clear cases. First, like all employers, it has a duty to take positive steps to safeguard an employee against risks of suicidal harm where they arise from the employee's working conditions.[71] Secondly, its agents owe duties not actively to cause physical or psychiatric injuries to a person that might in turn foreseeably cause that person to take his or her own life.[72] Thirdly, doctors and psychiatrists working in the public health system – for whose negligence the state is vicariously responsible – owe duties to their patients to take positive measures to safeguard them against suicide risk when dispensing medical advice and treatment. This is so both where the patient is seeking or receiving care in a health facility, and when he or she is subsequently discharged into the community.[73]

These three cases are unexceptional in so far as they replicate for the state the recognised duties (or vicarious liabilities) of private parties. Beyond this, however, there are some instances in which the state owes duties of care in relation to the exercise of special, public functions, which private citizens simply do not have. In this fourth category, prison and immigration authorities hence owe duties to take positive steps to protect prisoners and detainees against suicidal harm;[74] and police officers owe equivalent duties to persons in their custody, provided, again, that the suicide is foreseeable not just in a broad statistical sense, but in the victim's own, particular case.[75]

Beyond these instances, there is some weak authority suggesting that government departments investigating citizens they know to be vulnerable may owe duties to protect them against foreseeable self-harm resulting from an incompetent investigation.[76] And there is one English authority which suggests that police officers may have a duty to respond reasonably to emergency calls relating to suicide where they have given assurances that they will do so either to the person at risk, or to a person acting on his or her behalf.[77]

[71] *Corr v IBC Vehicles Ltd* [2008] UKHL 13, [2008] 1 AC 884. See also *Cross v Highlands and Islands Enterprise* 2001 SLT (CS) 1060.

[72] *Lisle v Brice* [2001] QCA 271, [2002] 2 Qd R 168; *Corr* (n 71); *RPY, XFL, QZT v Barnet, Enfield and Haringey Mental Health NHS Trust* [2021] EWHC 180 (QB).

[73] *Paterson* (n 18); *Warner* (n 18); *Brumen* (n 18); *Drake* (n 18); *Hyde* (n 26); *Smith* (n 18); *Baker* (n 18); *Walker* (n 18); *Rabone* (n 18) (negligence claim settled – patient on home leave after informal admission to hospital); *Savage* (n 18) (patient escaped from compulsory detention – Art 2 *ECHR*).

[74] *AYX18* (n 19); *FRX17* (n 19); *BAG18* (n 19); *Keenan* (n 20) (but nb Art 2 of the *ECHR* and no breach found).

[75] *Kirkham* (n 20); *Reeves* (n 20); *Quayle* (n 25); *Rigg v New South Wales* (1993) Aust Torts Reports 81-230 (but no breach); *Orange* (n 20) (but no duty to prevent plaintiff taking his own life because individual suicide risk not foreseeable; and no breach of duty to properly assess the risk).

[76] *McColley* (n 22). The case wisely settled before going to public trial, despite the existence of a line of potentially conflicting authority suggesting that police officers owe no duty to those they are investigating: *New South Wales v Plum* [2015] NSWSC 1566; *Batchelor* (n 24).

[77] *Sherratt* (n 23) (preliminary issue). Cf *Kent v Griffiths* [2001] 1 QB 36 (CA) (assurance given by ambulance call centre operator to the caller himself). *Sherratt* is probably more liberal than other courts (including

The existence of a duty in any of these instances is not, it is crucial to emphasise, the end of the story. A claim can still founder because the victim's family or estate is unable to prove on a balance of probabilities that a public official's conduct was unreasonable on the facts, or that it was the real cause of the relevant death. The death could also be so remote a consequence of the official's breach as to be beyond the scope of his or her liability, or a court might reduce the damages awarded where the victim was of sound mind, on the basis that he or she was partly responsible for his or her own demise.[78] Cases regularly falter on one or more of these grounds[79] and, in fact, my research to date has revealed only nine reported cases in England and Australia in which damages have been awarded since 1964.[80] Legislatures in Australia have further tinkered with the common law principles to make this negative outcome clearer – and in some instances, more likely – than ever, by explicitly requiring account to be taken of the resources and other responsibilities of a public decision-maker when adjudging the reasonableness of his or her conduct;[81] and by requiring any decision regarding the exercise of a special statutory function to be not just unreasonable, but absurdly so before any liability will attach to it.[82] The New South Wales version of the latter type of provision was, it should be noted, expressly introduced in order to ensure a wide margin of acceptable error for officers facing difficult decisions as to whether or not compulsorily to detain persons at (or posing) a risk of physical harm under the relevant mental health legislation.[83] It was designed, in others words, for precisely the type of controversial scenario with which we are about to deal, providing a less blunt solution than simply denying the existence of any duty of care in respect of the exercise of the relevant protective powers.

the UKSC in *Michael* (n 69)) have deemed appropriate. Dicta in the Court of Appeal in *Michael* [2012] EWCA Civ 981 [22] (Longmore LJ, Richards and Davis LJJ agreeing) suggested that direct contact with the victim is required for a duty to arise. Lord Toulson JSC in the UKSC at [138] went further, suggesting that there must be a specific *promise* about the timescale within which the police will respond, or an assurance that assistance will be arriving 'shortly', not simply an assurance that a call will be passed on to the relevant dispatch team.

[78] *Reeves* (n 20) (50 per cent reduction). It was, perhaps oddly, deemed irrelevant in this case that the conduct constituting contributory negligence was conduct which the defendant had a duty to prevent. In *Corr* (n 71), where the victim was suffering from a depressive illness caused by his physical injury, the court split on this issue, Lords Bingham and Walker being against any reduction, but Lords Scott, Mance and Neuberger favouring one (Lord Scott specifying 20 per cent as the appropriate figure, the others not specifying).

[79] See n 78; *Williams* (n 18) (no breach); *Smith* (n 18) (causation not proven); *Baker* (n 18) (no breach proven in respect of one allegation; causation not proven in respect of another); *AMP General Insurance Ltd v Road Traffic Association* [2001] NSWCA 186 (private defendant – causation not proven); *Hanaghan* (n 20) (breach and causation not proven); *Walker* (n 18) (no breach); *Warner* (n 18) (no breach or causation proven); *Cross* (n 71) (private defendant – no breach); *Orange* (n 20) (no breach); *Zinzuwadia* (n 20) (no breach); *Thorne* (n 18) (no breach); *Cowan v National Coal Board* 1958 SLT (Notes) 19 (too remote).

[80] *Kirkham* (n 20); *Quayle* (n 25); *Brumen* (n 18); *Reeves* (n 20); *Corr* (n 71); *Selfe* (n 18); *Drake* (n 18); *Walsh* (n 18); *Douglas* (n 21). Interlocutory injunctive relief was granted in a further three: *AYX18* (n 19); *FRX17* (n 19); *BAG18* (n 19). In another three, the case was settled: *RPY* (n 72); *Rabone* (n 18); *McColley* (n 22). In two, the court refused to strike out the claim: *Sherratt* (n 23); *Butchart* (n 20).

[81] Civil Liability Act 2003 (Qld) s 35; Civil Liability Act 2002 (Tas) s 38; Civil Law (Wrongs) Act 2002 (ACT) s 110; Civil Liability Act 2002 (NSW) s 42; Civil Liability Act 2002 (WA) s 5W. These provisions probably do not change the common law but make the point more explicit: Bell-James and Barker (n 68) 23.

[82] The original intention of the Ipp Committee, upon whose report these provisions were based, was that they should apply only in respect of 'policy' decisions, but legislatures went their own ways. Most such provisions are (bizarrely) confined to claims for breach of statutory duty, but others (see, eg, Civil Liability Act 2002 (NSW) s 43A and Civil Liability Act 2003 (Qld) s 36) have been found to include negligence claims. The provision in New South Wales extends to even operational negligence. See Bell-James and Barker (n 68) 24–37.

[83] *Parliamentary Debates*, New South Wales Legislative Council, 583–86 (4 December 2003, Della Bosca).

B. The Novel Case – Failures to Exercise Powers of Protective Detention

The above categories leave open a range of more controversial cases in which the state can foresee suicidal harm to an individual, including one that forms the particular focus of the rest of the chapter. This is the one in which a state agent has public powers to detain a person who is a known suicide risk but has failed to take him or her into protective care. Such powers are commonly held by doctors, police officers and ambulance staff in many jurisdictions as an extension of the protective functions of the welfare state.[84] The existence of any duty in such instances has been tested only once in England and Australia, in the case of *Stuart v Kirkland-Veenstra*.[85] The High Court of Australia in that instance held unanimously that no duty was owed by police officers to either the victim or his family on the facts, but the court's reasoning was divided and the scope and application of the governing principles has consequently been left unclear.

By way of background to our analysis of *Stuart*, when Australian courts are called upon to decide, in a novel case, whether a public agent owes a duty to use statutory powers to prevent a foreseeable risk of physical harm to a citizen, they nowadays consider a variety of different 'factors'. The range includes: (i) the foreseeability of the harm; (ii) the 'justiciability' of the agent's decision about how to use the power; (iii) whether or not the power was actually 'enlivened' on the facts; (iv) whether the power is designed to protect the interests of the individual concerned, or a specific class to which he belongs, as opposed to the 'public at large'; (v) whether it gives the agent 'control' over the risk; (vi) whether the agent knew about that risk; (vii) whether or not the victim was vulnerable in the sense of being unable reasonably to protect himself against the risk; (viii) whether the effect of imposing the duty would be unreasonably to interfere with a citizen's autonomy; (ix) whether or not the duty would be consistent with the purposes and provisions of the statutory framework granting the relevant powers, or with the agent's other duties; (x) whether the agent has 'assumed responsibility' for the citizen's protection (and whether the citizen has specifically relied upon him or her for such protection); (xi) whether recognising the duty would 'distort' discretionary public decision making or result in undesirable 'defensive practices'; and (xii) whether the duty would result in 'indeterminate' or 'massive' liabilities for the state that would divert valuable resources away from front-line service provision.[86]

[84] See, eg, Public Health Act 2005 (Qld) s 157B.

[85] *Stuart* (n 62). See also, analogously (but involving harm done to third parties by persons with a mental disorder, not self-harm) *Hunter Area Health Service v Presland* [2005] NSWCA 33; *Hunter & New England Local Health District v McKenna* [2014] HCA 44, (2014) 253 CLR 270.

[86] These factors stem not just from the suicide precedents considered in section IV.A, but from cases involving failures of public authorities to exercise powers in respect of public health risks such as fire, environmental contamination or asbestos: *Pyrenees Shire Council v Day* [1998] HCA 3, (1998) 192 CLR 330 [17], [25]–[26] (Brennan CJ); [72]–[77] (Toohey J); [102] (McHugh J); [168]–[169], [177] (Gummow J); *Crimmins* (n 70) [44]–[46] (Gaudron J); [93] (McHugh J, Gleeson CJ agreeing); [215]–[219] (Kirby J); *Barclay Oysters* (n 70) [84] (McHugh J); [149] (Gummow and Hayne JJ); *Stuart* (n 62) [62] (French CJ); [113] (Gummow, Hayne, Heydon JJ); [131]–[146] (Crennan, Kiefel JJ). Where the claim is for secondary, psychiatric harm, further criteria may be relevant, but in most cases involving close relatives, they are unlikely to be significant. For an exception, see *Morgan v Somerset Partnership NHS Foundation Trust* (29 February 2016, unreported), CC

This list is long and reflects the complexity of judgements about state responsibility for the use of public power where it may impact upon the autonomy of individuals, or impact upon public resources, as well as traditional hesitations about liability for omissions. Several of the 'factors' are less 'considerations' to be weighed in a court's reasoning, and more threshold *requirements* for the existence of a duty. A plaintiff's injury must hence always be foreseeable before a duty of care will arise. Similarly, if a court considers the failure to use a statutory power to be non-justiciable for either constitutional or practical reasons (factor (ii)), that is the end of the story. The court will simply refuse to assess the merits of the case.[87] Factors (iii)–(ix) are probably also best regarded as duty preconditions, although there is some doubt.[88] By contrast, the existence of an 'assumption of responsibility' is a positive factor which might be enough, in combination with the foreseeability of an injury, to give rise to a positive duty on the part of the state to act. An additional complication is that at least two of the factors ((xi) and (xii) in particular) are contentious and contested in the sense that some judges point to their importance, whilst others consider them wholly irrelevant,[89] which makes their weight in judicial reasoning very hard to predict.

Fortunately for us, only about half of these factors are likely to be in dispute in the difficult case with which we are concerned, where a state agent fails to use a power to detain a person who is known to be a foreseeable suicide risk. Such cases are very unlikely to raise 'non-justiciable' questions about public policy or general public resource allocation, because they inhabit the 'operational' end of the decision-scale. The powers in question are expressly designed to protect a particular class of vulnerable persons who may lack decisional autonomy; and there is no concern about indeterminate (uncertain) or 'massive' liability because only a single, identified person's life is at stake. There is also very little scope, on the current law, for any argument that the agent has 'assumed responsibility' for intervening, where he or she has never actually exercised the power, and gave no undertaking to do so. The mere fact, for example, that the state has used its powers in the past, or that it has, in a broad sense 'undertaken' particular public welfare functions, is insufficient to create the specific type of relationship required for such an 'assumption' to be found.[90]

The core principles in determining the existence of a duty in our difficult case in which an individual is known to be a suicide risk therefore relate to five, key questions: whether the power of intervention has been enlivened (factor (iii)); whether it gives an

(where the proximity in time and space between the suicide and the plaintiff's psychiatric reaction was too great to generate a duty of care). In *Stuart* the case was argued on the basis that a duty would only be owed to the suicide's wife, if a duty were first owed to him.

[87] Bell-James and Barker (n 68) 6–7, 10–12 and caselaw noted at fn 47.

[88] Whilst this was McHugh J's intention in *Crimmins* (n 70), courts have more recently implied a more flexible approach. See, eg, *Makawe Pty Ltd v Randwick City Council* [2009] NSWCA 412, (2009) 171 LGERA 165 [48] (Hodgson JA) (considering the features' 'cumulative effect').

[89] On defensive practice, compare, eg, *Brooks v Commissioner of Police of the Metropolis and Others* [2005] UKHL 24, [2005] 1 WLR 1495 [30] (Lord Steyn) and *Stewart v Ronalds* [2009] NSWCA 277 [101] (Handley JA) with *Van Colle v CC Hertfordshire*; *Smith v Chief Constable of Sussex Police* [2008] UKHL 50, [2009] 1 AC 225 [49] (Lord Bingham, dissenting) and *Robinson* (n 69) [75] (Lord Reed JSC, Lady Hale, Lord Wilson, Lord Hodge and Lady Black agreeing).

[90] *Stovin v Wise* [1996] AC 923 (HL) 935, 937–38 (Lord Nicholls). See also *Gorringe v Calderdale Metropolitan Borough Council* [2004] UKHL 15, [2004] 1 WLR 1057.

agent control over the risk of self-harm (factor (v)); the potential effect of recognising a duty of care on a suicide's physical liberty and decisional autonomy (factor (viii)); the compatibility or otherwise of such a duty with the statutory framework and the agent's other duties (factor (ix)); and (perhaps) whether recognising the duty will have a 'distortive' effect upon public decision-making (factor (xi)). The first three of these – power, control and autonomy – were central to the negative outcome in *Stuart*.

C. *Stuart v Kirkland-Veenstra*

The claim was brought by the wife of Mr Ronald Veenstra, a 37-year-old accountant, for psychiatric harm she suffered when he asphyxiated himself in his car outside their home at 2:30pm on 22 August 1999. Two police officers had discovered him only nine hours earlier, at 5:40am, parked up in a remote coastal car park, with a hose running from his car's exhaust pipe to its interior. The engine was turned off when they found him, and the bonnet was cold. When questioned, he admitted that he had been having marital problems and had been thinking of 'doing something stupid' (by which they understood him to mean taking his own life) but said that he had changed his mind. He also appeared to be in the process of writing a note, the contents of which he would not reveal, but which they suspected to be a suicide note. Unbeknown to them, he was being investigated and prosecuted for fraud and was expecting to be formally charged later the same day. The officers' notes recorded that they thought him to be 'depressed' (which one of them later clarified as meaning 'unhappy') but when they questioned him, they said that he appeared polite, co-operative and rational. They offered to contact a doctor, his family or a Crisis Assessment Team, but he declined, insisting that he would return home to discuss his problems with his wife and that he would contact a doctor later on. He then voluntarily removed the hose from his car. Satisfied that he was rational and trusting his word, they let him go.

Under the relevant legislation in Victoria at the time, an officer had the power to arrest and temporarily detain a person if: (i) he or she 'appeared [to the officer] to be mentally ill' and (ii) the officer had reasonable grounds for believing (did believe and had reasonable grounds to believe) that he or she had either recently attempted suicide, or was likely to do so.[91] The Act defined mental illness broadly as any 'medical condition … characterised by a significant disturbance of thought, mood, perception, or memory'[92] but stipulated expressly that officers were not required to exercise clinical standards of judgement in reaching their assessment of a person's mental state.[93]

It would be possible, on such difficult facts, to conclude that the officers' decision to let Mr Veenstra go was reasonable, given their limited knowledge, the acknowledged difficulty of accurately predicting suicidal harm, their lack of clinical expertise, their

[91] Mental Health Act 1986 (Vic) s 10(1). The clarifications provided in brackets reflect the meanings of the words found to be the correct construction by all members of the court. The provision has since been replaced by the Mental Health Act 2014 (Vic) s 351(1), which requires an officer to be satisfied that (i) a person appears to have mental illness; and (ii) because of that illness, the person needs to be apprehended to prevent serious *and imminent* harm to the person or another person (my emphasis).

[92] Mental Health Act 1986 (Vic) s 8(1A).

[93] ibid s 10(1A).

other potential commitments and Mr Veenstra's reassurances. But the High Court was not asked to determine that question and did not decide the case on that basis. The sole issue it had to decide was the more fundamental one of principle – whether the officers had any duty at all to be careful of Mr Veenstra in the first place, accepting that his suicide was a foreseeable risk. The Court unanimously held that they did not, but its reasoning was split. This conclusion, I shall suggest, is questionable and the reasoning of the Court defective in several, key respects. These defects evidence continuing confusions and hesitancies about the relationship between death, decisional autonomy, power and control that have so long been evident in our legal history, and which echo the uncertainties about these matters that are currently instantiated in our public laws.

i. The Enlivening of Power

Three members of the Court (French CJ, Kiefel and Crennan JJ) decided that, because the officers did not actually believe Veenstra to be mentally ill, the power to arrest him was never 'enlivened' and that no duty of care consequently arose: there could be no duty to be careful in respect of the exercise of a power that the officers did not, by virtue of their own subjective judgements, actually have.[94]

Whilst this sounds sensible, the effect is that an officer need take no care at all in deciding whether or not a protective detention power of this type is available for use, if he or she has personally decided that it is not. Subjective blindness to even the most obvious facts will immunise the officer against any obligation of reasonable precaution. To take an extreme example, if Mr Veenstra had been foaming at the mouth, speaking in tongues and threatening immediately to hang himself, an honest belief on the part of the officers that he was nonetheless rational and/or presented no risk of self-harm, would preclude them owing him any duty at all. This is a *reductio ad absurdum* of course, but it illustrates the logical consequence of riding this train of thought to the end of the line. It would be very odd, I think, if state officials could *never* have any obligation to be careful in considering whether or not they have a statutory power to protect a person against a foreseeable suicide risk. They might then have to take care in using the protective powers they know they have, but they could be as careless as they liked in determining whether or not they have them. Unless they were intended by Parliament to have some special statutory immunity that related solely to decisions of the latter type (which is highly unlikely, I will suggest below), that distinction appears to make no moral or pragmatic sense.

This does not mean that whether or not a power of arrest has been 'enlivened' is irrelevant to the agent's legal liability. If there is no authority to arrest, *failing to arrest* clearly cannot be unreasonable, because arresting someone without authority is both a tortious wrong and a crime. It would, as I suggest below, place the officer in a position in which he or she was faced with potentially conflicting legal obligations – to arrest and not to arrest. The point is nonetheless that the fact that an officer's subjective beliefs

[94] *Stuart* (n 62) [63] (French CJ); [146], [149]–[150] (Crennan and Kiefel JJ) (the absence of a live power rules out the possibility of the other factors, such as control of the risk, which might give rise to a duty to act). See, similarly, *Barclay Oysters* (n 70) [30] (Gleeson CJ); [183] (Gummow and Hayne JJ).

preclude any protective arrest power arising cannot be the end of the story as far as the existence of a duty to take reasonable care in respect of the power is concerned – it is relevant, I suggest, only to the question of breach in some cases in which it is the failure to apprehend itself that is the conduct alleged to be at fault.

ii. Control, Autonomy and Slippery Slopes

This is the view that appears to have been taken by the other three judges in the case (Gummow, Hayne and Heydon JJ), who indicated that whether or not the conditions for the exercise of the power had *actually been met* was not determinative of the duty of care question, being more relevant to breach.[95] Their Honours' own reasons for denying the existence of a duty were, in fact, broader and potentially more far-reaching. Even if the officers had actually had a 'live' power to arrest Mr Veenstra, they would *still* not have owed him any duty to exercise it carefully because: (i) they did not control the risk of his death, he did;[96] (ii) recognising a duty of care toward him would be incompatible with respect for his personal autonomy;[97] and (iii) if such a duty were recognised, it could not be limited to the type of case at hand, but would logically have to extend to the use of any power, statutory or otherwise, that *anyone* has to prevent another person harming themselves, including powers held by private parties.[98] The general rule in Australian law that no-one is liable for carelessly failing to save another would be eroded and the sky would fall in.

The last of these reasons is a 'slippery slope' argument[99] and is subject to the obvious rebuttal that no court need 'slip' into generalising a duty to save others if it is sufficiently surefooted and there are good reasons to distinguish one case from another. There might be perfectly good justifications for limiting the duty to cases in which the state has been granted powers for the specific purpose of safeguarding vulnerable individuals against suicide risk, but not to its other, more general statutory powers of arrest and detention, or to private powers of intervention. The matter is always one to be determined in the context of the purposes of the relevant legislation. Extending a duty to one case clearly does not necessarily entail extending it to all others.

That brings us to their Honours' concerns about control and autonomy, which they considered to be critical and connected. The police had no control over the death, they said, because Mr Veenstra did, being a person who must be assumed to be an autonomous agent.[100] The fact that he was known to have been contemplating suicide was, they stressed, insufficient to displace this assumption, since the historical connection

[95] *Stuart* (n 62) [103]. This is what I take their Honours to mean at [112] when they say that there can be 'no duty to act *in a particular way*' (my emphasis) unless there is authority to do so and that the existence of a power (to act in that way) is a 'necessary condition of liability' (for not having done so).

[96] ibid [114].

[97] ibid [97]–[98].

[98] ibid [99], [106]–[107]. Note also the suggestion at [107] that it would have to extend to a duty to prevent a person harming others, not just himself or herself.

[99] On which, see T Govier, 'What's Wrong with Slippery Slope Arguments?' (1982) 8 *Canadian Journal of Philosophy* 303; F Schauer, 'Slippery Slopes' (1985) 99 *Harvard Law Review* 361; E Lode, 'Slippery Slope Arguments and Legal Reasoning' (1999) 87 *California Law Review* 1469.

[100] *Stuart* (n 62) [114].

between suicide and mental illness that developed in the seventeenth and eighteenth centuries was, as we saw above, constructed for social reasons, not based on medical evidence.[101] Whilst the officers may therefore have been 'in a position to' control or minimise the risk in the sense that they knew about it and had a potential power of arrest,[102] this was *insufficient* to ground any positive duty to act in respect of an autonomous person. Unless an officer has actively contributed to the risk of a person's death by placing him 'in harm's way',[103] has actually taken him into custody[104] or has 'entered upon the exercise' of the arrest power,[105] he or she owes him no duty of care, even where his death is foreseeable and a protective power is 'live'.

This reasoning is problematic in at least three respects. First, the finding that the officers lacked control over the risk was clearly premised on a normative assumption that Mr Veenstra was autonomous, but the latter's actual mental state was never factually determined. Whilst their Honours were clearly right to deny any necessary connection between suicide and mental illness and to point out that no such correspondence was assumed in the Act,[106] the modern statistics nonetheless suggest that a mental or behavioural disorder is present in up to 90 per cent of cases.[107] There were also a number of clear risk factors in Mr Veenstra's own case that might well have borne upon the autonomy of his choice, including, potentially, a serious mood disorder associated with the decline of his relationship with his wife, and the pressures (clearly unknown to the officers) of his impending criminal trial. The problem, then, is that their Honours' insistence that Mr Veenstra's autonomy should be assumed cut off all possibility of that matter being properly decided on a full trial of the facts, and precluded the officers being under any duty to take him to a medical expert, so that his actual mental competence could be properly assessed.

A second problem lies in their Honours' assumption that control is a binary matter – something that lies either in the hands of a state agent, or in the hands of a suicide victim. The police lacked control, their Honours said, *because* Veenstra must be assumed to have had it. Control is not, however, a digital 'on/off' question – more than one agent can have *some degree* of control over a risk. Indeed, there are cases which show that, even where a victim is found to be of perfectly sound mind, state agents sometimes have *sufficient* control over the risk self-harm to be obliged to take reasonable care for his or her welfare.[108]

The third problem lies in their Honours' view that the state controls a suicide risk only when it has actually used its powers to take a person into physical custody.[109]

[101] ibid [96]–[97].
[102] ibid [116].
[103] ibid [116], distinguishing *Crimmins* (n 70) as a case in which the defendant put the plaintiff 'in harm's way'.
[104] ibid [116], distinguishing *Reeves* (n 20); *Savage* (n 18).
[105] ibid [117], distinguishing *Pyrenees* (n 86). See also [135] (Crennan and Kiefel JJ).
[106] ibid [98].
[107] See n 65 and accompanying text.
[108] *Reeves* (n 20). See, endorsing this conclusion in a rather different context, the observation of Beach J in *Minister for Environment v Sharma* [2022] FCAFC 35 at [660] that more than one entity can control a risk to varying degrees and that a public authority may owe a duty of care to a private person even where the latter has *more* control than the former.
[109] See similarly, *Presland* (n 85) (Sheller JA) (an agent who does not exercise a power to detain a person is not in control of that person).

This is, I suggest, far too restrictive. The views of a majority of the Court of the Appeal[110] and indeed of Crennan and Kiefel JJ in the High Court[111] were more realistic, suggesting that actual custody is inessential, provided at least that an officer has a live legal authority to detain and a factual opportunity to use it. This squares with the view of the United Kingdom Supreme Court in *Rabone*,[112] and with the view of Santow JA in the analogous case of *Presland*, who thought that control can exist over the physical risk that a person poses, even where there is only an unexercised, temporary power to detain him, provided the harm occurred during the period that the detention might legally have lasted.[113] Spigelman CJ in the same case took the (clearly non-binary) view that control can vary in degree in cases in which a detention power has not been exercised, but that it would probably exist in sufficient measure where the state *could* have exercised the power and the person posing the risk lacked the decisional capacity to admit himself or herself to care on a voluntary basis.[114] The best view, I suggest, is that the state can have a sufficient level of control over a risk of self-harm to attract a duty of care even without actually physical controlling the suicide victim, provided it knows about the risk and has access to a legal power that it could in fact have exercised to obtain such physical control at the time of death. It should be noted that, in this formulation, control over the risk sufficient to trigger a duty of care might exist even where a power has not actually been enlivened, if a state agent could reasonably have enlivened it.

iii. Compatibility with Statutory Frameworks

This leaves as residual, possible reasons to deny a duty the argument that it would be 'inconsistent with the statutory framework'; or that it might cause defensive policing and 'distort' officers' decisions whether or not to arrest. The defensive practice argument was put by counsel and had featured in the dissenting judgment of Chernov JA in the Court of Appeal, but did not count in the reasons of any member of the High Court. Its import in such cases therefore appears doubtful. All the judges did, however, give detailed consideration to the history, purposes and provisions of the relevant statutory framework.

The concern about the potential 'inconsistency' or 'incompatibility' of a duty of care with a statute can be understood in two ways. The first type of argument is that no duty can be owed at common law if a statute expressly or impliedly provides officers with a legal immunity (or liberty) in respect of the decision about how to use the relevant power. If it does, the decision will be said to lie within the officer's legal 'discretion' (although one must beware the slippery nature of this term[115]) and there can be no

[110] *Kirkland-Veenstra v Stuart* [2008] VSCA 32, (2008) 23 VR 1 [76] (Warren CJ); [88] (Maxwell P).

[111] *Stuart* (n 62) [138]–[140], [149] (Crennan and Kiefel JJ).

[112] *Rabone* (n 18) (the state can control a suicide risk 'in substance' even where its compulsory detention powers have not been exercised, at least where the suicide has previously been admitted to voluntary care, but then allowed to leave).

[113] *Presland* (n 85) [374] (obiter).

[114] ibid [30]–[31]. Control can hence be 'fluid': *Australian Capital Territory v Crowley* [2012] ACTCA 52 [311] (Lander, Besanko and Katzmann JJ).

[115] See further K Barker, 'Public Power, Discretion and the Duty of Care' in K Barker et al (eds), *Private Law and Power* (Oxford, Hart Publishing, 2017) 207.

further argument. In *Stuart*, there *was* an express immunity for good faith decisions under the Act,[116] but it did not apply to arrest decisions under section 10.[117] The existence of any immunity under the section could also not be implied merely from the permissive, as opposed to obligatory, terms in which the power was framed ('may' arrest, as opposed to 'must' arrest). The fact that a statute grants an agent a liberty and power to act does not necessarily imply that he or she is free of any obligation at common law to be careful in deciding whether or not to do so.[118]

The second version of the argument is that, irrespective of the immunity question, the common law must develop in harmony with the underlying balance of public values and priorities reflected in our public statutes. In this context, it means that courts deciding whether or not officers owe a new duty to use care in respect of their protective detention powers must take account of social judgements reflected in the scheme of the empowering legislation. In this way, contradictions between statute and judge-made law are avoided and the democratic consensus expressed about the relative values of decisional autonomy, state protection, and public risk in respect of suicide are respected. This is said to promote 'coherence' in the law.[119]

This is a good argument, but does not reveal any reason to reject a duty of care in cases like *Stuart*. Indeed, the existence of a duty on the part of officers to take reasonable care in using their powers of protective detention in respect of a person who may be mentally ill and at risk of death is wholly consistent with the core purposes of those powers as they were stated at the time.[120] It is true that the powers in section 10 were carefully limited, so as to ensure their use only as a measure of last resort. The Act therefore reflected a strategy, informed by public consultation, of using the 'least restrictive' means of dealing with suicide risk 'consistent with a person's proper protection and care',[121] striking a delicate balance between state intervention and public risk, on the one hand, and personal liberty, on the other. Gummow, Hayne and Heydon JJ placed an especially high level of importance on the Act's minimum intervention principle and the associated need to respect personal autonomy when developing the law.[122]

This stress on the value of personal autonomy under the Act appears, with respect, to be strangely overemphatic as a reading of its purposes and values. Yes, the Act limited powers of intervention so as to minimise *as far as possible* interference with personal freedom, but the primary purpose of the relevant provisions (so limited) was nonetheless to protect persons whose decisional autonomy may be lacking against the risk of suicidal harm. The Act contemplated and accepted the need, therefore, for even serious intrusions upon a person's physical liberty in some cases evidencing suicide risk, precisely because decisional autonomy *might* well be *absent*. Although the Act required

[116] Mental Health Act 1986 (Vic) s 122. Personal immunities for police officers acting in good faith also exist in most Australian jurisdictions (including Victoria – see Victoria Police Act 2013 (Vic) s 216), but the immunity does not extend to the state itself in respect of their conduct.
[117] *Stuart* (n 62) [43] (French CJ).
[118] *Crimmins* (n 70).
[119] On the various different types of coherence argument, see A Fell, 'The Concept of Coherence in Australian Private Law' (2018) 41 *Melbourne University Law Review* 1160.
[120] Mental Health Act 1986 (Vic) s 4(1)(a).
[121] ibid s 4(2); *Stuart* (n 62) [32] (French CJ).
[122] *Stuart* (n 62) [98]. See, similarly, *Hunter* HCA (n 85).

a respectful balance to be struck between risk and intrusion, there was therefore no obvious 'incompatibility' between its core purposes and values and the recognition of an obligation on the part of officers to use reasonable care in making decisions about how to use their powers under it.

The only way in which recognising a duty of care on the part of officers *might* result in contradiction, I suggested above, would be if they were held to be under a duty to arrest someone that they had no statutory authority to detain. This would involve a 'conflict' between their duty in tort law to detain and their duties in both the criminal law and tort law not falsely to imprison, or otherwise trespass upon, a citizen's person. Australian Courts have undoubtedly referred to the problem of potentially conflicting duties as a basis for denying the existence of a duty of care on the part of both public and private defendants,[123] but, even if one accepts this concern as a basis for denying a duty to arrest in some cases (including even *Stuart* itself), it would clearly not rule out a duty in any instance in which a power to arrest had actually been enlivened; nor would it rule out a duty carefully to consider whether or not such a power exists. Another way of dealing with the problem of potentially conflicting duties – which I personally prefer – is simply to leave the potential conflict to work itself out as an aspect of the breach question, rather than ruling out any duty of care *in limine* on the basis that a conflict 'might possibly exist'. It can clearly never be unreasonable for an officer to fail to arrest a person if doing so would involve an illegal trespass to their person, but that does not, surely, mean that he or she should in principle be free of any duty of care at all.

None of this is to suggest that the claim in *Stuart* should necessarily have succeeded at the end of the day, but the Court's reasoning on the basic duty question appears, with respect, to be beset with seriously problematic assumptions about the meaning and significance of a 'live' power and the question of 'control (on the one hand), and about the relationship between mental illness and decisional autonomy, on the other. In the latter respect, three members of the court (Gummow, Hayne and Heydon JJ) appear to have used the true fact that suicide can sometimes be an autonomous choice to justify an assumption that Veenstra's own death was such a choice without the issue being tested at trial; and, more worryingly, for denying the existence of any duty on the part of the state to use its powers positively to protect the large number of suicides who in practice do lack full decisional autonomy. That strikes me as both morally questionable and seriously undesirable from the social policy point of view.

The best approach, I suggest, is to recognise the existence of a duty of care in any case in which the state has an actual (live) or potential power to protect a specific individual who is a known suicide risk and whose death is reasonably foreseeable, and to leave all of the more difficult judgements about civil liability to the question of breach. In the vast majority of cases, this is likely to result in no liability, since the standard of care owed by

[123] *Tame v New South Wales* [2002] HCA 35, (2002) 211 CLR 317 (police officer); *Polar Aviation Pty Ltd v Civil Aviation Safety Authority (No 4)* [2011] FCA 1126 (aviation authority); *McKenna* (n 85) [31]–[33] (doctor under no duty to members of the public compulsorily to detain mental health patient since the duty would be inconsistent with an express statutory duty owed to the patient to release him unless doctor of the subjective opinion that no other care of a less restrictive kind was appropriate and reasonably available); *Dansar Pty Ltd v Byron Shire Council* [2014] NSWCA 364, (2014) 89 NSWLR 1 (development consent authority). See also *CAL No 14 Pty Ltd v Motor Accident Insurance Board* [2009] HCA 47, (2009) 239 CLR 390 [39] (hotelier).

an officer must take into account not just the difficulty of predicting suicidal harm, but the officer's limited clinical expertise; the resources available to him or her; any conflicting priorities; the exigency of the situation; and (crucially) the express limitations on his or her statutory authority to intervene by way of arrest. Not arresting a person where there is no live power to arrest clearly cannot constitute a breach, but failing to enliven a power when one could reasonably have done so might nonetheless be actionable on exceptional facts. If it is ultimately determined at trial that a suicide's decision was an autonomous choice unimpaired by associated mental disorder or other vitiating factors, then a fair conclusion is that it is the victim and not the state that is to be regarded as the cause of the death; or that he or she was at least partly responsible for it, so that damages should be significantly reduced. The idea, however, that the state in principle owes no duty of reasonable care at all in respect of the use of powers designed for the specific purpose of protecting vulnerable persons at risk of self-harm is in my view beyond the point of tolerance. With those powers must come a basic (reasonable) level of responsibility – a responsibility that the common law of negligence has a legitimate role in imposing.

V. Conclusions

The relationship between suicide, mental illness and the state is complicated and understandings of that relationship remain unsettled. The shift toward public acceptance of the act and greater understanding of its relationship with mental illness has impacted on both our public laws and on the gradual recognition of duties of reasonable care on the part of the state toward its citizens. As the welfare capacities and functions of the state have increased, more research has been done, and attitudes toward suicide become more empathetic, so too it has become appropriate and important to ask whether public powers to prevent self-harm can be attended by common law duties to take reasonable care to use those powers in specific cases in which its risk is known. Where these powers include the power compulsorily to detain a citizen for his or her own protection, the question is especially sensitive on account of the threat that such powers potentially pose to citizens' liberty, dignity and privacy – some of the key 'civil liberties' of our age. The basic answer suggested in this chapter is nonetheless a cautious 'yes'. That view is based in part on the modern statistics about the seriousness of suicide as a social concern and the frequency of its association with risk factors that tend to undermine the autonomy of personal choice. These statistics do not negate the real possibility of decisions to die being rational, powerful expressions of human agency and, in such cases, it is appropriate that the individuals concerned bear responsibility for the consequences falling upon themselves and others. But the figures nonetheless betray the danger of applying any assumption in tort law that empowered decisional choice is the paradigm case outside of the types of regulatory frameworks created by modern VAD laws.

The balance of reason, I suggest, therefore favours duties of reasonable care that extend even to persons who are not within the state's actual physical custody or control, and even where there has been no actual intervention, or express promise by a state agent to intervene. They should include the duty carefully to consider and exercise powers of arrest and detention in cases in which a particular individual has been identified as a foreseeable risk and the use of such powers is legally possible, even if we accept, as we must, that making the right call on whether or not to use such a power is in practice an extremely difficult task. One possible, additional limitation that might be considered out of deference to concerns about state resourcing is that the duty be limited to circumstances in which the risk of suicide is foreseeable as an *immediate* risk. There is precedent for that approach both in the form of the legislation that now frames the relevant protective powers in Queensland and Victoria,[124] and in the dissenting judgment of Lord Bingham in the *Van Colle* case.[125] Another possibility is to limit the standard of care required of officers in the way that it has been in New South Wales,[126] such that there is only a prospect of liability where a failure to intervene is proven to be entirely irrational. My personal view, however (which accords with the way in which the European Court of Human Rights approaches the duty to protect life[127]), is that the immediacy of a risk is more relevant to the question of breach, than duty, and therefore a matter to be considered alongside all others on a full trial of the facts. I also doubt whether, in practice, there is much difference between the standard of care of care that would be required of a state actor under the New South Wales provision and at common law, when all of the exigencies and difficulties attending the decisional question are taken into consideration.

[124] Public Health Act 2005 (Qld) s 157B(1)(a), and n 91 and text accompanying above.
[125] *Van Colle* (n 89) [44] ('specific and imminent threat').
[126] See nn 81–83 and accompanying text, above.
[127] *Osman v UK* (1998) 29 EHRR 245.

9

Death Can Be Fatal! The End of Empire and Survival of Actions Legislation in Queensland and New South Wales

MARK LUNNEY*

I. Introduction

In a chapter on 'Civil Wrongs' in the recently published *Cambridge Legal History of Australia*, I cited the survival of actions legislation (the Law Reform (Miscellaneous Provisions) Act 1934 (UK)) as an example where English legislation was simply incorporated into Australian law.[1] While I stand by this statement as a suitable, abstract description of the position, it undersells the convoluted and diffuse processes by which the legislation was introduced.[2] In fact, these processes reveal the complexity of the interplay between law generated in the metropole and its reception in its self-governing Dominion periphery. In the case of the survivorship legislation, there was no precise correlation between the factors that led the Westminster Parliament to introduce the legislation, and the timing and circumstances of its introduction in the various Australian jurisdictions. Australian lawyers and legislatures – the former along with their English counterparts post the 1934 Act – machinated over how the newly identified head of damage for loss of expectation of life was to fit with the survival of actions legislation. In 1940, when the Queensland Parliament passed the first survival of actions legislation in Australia, the controversy was at its height, and argument over the strength and weaknesses of allowing this head of damage to survive to the estate dominated the Parliamentary debates. Paradoxically, this remained the position even

* The author would like to thank staff at the Queensland State Archives (especially Laura Hartsuiker), the Queensland Law Society (especially Matt Dunn), and the State Archives Collection of New South Wales (especially Rhonda Campbell). Thanks are also due to Professor Paul Mitchell and Justice Mark Leeming for comments on earlier drafts.

[1] M Lunney, 'Civil Wrongs' in P Cane, L Ford, and M McMillan (eds), *The Cambridge Legal History of Australia* (Cambridge, Cambridge University Press, 2022) ch 28.

[2] A better description was provided in a 1949 article which described the survival of actions legislation as an 'outstanding' example of the 'bewildering variety in form and content' characterising Australian legislatures' copying or adaptation of English legislation: FR Beasley and RW Baker, 'The Need for Co-operation in State and Commonwealth Laws' (1949) 23 *Australian Law Journal* 188, 193.

after the House of Lords had largely quelled the debate in English law through the decision in *Benham v Gambling* in late 1940, which de facto capped the amount that could be awarded.[3] But even apart from this issue, other changes in Australian law made some of the English justifications for introducing the legislation much less powerful. To that extent, the Australian discussions could seem somewhat unreal, divorced from the wider legal question that underpinned the substantive debate in Australia about the level of compensation available where a tort resulted in the victim's death.

It is tempting to see this dissonance – between the perceived need to follow English law and the reality that the grounds for English legislation were not always mirrored in Australia – as characteristic of legal cultural cringe. Through the cultural cringe lens, Australian legislatures were only capable of rehashing the same arguments as had been used in the mother country. But such a view is quite mistaken. At a granular level, Australian legislation rarely mimicked the 1934 Act perfectly and, when it did so, it was with the knowledge of consequences that were most likely beyond the contemplation of the drafters of the 1934 legislation. More broadly, however, Australian legislatures never thought that the best way to solve the accepted problem was unquestioningly to adopt the English reform. That would, of course, be a starting point, but it could, even formally, be nothing more because the legislatures of Australian states had enjoyed a very wide discretion to depart from English law since the Colonial Laws Validity Act 1865.[4] That they did not vary too much from the English model was not because they had limited legal wriggle-room, but because of the cultural and intellectual constraints of British race patriotism. To Australian lawyers, English law was not foreign law, but was *their* law, the common law, to which they were entitled as members of the British race.[5] Australian lawyers' primary commitment was thus to their common law. Usually, that corresponded to the common law of England. Where it did not, within the bounds allowed by being a member (and ultimately a Dominion) of the British Empire, English law was adapted and modified as part of an 'Australia First' approach, a stance of 'first among equals', rather than one based on a sense of superiority. This was still the dominant sentiment at the time when the survival of actions legislation was being introduced in Australia. So when, in August 1940, a Victorian lawyer wrote about the one overarching war aim as being the preservation of British law, this involved no sense of undue deference:

> When war was declared in September last it was prophesised that the lights would go out over Europe, and they have. But while we maintain for every British subject 'leave to live by no man's leave underneath the law' the lights shall not go out over the British Empire and we shall in due time rekindle the lights over Europe. For British law is the light of the world and British lawyers should be proud of that thought.[6]

[3] *Benham v Gambling* [1941] AC 157 (HL). The conventional amount was £200.

[4] (28 & 29 Vict c 63). On the discretion to depart from English law, see V Windeyer, 'Unity, Disunity and Harmony in the Common Law' in B Debelle (ed), *Victor Windeyer's Legacy: Legal and Military Papers* (Sydney, Federation Press, 2019).

[5] V Windeyer, '"A Birthright and Inheritance": The Establishment of the Rule of Law in Australia' (1962) 1 *University of Tasmania Law Review* 635. On the slow demise of this influence, see M Lunney, 'From *Parker* to the Australia Acts: Sir Victor Windeyer and the Short-Lived Triumph of the Independent Australian Britons' (2021) 74 *Current Legal Problems* 61 and more generally A Clark, *Making Australian History* (Melbourne, Vintage Books Australia, 2022) ch 4.

[6] 'Our War Aims and the British Empire: From a Lawyer's Point of View' (1940) 14 *Law Institute Journal* 128.

Accordingly, presenting the movement of the law as a one-way journey from London to the colonies and the Dominions is too crude a story. Australian lawyers were aware of the connotations of inferiority – which they understandably disliked – but it never shook their confidence that they could handle the common law (including statutory change to it) as well as their English counterparts. At the risk of being parochial, anyone who reads a judgment of Justice Griffith, Dixon, Isaacs, Evatt or Jordan from the first half of the twentieth century would be hard pressed to argue otherwise. So while it was perfectly natural to start with the 1934 Act – itself the result of the First Interim Report of the Law Review Committee made up of eminent English lawyers (including academics) – it was not necessary to end there. Indeed, what is striking about the Australian parliamentary debates around the survival of actions legislation is that the weight to be given to English law was largely a political, rather than a legal, question. The lesser the change to be the made to the 1934 Act, the greater the emphasis placed on its English source; the more substantial the change, the more equivocal the reference. This is characteristic of Australian lawyers' engagement with English precedents in private law throughout the first half of the twentieth century.[7]

This chapter is concerned with the introduction of the survival of actions legislation in Queensland – the first state to do so in Australia – and New South Wales – the last. The reason for the choice needs some explanation, given that each Australian jurisdiction has an implementation story of its own that is worth telling. One reason is that the complexity and variance of the implementation story in at least two other jurisdictions – South Australia and Victoria – requires more extensive treatment than can be given in this chapter. In each of those jurisdictions, the starting point for reform was that the 1934 Act should not be implemented in *toto*, and various more or less radical solutions were introduced, or at least mooted.[8] This was not the case for Queensland and New South Wales. The Australian Labor Party (ALP) governments in both states were committed to introducing the 1934 Act, complete with the knowledge of how it operated in respect of damages for loss of expectation of life. By 1940, however, there were, in effect, dual representations of what English law was: the formal representation of the black-letter extant law, and the desirable representation of what the law should be, rather than what it was. By the time the McKell government of New South Wales put its first bill on survival of actions to the Parliament in late 1943, it also had – in theory if not in practice – the experience of every other Australian jurisdiction to call on in determining what legislative solution to adopt. The result was that the authority of the 1934 Act in one sense competed against a variety of legal and political imperatives from each Australian jurisdiction that had considered the issue; and that turned the debate into something very different from the one which had taken place in England. The calm reflection and professional (legal) expertise that underpinned the 1934 Act in England were replaced by the hard-edged politics of insurance and compensation for death. A focus on the final form of the legislation in both jurisdictions masks both how English

[7] See, generally, M Lunney, *A History of Australian Tort Law 1901–1945: England's Obedient Servant?* (Cambridge, Cambridge University Press, 2018) ch 2.

[8] See, eg, Wrongs Act Amendment Act 1940 (SA) s 5 and more generally, M Lunney, 'Subversion Down-Under: Innovation, Ambition and the Introduction of Survival of Causes of Action Legislation in South Australia and Victoria' (2024) 45 *Journal of Legal History* 55.

law was portrayed in the debates, and how it was invoked to support a preferred political result, and risks mischaracterising the nature of the agency exercised by the state legislatures in the legislative choices made. In other words, it risks making the same oversimplification that I made in my chapter on 'Civil Wrongs'.

II. The English Problem

While this chapter is not about English law as such, it is impossible to discuss the Australian reforms without understanding the position that English law had reached by 1940 (the date of the first Australian statute). The starting point for any discussion is the Interim Report of the Law Revision Committee of 1934. In it, a distinguished body of lawyers, academics and civil servants recommended the abolition of the *actio personalis moritur cum persona* rule that personal actions died with the death of either party to the action.[9] The rule was universally reviled, the Committee itself quoting a great authority which 'described the rule as one which has been made at all tolerable for a civilised country only by a series of exceptions'.[10] The Committee identified the problems it created for those injured by road accidents which made reform an issue of urgent national importance. Put simply, in situations where the defendant motorist died before judgment, anyone injured through that negligence would be denied the benefit of the compulsory third party liability insurance which owners of motor vehicles had been required to possess since 1930. The insurer was only liable for the liability of the insured, and the death prevented the insured from incurring that liability. This was manifestly inconsistent with the compensatory aims of the 1930 legislation.[11]

Paul Mitchell has explored the relationship between the Interim Report, members of the Law Revision Committee and the Parliamentary Draftsman in drafting and ensuring the passage of the 1934 Act.[12] It is not necessary to repeat that here. What is relevant, however, is how the drafters dealt with non-pecuniary loss claims by the estate. The initial draft provided for an exclusion for 'any sum in respect of the mental or bodily suffering of that person before his death', but this was omitted from the final version. Mitchell found no specific discussion relating to the original inclusion, and later omission, of this clause. Whatever motivated the drafters, it was no doubt thought that it was a relatively minor issue because it was the reimbursement of economic losses to the estate that was at heart of the reform, and awards of non-pecuniary loss would be moderate by comparison.[13] The 1934 Act was thus passed without any express exclusion of estate claims for non-pecuniary loss.

[9] Actions claiming damages for personal injury fell within this rule irrespective of whether the action was in contract or tort: *Woolworths Ltd v Crotty* (1942) 66 CLR 603 (HC) 613–15 (Latham CJ).

[10] Law Revision Committee, *Interim Report* (Cmd 4540, 1934) para 3.

[11] On the wider issue, see P Bartrip, 'Pedestrians, Motorists and No-Fault Compensation for Road Accidents in 1930s Britain' (2010) 31 *Journal of Legal History* 45; P Bartrip, 'No-Fault Compensation on the Roads in Twentieth Century Britain' (2010) 69 *CLJ* 263.

[12] P Mitchell, *A History of Tort Law 1900–1950* (Cambridge, Cambridge University Press, 2015) ch 10.

[13] Claims for damage to real and personal property survived for the benefit of the estate before the 1934 Act, and in the Interim Committee's Report it was the inability of the estate to claim for economic losses (funeral, medical expenses) that was thought to justify extending a claim to the deceased's estate.

Unfortunately for the drafters of the 1934 legislation, their timing was poor. Later in 1934, the Court of Appeal decided *Flint v Lovell*,[14] recognising a new head of damages for non-pecuniary loss. In what was otherwise an unexceptional case, the trial judge awarded the 70-year-old plaintiff an amount of £4,000 to reflect the fact that his life had been shortened from 'a number of years' to probably less than one.[15] By a 2–1 majority, the Court of Appeal upheld the claim for loss of expectation of life in both principle and amount. In June 1937, the House of Lords in *Rose v Ford*[16] unanimously decided that *Flint v Lovell* was correct to recognise loss of expectation of life as a head of damages; that the award was for non-pecuniary loss and assessed objectively, not subjectively; and that this award survived for the benefit of the estate under the 1934 Act, alongside more conventional awards for non-pecuniary loss comprising pain and suffering, and loss of amenity.

It is not necessary for present purposes to delve in detail into the short-term furore that surrounded the decision in *Rose v Ford* before it was subdued four years later in *Benham v Gambling*.[17] What is important is that this furore provided the background to the debates over how the 1934 Act should be incorporated in Australian jurisdictions. There were two main themes of the English criticism. The first was that it was simply impossible to give a value to the loss of expectation of a life. As CK Allen put it:

> The dilemma is complete, for, on the one hand, the subjective test is impossible, since nobody can apply it except the dead man himself; and on the other hand, an objective test of what is essentially subjective is a contradiction in terms.[18]

Allen also identified the other, primary difficulty: 'The result, as everybody knows, has been confusion and despair in the Courts and among the insurance companies'.[19] Novel tort decisions increasing the potential liability of insurers were not a new phenomenon, but compulsory third-party liability insurance for motor vehicles gave *Rose v Ford* a particular edge. Throughout the second half of the 1930s, in a variety of forums, third party liability insurers expressed their discontent and the need, in the absence of reform, for there to be a rise in premiums for this kind of insurance.

[14] *Flint v Lovell* [1935] 1 KB 354 (CA).

[15] It appears that the medical prognoses for his future were unduly pessimistic, it being noted by Langton that 'some three years after his accident, he appeared to have been still alive, and even in a condition of health to justify the expression usually associated with a certain Mr John Walker of the Regency period': G Langton, 'Damages for Loss of Expectation of Life: A Suggestion' (1942) 58 *LQR* 53, 54.

[16] *Rose v Ford* [1937] AC 826 (HL). While the loss of expectation of life aspect of *Flint v Lovell* seems not to have been formally cited at all during this period in Australian reported cases, newspaper reports of cases indicated that this head of damages was claimed by Australian plaintiffs (including in New South Wales): see, eg, 'Collision at Hurstville' *The Propeller* (Sydney, 9 April 1936) 4; 'KC's Claim Fails' *Newcastle Morning Herald and Miners' Advocate* (Newcastle, 19 April 1939) 10; 'Young Woman Completely Paralysed for Rest of Life Sues for £10000' *Border Morning Mail* (Albury, 24 May 1938) 1; 'Youth Claims Damages' *News* (Adelaide, 11 March 1937) 7.

[17] (n 3). It certainly did not end criticism of the loss of expectation of life head of damage: see, eg, 'Damages for the Dead' (1940) 90 *Law Journal* 246; 'Loss of Expectation of Life' (1941) 91 *Law Journal* 34; Langton (n 15).

[18] CK Allen, 'Is Life a Boon?' (1941) 7 *LQR* 462, 465.

[19] ibid 464.

Writing in *The Financial Times*, Dr CE Golding began his analysis of *Rose v Ford* with the following:

> For this reason it is also of particular interest to insurance companies and is likely to have a definite effect on the claims. Hardly a single chairman of the big insurance offices has failed to refer to this case in addressing the general meeting this year, and the views which have been expressed on its probable influence on the course of motor insurance have been extremely pessimistic.[20]

Within this genre, *The Economist* was particularly scathing. From creating mock tariffs to assist the judiciary in valuations,[21] to penetrating analysis of the perceived incoherence of the position reached in *Rose v Ford*,[22] the power of the critique was such that Australian legislators made reference to it when arguing for a departure from the English status quo.[23] But it was not quite so simple – in either theory or practice – to transplant these arguments from England to Australian jurisdictions.

III. Queensland – The First Cab off the Rank

It is somewhat surprising that Queensland was the first state to enact survival of actions legislation in Australia.[24] While the extant records may be incomplete, it is striking that there is no reference to survival of actions legislation in any of them until the legislation was before the Queensland Parliament in September 1940.[25] The Acting Attorney-General, the Hon J O'Keefe, began his speech in the Invitation in Committee (where bills were initiated) by saying that there was a 'great need for the introduction of a measure

[20] CE Golding, 'Case of Rose v Ford: Effect of House of Lords Decision' *Financial Times* (London, 20 June 1938) IV. See also 'Insurance Topics' *Financial Times* (London, 31 January 1938) 6; 'City Men and Matters' *Financial Times* (London, 7 June 1938) 4; GF Johnson, 'Insurance Review IV – Accidents and Motor Departments: Premiums and Claims' *Financial Times* (London, 20 June 1938) IV; 'Motor Claims Heavier – Fresh Forms of Liability' *The Times* (London, 13 July 1938) 23; 'Advance Likely in Motor Business Premiums' *Financial Times* (London, 20 January 1939) 5; WA Mackenzie, 'Fight is On to Stop Dearer Motoring – Third Party Law is Crippling Companies' *Daily Mail* (London, 29 March 1939) 11. Concerns of insurers were also reported in the law professional journals: 'Motor Insurance and the "Accident-Prone"' (1938) 82 *Solicitors' Journal* 181; 'Company Meeting: The London Assurance' (1938) 185 *Law Times* vi (30 April 1938).

[21] The value of judges' lives was suggested at £100,000, that of Motor Car Underwriters, in the present condition of the law, at 10d: 'Is Life a Boon?' *The Economist* (London, 11 December 1937) 518.

[22] 'Under the Law Reform Act as interpreted by the House of Lords in Rose v. Ford, a dead person's representatives can recover the damages which he would have claimed, if he had been alive, for the loss he suffers through being actually dead.': 'Torts and Corpses' *The Economist* (London, 24 December 1938) 649.

[23] *Parliamentary Debates*, Queensland Legislative Assembly, 435 (1 October 1940, Russell).

[24] It may be linked to the absence of any relief from the rule in the compulsory third party motor vehicle insurance legislation: Motor Vehicles Insurance Act 1936 (Qld). By 1940, South Australia and Victoria allowed a direct claim against the third-party liability insurer when the insured driver died before the claim: Road Traffic Act Amendment Act 1936 (SA) s 31; Motor Car (Third Party Insurance) Act 1939 (Vic) s 12.

[25] Unlike in New South Wales (see discussion below), South Australia, and Victoria, where attempts had been made to introduce a version of the 1934 Act: see State Records of South Australia, AGO 186/1936 – Wrongs Act 1936, Letter from Secretary Law Society of South Australia to Attorney-General (29 April 1936); State Record of South Australia (n 25), Letter from Secretary Law Society of South Australia to Attorney-General (25 October 1938); 'Statute Law Revision' (1939) 13 *Law Institute Journal* 115; 'Statute Law Revision' (1942) 16 *Law Institute Journal* 12, referring to a debate in the Legislative Council of Victoria in November 1941.

of this kind',[26] but the motivation seems to have been a concrete case, rather than formal representations of interested parties. In July 1939, 19-year-old Arthur Farlow was injured when the bicycle he was riding was struck by a car being driven negligently by one JJ Munro.[27] Munro was insured against such liability with the General Accident, Fire and Life Assurance Corporation. A settlement with the insurer was being negotiated, and was on the point of final agreement, when it was discovered that Mr Munro had died. The insurer then denied liability under the policy.[28] The plaintiff's father wrote to O'Keefe which, it seems, prompted him to move, quite quickly, to enact amending legislation.

There was one, uniquely Queensland argument for passing the legislation. As one of the Bill's supporters said in the second reading speech, the root of the problem in the Farlow case came because the head-office of the company was in Sydney. While the Brisbane office wanted to put the question of an ex-gratia payment to a Committee, the proposal was turned down in Sydney, where the company 'made the boast that it has not yet made an ex-gratia payment and does not intend to make one'.[29] By way of contrast, the same supporter argued that, although the company was acting within the laws of Queensland, 'as it was carrying on business in Queensland, it was morally bound to pay this compensation'.[30] The juxtaposition of the moral position being taken by introducing the legislation with the immoral conduct of the southerners from New South Wales, did its credibility no harm.

More broadly, the debate over the introduction of the equivalent of the 1934 Act foreshadowed the arguments that would largely characterise the debates in other Australian jurisdictions, as they considered such legislation. In Queensland, the Bill that was put forward mirrored exactly the English legislation. To the extent that this Bill remedied the Farlow-type situations, it was uncontroversial. But when the Bill reached the Committee stage in the Legislative Assembly – the last real place for legislative debate in Queensland's unicameral parliament – the conservative opposition parties tabled a motion to exclude the estate claiming for pain or suffering, or for any bodily or mental harm suffered by him, or for the curtailment of his expectation of life.

O'Keefe responded in three ways. The first was to point out that denying full damages to the deceased's estate simply reinforced the criticism under English law that it was cheaper to kill, than to wound.[31] This overcame any concerns over whether people unconnected to the deceased personally – such as creditors – would benefit if the estate could claim for these non-pecuniary losses. To the contrary, the Acting Attorney-General thought the prospect of the estate recovering damages for the benefit of creditors a desirable consequence of the reform.[32]

The second was to suggest that the amendment sought was pressed solely in the interests of insurers. When the legislation had been introduced, the Fire Underwriters

[26] *Parliamentary Debates*, Queensland Legislative Assembly, 174 (3 September 1940, O'Keefe).
[27] 'Cyclist Seriously Injured' *The Telegraph* (Brisbane, 26 July 1939) 17.
[28] *Parliamentary Debates*, Queensland Legislative Assembly, 322–23 (11 September 1940, O'Keefe).
[29] ibid 323 (Williams).
[30] ibid.
[31] *Parliamentary Debates*, Queensland Legislative Assembly, 437 (1 October 1940, O'Keefe).
[32] ibid 438.

Association wrote to O'Keefe suggesting amendments. The letter has not survived, but at least one part of the argument cited Lord Roche's speech in *Rose v Ford*, where he expressed concern over the estate claim for loss of expectation of life.[33] Five days before the Committee hearing, the same association had spent two and a half hours trying to convince O'Keefe that the Bill should be amended, and amendments were later tabled in Committee. The idea that the amendments were insurer-driven was taken up by one of O'Keefe's ALP colleagues, asking the proposers of the amendment 'have you a brief from the insurance company?',[34] later interjecting that they 'evidently have a brief for the underwriters',[35] and finally: 'The whole of the case put forward by the hon. Member for Hamilton has been in the interests of the Underwriters' Association and not on behalf of those who are dependants of the victim of the accident'.[36]

The final response was to use the fact that the legislation had an English precedent as reason enough for introducing it. But it would be quite wrong to see this as some form of blind obeisance to the mother country. As O'Keefe described, 'We look upon the English laws as a guide to us, and there is nothing even in the quotations from the highest authorities given by the hon. member for Hamilton to show that this Bill is wrong'.[37] The House of Lords in *Rose v Ford* adopted an interpretation that was reasonable, fair, and equitable to all parties and, as a result, 'we cannot do better than adopt the English Act seeing that it has already been interpreted by the highest authority in the Empire'.[38] He summed up his view in this way:

> There is nothing wrong in giving effect to the decisions of those authorities that I and other hon. Members have quoted, from the Old Country. If they are good enough for England, I cannot see that there is any harm in our accepting them in Australia.[39]

Proponents of the amendments also drew on English experience, but that experience was of the dissatisfaction with the law that the decision of the House of Lords had created. While the rise in insurance premiums that the change would produce was always in the background,[40] the ostensible ground for criticism was that English *lawyers* were complaining of the state of the law.[41] There was certainly evidence to support this view, and the battle lines were drawn over what the best interpretation of the English position actually was.[42] But the position in another Dominion, New Zealand, was unequivocal.

[33] *Rose v Ford* (n 16) 861–62. More generally, see 'Higher Premiums for Car Insurance Will Costs Motorists Here £100,000 for Year' *The Telegraph* (Brisbane, 24 June 1939) 9.

[34] *Parliamentary Debates*, Queensland Legislative Assembly, 433 (1 October 1940, Power).

[35] ibid 434.

[36] ibid 441.

[37] ibid 437 (O'Keefe).

[38] ibid.

[39] ibid 438.

[40] ibid 432, 433, 435, 440 (Russell).

[41] *The Economist* article (n 22) formed the main thrust of the Opposition critique on this point: *Parliamentary Debates*, Queensland Legislative Assembly, 435, 436 (1 October 1940, Russell).

[42] 'Apparently, it is founded on the English amendment, but it is fairly common knowledge that a grave mistake was made in the English amending Act'; 'It was never intended by the English Act that these benefits should go to the estate of a deceased person, particularly as the estate might consist of legatees not connected by blood, and who certainly should not claim damages for the curtailment of expectation of life'; 'As a matter of fact, we have definite information that it is intended to amend the English Act, although, naturally, details of that kind are not being attended to over there to-day': *Parliamentary Debates*, Queensland Legislative Assembly, 433, 439 (1 October 1940, Russell), 441 (Nimmo).

There, the English legislation had been introduced in 1936, only to be amended as suggested in Queensland two years later after stinging judicial criticism of allowing the estate to claim damages for loss of expectation of life.[43] The Opposition used this as evidence as to why Queensland should adopt the amendment but, on its own, it did not persuade the Acting Attorney-General. This was partly because of a lack of information about why the amendment was passed, but it was also about status: 'Never mind what New Zealand did; it is not necessary that we should follow New Zealand'.[44] The Opposition 'quoted a suppositious case from New Zealand, but they have never honestly quoted a case from England'.[45] That was reason enough for Queensland to differ from the reform of a fellow antipodean jurisdiction.

IV. New South Wales – The Politics of Law Reform

Unlike in Queensland, in New South Wales there was a history of concern with the *actio personalis* rule that pre-dated the 1934 Act. In June 1925, the New South Wales Parliamentary Draftsman, Allan Uther, prepared a memorandum for the Commission on Law Reform, chaired and effectively run by Professor John Peden, the Dean of the Law School at the University of Sydney, on amendments to the New South Wales equivalent of Lord Campbell's Act,[46] the Compensation to Relatives Act 1897. One amendment related to the survival of actions:

> I would also suggest for consideration whether a provision should not be introduced preserving the right of action against executors or administrators of the defendant for, owing to the operation of the rule *actio personalis moritur cum persona* it would seem the relations lose their remedy under the Act if the wrongdoer dies whether he dies before or after the death of the person whom he injured, for the Act supplies no remedy either to the person injured while he lives or to his relations after his death against the executors or administrators of the wrong doer.[47]

Peden approved the suggested reform and drafted a bill for introduction in 1925. As was characteristic of statutory law reform in this period, advice was sought from the profession. The secretary of the Bar Council obliged, and the section was altered to make sure it caught both actions commenced but not completed, and those where there was a merely prospective cause of action. The introduction of the Bill was delayed but

[43] It was introduced in 1936 (Law Reform Act 1936 (NZ) pt I). In *McLeavey v Marris and Campbell* (3 February 1938, unreported), NZSC, in instructions to a jury in an action where NZ£7500 was claimed by the estate for loss of expectation of life, Myers CJ in the New Zealand Supreme Court said there was 'something revolting in the idea of living persons making a profit out of another person's death'. More generally, see 'New Zealand Letter' (1938) 11 *Australian Law Journal* 518. The amending legislation was the Statutes Amendment Act 1937 (NZ), passed on 15 March 1938.

[44] *Parliamentary Debates*, Queensland Legislative Assembly, 438 (1 October 1940, O'Keefe).

[45] ibid 443.

[46] Fatal Accidents Act 1846 (9 & 10 Vict c 93).

[47] State Archives Collection of New South Wales, NRS 302/NRS 333: Attorney-General (and Justice) Special Bundles, 1822–1984 – Law Reform (Miscellaneous Provisions) Bill (to amend the law in relation to actions for the recovery of damages, etc – 51/2587), 1925–1952 [12/1352.2] (NSW Archive File), Memorandum from Parliamentary Draftsman to Under-Secretary, Department of Attorney-General and Justice (19 June 1925).

was eventually passed in 1928, extending the coverage of the legislation beyond that of its English counterpart.[48]

When the 1934 English legislation was passed, interest in introducing it in New South Wales was swift. In September 1934, a formal request for reform was made by the firm of solicitors McLachlan Westgarth & Co, citing the seventh edition of *Pollock on Torts* for the inadequacy of the rule. A concrete case was cited involving the serious injury of a nurse being transported by a wealthy grazier, who was killed in the same accident. The grazier's estate was substantial and was administered by a trustee company in Adelaide, which denied liability and offered £25 as an *ex gratia* payment in full settlement.[49] The authors of the letter were vaguely aware of 'a Committee of the House of Lords' being deputed to consider reform, but were unaware of what had happened. Six weeks later, they wrote again to the Minister for Justice. The letter included extracts from the *Law Times*, which highlighted the Law Revision Committee's Interim Report, and the criticism that report made of the operation of the *actio personalis* rule in motor vehicle accident cases. The Minister was pointedly asked whether any legislative action was contemplated 'on the lines suggested'.[50]

While a holding letter was sent to the firm,[51] within government things were moving. Advice was sought in relation to the correspondence by the Under-Secretary of Justice from the Crown Solicitor, who responded by affirming that legislation would be required to deal with the case raised and summarising the report of the Interim Committee. The Assistant Law Officer noted on the reply that the probability of English legislation being passed in England suggested that any New South Wales legislation should be deferred until the former could be seen.[52] In late February 1935, a minute on the subject of 'extending the scope of the Compensation to Relatives Act 1897 in the direction that action for damages may be taken against the estate of a deceased person' was sent to the Under-Secretary of the Premier's Department.[53] It contained a copy of the Interim Committee's Report, and seems to have prompted the Premier's Minute to the Governor in March 1935, seeking a copy of the 1934 legislation through vice regal channels.[54] This arrived in Sydney at the end of August[55] and less than a week later, the Assistant Law Officer summarised the legislation and argued for its enactment, citing

[48] Compensation to Relatives (Amendment) Act 1928 (NSW).

[49] NSW Archive File (n 47), Letter from McLachlan Westgarth & Co to Minister of Justice, 27 September 1934.

[50] NSW Archive File (n 47), Letter from McLachlan Westgarth & Co to Minister of Justice, 6 November 1934.

[51] NSW Archive File (n 47), Letter from Under-Secretary of Justice to McLachlan Westgarth & Co, 9 November 1934.

[52] NSW Archive File (n 47), Annotation of 14 February 1935 of CJ Weigall, Solicitor-General, to letter from Crown Solicitor to Under-Secretary of Justice, 8 February 1935. Confusingly, Weigall signed above an 'Assistant Law Officer' stamp (Assistant Law Officer in the Ministry of Justice) but it seems this was in recognition that his role involved at times standing in for the Attorney-General: K Mason, 'The Office of Solicitor General for New South Wales' [1988] (Autumn) *Bar News – Journal of the New South Wales Bar Association* 22, 25.

[53] NSW Archive File (n 47), Minute, Department of Attorney-General and of Justice to Under-Secretary, Premier's Department, 26 February 1935.

[54] NSW Archive File (n 47), Minute for His Excellency the Governor, Premier's Department, 1 March 1935.

[55] NSW Archive File (n 47), Letter from JH Thomas, Dominions Office to Sir Alexander Hoare-Ruthven, 31 July 1935; Correspondence note from Under-Secretary, Premier's Department to Under-Secretary of Justice, 29 August 1935.

the importance of maintaining unity of law in British communities in regard to the enforcement of civil rights of actions, as well as the distinguished source of the legislation in the Interim Report.[56]

Three days later, the Under-Secretary of the Ministry of Justice prepared a minute for the Attorney-General detailing all of the background – from the initial correspondence from McLachlan Westgarth & Co, to the Assistant Law Officer's recommendation – and sought advice from the Attorney-General whether 'he desires such legislation to be introduced'.[57] A handwritten notation of approval on the Minute made by the Attorney-General was then actioned by a letter to McLachlan Westgarth & Co, advising that he had 'approved the introduction of appropriate legislation and has given instructions for the preparation of the necessary Bill'.[58] But, while the papers appear to have been sent to the Parliamentary Draftsman, nothing further seems to have been done to prepare the legislation. A similar scenario played out in early 1937. A firm of solicitors wrote to the Minister of Justice, highlighting another example of the injustices of the rule in relation to the death of all parties to a claim in the same accident.[59] The Under-Secretary of Justice wrote to the firm, advising that amending legislation to deal with the question was being contemplated, with a view to being introduced into Parliament in the next session.[60] Indeed, the Attorney-General, Sir Henry Manning, directed that the relevant papers, including the previous recommendation for legislation, be referred to the Parliamentary Draftsman 'for preparation of the necessary Bill of which Mr Manning has already approved'.[61] Again, no further steps were taken.

By the time the McKell ALP government came to power in New South Wales in May 1941, nothing had been done to reform this (or any other) area of private law. This lack of progress across the board on law reform meant the abolition of the *actio personalis* rule competed with a variety of other reforms for government attention. These included reform of the class of dependants for Lord Campbell's Act claims; changes to the all-or-nothing contributory negligence defence; abolition of the common employment defence; abolition of the rule that a husband was liable for his wife's torts; awards of interest on damages; abolition of the rule prohibiting contribution between tortfeasors; and the abolition of the restrictions imposed by *Victoria Railway Commissioners v Coultas*[62] on awards of damages for nervous shock. After some changes of mind – and some changes forced by political necessity – survival of actions was paired with

[56] NSW Archive File (n 47), Assistant Law Officer, Law Reform (Miscellaneous Provisions) Act 1934, 3 September 1935.

[57] NSW Archive File (n 47), Minute, Under-Secretary, Department of the Attorney-General and of Justice, 6 September 1935.

[58] NSW Archive File (n 47), Letter from Under-Secretary of Justice to McLachlan Westgarth & Co, 18 September 1935.

[59] NSW Archive File (n 47), Letter from McCaw, Moray & Co to Minister of Justice, 15 January 1937. A later letter recognised that the 1928 amendments to the Compensation to Relatives Act made some improvements where the tortfeasor died but did not solve the whole problem: NSW Archive File (n 47), Letter from McCaw, Moray & Co to Under-Secretary of Justice, 23 February 1937.

[60] NSW Archive File (n 47), Letter from Under-Secretary of Justice to McCaw, Moray & Co, 20 January 1937.

[61] NSW Archive File (n 47), Minute from Under-Secretary of Justice to Attorney-General, 19 January 1937. For contemporary press criticism of the rule see A Barrister, 'The Lawyer's Day Book' *The Sun* (Sydney, 25 July 1937) 5.

[62] *Victoria Railway Commissioners v Coultas* (1887) 13 App Cas 222 (PC).

reform of the *Coultas* rule in amending legislation. Both proposals ending up being controversial.

The first record in the archives of the general abolition of the *actio personalis* rule coming back onto the political landscape is a memo of 27 October 1941 from the Solicitor-General, CE Weigall, to the Under-Secretary of Justice. Under the heading, 'Compensation to Relatives Act 1941', Weigall opined that the *actio personalis* rule should be abolished.[63] By December 1941, the new Attorney-General, CE Martin, had arranged for a minute to be prepared for Cabinet, advocating the abolition of the rule, and referencing the 1934 Act and the New Zealand legislation that adopted it in 1936.[64] No decision by Cabinet on the proposal appears in the records. By July 1942, an updated memo adding further areas for reform was planned for Cabinet,[65] but it was held back and only amendments relating to Lord Campbell's Act proceeded to Cabinet in October.[66] When Dudley Westgarth, a solicitor who had written to a previous Attorney-General advocating reform of the rule, wrote again in December 1942 along the same lines,[67] Martin authorised a response which stated he was 'well aware' of the need for reform of the maxim, that Cabinet was not able to deal with it yet, but that he was hoping it would do so early next year.[68] Curiously, both parties seemed to be unaware that the specific problem that Westgarth raised had now been solved. Following South Australian and Victorian examples, the New South Wales legislation requiring the taking out of third party liability insurance in relation to the use of motor vehicles allowed a direct claim against the third party liability insurer, when the insured driver died before the claim.[69] That legislation was passed in June 1942, and, although it required a commencement order to come into effect, the proclamation giving the commencement date as 1 March 1943 was gazetted on 23 December, only five days after Martin authorised the reply to Westgarth.[70] Given that Martin was considering a range of general reforms at the time, no doubt the prospect of abolishing the rule across the board was the preferred policy option. But it also speaks to the dynamic environment in which the *actio personalis* reform was taking place.

By January 1943, the indefatigable Martin had placed another minute before Cabinet on tort reform which included abolition of the *actio personalis* rule.[71] As with the

[63] NSW Archive File (n 47), Memo from CE Weigall, Solicitor-General, to Under-Secretary of Justice, 27 October 1941.

[64] NSW Archive File (n 47), Memo, CE Martin, Proposed Law of Tort (Compensation to Relatives and Miscellaneous Provisions) Bill, 28 November 1941; NSW Archive File (n 47), Minute for Cabinet, 22 December 1941.

[65] NSW Archive File (n 47), Minute for Cabinet (supplementary to Minute of 24 December 1941), 6 July 1942.

[66] NSW Archive File (n 47), Annotations on Minute, Department of Attorney-General and of Justice, Legislative Council's Amendment to Motor Vehicle (Third Party Insurance) Bill: Proposal to amend the general law, 3 July 1942.

[67] NSW Archive File (n 47), Letter from Dudley Westgarth to CE Martin, 17 December 1942. The letter was prompted by press reports on the introduction of a bill to mitigate the effect of the *Coultas* case. Westgarth suggested that the bill might also include an amendment of the *actio personalis* rule.

[68] NSW Archive File (n 47), Annotation to copy letter, Frank Murphy to D Westgarth, 18 December 1942.

[69] Motor Vehicles (Third Party Insurance) Act 1942 (NSW) s 15(2)(a).

[70] Motor Vehicles (Third Party Insurance) Act 1942 – Proclamation (1502), New South Wales Government Gazette No 172 (24 December 1942) 3238.

[71] NSW Archive File (n 47), Minute for Cabinet, 'Suggested Amendment to the Law of Torts', 1 January 1943.

December 1941 memo, the listing of comparator jurisdictions in the case for reform is striking. Paragraph 2 noted that the rule formed 'no part of continental law, nor the law of Scotland, and was abolished in England in 1934 and in New Zealand in 1936. Legislation abolishing it is also in force in many States of the USA'.[72] Nowhere was it mentioned that the other five Australian state jurisdictions had abrogated the rule, largely in similar form, but also with some differences between each other, and also from the 1934 Act. There is also no sense that there had been any controversy associated with the passage of the legislation in any of those jurisdictions. All that was noted was that, in September 1935, a previous Attorney-General had approved the drafting of a bill on the English lines, but that it was never presented to Parliament.[73] Given this background, it was perhaps unsurprising that, when Cabinet approved a version of the suggested reforms which included the abolition of the *actio personalis* rule in March 1943,[74] Martin directed that the draftsman should 'Follow the provisions of the English Act'.[75]

The focus on the English legislation also underpinned the more detailed preparation for the bill. When the senior civil servant in the Department of Attorney-General and of Justice, Holmwood, prepared a memo for Martin, the emphasis was on the causes of action that were caught or exempted from the legislation. Winfield's views on the question in the *Canadian Bar Review* were cited, as was an extract from the *Harvard Law Review* critiquing the treatment of exemplary damages.[76] No reference was made to the controversy that surrounded the applicability of the legislation to non-pecuniary loss, or to any Australian legislation that considered this question (or indeed the question of which causes of action were affected, which had been debated in a number of jurisdictions).[77] Thus, the table which Holmwood prepared to illustrate the different approaches to causes of action had columns for English and New Zealand Acts, the English Law Revision Committee, the *Harvard Law Review* and Percy Winfield, but had nothing on the approach of its sibling Australian jurisdictions.[78]

Almost 10 years after it had been first mooted, it seemed the 1934 Act would be implemented in New South Wales. A further delay arose when Martin left for active

[72] ibid.

[73] ibid para 2. See also NSW Archive File (n 47), Minute for Cabinet, December 22 1941, para 13.

[74] NSW Archive File (n 47), Letter from WJ McKell to CE Martin, 17 March 1943.

[75] NSW Archive File (n 47), Annotation of 6 April 1943 to Minute, Department of Attorney-General and of Justice, 'Proposed Bill to abolish the doctrine "Actio Personalis Moritur Cum Persona"', 29 March 1943.

[76] NSW Archive File (n 47), Memo by Holmwood, 'Proposed Bill to Abolish the Doctrine "Actio Personalis Moritur Cum Persona"', 24 March 1943.

[77] See, eg, *Parliamentary Debates*, South Australian House of Assembly, vol 1, 900 (10 October 1940).

[78] NSW Archive File (n 47), Memo by Holmwood, 'Proposed Bill to Abolish the Doctrine "Actio Personalis Moritur Cum Persona"', Comparative Table, 24 March 1943. In no Australian jurisdiction was the position in Canadian jurisdictions discussed. Ontario first passed legislation abrogating the rule in 1886 and there were differences between this legislation and the 1934 Act. Nonetheless, once these differences were held not to prevent the application of *Rose v Ford* to the legislation, the Ontario legislature abolished the estate claim for loss of expectation of life. For discussion, see FA Brewin, 'Loss of Expectation of Life' (1938) 16 *Canadian Bar Review* 119; CA Wright, 'The Abolition of Claims for Shortened Expectation of Life by a Deceased's Estate' (1938) 16 *Canadian Bar Review* 193; 'Case and Comment: Damages – Shortened Expectation of Life' (1941) 19 *Canadian Bar Review* 141. In 1939, New Brunswick also introduced survival of actions legislation, excluding the estate claim for loss of expectation of life: 'Legislation: The New Brunswick Survival of Actions Act 1939' (1940) 18 *Canadian Bar Review* 137.

service in New Guinea.[79] It was initially agreed that, while Martin was away, the measure would not be proceeded with in the current Parliament.[80] However, motivation for a more urgent attitude came from an unusual source. In August 1943, the Chief Justice of the New South Wales Supreme Court, Sir Frederick Jordan, wrote to the Attorney-General – now RR Downing – noting an anomaly under the Compensation to Relatives Act which allowed actions to survive where the wrongdoer died after the deceased whose death gave rise to the dependant's claim, but not before.[81] It was decided that, rather than make a piecemeal amendment to cover the problem under the wrongful death legislation, the bringing forward of the general abolition of the *actio personalis* bar included in Martin's original draft omnibus Bill earlier in 1943 would be preferable.[82] Thus a bill was drafted in October that included this, along with provisions allowing and extending the recovery of damages for nervous shock.[83] On the *actio personalis* rule, the English Act was adopted (unsurprisingly, given the history of the discussions) except that various time limits were doubled from six months to 12 months.

The Law Reform (Miscellaneous Provisions) Bill was introduced by Premier McKell in November 1943. The introductory comments suggested that McKell thought the Bill was uncontroversial:

> This measure is an earnest of the Government's resolve to review, and, where necessary, to revise general legal principles which have outlived their usefulness and have ceased to serve the needs of society. The law should be the servant of the people, not their master; it should be moulded to serve the changing needs of society, not allowed to become and to remain a straitjacket. … I might say, in passing, that I do not anticipate that this bill will prove contentious, and I feel that the House will agree that it is in no sense a party measure.[84]

McKell took the same tone in an article for the ALP newspaper, the *Australian Worker*, in early December.[85] The bill would help 'free us from many of the remaining fetters of the Victorian era' and allow justice to be delivered in a direction 'all agree is deserving'.[86] As far as the abolition of the *actio personalis* rule was concerned, McKell's reference to the wealthy grazier example which Dudley Westgarth had first raised in the mid-1930s closed the loop fittingly on what must have seemed a powerful case for reform. Yet it is difficult to believe McKell thought the bill's passage would be all plain sailing. The Leader of the Opposition, Mair, conceded that, if the legislation was for the purpose of making a desirable objective more readily achievable, there could be no objection to it. Ominously, though, he noted that the nervous shock provisions had indeed been discussed during the passage of the compulsory third party motor vehicle legislation

[79] 'Rumours of Change in Cabinet' *Truth* (Sydney, 2 May 1943) 16; 'State Minister on Active Service' *Sydney Morning Herald* (Sydney, 19 May 1943) 6.
[80] NSW Archive File (n 47), Minute for Cabinet, Law Reform (Miscellaneous Provisions) Bill, annexure to Letter from Under-Secretary Premier's Department to Under-Secretary of Justice, 8 October 1943.
[81] NSW Archive File (n 47), Letter from Chief Justice to RR Downing, Attorney-General, 25 August 1943 (citing the case of *Kebby v Waldron* (1943) 43 SR (NSW) 342).
[82] Minute for Cabinet (n 80).
[83] Despite no longer being Attorney-General, it seems Martin's approval for proceeding was obtained: NSW Archive File (n 47), Annotation to file note of response to letter of Chief Justice Jordan, 21 September 1943.
[84] *Parliamentary Debates*, New South Wales Legislative Assembly, 880 (18 November 1943, McKell).
[85] 'The Law Should Serve the People: Amendments to NSW Enactments' *Australian Worker* (Sydney, 1 December 1943) 8.
[86] ibid.

several years earlier.[87] Whether McKell expected similar controversy over the survival of actions legislation is harder to gauge. The complete lack of discussion of the position in other Australian jurisdictions, and the controversies that had surrounded the non-pecuniary loss issue in the preparation of the bill, at least suggest that he might have been. But it is hard not to read the capitalised and bold text at the end of the article – that the 'endeavour to improve the law as it stands should not involve any questions of party-political principle' – as evincing some foreboding of future difficulties.[88]

The detail of the Bill was left to the second reading in early March 1944. It is not necessary to set out McKell's detailed analysis of the *actio personalis* provisions, but the alignment of the New South Wales suggested amendment with that of England was a strength:

> Its enactment will bring New South Wales into line with the modern developments of the law in England, following the Law Revision Committee's first report. Great Britain seems to be somewhat ahead of us in dealing with law reform.[89]

When McKell was questioned on the relationship between the survival of actions claim and the Lord Campbell's Act claim, he simply said that the recent House of Lords cases, which had a 'far-reaching effect' on the law on the matter, had been given close and detailed consideration. Cryptically, he finished by saying, 'Apparently the last decision of the House of Lords in this respect was revolutionary, having in mind what had been considered to be the law up to that time'.[90] If consideration was given to the revolutionary decision (*Benham v Gambling*?), it does not survive in the official records.

Opposition members immediately commented that McKell had said nothing about what had happened in other Australian states. The Premier had noted the Bill was based on the recommendations of the English Law Revision Committee:

> and he expressed the view that the safest course was for the House to accept it. I think he went so far as to say that we ought to accept it. I appreciate the fact that the committee referred to by him has done excellent work, but regret that the Premier himself has not traced the history of this kind of legislation in the Australian State Parliaments, because in recent years there have been before most of the State Houses, the very questions involved in this measure. … Amending legislation has been passed by other Australian Parliaments, and hon. members should be fully informed on the matter. This is a deliberative assembly. We should have more information from the head of the Government following upon the investigation regarding similar legislation in the other States, and I should like to know why this matter has been overlooked.[91]

It was pointed out that the suggested changes on non-economic loss were not a matter of party politics: ALP and Labour governments in Western Australia and New Zealand respectively had derogated from the English model.[92] The suggested amendments would appeal 'not only to the crusted conservatives, but also to the radicalism of those

[87] *Parliamentary Debates*, New South Wales Legislative Assembly, 880 (18 November 1943, Mair).
[88] 'The Law Should Serve the People' (n 85).
[89] *Parliamentary Debates*, New South Wales Legislative Assembly, 1428 (1 March 1944, McKell).
[90] ibid.
[91] *Parliamentary Debates*, New South Wales Legislative Assembly, 1432, 1434 (1 March 1944, Richardson).
[92] ibid 1435.

who carry on the Government in other parts of our Empire'.[93] The Bill passed the second reading, but, on initiation in Committee, McKell agreed to consider the cases and Australian legislation in connection with another Bill.[94] The incorporation of the 1934 Act into New South Wales law would not be affected. The Bill was read a third time in the Assembly the next day, without debate.[95]

While the McKell government had the numbers in the Assembly, it did not have a majority in the Legislative Council, and it was there that the attack on the legislation was concentrated. The Attorney-General, RR Downing, repeated McKell's justification: the *actio personalis* provisions would bring the law into line with modern English developments.[96] This time, other states were not ignored: the legislation followed the overdue reform effected in England and by the other states, as well as New Zealand thereafter.[97] This was hardly helpful because, as Sir Henry Manning for the Opposition pointed out, the majority of those jurisdictions had excluded the estate claim for damages for non-pecuniary loss.[98] As in other states, the error of the English legislation was put down to the failure of the Law Revision Committee to see the step taken in *Rose v Ford*.[99] In reply, Downing now recognised that other Australian jurisdictions had indeed amended the legislation so a new tack was taken:

> It is necessary, I suggest, to look at this matter in a different light. I have discussed it with the Premier as suggested and I now put to the House some considerations that appeal to me. It has been suggested that when a person is killed his estate should not be able to secure damages for pain and suffering of the deceased or for the curtailment of his expectation of life. If that provision were inserted into the measure it would be cheaper to kill than to maim.[100]

In support of the English status quo, Downing rehearsed familiar arguments: Lord Wright was on the Law Revision Committee and sat in *Rose v Ford* so the 'unanticipated consequences' argument was hard to make;[101] *Benham v Gambling* had clarified any ambiguities;[102] and there had been options for legislative reversal of the *Rose v Ford* position, but nothing had been done.[103] More novel was the selective citing of English

[93] ibid (Treatt).

[94] ibid 1436. Presumably this was the Bill that proposed a widening of the class of dependants under the Compensation to Relatives Act 1897 (NSW). An extension of the class was made in the Committee stages of the Motor Vehicles (Third Party Insurance) Act 1942 (NSW), which was enacted as s 44 of that Act, but there were continuing discussions in the Department of the Attorney-General and of Justice about extending the class further.

[95] And received support from parts of the non-ALP, if popular, press: 'Reforms in Law on Injury Timely Move' *Truth* (Sydney, 5 March 1944) 15.

[96] *Parliamentary Debates*, New South Wales Legislative Council, 1691 (15 March 1944, Downing).

[97] ibid 1695.

[98] ibid 1698, 1699. See also 1705, 1706 (Holden).

[99] ibid 1699.

[100] ibid 1708 (Downing).

[101] ibid 1708–09.

[102] ibid 1709. Sir Owen Dixon was not impressed with the decision (O Dixon, 'The Survival of Causes of Action' (1948) 1 *University of Queensland Law Journal* 1, 2) but what little contemporary Australian commentary there was broadly, if pragmatically, supported the outcome: JH Arundell, 'Loss of Expectation of Life' (1939–41) 1 *Res Judicatae* 245; 'Recent Cases: Notes and Comments: Loss of Expectation of Life – Measure of Damages' (1941) 15 *Australian Law Journal* 88.

[103] *Parliamentary Debates*, New South Wales Legislative Council, 1710 (15 March 1944, Downing).

academic support for that position.[104] The final affirmation, however, was again a reference to the efficacy of English law: 'the correct action is to follow the law as it exists in England, particularly in view of the eminent persons who recommended the original legislation in England'.[105]

While the Bill passed its second reading, the attack on it continued when it returned to the Legislative Council in Committee with a proposed amendment to exclude the estate claim for non-pecuniary loss. The amendment took the South Australian form: non-pecuniary loss was to be excluded irrespective of whether the cause of death was the original wrong, or not. The second reading arguments were largely rehearsed: the 'cheaper to kill than to maim' assertion (on the one hand) against the protest that giving the estate a claim for non-pecuniary losses provided damages for a personal loss that the recipients had not suffered (on the other). Only rarely were wider, and arguably more pertinent, issues raised. Downing noted the absence of any claim for non-financially dependent family members under the Compensation to Relatives Act, but only for the purpose of reinforcing the 'cheaper to kill than maim' argument.[106] For the same purpose, he argued that, even if the beneficiaries received something to which they may not otherwise have been entitled, as between the wrongdoer and the beneficiaries the latter had the better claim: 'they have done nothing wrong. Who started all the trouble? The wrongdoer. Therefore, if anybody should be prejudiced, it should be the wrongdoer'.[107] But the trump card remained English law:

> I suggest to the House that possibly the most eminent legal committee ever constituted in the British Empire recommended these provisions in the English law. … There has been no suggestion of an amendment of the law in England. … On the contrary, the most recent edition of Winfield's book on torts, published last year, strongly supports the retention of the English law in its present form. I, therefore, say that our law should be brought into conformity with the law in England.[108]

It was to no avail. The Legislative Council voted, by a majority of two, to accept the amendment. The Cabinet decided to oppose the amendments[109] and when the Council's amendments came back before the Assembly, McKell's critique was brutal.[110] The Council insisted on its amendment,[111] however, and as Cabinet decided that the Council's amendment should still be rejected,[112] the Bill was dropped.[113]

[104] No detailed reference was provided in Hansard but the reference to Goodhart was to the second part of an article written in 1936 on the American position on damages for loss of expectation of life. Only the Court of Appeal decision in *Rose v Ford* was available when it was written (A Goodhart, 'Damages for Loss of Life Under American Law' (1936) 82 *Law Journal* 293, 311. The other contributor was in fact the author of a short 'Letter to the Editor', responding to an earlier longer article advocating abolition: see H Munro, 'Negligent Homicide and Loss of Expectation of Life' (1941) 91 *Law Journal* 246; F Gates, 'Negligent Homicide and Loss of Expectation of Life' (1941) 91 *Law Journal* 235.

[105] *Parliamentary Debates*, New South Wales Legislative Council, 1710 (15 March 1944, Downing).

[106] *Parliamentary Debates*, New South Wales Legislative Council, 1855 (22 March 1944, Downing).

[107] ibid.

[108] ibid 1856.

[109] NSW Archive File (n 47), Letter from McKell to Downing, 28 March 1944.

[110] *Parliamentary Debates*, New South Wales Legislative Assembly, 2249–53 (30 March 1944, McKell).

[111] *Parliamentary Debates*, New South Wales Legislative Council, 2297–302 (4 April 1944).

[112] NSW Archive File (n 47), Letter from McKell to Downing, 13 April 1944.

[113] 'Law Reform Bill Out: Withdrawn by Premier' *Sydney Morning Herald* (Sydney, 14 April 1944) 6.

The debates on the proposed Council amendments, while increasingly bad-tempered, did (eventually) get to some of the key legal points of difference. In his rejection of the Council's amendment, McKell said that 'most of us' accepted that opportunities for profit by another's death should not be enlarged, but that this had to give way to the weightier principle 'that killing should not be cheaper than the infliction of injury'.[114] To the argument that the beneficiaries of the deceased had no interest in the non-pecuniary loss damages, McKell observed that exactly the same could be said for a living plaintiff who recovered non-pecuniary loss damages and died the next day, so that the beneficiaries inherited those damages.[115] Rather, as he did in response to an Opposition speech during the second reading debate, he raised the issue of equivalence: whether a living plaintiff would receive less than on the basis determined in *Rose v Ford*.[116] Conversely, Manning's argument was, at base, that this was the wrong analogy. Once death had occurred, the Compensation to Relatives Act was the comparator and, under that legislation, the dependants would receive nothing for non-pecuniary loss. To alter this rule through the subterfuge of allowing the estate claim for non-pecuniary loss was unacceptable.[117] Hence Manning's focus, during his second reading speech, on the impossibility of envisaging that it was intended that every head of damages would survive for the benefit of the estate.[118]

Even with the invocation of English law in support, the Council's attitude nonetheless provoked McKell to go on the political attack. A letter to his support base in the *Australian Worker* on 5 April – the day after the Council rejected the Assembly's attempts to insist on its original provisions – built on the already politicised response he had made in the Assembly to the Council amendment. The Council's attitude was about protecting insurance companies and their profits. Starting by saying that the attitude of the Council 'callously demonstrated its complete indifference to the welfare of the community', he argued that the Council was simply protecting the interests in big business in the form of insurance companies:

> I unhesitatingly state that seldom in the history of this Parliament has there been such a sacrifice of personal rights on the altar of Mammon as that perpetrated by the Legislative Council in dealing with this particular measure. The Council's amendments are totally unacceptable to the Lower House, and, if the Upper House is looking for a fight, my Government could not ask for a better cause upon which to join issue with those members who, in their capacity as guardian angels of the profits of insurance companies and other allied business interests, seek to sabotage the major provisions of the Government's humane bill.[119]

McKell was a good as his word. In his April article, he expressly noted that the legislative changes did not form part of any ALP policy platform and hence should have been treated as non-party. However, in his election pitch for the upcoming New South Wales election in May, the re-introduction of the Law Reform (Miscellaneous Provisions) Bill

[114] *Parliamentary Debates*, New South Wales Legislative Assembly, 2249 (30 March 1944, McKell).
[115] ibid 2251.
[116] *Parliamentary Debates*, New South Wales Legislative Assembly, 1435 (1 March 1944, McKell).
[117] *Parliamentary Debates*, New South Wales Legislative Council, 2299–301 (4 April 1944, Manning).
[118] *Parliamentary Debates*, New South Wales Legislative Council, 1698 (15 March 1944, Manning).
[119] 'Political Guardians of Big Business: Who is the Upper House Protecting?' *The Australian Worker* (Sydney, 5 April 1944) 9.

(which included survival of actions) was now party policy.[120] And, when he convincingly won the election, the battle lines were quickly redrawn. When McKell indicated that the Bill would be introduced in the first session of Parliament, a spokesman for the insurance industry estimated that the liability costs associated with a death if the Bill was introduced (which also included the extended claim for nervous shock, as well as non-pecuniary loss claims for the estate) would be tripled.[121] McKell responded by criticising the anonymity of the spokesman – in contrast to the political opponents who were prepared to be judged on the stand they took – and noting that the 'real opposition' to the Bill was from the insurance companies.[122]

When the Bill was re-introduced in October 1944, it was immediately trench warfare, with a long first reading debate on whether the election result had indeed given McKell a mandate for the Bill.[123] The second reading, a week later, did little more than repeat the well-rehearsed arguments except that, this time, the significance of the *Benham v Gambling* clarification was given much greater prominence by McKell than it had been given when it was raised late in debates on the previous Bill. On the conduct of the other Australian states, after *Rose v Ford* they had run for cover but 'England, rightly, did not'.[124] While the Opposition maintained its approach that the Law Revision Committee had not anticipated the consequences (and, seemingly, that the House of Lords in *Rose v Ford* was incorrect), there was greater explicit recognition that a divergence from English law might be required:

> The House must accept responsibility for making up its mind on whether it is impressed with the bill and it will not be unduly influenced by the circumstance that a committee of legal men in England expressed one opinion. Legislatures of democratic outlook expressed a contrary view.[125]

The Bill passed its second reading but, in Committee, substantive debate ended when McKell agreed to consider possible changes for damages 'in respect of pain or suffering'.[126] But nothing was offered to the Opposition when the Bill was introduced into the Council, and the arguments in the second reading debate simply settled into the now familiar pattern and the debate was adjourned.[127] However, by the time debate resumed three weeks later, a compromise had at last been reached: the second reading debate was truncated when it was realised the long struggle was over, and, in Committee, the Victorian provision (which excluded the estate's claim for non-pecuniary loss only where the death resulted from the tort) was adopted by

[120] '"Cheaper to Kill than to Maim": Council Amendment to Compensation Bill.: Premier McKell's Indignation' *The Australian Worker* (Sydney, 19 April 1944) 7; 'Mr McKell States Labour's Policy' *Sydney Morning Herald* (Sydney, 11 May 1944) 3.

[121] 'Law Reform Bill: "Lawyers' Feast"' *Sydney Morning Herald* (Sydney, 26 August 1944) 5.

[122] 'Criticism of Law Bill: Premier's Reply' *Sydney Morning Herald* (Sydney, 28 August 1944) 4.

[123] *Parliamentary Debates*, New South Wales Legislative Assembly, 399 (11 October 1944).

[124] *Parliamentary Debates*, New South Wales Legislative Assembly, 520 (18 October 1944, McKell).

[125] ibid 523 (Treatt). He later said: 'After all, the argument of the Premier that the English legislature has not amended their Act is no better argument than mine, that Legislatures in Australia have seen fit to alter the law. However, I suppose we must carry our own responsibility in New South Wales and consider what is the best provision to make': at 525.

[126] ibid 530 (McKell).

[127] *Parliamentary Debates*, New South Wales Legislative Council, 826–37 (8 November 1944).

agreement.[128] Other compromises on the nervous shock provisions ended any opposition to the Bill. The bitter struggle that had gone on over two bills, interrupted by a state election, rather petered out; it took three days from the Committee stage in the Council until Royal Assent.[129] Downing justified the compromise by not letting the perfect be the enemy of the good. Ultimately, he thought the consequences of the *actio personalis* rule were sufficiently unfortunate that it was still advantageous to pass the Bill, despite the departures from the 1934 Act it contained.[130]

V. New South Wales in Retrospect

The New South Wales experience of passing survival of actions legislation is unique among the Australian jurisdictions. It was the final state to introduce legislation on the issue, so it ought to have had the benefit of the consideration of the question in the other Australian jurisdictions. Yet the discussion in those jurisdictions was almost completely ignored.[131] Even the Opposition saw the comparative data as a numbers game: more states had excluded non-pecuniary loss from the estate claim than had allowed it. This required adherence to the 1934 Act to be justified by the McKell government by the singular quality of English law, a tricky balancing act, given the fact that the other section of the Bill on nervous shock was explicitly departing from that law. Conversely, the Opposition conservatives struggled to align themselves too much with the idea that the changes they were suggesting were directly contrary to English law. On one level, the debate turned into a somewhat surreal exercise in arguing over how much English law knew what it was actually doing, and whether it was the result of the exigencies of the wartime restrictions on legislative time in Westminster. As the underlying political reality – that the insurance companies, many with English affiliations, were opposed to the estate claim for loss of expectation of life – was never far from the surface, the political representation of English law in support of the opposing positions was a characteristic of the parliamentary debate over the issue. The contingent gravitas of English law was graphically illustrated within the Law Reform (Miscellaneous Provisions) Bill itself, in clause 4, which extended the right to claim damages for nervous shock beyond the English law. It was not unfair of one member of the Opposition in the Legislative Council to note,

> We were told by the Minister that it was wrong to amend clause 2 because that was the law of England. … One should be consistent and when an argument is advanced that one clause should be passed because it is the law of England, the same principle should be applied to other clauses.[132]

[128] *Parliamentary Debates*, New South Wales Legislative Council, 1487–89 (5 December 1944).

[129] The Assembly accepted Council's amendments two days later (*Parliamentary Debates*, New South Wales Legislative Assembly, 1672 (7 December 1944).

[130] *Parliamentary Debates*, New South Wales Legislative Council, 1489 (5 December 1944, Downing).

[131] And where mentioned, confused. Even at the end of the long debates on the issue, in November 1944, Sir Henry Manning thought that Tasmania had followed Queensland in enacting the 1934 Act (*Parliamentary Debates*, New South Wales Legislative Council, 834 (8 November 1944, Manning)). In fact, the Tasmanian legislation of 1943 adopted the South Australian provision on the survival of non-pecuniary loss (Administration and Probate Act 1943 (Tas) s 2, introducing s 27(3)(IV) into the Administration and Probate Act 1935 (Tas)).

[132] *Parliamentary Debates*, New South Wales Legislative Council, 1862 (22 March 1944, Holden).

The New South Wales reform also illustrates a feature common to the reform in other jurisdictions. There was genuine confusion over what, exactly, allowing the estate claim for non-pecuniary loss would achieve, especially the claim for loss of expectation of life. Ultimately, this reflected the problem identified by Sir Owen Dixon in an article on the topic he wrote in 1948: damages to the estate under the survival of actions legislation were being used as a means of fixing a flaw with the damages limitation in Lord Campbell's Act actions.[133] While McKell and Downing did at times refer to the inadequacy of damages awarded under the Compensation to Relatives Act, it was never seriously contemplated that a solution along the South Australian lines might have been one way of solving the impasse.[134] Taking that route would also have addressed one strand of the Opposition argument: that the relatives of the deceased were taken care of by a claim under the Compensation to Relatives Act. While the archive is largely silent after the original Bill was introduced in late 1943, what it does show, along with McKell's speech on introducing the Bill, is either ignorance or disinterest in the efforts of other states. This resulted in the key legal problem being masked by the other arguments, raised on both sides, about the efficacy of the English law, about beneficiaries inheriting non-pecuniary loss damages in which they had no interest, and so on, which have been discussed above. The result is that there is a strong sense in the New South Wales debates of the parties fencing with shadows.

VI. Conclusion

The introduction of the survival of actions legislation in Queensland and New South Wales reveals many facets characteristic of the wider interaction between English law and its diaspora legal community. To those who look for grandiose statements as evidence of legal independence, the evidence will reveal the imperial deference that required Australian legislatures to look to the 1934 Act as first port of call to reform. As this analysis has showed, however, both the legal and especially the political dynamics of this statutory reform of private law played out very differently in Queensland and New South Wales than they did in England. Put simply, the 1934 Act in England was seen as a lawyer's reform, supported by the eminence of the members of the Committee on which it was based. Other than the Solicitor-General who introduced the Bill, only four other members spoke inconsequentially. One said the Bill was 'entirely a non-party matter'.[135] When, in the House of Lords, Lord Danesfort – who made the only substantive comments on the Bill as it passed through the Westminster Parliament – was told by the Chair of the Committee, Lord Hanworth, that 'nobody who has not given continuous attention to the problems involved can speak with any authority', the latter was asserting the primacy of professional competence.[136]

[133] Dixon (n 102).
[134] A limited claim for solatium to surviving spouses and parents of deceased children: Wrongs Act Amendment Act 1940 (SA) s 5.
[135] Mitchell (n 12) 267.
[136] ibid 265.

By the time the question of adopting the legislation reached Australian shores, the scene was very different. Even when the 1934 Act was passed, there was already a history of limited abrogation and attempts at abolition of the rule. The 1934 Act could not be adopted without the legal baggage and economic expense (to insurers) that *Rose v Ford* added. Such a change was no longer a question for the lawyers, and while the legal arguments were extensively canvassed, they competed against broader policy issues about the costs and extent of compensation associated with death. In that political contest, the relative authoritativeness of English law was co-opted, depending on the answer that was wanted to that wider political question. Perhaps deference to English law did prevent consideration of more radical responses to the challenges which the English Law Reform Committee had been asked to tackle. But it was the local political dynamics that shaped the way the question was framed, argued and resolved before the legislatures of Queensland and New South Wales. At a superficial level, it is accurate to say that Queensland strictly conformed to the 1934 Act, and New South Wales did not. As the above analysis suggests, however, it would be wrong to see the end result as a proxy for the extent of the deference to English law that each legislature showed. Certainly, both jurisdictions began with English law – as the cultural and intellectual milieu in which lawyers and legislatures operated required – but that starting point was a springboard into wider discussions about whether the 1934 Act, as applied in England, was best for them. Whatever final result was reached, it was plainly not a simple case of excessive deference to the superiority of the metropole over the periphery.

All Australian states and territories now have survivorship legislation that excludes estate claims for non-pecuniary loss.[137] New South Wales retains the legislation that it adopted in 1944. However, Queensland's adoption of this position is more recent. In 1971, a working paper of the Queensland Law Reform Commission, after noting that little was recovered under these heads, nonetheless decided to abolish them for estate claims. The one-paragraph justification referred to only one of the arguments frequently raised in the 1940s debates – that these damages were personal to a living plaintiff – but, with the academic support of John Fleming, recommended falling into line with the other Australian states and territories. Paradoxically, the authors argued it would be more consistent, and remove doubts, if the exclusion was general, so exclusion was recommended in all cases.[138] The Common Law Practice Amendment Bill was

[137] Administration and Probate Act 1935 (Tas) s 27(3)(c)(ii); Law Reform (Miscellaneous Provisions) Act 1944 (NSW) s 2(2)(d); Administration and Probate Act 1958 (Vic) s 29(2)(c)(ii); Civil Law (Wrongs) Act 2002 (ACT) s 16(3)(b)(i); Survival of Actions Act 1940 (SA) s 3; Law Reform (Miscellaneous Provisions) Act 1941 (WA) s 4(2)(d) (other than for where the death is caused by tortious exposure to asbestos when the fact the death *is* caused by the tort allows the estate a claim for non-pecuniary loss); Law Reform (Miscellaneous Provisions) 1956 (NT) s 6(1)(c)(ii) (and Compensation (Fatal Injuries) Act 1974 (NT) s 10(3)(f) for solatium to a member of the deceased's persons family). For a modern critique of the Australian jurisdictions that do not allow awards for solatium see I Field, 'In Mourning of Bereavement Damages' (2014) 22 *Torts Law Journal* 95.

[138] Queensland Law Reform Commission, *An Examination of the Provisions of the "Fatal Accidents Acts" with a View to the Elimination of Anomalies* (Working Paper 7, 1971) 8. The recommendation was adopted verbatim in the final report: Queensland Law Reform Commission, *An Examination of the Provisions of the "Fatal Accidents Acts" with a View to the Elimination of Anomalies* (Report No 9, 1971) 6. This was, and is, the position adopted in South Australia and Western Australia, but the more common provision is to exclude

passed on the second last sitting day of 1972. There were only two contributors to the debate – the Minister of Justice who introduced the Bill, and the Opposition spokesman for that portfolio. There was a half-hearted attempt from the latter to oppose the abolition of the estate claim for non-pecuniary loss but, in the end, it was abolished without a whimper. Ironically, the claim was now worth so little that it was not worth fighting about and was seen as a question of tidying up the law – a reform for the lawyers and not the politicians.[139] That the amendment of the legislation was largely unremarkable shows how much the legal and political landscape had changed since the original legislation was passed. Thirty years on from the 1940 Act, the passage of this legislation through the Queensland Parliament now looked a lot like the passage of the 1934 Act at Westminster. The contrast with the 1940 Act could not have been greater.

the claim for non-pecuniary loss only where the death results from the tort, the action for which survives by virtue of the legislation.

[139] *Parliamentary Debates*, Queensland Legislative Assembly, 2576–79 (12 December 1972). The survival of actions provisions are now located in the Succession Act 1981 (Qld) s 66(2)(a).

10

Dealing with the Dead and Familial Discord: Contested Funerals and the Challenges for Private Law

HEATHER CONWAY*

I. Introduction

> A deceased loved one … bequeaths an array of emotional and practical problems that a bereaved person must solve.[1]

Though writing about clinical understandings of grief and bereavement, Shear's observations are equally apt in a legal setting when it comes to dealing with the 'things' that are left behind when someone dies. Perhaps the first that springs to mind is the person's inheritable estate, passing under the distributive contents of a validly executed will or the default system of intestacy. However, dealing with the dead body itself is a more urgent issue, and one that can trigger highly emotive and bitter disputes where the deceased's family are divided over the funeral arrangements. It is these disputes, and private law's treatment of them where feuding families resort to litigation, that are the focus of this chapter.

Of course, not all deaths result in disputes of this nature. There may be disagreements and differences of opinion, but not disputes in the more intractable sense of the word; and not all such disputes end up in a courtroom. When they do, however, a resolution is needed. What makes the resultant cases so intriguing is not just the subject-matter. It is the underlying family dynamics and the uniquely complex and distinctive emotions (both past and present) that spark, propel and sustain these disputes – inherent traits that transcend the legal issues, but cannot be resolved quite so easily – that make contested funerals so problematic.

* I am grateful to Professor Sharyn Roach Anleu, Flinders University for her insights on the emotional aspects of this chapter. Thanks also to my colleagues Sheena Grattan and Dr Ciara Hackett, and to Dr Kate Falconer, for their extremely helpful comments on an earlier draft.

[1] MK Shear, 'Grief and Mourning Gone Awry: Pathway and Course of Complicated Grief' (2012) 14 *Dialogues in Clinical Neuroscience* 119, 121.

Whether 'family' denotes the traditional nuclear model, or more diverse, fluid structures that embrace a range of personal relationships and living arrangements beyond institutionalised norms,[2] the central characters are connected to the deceased and to each other by some sort of relational tie.[3] This has significant consequences. First, we know that families are more prone to conflict than other social groupings, because of their shared personal histories and group interactions.[4] A propensity for conflict creates a perfect breeding ground for the type of disputes that we are considering here.[5] Second, all families comprise a group of interconnected individuals who function – for better or worse – as an emotional unit.[6] Individual family dynamics can also trigger their own distinct emotions, based on how the members interact with each other.[7] Third, this delicate emotional ecosystem is thrown off balance by the deceased's passing. Relationships that anchored 'normal' family life are destroyed,[8] adding instability to emotional upheaval as each person grieves the loss in their own unique way.[9]

Contested funerals are thus highly individualised experiences within a collective setting. They also speak to the theme of dead bodies and public displays of power. Much has been written on this phenomenon in the political and social contexts, most notably in the works of Katherine Verdery.[10] However, similar traits are apparent in funeral disputes as more localised power struggles riven by family politics, and imbued with symbolism for what the parties are fighting over. Funerals are not just about dealing with the dead; as socially constructed ceremonies that frame the ritual in the minds of participants, they cement the deceased's place in the lives of family, friends and community.[11] This normative component can be a powerful public statement about who was seemingly closest to the deceased in life – hence the desire, by certain family

[2] See, eg, J Finch and J Mason, *Passing On: Kinship and Inheritance in England* (London, Routledge, 2000) and M Gilding, 'Reflexivity Over and Above Convention: The New Orthodoxy in the Sociology of Personal Life, Formerly Sociology of the Family' (2010) 61 *British Journal of Sociology* 757.

[3] Since concepts of family are also culturally influenced, indigenous families are frequently not captured within standard western definitions: see BY Tam, LC Findlay and DE Kohen, 'Indigenous Families: Who Do You Call Family?' (2017) 23 *Journal of Family Studies* 243. This is part of a wider issue around the recognition of cultural variances in private law, something that Prue Vines highlights in ch 11 of this collection.

[4] See A Taylor, *The Handbook of Family Dispute Resolution: Mediation Theory and Practice* (Hoboken, John Wiley & Sons, 2012) chs 1–2.

[5] In discussing why people take their disputes to law, Felstiner, Abel and Sarat note that 'the antecedents of disputing are as problematic and as interesting as the disputes that may ultimately emerge': WLF Felstiner, RL Abel and A Sarat, 'The Emergence and Transformation of Disputes: Naming, Blaming, Claiming …' (1980–81) 15 *Law & Society Review* 631, 633.

[6] Something that Bowen emphasised in his well-known family systems theory: see, eg, M Bowen, *Family Therapy in Clinical Practice* (New York, Aronson, 1978).

[7] In putting forward a 'relational conception of emotions', Burkitt argues that 'emotions are not "things" internal to the individual and their biological constitution, but are to do with the social relations and interdependencies between people': I Burkitt, 'Social Relationships and Emotions' (1997) 31 *Sociology* 37, 52. See also K Gergen, *Realities and Relationships: Soundings in Social Construction* (Cambridge, Harvard University Press, 1994).

[8] The resultant 'emotional shock wave' can be felt over a period of months, or even years: M Bowen, 'Family Reaction to Death' in F Walsh and M McGoldrick (eds), *Living Beyond Loss: Death in the Family* (New York, W W Norton and Co, 1991) 78, 82.

[9] See section II.

[10] K Verdery, *The Political Lives of Dead Bodies: Reburial and Postsocialist Change* (New York, Columbia University Press, 1999).

[11] See, eg, T O'Rourke, BH Spitzberg, and AF Hannawa, 'The Good Funeral: Toward an Understanding of Funeral Participation and Satisfaction' (2011) 35 *Death Studies* 729 and WG Hoy, *Do Funerals Matter? The Purposes and Practices of Death Rituals in Global Perspective* (New York, Routledge, 2013).

members, to control the funeral arrangements. For both sides, the legal outcome can be seen as a permanent and judicially authenticated articulation of a particular family narrative.

Against this backdrop, the challenges that contested funerals pose for private law are all too apparent. At the risk of over-simplifying, the task is to resolve the practical issue of dealing with the dead while handling the emotional aspects of the conflict. From a practical perspective, the applicable legal rules allow the matter to be resolved as quickly as possible so that the funeral can take place. This is not just because of the time-honoured principle of respect for the dead;[12] from a societal perspective, decaying corpses pose a risk to public health and should not be stored indefinitely while feuding relatives engage in litigation.[13] From an emotional perspective, the issues are just as pressing, even if the solutions are not as obvious: how to deal with distressing cases, conducted against an emotionally volatile backdrop and in the emotion-generating settings of both the family and the courtroom, with outcomes that are likely to exacerbate familial conflicts instead of resolving them (beyond the purely legal sense).

Adopting this 'dual purpose' approach as its basis, the first substantive part of this chapter (section III) focuses on the legal rules. It offers a fresh perspective on these rules by looking at their content and efficacy, and draws on broad principles of legal theory to assess the practical utility of both the set rules that dominate the decision-making process in contested funerals, and the default principles that are invoked where set rules do not provide a solution. The second substantive part of the chapter (section IV) moves beyond the application of established legal doctrine to focus on matters that law is not as well-equipped to deal with: limiting the emotional fallout when families are fighting over contested funerals. Drawing on existing techniques in law and emotion literature, this part of the chapter suggests a number of strategies linked to the courtroom proceedings themselves. It also offers a novel perspective on the reported cases on contested funerals, suggesting that judges can temper the emotional impact of their decisions by conveying them to the parties in a particular way.

Though the emphasis throughout this chapter – like many others in this collection – is on the Anglo-Australian position,[14] the subject-matter has a much wider resonance.

II. Emotional Backdrops and Dispute Drivers

To gain a deeper understanding of what lies at the heart of contested funerals, we begin by looking more closely at the emotions associated with death and grieving, and what families are typically fighting over in these disputes.

[12] Respect for the dead is a universal standard that is reflected in numerous judicial statements. See, eg, Martin J in *Calma v Sesar* (1992) 2 NTLR 37, 42 (the dead must be 'disposed of without unreasonable delay, but with all proper respect and decency').

[13] The public health risk is reduced where bodies are kept in cold storage for a short time, pending the outcome of any legal action. However, there is also a 'general public interest' (linked to respect for the dead) that deceased persons 'not be permitted unnecessarily to decompose' before burial or cremation: Gorton J in *Re Ghosh* [2022] VSC 210 [18].

[14] With 'Anglo' denoting both England and Wales here. Although separate legal jurisdictions, the two are amalgamated – for convenience – because the exact same laws apply in both.

Occurring in the immediate aftermath of death, funeral disputes coincide with the acute initial phase of grief when those affected are confronted with a range of intense and complex emotions.[15] There may be sadness, shock, guilt, anxiety, relief, contentment or even happiness;[16] and different feelings might be experienced at different times, or as part of a more ambiguous and seemingly contradictory mix.[17] Much will also depend on the nature of the death, and the relationship of the deceased to the person grieving: the sudden death of a child will evoke different emotions than the loss of a parent of advanced years, just as the death of a sibling is different to that of a spouse or partner. However, the end of any life is a highly emotional experience for those who are bereaved, and one that is typified by predominantly negative emotions such as anger, hostility, pain and despair.[18]

In the family context, grief is experienced both intrapersonally and interpersonally: each individual reacts to the loss of a loved one in their own particular way, but within the group setting of the family as it slowly adapts to the loss of a key figure.[19] Adding relational dynamics to the mix ensures that the stage is perfectly set for conflict – and the potential for consensus or compromise severely diminished – when families discuss the time-sensitive issue of funeral arrangements.

A perusal of contemporary English and Australian cases reveals clear points of contention.[20] There is the fundamental question of whether to bury or cremate the deceased.[21] Then there is the type of funeral ceremony, where to hold it, and whether to incorporate specific religious or cultural elements.[22] A decision to bury inevitably raises the question of which grave, or perhaps which cemetery, churchyard or burial ground;[23]

[15] Seminal works on grief include J Bowlby, 'The Process of Mourning' (1961) 42 *International Journal of Psychoanalysis* 331; E Kubler-Ross, *On Death and Dying* (New York, Macmillan, 1969); and CM Parkes, *Bereavement: Studies of Grief in Adult Life* (London, Tavistock Press, 1972). For more recent authorities, see J Archer, *The Nature of Grief: The Evolution and Psychology of Reactions to Loss* (London, Routledge, 2003) and L Granek, 'Grief as Pathology: The Evolution of Grief Theory in Psychology from Freud to the Present' (2010) 13 *History of Psychology* 46.

[16] Some of these 'nontraditional' grief responses are explored in J Elison and C McGonigle, *Liberating Losses: When Death Brings Relief* (Boston, Da Capo Lifelong Books, 2004).

[17] See, eg, C Lloyd, *Grief Demystified: An Introduction* (London, Jessica Kingsley Publishers, 2018).

[18] See the various sources cited at n 15.

[19] See MS Stroebe, 'Bereavement in Family Context: Coping with the Loss of a Loved One' (2010) 1 *Family Science* 144.

[20] It also suggests a shift in emphasis from the older case law on funerals, which focused predominantly on costs (see, eg, *Green v Salmon* (1838) 8 Ad & E 348; 112 ER 869 and *Ambrose v Kerrison* (1851) 10 CB 777; 138 ER 307) to who has decision-making authority over the arrangements. This is not to suggest that costs are not an issue today, just that they do not seem to be the main driver for funeral disputes ending up in court.

[21] As in *Donahue v Morleys Funerals Pty Ltd* [2016] QSC 137 (de facto spouse's decision to cremate challenged by the deceased's mother). In *Re JS (Disposal of Body)* [2016] EWHC 2859 (Fam), [2017] 4 WLR 1 separated parents fought over whether their teenage daughter should be cryogenically frozen; while this option is rare, new and emerging methods of bodily disposal (eg alkaline hydrolysis (often referred to as Resomation™) and natural organic reduction (or 'human composting')) will trigger similar disagreements.

[22] See, eg, *Re Lochowiak (Deceased)* [1997] SASC 6301 (deceased's adult son challenged the deceased's partner, the former arguing that his Catholic father would not have wanted to be cremated). Australian courts have dealt with numerous cases where non-adherence to Aboriginal traditions and death rituals has triggered conflict within families and the wider community. See, eg, *Calma* (n 12); *Reece v Little* [2009] WASC 30; *Dann v Office of the State Coroner* [2020] WASC 486; and *Frail v Shorey* [2021] NSWSC 122, (2021) 20 ASTLR 437.

[23] See, eg, *Scotching v Birch* [2008] EWHC 844 (Ch) (mother who pleaded guilty to the unlawful killing of her son wanted to bury him in the local churchyard, close to the family home; the boy's father (the couple

sometimes the disagreement can be over which country.[24] However, closer analysis suggests that many disputed funerals are actually a lightning rod for issues that have been festering for some time.[25] Old family grievances can be projected onto funeral arrangements and create new rifts in the process. Classic examples are siblings fighting over a dead parent, when childhood jealousies and rivalries reappear, or separated parents resuming hostilities over a dead child by embarking on one final and decisive custody dispute.[26] Another significant factor is the rise in second and blended families; disputes between children from different relationships on the death of a parent are a perfect illustration, as are tussles between a child and their deceased parent's new spouse or partner.[27]

This combination of grief and family strife militates against self-restraint, and propels the two sides towards the adversarial setting of the courtroom when agreement cannot be reached. The emotional costs are high and diffuse, as the resultant legal process impacts on the parties and on wider family relationships.[28] But when the dispute goes this far, a solution must be found.

III. The Legal Solution

The role of private law in contested funerals is primarily one of adjudication in deciding who has the legal right to possession of the deceased's remains, and consequent entitlement to make the funeral arrangements.[29] In the first instance, judges rely on fixed rules that invoke familiar notions of status and control. Where these fail to provide a solution, the emphasis shifts to a judicially crafted default framework to resolve the matter.

A. The Dominant Approach: Fixed Rules and Legal Formalism

Both English and Australian courts rely on succession law rules that favour the deceased's personal representatives in contested funerals, even if the justificatory

were separated) insisted on a grave plot close to where he lived). See also *Kitchener v Magistrate Thomas* [2019] NSWSC 701 (deceased's mother insisting on burial in his Aboriginal homeland; de facto spouse (and mother of his children) wanting to bury the deceased close to where they had lived).

[24] As in *Anstey v Mundle* [2016] EWHC 1073 (Ch) (deceased's daughters divided over burial in England or in Jamaica) and *Pangou v Nzoulou* [2022] EWHC 147 (Ch) (deceased's long-term partner wanted burial in England, while his daughter wanted her father's body to be buried in France). Post-cremation, there is also the issue of what happens to the ashes: should they be interred or scattered (and where), or retained by one family member or divided between others? See, eg, *Fessi v Whitmore* [1999] 1 FLR 767 (Ch) and *Doherty v Doherty* [2006] QSC 257, [2007] 2 Qd R 259 for an illustration. For now, however, the focus is on the more pressing issue of the funeral itself.

[25] For an overview, see H Conway and J Stannard, 'The Honours of Hades: Death, Emotion and the Law of Burial Disputes' (2011) 34 *University of New South Wales Law Journal* 860.

[26] There are numerous examples of each. For feuding siblings see, eg, *Anstey* (n 24); *McCredie v Batson* [2020] NSWSC 1913; and *Marinucci v Condo* [2020] VSC 613. For parental disputes over dead children, see *Fessi* (n 24); *Joseph v Dunn* [2007] WASC 238; *Re JS* (n 21); and *Nayacakalou v Vincent* [2020] NSWSC 24.

[27] See, eg, *Burnes v Richards* (1993) 7 BPR 15,104 and *Pangou* (n 24).

[28] For an overview of the psychological effect of engaging in litigation both generally and where families are involved, see M Keet, H Heavin and S Sparrow, 'Anticipating and Managing the Psychological Cost of Civil Litigation' (2017) 34 *Windsor Yearbook of Access to Justice* 73.

[29] See H Conway, *The Law and the Dead* (Abingdon, Routledge, 2016) ch 3.

basis of these rules is estate distribution as opposed to dealing with the dead.[30] The first point to note is that, despite the centrality of the deceased's wishes on inheritance matters,[31] it has long been established that funeral preferences are not legally binding.[32] There are recent signs of a less dogmatic stance, in both law reform agendas[33] and in the cases themselves as judges treat the deceased's own views as a persuasive factor in family funeral disputes.[34] This seems instinctively right. One could argue that the moral obligation to do what the deceased wanted is a strong normative force, which should be legally validated – especially where the dispute in question has been triggered by one side's insistence on honouring the deceased's wishes.[35] As things currently stand, however, there is no guarantee that this will be the outcome.

Instead, where the deceased made a will, the final say on the funeral arrangements lies with the executor.[36] For intestate deaths, the decision lies with the presumptive estate administrator – that is, the highest ranking individual(s) who would be entitled to letters of administration in respect of the deceased's estate. Much depends on the relevant intestacy statute, but in most instances a surviving spouse or civil partner takes priority, followed by the deceased's children, then parents, then sisters or brothers,[37] though individual Australian states also include cohabiting or de facto partners as a separate secondary category after surviving spouses or civil partners.[38] Delineating rights by a descending order of relational ties means, for example, that courts will favour a spouse over the deceased's parents or siblings where the two sides clash over funeral arrangements.[39] In short, there is a hierarchy of preference, albeit one that is largely based on a standardised view of contemporary family relationships.[40]

[30] Contrast this with other jurisdictions that have bespoke statutory regimes for resolving funeral disputes – see, eg, s 65 of the Burial and Cremation (Scotland) Act 2016 (asp 20).

[31] The core principle of testamentary freedom dominates common law succession regimes.

[32] As is well-known, this stems from the nineteenth-century case of *Williams v Williams* (1882) 20 Ch D 569 which held that, since a dead body is not property in any legal sense, directions that seek to control its fate are not legally binding. See H Conway, '*Williams v Williams* (1882): Succession Law Rules and the Fate of the Dead' in B Sloan (ed), *Landmark Cases in Succession Law* (Oxford, Hart Publishing, 2019).

[33] See, eg, Victorian Law Reform Commission, *Funeral and Burial Instructions* (Report, 2016).

[34] See, eg, *Burrows v HM Coroner for Preston* [2008] EWHC 1387 (QB), [2008] 2 FLR 1225 and *McCredie* (n 26). Funeral instructions aside, the dead assume a central role in the courtroom narrative as discussed by Kate Falconer in her chapter in the current collection: see ch 12.

[35] Though this often creates a secondary layer of dispute around what the deceased actually wanted, especially when relying on oral statements. Surviving relatives often claim that the deceased said different things to different people at different times: see, eg, *Smith v Smith* [2021] WASC 15.

[36] See *Grandison v Nembhard* [1989] 4 BMLR 140 (EWHC); *Kak v Kak* [2020] NSWSC 140, (2020) 20 ASTLR 425; and *Otitoju v Onwardi* [2023] EWHC 2665 (Ch).

[37] In England and Wales, see s 46 of the Administration of Estates Act 1925 and (more importantly) r 22 of The Non-Contentious Probate Rules 1987, SI 1987/2024.

[38] See, eg, *Reece* (n 22) (de facto partner granted custody of the deceased's remains as the person entitled to seek letters of administration and consequent presumptive administrator under ss 15 and 25 of the Administration Act 1903 (WA)). In contrast, cohabiting partners have no rights under English intestacy laws.

[39] See, eg, *Threlfall v Threlfall* [2009] VSC 283 (coroner erred in releasing the deceased's body to his brother instead of his widow) and *Dann* (n 22) (deceased's wife and mother of his 16-year-old son entitled to decide the funeral arrangements over the deceased's sister).

[40] See, eg, K Woodthorpe and H Rumble, 'Funerals and Families: Locating Death as a Relational Issue' (2016) 67 *The British Journal of Sociology* 242. We will return to this theme below.

i. *The Benefits of Legal Formalism: Practical and Emotional*

The task for private law in funeral disputes is to resolve the matter swiftly, in the interests of everyone involved. It is clear that the rules achieve and promote the objectives of the law: that is, ensuring that the dead are dealt with, by awarding control of the funeral arrangements – through the medium of possessory entitlements – to a particular individual, or individuals.[41] What we see here is adherence to established doctrine that sits firmly within the formalist tradition of legal theory. Judges are using 'clearly defined, highly administrable rules, [with] an emphasis on uniformity, consistency and predictability'[42] to produce a decisive outcome.

A foray into the merits of legal formalism is beyond the scope of this chapter.[43] Though often heavily criticised (and occasionally reviled) as a theory of adjudication,[44] it is suggested that there are benefits to what Schauer describes as 'decisionmaking according to *rule*'[45] when judges are dispensing with funeral disputes. Focusing on the executor or presumptive administrator is a straightforward exercise: the person with the legal right to arrange the funeral is easily identifiable, and a quick decision can be made. It is not just an exercise in judicial expediency. What we see here is an emphasis on the practicalities of allowing the funeral to proceed because contested corpses are physical and material presences that must be dealt with in a compressed timeframe. As already noted, the dictates of public health, combined with the fundamental tenet of respect for the dead, demand that the funeral takes place as quickly as possible.[46]

This is not to suggest that what happens here is a process of 'mechanical deduction', whereby rules of law are rigidly applied to the facts.[47] Advocates of legal formalism point to more sophisticated processes of identifying and interpreting the law, before applying it to the individual factual scenario to produce a reasoned decision,[48] something that is apparent across the case law on contested funerals. And while the majority of said cases adhere to the aforementioned rules, judges can depart from these set legal norms on the facts before them.[49] For instance, a number of Australian cases have suggested that the

[41] The court's function is to decide this matter, not to micro-manage the funeral: see, eg, *ND v LD* [2019] EWHC 3639 (Fam). However, there are isolated examples of courts issuing specific directions about the funeral: see text to nn 101–104.

[42] D McBarnet and C Whelan, 'The Elusive Spirit of the Law: Formalism and the Struggle for Legal Control' (1991) 54 *Modern Law Review* 848, 849. See also F Schauer, 'Formalism' (1989) 97 *Yale Law Journal* 509.

[43] And beyond the capabilities of its author!

[44] See, eg, M Stone, 'Formalism' in J Coleman and S Shapiro (eds), *The Oxford Handbook of Jurisprudence and Philosophy of Law* (Oxford, Oxford University Press, 2002) 166 ('few terms have been used more often to criticize legal thought and practice'), as well as the sources cited throughout the chapter. For a contrary view, see, eg, Schauer (n 42) and P Troop, 'Why Legal Formalism is Not a Stupid Thing' (2018) 31 *Ratio Juris* 428.

[45] Schauer (n 42) 510.

[46] For recent affirmation of this basic principle, see *Otitoju* (n 36).

[47] See B Leiter, 'Legal Formalism and Legal Realism: What is the Issue?' (2010) 16 *Legal Theory* 111, 111. See also C Guthrie, JJ Rachlinski and AJ Wistrich, 'Blinking on the Bench: How Judges Decide Cases' (2007) 93 *Cornell Law Review* 1, 2 (referring to the formalist model of applying law to facts in a 'mechanical and deliberate way').

[48] See Leiter (n 47) and RJ Sharpe, 'How Judges Decide' in R Assy and A Higgins (eds), *Principles, Procedures and Justice: Essays in Honour of Adrian Zuckerman* (Oxford, Oxford University Press, 2020).

[49] See Sharpe (n 48) 92 (discussing the role of the judge in interpreting and applying the law).

personal representative rule is not absolute where the deceased leaves no estate, or if the circumstances of the case call for a different approach.[50]

One might also argue that a 'retreat to legal formalism'[51] has certain advantages in the emotionally charged arena of funeral disputes. Judges have clear rules, allowing them to reach their decisions on the legal merits of the case. There is no need to unravel complicated family histories, or make difficult subjective value judgments about the state of lifetime relationships between the deceased and the feuding parties; isolated comments in the case law suggest a certain judicial reticence around dealing with such highly charged issues and unleashing a Pandora's box of emotions on which the lid is already dangerously ajar.[52] Justice can be dispensed in a 'mechanical, detached way compelled by law, fact and reason',[53] and without getting too embroiled in messy family dynamics and emotionally-laden narratives.[54]

ii. The Boundaries of Formalism

Of course, legal formalism has its limitations, and this is also apparent in the treatment of funeral disputes. One could argue that a purely rules-based approach is inherently flawed, because the decision-maker is shielded from 'factors that a sensitive decision-maker would otherwise take into account'.[55] Close inspection of the case law suggests, however, that judges dealing with funeral disputes are understanding of things like the nuances of family life, and religious and cultural imperatives, when dealing with funeral disputes.[56] A more valid argument is that the content of the actual rules is open to criticism, and intestacy rankings illustrate the point perfectly. The idea of a relational framework that prioritises certain individuals is a familiar one, and not just in a legal setting.[57] Yet intestacy laws are often decried as 'privileging the nuclear family, to the

[50] See K Falconer, 'Australian Burial Law 25 Years On From Smith v Tamworth City Council' (2022) 96 *Australian Law Journal* 581, 584–88 and the cases cited therein. For another recent example of this approach, see *Re Ghosh* (n 13).

[51] K McEvoy and H Conway, 'The Dead, The Law, and the Politics of the Past' (2004) 31 *Journal of Law and Society* 539, 541.

[52] See, eg, the comments of Debelle J in *Re Lochowiak* (n 22) [8] ('A court is … reluctant to enter into disputes of this kind which, clearly, involve emotional issues of a high degree').

[53] JM Shaman, 'The Impartial Judge: Detachment or Passion?' (1996) 45 *DePaul Law Review* 605, 606 and cited in S Roach Anleu and K Mack, 'Judicial Performance and Experiences of Judicial Work: Findings from Socio-legal Research' (2014) 4 *Oñati Socio-Legal Series* 1015, 1029.

[54] Might this trigger suggestions that artificial intelligence (AI) should supplement – or even replace – the judicial role here? The current author is definitely not suggesting this, given the sensitive and emotionally complex nature of funeral disputes and the arguments presented in section IV. However, it would be wrong to ignore the debates around AI reshaping the process of judging – see, eg, T Sourdin, *Judges, Technology and Artificial Intelligence: The Artificial Judge* (Cheltenham, Edward Elgar Publishing, 2021).

[55] Schauer (n 42) 510 who describes this as a 'supposed' failing of formalism.

[56] There are various instances of judges allowing religious and cultural imperatives to shape the outcome when these are central to the factual and legal narratives. For an illustration, see *Darcy v Duckett* [2016] NSWSC 1756; *Bertani v Bertani* [2017] WASC 78; *Abraham v Magistrate Stone, Deputy State Coroner* [2017] NSWSC 1684; and the decision of the New Zealand Supreme Court in *Takamore v Clarke* [2012] NZSC 116, [2013] 2 NZLR 733.

[57] For instance, when someone dies there is a 'ranking of grief' within the family whereby it is deemed acceptable for certain people to experience a stronger sense of loss than others because of their relationship to the deceased (eg a spouse and/or children, compared with the deceased's cousin). See, eg, H Peskin, 'Who has the Right to Mourn?: Relational Deference and the Ranking of Grief' (2019) 29 *Psychoanalytic Dialogues* 477.

exclusion of modern forms of associations and relationships'[58] in their articulation of next-of-kin. Extrapolating these rules onto funeral disputes creates the same problem: that is, an unduly narrow hierarchy of entitlement that does not align with contemporary family structures.[59]

Legal rules that facilitate an inward decision-making process are problematic for other reasons. Applying blunt succession law rankings means that certain people are legitimised despite not being the person who neutral observers would instinctively favour on the merits of the case – nor on the emotional narratives. A classic example is the English case of *Holtham v Arnold*,[60] where the deceased's estranged wife was allowed to cremate his remains, despite opposition from the deceased's long-term partner, who wanted to bury him in accordance with what she claimed were his last wishes. That result jars somewhat, even if it is legally correct; the deceased died intestate and his wife was entitled to letters of administration in respect of his estate because English law does not include cohabiting partners within its intestacy rules.[61]

The old problem of a 'literal application' of rules 'not produc[ing] the desired end'[62] has triggered workaround solutions. As mentioned, some Australian judges have downplayed the extrapolative effect of intestacy rules in contested funerals, resulting in different outcomes on the facts of individual cases.[63] English judges will also occasionally grant possession of the deceased's remains to someone other than the executor or presumptive administrator, though by different means. Using the inherent jurisdiction of the court is one option;[64] invoking succession law procedures to 'pass over' a personal representative and appoint someone else solely for the purposes of arranging the funeral is another.[65] Overall, one might argue that the problems associated with legal formalism are not as insurmountable as they might initially appear. However, the fact remains that, as with any system of rules, 'there may be gaps, omissions or loopholes … which undermine their effectiveness',[66] and these are exposed where two or more individuals

[58] See S Kreiczer-Levy, 'Big Data and the Modern Family' (2019) 2019 *Wisconsin Law Review* 349, 349.

[59] This is a recurrent theme in contemporary succession law – see, eg, R Kerridge, 'Intestacy Reform in 2014 – Unfinished Business' in B Häcker and C Mitchell (eds), *Current Issues in Succession Law* (Oxford, Hart Publishing, 2016). Additionally, the legal classification of next-of-kin may not reflect cultural notions of kinship, authority and extended family ties in funeral disputes where the deceased was a member of a particular indigenous community: see, eg, P Vines, 'Consequences of Intestacy for Indigenous People: The Passing of Property and Burial Rights' (2004) 8 *Australian Indigenous Legal Reporter* 1.

[60] *Holtham v Arnold* [1986] 2 BMLR 123 (EWHC).

[61] See n 38. Even if it did, the surviving spouse would probably have 'outranked' the cohabiting partner by virtue of sitting higher in the intestacy ranking and the spouses having never formally separated.

[62] McBarnet and Whelan (n 42) 850.

[63] See text to n 50 above.

[64] See *Re K (A Child) (Disposal of Body)* [2016] EWHC 1083 (Fam), [2017] 4 WLR 112 and *Y v Z* [2018] EWHC 4026 (Ch).

[65] Though there is something ironic in invoking formal and technical succession law processes to undo the consequences of formalistic rules! In England and Wales, the relevant legislation can be found in s 116 of the Senior Courts Act 1981 which allows the court to appoint a different personal representative where it is 'necessary or expedient' to do so. Although Hoffmann J (as he then was) in *Holtham* (n 60) was of the opinion that s 116 was not intended to deal with funeral disputes, other English cases have taken the opposite view and used s 116 accordingly: see, eg, *ND* (n 41) and *Pangou* (n 24). In the latter case, the deceased's long-term cohabiting partner was granted control of the funeral arrangements under s 116, despite the deceased's adult daughter from a previous relationship being entitled to act as estate administrator.

[66] McBarnet and Whelan (n 42) 850.

have equal rights to possession of the deceased's remains but clash over the funeral arrangements. Joint executors, most usually adult siblings under a parental will, provide one example.[67] The more usual scenario, and the focus of what follows, involves disputes between the parents or adult children of an intestate deceased.[68] Since intestacy laws do not distinguish between individuals within the same relational class (both parents and children have the same entitlements vis-à-vis each other), alternative 'tie-breaker' solutions have had to be found.

B. The Default Mechanism: Judicially Devised Factors

In some jurisdictions, discrete legislative enactments impose blunt rules. For instance, the Canadian province of British Columbia looks at birth order and gives the elder or eldest protagonist the final say on funeral arrangements,[69] while the US state of New Jersey favours majority rule where numerical advantage is possible.[70] This metaphorical equivalent of cutting the Gordian knot depersonalises the issue,[71] but has not been embraced in England and Wales, or in any part of Australia. Instead, judges have filled the legal void by devising a default framework to determine which parent or adult child gets possession of the deceased's remains and consequent control of the funeral arrangements.

A deep dive of the case law reveals a clear set of guiding factors,[72] one or more of which can have magnetic importance on the facts of the particular case. Because the ultimate task remains the same – to resolve the dispute, so that burial or cremation happens as quickly as possible – the question of who will expedite the funeral often dominates.[73] Emphasis has also been placed on the deceased's own funeral preferences;[74] the religious and cultural sentiments of the deceased (and/or their family);[75] and choosing a final resting place that has some sort of positive meaning for the deceased (and/or the bereaved), or facilitates future visits to the grave.[76] More controversially, perhaps, judges have also decided a number of these cases on the basis of which parent or adult child

[67] Though relatively infrequent, this does occur. See, eg, *Leeburn v Derndorfer* [2004] VSC 172, (2004) 14 VR 100; *Marinucci* (n 26); *McCredie* (n 26). The latter case is discussed below: see text to nn 101–103.

[68] In other words, parents fighting over the funeral arrangements for a dead child, or siblings fighting over a dead parent. These form the bulk of the reported cases; for a detailed exposition see H Conway, '"First Among Equals": Breaking the Deadlock in Parental and Sibling Funeral Disputes' (2018) 39 *Liverpool Law Review* 151. Siblings fighting over another dead sibling is also a possibility, where the deceased died without legally closer kin.

[69] Section 5(3) of the Cremation, Interment and Funeral Services Act, SBC 2004, c 35 (BC). Similar provisions are in force in Alberta and Saskatchewan: see, eg, s 91(2)(b) of the Funeral and Cremation Services Act, SS 1999, c F23.3 (Sask).

[70] NJ Rev Stat § 45:27-22.

[71] The various pros and cons are analysed elsewhere: see Conway (n 68) 165–67.

[72] ibid 155–59.

[73] See *Hartshorne v Gardner* [2008] EWHC B3 (Ch); *Calma* (n 12); *Smith* (n 35). The current author does not share Falconer's view (n 50, 588) that the emphasis on burial (or cremation) without reasonable delay is largely redundant (at least in Australia).

[74] See *Anstey* (n 24) and *Nayacakalou* (n 26).

[75] As in *Frail* (n 22) and *Nayacakalou* (n 26).

[76] See *Hartshorne* (n 73). Religious and cultural factors can also exert a strong influence here: see, eg, *Frail* (n 22).

was closest to the deceased in life,[77] looking at emotional ties and the strength of each person's relationship with the deceased.[78]

Again, there is a wealth of jurisprudential literature on the process of common law decision-making more generally: how rules are established and modified, the different methods of reasoning, and how precedent constrains and assists judges, to list but a few.[79] All of these things raise interesting questions in contested funerals, and the types of cases that we are looking at here, though the present focus is inevitably more limited.[80] From analysing the judgments, what we have is a set of judicially-constructed norms that acknowledge the practical necessity of dealing with the dead, prioritise the deceased's wishes where possible, and incorporate wider (though often contradictory) familial views on specific funerary rites and the quality (and duration) of lifetime relationships with the deceased. There is a sense of 'doctrinal coherence'[81] in that the factors are circumscribed and well-defined; the fact that they align with what might be considered key elements of funeral choice – both for the deceased, and for those that he/she leaves behind – gives legitimacy to the decision-making process. The resultant framework is certainly more fluid than the executor or presumptive administrator rule, and allows for individualised solutions. However, the outcomes are much less predictable: because each case necessarily turns on its own facts, the various judgments do not reveal clear trends, and what tips the scales in favour of a particular result is much harder to predict. This might encourage litigation between feuding parents or adult siblings, and make both sides less inclined to settle the contest or back down, if they think there is a chance of winning.

When resolving individual disputes, there is more work for judges to do and not just because they have to adjudicate on a case-by-case basis with limited assistance from previous case law.[82] Judges have to make more taxing assessments about whether the deceased's wishes were unambiguous, and what significance to attach to things like cultural values, or the different burial locations proposed by the parties. Sidestepping the tangled mess of emotion and conflicting family narratives is not as straightforward, even if the emphasis on finding a quick and pragmatic resolution may help to focus minds. Meanwhile, deciding who was closest to the deceased in life opens up its own

[77] The person who had the 'closest relationship with the deceased' is actually the designated legislative test in the US state of Pennsylvania: see 20 PA Const Stat § 305(d)(2).

[78] *Keller v Keller* [2007] VSC 118, (2007) 15 VR 667 shows the test being applied between adult children fighting over a dead parent, though it is more prevalent in parental disputes over infants or minor children. See, eg, *AB v CD* [2007] NSWSC 1474; *Re JS* (n 21); and *AG v JB* [2022] NSWSC 326. The latter case involved the funeral arrangements for a baby son who died a few days after he was born; in ruling for the mother, the court emphasised her connections to her child in utero – and the fact that it was hard to imagine a 'more intimate connection': at [39].

[79] For a flavour see, eg, MA Eisenberg, *The Nature of the Common Law* (Cambridge, Harvard University Press, 1988); N MacCormick, *Legal Reasoning and Legal Theory*, 2nd edn (Oxford, Clarendon Press, 1994); E Sherwin, 'Judges as Rulemakers' (2006) 73 *University of Chicago Law Review* 919; and F Schauer, 'Do Cases Make Bad Law' (2006) 73 *University of Chicago Law Review* 883.

[80] For instance, the normative basis of these judicially formulated tests could be the subject of another article or book chapter in itself!

[81] A core element of common law decision-making, alongside legitimacy, objectivity and predictability: see P Sales, 'The Common Law' (2019) 135 *LQR* 47.

[82] Because the factual scenario – and the manner in which a previous judge reached their decision – will always be different.

proverbial can of worms, forcing judges to make difficult value judgements about the affective connections between each party and the deceased.

IV. Limiting the Emotional Fallout?

We know that emotions are rampant when families are fighting over funerals, and not just because of the parties' relationships with each other and the deceased. Combining this with the acute phase of grief, when feelings of anger and hostility dominate, creates a contentious and highly emotional legal dispute.

Judges are often 'exposed to highly emotional topics and people',[83] and the question of how they handle these emotions is a complex one that receives extensive coverage in law and emotion literature.[84] What is clear is that judges do not, cannot and should not operate in an emotional vacuum. With this in mind, it is suggested that judges who deal with contested funerals must find a way of acknowledging and – insofar as this is possible – managing the complex emotions that fuel these disputes in the interests of everyone involved.[85] Given the high risk of aggravating and perpetuating the conflict, damage limitation is paramount; and judges have a number of tools at their disposal.[86]

A. The Courtroom Setting

How the case is conducted in court is important. For instance, relying solely on affidavits[87] makes it easier to preserve the emotional equilibrium of the courtroom than parties giving evidence in person.[88] In the latter scenario, how judges deal with outward expressions of emotions in an adversarial setting – including those of other family members also present at the hearing – is part and parcel of what Roach Anleu

[83] See KM Snider, PG Devereux and MK Miller, 'Judges' Emotion: An Application of the Emotion Regulation Process Model' (2022) 29 *Psychiatry, Psychology and Law* 256, 268.

[84] There is a wealth of literature on how judges deal with emotions in the courtroom setting – both their own, and those of the various legal actors and participants. See, eg, TA Maroney, 'Emotional Regulation and Judicial Behavior' (2011) 99 *California Law Review* 1485; S Bergman Blix and A Wettergren, *Professional Emotions in Court: A Sociological Perspective* (Abingdon, Routledge, 2018); and S Roach Anleu and K Mack, *Judging and Emotion: A Socio-Legal Analysis* (Abingdon, Routledge, 2021). For clarity, the discussion that follows is *not* looking at how judges manage their own emotions; this raises different issues entirely.

[85] Of course, judges must walk a fine line between acknowledging the emotive content of the litigation, and creating any sense that they are legitimising the outcome based on emotion. Law and emotion literature clearly demonstrates that judges can be aware of emotions, but still be dispassionate and impartial applicators of law: see, eg, S Roach Anleu and K Mack, 'Impartiality and Emotion in Everyday Judicial Practice' in R Patulny et al (eds), *Emotions in Late Modernity* (Abingdon, Routledge, 2019).

[86] Naturally, there are limits to what can be achieved in the adversarial setting of contested funerals. Though focusing on family disputes more generally, Huntington and others have argued that the law could do more to repair family relationships, and cultivate more positive emotions where possible: see C Huntington, 'Repairing Family Law' (2007) 57 *Duke Law Journal* 1245 and K Abrams, 'Barriers and Boundaries: Exploring Emotion in the Law of the Family' (2009) 16 *Virginia Journal of Social Policy & Law* 301.

[87] A not infrequent occurrence in contested funerals: see L Griggs and K Mackie, 'Burial Rights: The Contemporary Australian Position' (2000) 7 *Journal of Law and Medicine* 404, 404–05.

[88] With affidavit evidence, a large part of the emotional narrative is lost- see K Mack and S Roach Anleu, 'Performing Impartiality: Judicial Demeanor and Legitimacy' (2010) 35 *Law & Social Inquiry* 137.

and Mack describe as 'judicial emotion work'.[89] Judges can deploy a range of strategies, beginning with the interpersonal (for example, patience, expressions of empathy, allowing the parties to 'have their say' and to express emotion, within limits[90]). This moves to courtroom management (for example, allowing breaks in the hearing) and invoking legal rules (for example, focusing solely on the facts) to deal with 'emotionally dense'[91] situations – and the type of dispute that we are considering here is certainly an example of that.

However, in the emotional cauldron of contested funerals, there is one distinct feature of the proceedings that constrains the parties and assists judges: the emphasis on resolving the dispute as quickly as possible. This may be something that limits the use of formal mediation, because both sides do not have the necessary time to reflect and accept the compromises that are crucial to agreeing a settlement.[92] But, in the courtroom setting, time constraints are advantageous. In theory, corpses could be kept in cold storage to allow discordant relatives to litigate (or mediate) at leisure. From a societal perspective, this probably offends some basic sense of social mores and raises public health issues, since refrigeration can only slow the natural process of decay.[93] More importantly, from a familial perspective, a speedy resolution limits the scope for further infighting and consequent infliction of emotional harm. As McKechnie J summarised in *Ugle v Bowra & O'Dea*:[94]

> There has to be a balance between the need for prompt expedition of a matter that involves grief and loss to many people, together with the need to secure burial of a person reasonably promptly, and the need for a full exploration of disputed matters. In this case, given much time, many issues could be ventilated and explored, but time is one thing that is simply not available. Pressures of time, stress and pain add to an already emotional situation where there are no winners and losers, only deeply held and legitimate feelings that are exacerbated by uncertainty.[95]

B. Reaching and Communicating the Decision

Most court decisions will have a negative emotional impact on someone, and on the losing party in particular.[96] With contested funerals, one might argue that rules-based

[89] See Roach Anleu and Mack (n 84) ch 5. See also S Roach Anleu et al, 'Judicial Ethics, Everyday Work, and Emotion Management' (2020) 8 *Journal of Law and Courts* 127.

[90] Disruptive behaviour (eg shouting at the other parties and witnesses) would not be tolerated.

[91] Roach Anleu and Mack (n 84) 124. Snider, Devereux and Miller (n 83) emphasise the importance of regular breaks and keeping hearings formal where a case elicits strong emotions.

[92] Previous attempts at mediation are mentioned in a small number of contested funeral cases, though with seemingly little success and subsequent challenges to agreed settlement terms: see, eg, *Garlett v Jones* [2008] WASC 292; *Reece* (n 22); *Raggio v Horlock* [2016] SADC 69 (though the last case was dealing with disputed rights to a burial plot).

[93] Something that was emphasised recently in *Eastern Health v Bruinink* [2022] VSC 772 where storing the deceased's remains for two years in a hospital mortuary posed a health risk to its staff.

[94] *Ugle v Bowra & O'Dea* [2007] WASC 82 [1].

[95] See also the comments of Hale J (as she then was) in *Buchanan v Milton* [1999] EWHC B9 (Fam), [1999] 2 FLR 844, 854: '[these disputes] delay the proper disposal of the body and the normal processes of grieving while bringing further grief in themselves'.

[96] The late and eminent English judge Sir Robert Megarry used to say that the most important party in any case was the loser; insofar as he or she went away feeling unhappy with the court's decision, the case to some extent remained unresolved.

outcomes might lessen this impact: the systematic choice of executor or presumptive administrator may be easier to accept, because it invokes strict and value-neutral rules that say nothing about the merits of the case, or the nuances of family relationships.[97] Perhaps this is being over-optimistic, because the content and application of these rules can produce unjust outcomes and workaround solutions have often been sought, as discussed above.[98] Whether the default rules, in the limited circumstances that they apply, offer more emotional solace to the parties – and to the losing side in particular – simply because judges engage in reflective assessments of discrete factors to reach their decisions – is impossible to say.[99] One might, however, question the impact of being told that someone else will have the final say on funeral arrangements because that person was deemed to have been closer to the deceased.[100]

Of course, the bigger issue here is the outcome, and not the legal rules that generate it. Another option would be for judges to move beyond simply determining who has the legal right to conduct the funeral and make all the relevant decisions, to judges actively deciding how the body will be dealt with – for instance, whether the deceased should be buried or cremated, the content of the funeral ceremony, and who can attend. There are isolated examples of this in the case law, with *McCredie v Batson*[101] being the most notable. Faced with a dispute between joint executor siblings over who should attend their mother's cremation,[102] the court issued detailed instructions for the cremation: only close and extended family could attend; neither the plaintiff nor the defendant could give the eulogy; and the deceased's ashes would be placed in a niche with those of her late husband.[103] One can see the potential advantages of this approach, in trying to suppress further familial infighting (and consequent emotional damage) while moving the parties away from a 'winner takes all' mentality, which might be beneficial in the longer-term. A counter-argument is that forcing a compromise solution that no-one likes could exacerbate the emotional issues, because everyone is unhappy with the outcome.[104]

[97] Though the moral and practical dilemmas created by authoritative rules have been widely analysed: see, eg, L Alexander and E Sherwin, *The Rule of Rules: Morality, Rules, and the Dilemmas of Law* (Durham, Duke University Press, 2001).

[98] See text to nn 62–68.

[99] These hypotheses are somewhat speculative, and would need an in-depth, targeted study.

[100] When presenting this idea at an event several years ago, one participant said that if she and her several siblings disagreed about her parents' funeral arrangements, she could cope with losing for other reasons – but not because a judge decided that she was not as close to her parents as her other siblings.

[101] (n 26).

[102] This stemmed from 'residual underlying resentment' linked to the father's funeral some nine years earlier: ibid [6].

[103] These were part of a lengthy list of conditions imposed by the court: ibid [28], and see *Smith* (n 35) for a slightly less interventionist approach. For an English illustration of judges imposing specific funeral arrangements, see *Oldham Metropolitan BC v Makin* [2017] EWHC 2543 (Ch), [2018] Ch 543 in which the court ordered that the body of Ian Brady, the child killer responsible for the infamous 'Moors murders' in the 1960s, be cremated at night in an undisclosed location, with no music or ceremony, and the resultant ashes scattered at sea. The court's motivations were fundamentally different here: ie easing community tensions following claims that Brady had wanted satanic music played at his funeral and his ashes to be scattered on the same moors where he had buried his victims.

[104] There is a world of difference between an agreed compromise by, eg, mediation (however reluctantly it might have been reached through) and a forced compromise at the behest of a court order.

Much more important, for present purposes, is the way in which the decision is communicated to the parties, and the observations that judges make in their judgments.[105] As Maroney points out, 'the proper resolution of many legal questions relies on perception and assessment of the presence, content … and impact of emotional states'.[106] This has added resonance in contested funerals, given the centrality of emotions to the dispute and the long-term repercussions of the court's decision. If a thoughtfully crafted judgment can limit the emotional fall-out of the ruling in any meaningful way, then this is surely a good thing.

Constraints of space prevent a fuller discussion of the other novel perspective on contested funerals case law that is offered here. However, two things are clear. The first is that the parties (and wider family circle) are the primary audience of the legal process and its outcomes, and receive 'special attention'[107] in the judgments. The second is that a textual analysis of the cases reveals a variety of judicial approaches, some of which are less helpful than others. For instance, there are examples of judges being highly critical of the parties for fighting over their loved one's funeral arrangements;[108] and numerous judicial references have been made to disputes such as these being 'unseemly'.[109] Context is important, and admonishing the parties in such a public manner might seem outwardly acceptable where, for instance, both sides have been guilty of poor courtroom behaviour, or particularly spiteful towards each other. The reality is that, in most of the cases, the parties are reacting to a significant loss; each one of them will have strong feelings about the deceased's funeral, and a fervent belief that they are doing the right thing. In this respect, a public admonishment or judicial 'dressing down' may be neither appropriate, nor warranted.[110]

A more constructive use of judicial rhetoric is to acknowledge the tragic situation that the parties find themselves in, and the resultant pain and sadness that these disputes bring to everyone involved.[111] Better still are judicial statements that attempt to bring some emotional solace to the parties – and to the losing side especially – by admitting the shortcomings of any legal solution and the judge's own limitations in striving to resolve the impossible. For example, Harrison J in *AB v CD*[112] emphasised that the

[105] There is a wealth of literature on how judges write judgments, and their intended audience: see, eg, A Mikva, 'For Whom Judges Write' (1987) 61 *Southern California Law Review* 1357.

[106] T Maroney, 'Lay Conceptions of Emotion in Law' in S Bandes et al (eds), *Research Handbook on Law and Emotion* (Cheltenham, Edward Elgar Publishing, 2021) 17.

[107] FP Shecaira and N Struchiner, 'Legal Audiences' (2018) 32 *Argumentation* 273, 275.

[108] In *Keller* (n 78), where the deceased's daughter favoured cremation and the deceased's son wanted burial in accordance with Jewish law, Hargrave J described the dispute as a 'bitter and spiteful' one that was 'disrespectful of the deceased and offensive to ordinary standards of common decency': at [1].

[109] See, eg, *Buchanan* (n 95) 854; *Leeburn* (n 67) [10]; *Keller* (n 78) [15]; and *Eastern Health* (n 93) [26].

[110] Perhaps these sorts of judicial comments are reflective of the judge's own feelings towards the dispute, where this has triggered some sort of negative emotional response such as anger or disgust.

[111] See *Joseph* (n 26) [2] ('The tragic circumstances of this case are … apparent to everyone. I have the most profound respect and sympathy for both the plaintiff and the defendant') and *AG v JB* (n 78) [22] ('[A] dispute such as the current one might be described as unseemly. Whether or not that is apt, there is little doubt that it is sad, indeed tragic'). The cases involved separated parents fighting over the funeral arrangements for a young son and infant child respectively.

[112] (n 78) [66].

court's ruling was 'not, and should not appear to be, a prize for who was the better parent', sentiments echoed by the deputy judge in *Hartshorne v Gardner*:

> [A] decision between the earnest wishes of two grieving parents requires the wisdom of Solomon, which I do not profess to have. Any decision will be hard to take for the losing party, but I must make it absolutely clear at the outset that the decision I am making involves no criticism of either parent.[113]

Such comments go beyond separated parents fighting over their dead child. As Doyle CJ remarked in *Dodd v Jones*, when dealing with a dispute between the deceased's father and the mother of the deceased's minor children:

> Sadly the problem before me is really insoluble in one sense. It is impossible in any realistic sense to weigh the competing claims and arrive at what one would truly call a legal judgment. I understand and respect the wishes and beliefs [of the parties]. There is no solution or compromise available to me that will satisfy each side. I can only make a decision and indicate my regret that it will cause pain to the losing party.[114]

Such statements suggest judges are acutely aware that their rulings will only intensify the anguish and sense of grievance felt by the losing side, and that trying to lessen the emotional fallout is a good thing. Of course, there are limits to any such textual analysis, and more work could be done to probe and validate these claims.[115] However, appropriate displays of empathy and understanding that do not compromise judicial impartiality[116] have an important role to play in contested funerals. Whether or not this can pave the way for some sort of family reconciliation is another matter entirely, as expertly summed up by Campbell J in *Munro v Pitt*:

> I appreciate that at times like this in the life of a family feelings run high, even though it would be far preferable that they did not. These significant events in the life of families, in our community, are truly a time for bringing people together, for putting aside old scores and for the healing of old wounds. It is unrealistic perhaps to accept that this will always occur.[117]

V. Conclusion

> People never fully relegate disputes to the past, never completely let bygones be bygones … [T]here is a continuity to disputing that may not be terminated even by formal decision. The end of one dispute may create a new grievance.[118]

Contested funerals are a peculiar species of private law dispute that pose all sorts of challenges, and not just because the subject-matter is the deceased's mortal remains. Set

[113] (n 73) [2]–[3].
[114] *Dodd v Jones* [1999] SASC 458 [36].
[115] Testing, for instance, what judges hope to achieve by crafting their judgments in this manner, and the emotional impact (if any) on the parties – and the losing parties in particular. From a research perspective, the latter would be more difficult.
[116] A recurrent theme in law and emotion literature on the legitimacy of empathy in the practice of judging. See, eg, SA Bandes, 'Empathetic Judging and the Rule of Law' [2009] *Cardozo Law Review De Novo* 133.
[117] *Munro v Pitt* [2019] NSWSC 1374 [19].
[118] Felstiner, Abel and Sarat (n 5) 639.

against a backdrop of death, personal loss and familial upheaval, these disputes often have their origins in something unrelated to the issue at hand, and neither side will be prepared to 'back down' or compromise regardless of the consequent delays to the funeral.

Writing in a different context, Bosley and Cook describe funerals as fusing the 'practical and emotional tasks associated with death'.[119] A central theme of this chapter is that private law's treatment of contested funerals should operate on a similar basis. The first and more pressing task is routinely performed in the numerous cases cited here. Judges use discrete legal rules, or multi-factorial approaches, to award possession of the deceased's remains to a particular individual; and while the decision-making frameworks may not be perfect, a solution can be found that allows the funeral to proceed. Dealing with the emotional aspects of these disputes is a less straightforward, but nonetheless vital, task. To begin with, judges (and legal advisors) need to understand why emotions are running so high, and that it is not just because the parties are grieving (though this is obviously an important aspect). More often than not, fraught and dysfunctional family relationships are the root source of the problem, and death does not automatically (re)unite those who loved the deceased in life. Again, the volume of case law referenced throughout this chapter makes this abundantly clear.

The danger in all of these cases is that the formal resolution of the matter does not actually end the dispute, given everything that has happened and the significance that comes (both privately and publicly) with having the final say on funeral arrangements. Damage limitation strategies are imperative here, and the manner in which the decision is communicated in particular. Of course, it is naïve to assume that any of this will bring closure to the losing party, or achieve family unity in the long-term; the emotional fissures run deep in contested funerals, and the parties' relationships with each other (and wider family circle) are often irreparable long before they end up in a courtroom. Yet, there may still be a glimmer of hope. Attempting to diffuse the emotionally charged situation that the parties find themselves in could have a positive impact in the longer-term, once the proverbial litigation dust has settled and the deceased laid to rest.

Looking beyond the subject-matter, this chapter demonstrates the ongoing challenges for private law in presenting an ideal framework for the various disputes it is tasked with resolving. There is also the legitimate question of how private law engages with emotion and integrates emotion in its legal processes. These are both major themes for another day, with others setting the research agenda for any such process of internal reflection. For now, contested funerals are a useful means of bringing both to the fore, as part of a wider debate around the issues facing private law today[120] and beyond the constructs of life and death that dominate this collection.

[119] GM Bosley and AS Cook, 'Therapeutic Aspects of Funeral Ritual: A Thematic Analysis' (1994) 4 *Journal of Family Psychotherapy* 69, 69.

[120] See, eg, K Barker, R Grantham and K Fairweather (eds), *Private Law in the 21st Century* (Oxford, Hart Publishing, 2017).

11

Cultural Negotiation of Inheritance Law in Australia

PRUE VINES

'He that begins to live, begins to die.'

Francis Quarles (1592–1644), Hieroglyphikes of the Life of Man[1]

I. Introduction

Death is the only certainty for us. Even taxes don't come to everybody. The quote above by Francis Quarles reminds us not only that all people must die, but also that life and death are inextricably interlinked; and indeed that there is actually no gap between them. The purpose of succession rules is to ease the passage of property from one generation to the next, and, in doing so, to also ease the monstrous fact of death in every life – the death the individual suffers which takes away everything and everybody else; and the response those left behind have to the loss of the person who has died, which includes the reminder that death will come for them too. The loss of the deceased is the loss which succession law (itself a form of culture) and cultural patterns of behaviour mostly respond to.

Cultural attitudes to death differ and, within cultures, attitudes also differ over time. In Western Europe up until the nineteenth century, death was reluctantly accepted as something which had to be dealt with. There was no possibility of denying something so prevalent. It was also thoroughly embedded in religion. The concept of 'the good death' became significant and was strongly associated with the last confession, which in turn was strongly associated with the making of a will.[2] Intestacy itself could be regarded as a sin.[3]

[1] (London, printed by M Flesher, 1638) 5.

[2] See generally TSR Boase, *Death in the Middle Ages: Mortality, Judgment and Remembrance* (London, Thames and Hudson, 1972); P Binski, *Medieval Death: Ritual and Representation* (New York, Cornell University Press, 1996); B Gordon and P Marshall (eds), *The Place of the Dead: Death and Remembrance in Late Medieval and Early Modern Europe* (Cambridge, Cambridge University Press, 2000).

[3] R Croucher and P Vines, *Succession: Families, Property and Death*, 5th edn (Sydney, LexisNexis, 2019) 28.

After the nineteenth century and into the twentieth denial of death became the norm. Death was hidden:

> Before 1959 when Herbert Feifel wanted to interview the dying about themselves, no doubt for the first time, hospital authorities were indignant. They found the prospect 'cruel, sadistic, and traumatic'. In 1965 when Elisabeth Kübler-Ross was looking for dying persons to interview, the heads of the hospitals and clinics to whom she addressed herself protested, 'Dying? But there are no dying here!' There could be no dying in a well-organised, respectable institution. They were mortally offended.[4]

These cultural stances, such as denial or acceptance of death, may exist independently of the law of succession, which might remain the same in the face of that stance. Even in the twentieth century, traditional succession law courses rarely mentioned death. Of course, death had to be proved, because that was a pivot for jurisdiction,[5] but it was not really explored. The culture has now changed and now most succession courses pay more attention to the dying testator, funerals, how the body is treated, and so on. However, it is also true that, over time, cultural matters will have an impact on the law and change it.

The Anglo-centricity of succession law refers to the law itself, to the legal culture surrounding it, and to the general culture surrounding the legal culture. Australian succession law is Anglo-centric in that it is part of the common law in which we expect judges to write judgments which make law; it draws on elements of the English law of equity, which gave us trusts and a number of remedies such as estoppel and injunctions which did not exist elsewhere. Where there is a dispute, it is adversarial in the way the dispute is determined. The legal culture also includes the use of solicitors for advice and barristers as advocates in court. English succession law's most obvious characteristic was its insistence on freedom of testation – that is, that the testator, as long as s/he had capacity, was free to make as idiosyncratic a will as s/he liked. The legal culture is also embedded in a social culture which, in many ways, has its roots in the English culture – this includes a level of individualism shared by many Western societies, views about families and how they deal with each other which focus on the nuclear rather than the broader family, views about when children are old enough to transact business, or own property; and views about property which see it as alienable, and (in relation to land) mostly as based on feudal tenure. It also draws on the historical, religious foundations of England, which include the move from Roman Catholicism to Protestantism, and indeed to an established church (although Australia does not have an established church). Because the Anglican Church was the establishment, it did affect law. It is arguable that Protestantism in its later nineteenth-century form had an enormous impact on burial rights, treatment of burial grounds and treatment of the dead, as Protestantism took more and more to the idea that the body is a mere 'envelope' and therefore not so important.[6] All of these factors may contribute to an individual, family or community's response to the fact of death and the need to deal with the dead, the deceased's estate and those left behind. Culture needs to be taken seriously.

[4] P Ariès, *The Hour of Our Death*, 2nd edn (New York, Vintage Books, 2008) 589.

[5] See, eg, Probate and Administration Act 1898 (NSW) s 40.

[6] See P Vines, 'Resting in Peace? A Comparison of the Legal Control of Bodily Remains in Cemeteries and Aboriginal Burial Grounds in Australia' (1998) 20 *Sydney Law Review* 78.

The most recent census emphasised the fact that over half of Australians were born – or had parents born – overseas.[7] This suggests that people bring different cultures with them to Australia, which might well affect attitudes or expectations about inheritance, our law of succession on death. This is partly because people tend to go back to their roots, first language and so on as they age, or come close to death.[8] This chapter will explore how different values and meanings attached to death (and to life) in various cultural contexts lead to the need to negotiate with the dominant, Anglo-centric legal culture.

II. Legal and Social Culture

Culture is hard to define, since it can be a mere label – for example 'Australian' – without much detail in how it is constituted. The most usual meaning of the word in sociology now is 'the entire way of life, activities, beliefs and customs of a people, group or society'.[9] Clifford Geertz's view of culture can be characterised as a way of including more than a 'nominal' or 'thin' approach into the study of a group of people, thus incorporating more context and, often, the perspective of the observer.[10] He uses 'thick description' to describe cultures, moving away from Talcott Parson's 'forms' and 'values' as making up culture:[11] 'man is an animal suspended in webs of significance he himself has spun. I take culture to be those webs and the analysis of it to be therefore … an interpretive one in search of meaning'.[12] Similarly, 'expressive' theories of law can add to the understanding of a culture, or culture in general, by being willing to incorporate emotional responses along with moral and cultural values as they are traditionally understood.[13] This gives a richer view of the culture being considered. In this chapter, I use the term 'culture' to encompass groups which identify as having distinct values.

[7] According to the 2021 Census, the highest ancestries for the population were English 33 per cent, Australian 29 per cent, Irish 9.5 per cent, Scottish 8.6 per cent and Chinese 5.5 per cent. Nearly half of Australians had a parent born overseas and 27.6 per cent were themselves born overseas. The most common languages spoken at home are English, Mandarin, and Arabic: Australian Bureau of Statistics, '2021 Census: Nearly Half of Australians Have a Parent Born Overseas' (28 June 2022) www.abs.gov.au/media-centre/media-releases/2021-census-nearly-half-australians-have-parent-born-overseas. For our purposes, the most interesting statistic is that, before the 2016 census, the Asian born population over 65 years old was low and the European born population of the same age was high. The position reversed in 2016, when the median age of the Asian born population was 35 and the median age of the European born population was 59.

[8] For example, when people have to consider an autopsy on a loved one who has died, their background religion may suddenly be more important than it seemed to be during ordinary life. Thus, objections to autopsies become more prevalent where people's background is Aboriginal Australian, Jewish, Muslim or Buddhist: P Vines, 'Objections to Post-Mortem Examination: Multiculturalism, Psychology and Legal Decision-Making' (2000) 7 *Journal of Law and Medicine* 422.

[9] P Smith and A Riley, *Cultural Theory: An Introduction*, 2nd edn (Oxford, Blackwell Publishing, 2009) 23–24.

[10] See C Geertz, 'Thick Description: Toward an Interpretive Theory of Culture' in C Geertz (ed), *The Interpretation of Cultures* (New York, Basic Books, 1973).

[11] See T Parsons, *The Structure of Social Action* (New York, Free Press, 1968).

[12] Geertz (n 10) 5.

[13] See, eg, C Sunstein, 'On the Expressive Function of Law' (1996) 144 *University of Pennsylvania Law Review* 2021; ES Anderson and RH Pildes, 'Expressive Theories of Law: A General Restatement' (2000) 148 *University of Pennsylvania Law Review* 1503.

These may be legal, social, moral or political in nature, and may derive from geography, religion, ethnicity or even being part of a football club (for example). We are less likely to think that membership of a football club is a central cultural marker than religion or ethnicity, but such groups also have their own cultures, although football clubs are less likely to have cultural views about death that differ from the those of the general spread in society. The dominant culture for the purpose of this chapter is the common law legal culture of Australia, drawing on common law and equity, and the church law of England, with an emphasis on the rule of law, and based on views of the nuclear rather than broad family, an individualist rather than collectivist culture and morality; and of course, emphasising freedom of testation.

The effects of conflicting cultural expectations are real. In the area of succession law, they also exist and can have considerable impact. In this chapter, I will attempt to consider how the Australia law of succession has managed – and responded to – the interaction between itself and the cultural values of other groups; and how those other groups' expectations affect their interactions with Australian succession law while they are living in Australia. Three, major groups come to mind – Indigenous people, Jewish people and Muslims, and a fourth one which has been a major source of immigration to Australia, people from civil law countries, such as those in Western Europe. The first three are the most different from the Anglo-centric succession law we are speaking of. Each involves a view of law that connects it deeply, if not completely, with religion.

III. Religion and Law as Culture

The Anglo-centricity of Australian succession law is no surprise because it is a derivative of English succession law, the origins of which lay in the church. The mediaeval English will was deeply religious. Originally, wills were part of the confession the deceased made to God when he or she was dying, in conjunction with the last rites given by the priest. The church managed the distribution of the estate, part of which was given to the church to pray for the soul of the deceased. Indeed, right up until the mid-nineteenth century in common law jurisdictions, wills began with a religious exhortation,[14] for example:

> In the name of God Amen the 8th day of September and in the year of our Lord God 1558 I Thomas Ruddock the elder of Bridgham dwelling in the county of Norfolk being whole of mind and good of remembrance to God be praised do make this my last will and testament in this form following First I commend my soul into the hands of my lord God to our lady Saint Mary and all the holy company of heaven and my body to be buried in the churchyard of our lady in Bridgham aforesaid Item I will have at the day of my burial dirge and mass and the poor people of Bridgham to have among them to pray for my soul and all … share 6 s 8 d.[15]

[14] Ariès suggests that this move away from religious exhortations came earlier in the European context. He tracks the change to the second half of the eighteenth century: (n 4) 471.

[15] Will of Thomas Ruddock, 1558. From the Roudham Wills collection transcribed and translated by Peter and Miriam Barry. The original Will is held in Norfolk Records Office. Copy in the author's possession.

Here, Thomas Ruddock commends himself to God and Mary the mother of Jesus Christ – a characteristically Catholic way of considering religion. He then goes on to ask that his body be buried in the churchyard, that is, in sacred ground, and requests that mass for his soul be performed on the day of his burial. This mass was to assist his passage to Heaven.

A later will reflects a different view of religion:[16]

> In the name of god Amen; [date 1586] And in the eight and twentith yeare of the raigne of o[ur] Soveraign Ladie Elizabeth by the grace of god Queene of England, Fraunce and Ireland etc / I John Sparke the elder of Rowdehame in the Countty of Norff husbandma[n] and in the dioces of Norwich being of whole mynd and of good and perfecte remembrance thanckes be to Almightie god trustinge assuredlie that of his infinite goodness and mercie through the merrittes and passion of his deare sonne my Lorde and Saviour Jesus Christ hee will after the course of thys mortall life fulfilled receave my Soule unto the blessed reste of his eternall and everlastinge kingdome of heaven: And my bodie to be buried in the Churchyarde of Rowedeham aforesaide Item I geve and bequeathe to the rep[ar]acion of the Churche of Rowdeham aforesaide three shillings and foure pence of good and lawful englishe money to be paid within one whole yeare next after my decease / Item I geve and bequeathe to the poorest people within the parrishe of Rowdeham aforesaide three shillings and foure pence to be geven at the daie of my burial.

These two testators came from the same village of Roudham in Norfolk, England. They are separated by some 30 years – but those 30 years were the years of the Reformation in England. The second fragment emphasises the saving power of Jesus Christ and does not mention Mary, his mother. The earlier fragment reflects the dominant Christian (Roman Catholic) view of death and the body in mediaeval times across Europe and the British Isles, which was based on a belief that the body and soul remained connected to each other after death, and that prayers for the dead in between the time of death and the bodily resurrection at the end of time would make a difference to whether the deceased went to Heaven or Hell on the Last Day. Before the Reformation, prayers for the dead were said every day in every church. But, after the Reformation, praying for the dead became illegal[17] and a shift occurred from praying for the dead by referring them to the Virgin Mary, to an emphasis on the importance of faith in the saving power of Jesus Christ.

This was a forced, top-down change of culture. It took time for such a radical change to filter through to the common people, but the change is manifest in these two wills, which would, of course, have been written for the testator by the village priest. After the Reformation, England became a profoundly Protestant country, and eventually the link between church and state was manifested in the concept of the established church. In Australia, although there is no established church, the common law was already imprinted with its religious, especially Protestant background.[18] The English

[16] Will of John Sparke, 1586. From the Roudham Wills collection transcribed and translated by Peter and Miriam Barry. The original Will is held in Norfolk Records Office. Copy in the author's possession.

[17] Henry VIII made this illegal in 1529, as a statute passed in 1547 makes clear: (Public Act, 1 Ed VI, c 14). Chantries (places where one prayed for the dead) were abolished and the proceeds went to the Crown.

[18] Today, in Australia and other common law countries, the preamble to a will rarely contains a religious statement, but this is a relatively recent phenomenon. The early New South Wales wills (as late as 1836) still began 'In the name of God Amen'. See, for example, the Will of William Hill, 12 February 1836, New South Wales Probate Registry. Note that the inscription on the probate copy of the will states that it is in the Ecclesiastical Jurisdiction of the Supreme Court of New South Wales.

industrial revolution altered the culture again and, by the nineteenth century, England was renowned for its emphasis on both freedom of contract and freedom of testation. Both these concepts emphasised the freedom of the individual. Freedom to contract meant that both parties to a contract were regarded as having equal power, which meant that, once there was agreement, there could be no reason not to meet the terms of the contract. Despite the fact that parties often were *not* equal, this fiction was used to reinforce and develop systems of trade which reinforced the industrial revolution. Similarly, freedom of testation emphasised the idea that everyone should equally be able to pass their own property to whomever they pleased. This conveniently ignored the fact that many people (often women) simply did not have property to leave, or that this freedom – in the context of married women being regarded as not having legal personality – meant that they and their children could be left destitute.[19]

Freedom of testation was not emphasised in the civil law countries of Europe. They limited the use of wills to a portion of the estate and otherwise had patterns of forced inheritance. Despite this major difference, the common Christian religious background means that immigrants who came to Australia in the 1950s and 60s (often from Greece, Italy and the Baltic states) had similar cultural and religious understandings of death and succession law. There was relatively little difficulty in understanding how it worked, despite the differences between Protestant, Roman Catholic and Orthodox Christian Churches.

Other groups where religious culture makes a difference to attitudes to death and succession law include Indigenous people, and Jewish, Muslim, Hindu and Buddhist immigrants. For Indigenous people, the vital connection to land and the complex customary laws concerning 'sorry business' and rituals of mourning for kin to observe are difficult to fit into the secular Australian world which now exists. Jewish people also have their own practices, such as burial within 24 hours, and other customs to comfort the bereaved, as well as their own succession law. Muslims also prefer speedy burial and have rituals for comfort which differ from secular Australian culture. All three of these groups have a major aversion to autopsy which is part of their attitude to death – that the body is sacred.[20]

One would not call modern Australia a religious culture, although its roots still lie in Christianity; rather, Australia is now a very secular society, with approximately 38.9 per cent of respondents to the 2021 Census saying they had no religion.[21] Those who did say they had a religion were predominantly Christian (43.9 per cent), followed by Muslim (3.2 per cent) and Hindu (2.7 per cent). The percentage of Indigenous people is now 3.2 per cent. How is the succession law of Australia to be negotiated by people from very different laws and cultures?

[19] Eventually, equity assisted with the most egregious of the inequalities in contractual power with doctrines such as undue influence, fraud, duress etc; while in succession law, not until the development of Testator's Family Maintenance (now often 'family provision') legislation were limits placed on the testamentary freedom which could leave every bit of property away from spouse and children: the Testator's Family Maintenance Act 1900 (NZ) was the first of these; it was followed in Australia shortly after.

[20] Vines (n 8).

[21] Australian Bureau of Statistics, 'Snapshot of Australia' (28 June 2022) www.abs.gov.au/statistics/people/people-and-communities/snapshot-australia/2021.

IV. How Does Australian Law Deal with the Law of Religious and Other Groups in Relation to Inheritance?

The short answer to this question is that it ignores other laws and religions, including, until very recently, Indigenous customary law. The content of the will is largely left to the testator in the name of testamentary freedom. The exception to this is that, where religious or other conditions have been placed on wills, the court may scrutinise the condition, in order to determine whether the condition may be allowed or should be struck down as uncertain, or because it is against public policy. This is a matter of construction of the will. Many conditions in wills have been religious in nature. It has been common in the past for gifts in wills to be made on condition that a person marry, or not marry, into a particular religion – Roman Catholicism, Anglicanism, Jehovah's Witnesses, the Brethren, and so on. Generally, such clauses will not be struck down for public policy reasons, but because it is uncertain how to determine whether a person has become a member of a religion.[22] Clearly, these cases are not directed at issues of recognition of those religions as law even when they do have their own law, as do Judaism and Islam. Australian inheritance law, apart from religious conditions, has simply ignored the needs of Muslims, Indigenous people, Jewish people, and so on, simply assuming they will conform to the law of the land. This means that these groups have to negotiate the dominant legal system for themselves.

A. Muslim Inheritance in Australia

The Muslim percentage of the population of Australia is now 3.2 per cent. It is a relatively young population, but the need to deal with succession law remains important. The Muslim population is also quite diverse in Australia, coming from many countries. The major divisions between Sunni and Shi'a are significant in inheritance. Muslim Australians come from a wide range of schools (*madhabs)* and cannot be categorised as one, homogenous group. There are three major schools within the Shi'a grouping: *Ismailis* ('seveners'), *Ja'fari* ('twelvers') and *Zaydi*. Within the Sunni population, some may not distinguish amongst the schools, just calling themselves Sunni; others will designate a school to which they belong. The four major schools are *Hanafii*, *Shafi'i*, *Maliki* and *Hanbali*. Although the schools may have substantial similarities, they also have different interpretations of the law, which must be considered for a particular person. *Ja'fari*, *Hanafi* and *Shafi'i* appear to be the most common schools in Australia.[23]

Interestingly, in a recent survey of Muslim Australians, 63.6 per cent simply answered 'Sunni' to a question about which tradition they identified with, and 34 per cent

[22] See, eg: *Clayton v Ramsden* [1943] AC 320 (HL); *Re Orr* [1940] SASR 395; *Hickin v Carroll (No 2)* [2014] NSWSC 1059.

[23] A Saeed, *Islam in Australia* (Crows Nest, Allen & Unwin, 2003) 69, cited in B Thompson, 'Navigating Dual Legal Systems: Islamic Inheritance Law in Australia's Secular Framework' (2022) 41 *University of Queensland Law Journal* 89, 101.

answered 'Muslim'.[24] My own anecdotal experience of students is that, to the question 'which school?' they may answer just 'Sunni' – and may tell me that they don't know more than that. It should be noted that in many religious groups only the priest, or imam, is expected to know all the detail of the religion, the laity simply following along.

A case study of Muslims who were contemplating using Shari'a in their will in Australia showed that the participants had various views about how they could make a Shari'a-compliant will. The survey was part of a much larger one, and only 16 Muslim participants could be found. A small number of these said that Islam required the making of a will, that it required a specialist in Islamic law to assist, and that they needed a lawyer but would instruct them carefully. Some had written wills which they felt met the requirements of Islam, but some had done this in a detailed way, and others had made wills that they considered fair, 'seen as the underlying intent of Shari'a-compliant wills'.[25] Some considered that there was a conflict between Islam and the Australian succession system. In most cases where perceived Shari'a was to be followed, sons were to receive twice as much as daughters, although one participant commented: 'I have to do it according to the Sharia, even though I am not happy with that. I would like to give the boy 50% and the girl 50%'.[26]

Islamic inheritance is very complex – so complex that Islamic legal scholars regard knowledge of it as 'constitut[ing] one-half of all knowledge.'[27] Its precision and detail make it hugely daunting. First, there is an obligation to make a will covering only one third of the estate, which should not include certain heirs. Then the other two-thirds of the estate should be passed as follows (note debts and funeral expenses should be paid before distribution to heirs). In Sunni groups, the basic principle is that there are three classes of inheritors: *Qur'anic* heirs ('sharers'), agnatic ('residuaries') and uterine heirs ('distant kindred'). Broadly speaking, the emphasis is on the *Qur'anic* heirs in Shi'a[28] and on agnatic heirs in Sunni Islam. The sharers are specified in the Qur'an and cannot be excluded by other heirs. They get a specified share. This group includes husband, wife, father, true grandfather, mother, true grandmother, daughter, son's daughter, full sister, consanguine sister, uterine brother and uterine sister. You will notice that son is not mentioned in this group. That is because he is a residuary heir – only traced through male links. In Sunni schools, this group gets the bulk of the estate, the true heirs only getting their designated shares. Only if there are no other relatives (except a spouse) does the estate go to distant kindred.

[24] H Rane et al, 'Islam in Australia: A National Survey of Muslim Australian Citizens and Permanent Residents' (2020) 11 *Religions* 419, 425. 84.2 per cent of the survey respondents were born Muslim and 15.8 per cent had converted to Islam: ibid.

[25] J Wilson et al, 'Cultural Considerations in Will-Making in Australia: A Case Study of Islamic or Sharia-Compliant Wills' (2016) 41 *Alternative Law Journal* 23, 25.

[26] ibid.

[27] Z Chaudhry, 'The Myth of Misogyny: A Reanalysis of Women's Inheritance in Islamic Law' (1997–98) 61 *Albany Law Review* 511, 527. See also M Keshavjee, *Islam, Sharia and Alternative Dispute Resolution: Mechanisms for Legal Redress in the Muslim Community* (London, IB Tauris, 2013).

[28] Details of Shi'a inheritance are not discussed in this chapter. The fundamental difference from Sunni law is that, for Shi'a, the *Qur'anic* rules are regarded as the fundamental principles of the inheritance system. This means that the strength of agnatic ties in Sunni are ignored in Shi'a inheritance, thus allowing those who are *Qur'anic* heirs, such as daughters, to exclude those who are only agnatic heirs. In general, women receive a greater share under Shi'a law than Sunni.

This explanation is, of course, too simple. There are further laws; and the effect of complex relationships may alter the fractions an heir is entitled to. The share a person takes will vary according to the presence of different relatives. It may also alter which class relatives will be in. For example, if a Sunni man dies leaving a son and a daughter, the presence of the son will convert the daughter from a *Qur'anic* heir to a residuary heir.

The scope of the conflict between Islamic inheritance law and Australian inheritance law is not simple. First, and as noted above, there is the requirement under Shari'a law that a will not cover more than one third of the estate. Doing this literally will lead the testator to be treated as an intestate as to the rest of the estate by the succession law of Australia. The answer to this is usually to make a will (including to prevent intestacy) according to the requirements of the particular *mahdab*. Presumably, this should be a composite will – one third as if it were the only will, and the other two thirds as prescribed shares in accordance with the principles set out above. This is what the Imams of the Australian National Imams Council were referring to when they said 'Death has no time, place or age. As Australian Muslims, it is our duty to ensure that we have a Will in place which conforms with Islamic guidelines and Australian law'.[29]

However, there may be clashes between a will and family provision requirements, and, where shares given between siblings are unequal, the family provision jurisdiction is unlikely to allow them to remain.

The family provision legislation across Australia provides for eligible applicants who have not been left with sufficient assets to support their maintenance, education and advancement in life to apply to the court for the will or intestacy to be varied according to the law.[30] The most common eligible applicants are the spouse and then the children of the deceased. Children often seek to claim where they have been treated unequally. This raises the issue for those who make wills giving one share to daughters and two shares to sons as to whether the testator's view will prevail. It is, of course, true that Muslims who have lived in Australia all their lives may have developed cultural expectations which differ from those of their parents, and this may cause problems.

[29] The statement continues:

> Drafting a Will gives you the opportunity to specify how your funeral arrangements are carried out, how your Estate will be distributed and even matters concerning guardianship of minors.
>
> The Australian National Imams Council (ANIC) in partnership with [a particular law firm] now provides this much needed service to the Australian Muslim Community a Will endorsed by the Imams and drafted by Professional Muslim Lawyers.
>
> Narrated Abdullah bin Umar: the Messenger pbuh said, "It is not permissible for any Muslim who has something to Will to stay for two nights without having his last Will and testament written and kept ready with him." Bukhari.
>
> Get your Islamic and legal Will NOW.
>
> For more information please Email: wills@anic.org.au

Australian National Imams Council, 'Islamic and Legal Wills' www.anic.org.au/islamic-and-legal-wills/.

[30] See Succession Act 1981 (Qld) pt IV; Testator's Family Maintenance Act 1912 (Tas); Administration and Probate Act 1958 (Vic) pt IV; Family Provision Act 1969 (ACT); Family Provision Act 1970 (NT) s 8(1); Succession Act 2006 (NSW) s 59(1)(c); Inheritance (Family Provision) Act 1972 (SA); Family Provision Act 1972 (WA).

The case of *Omari v Omari*[31] raised all these issues simultaneously. This case was not a family provision case, but it could easily have been. It concerned the situation where an elderly Muslim testatrix's will was drafted by one of her sons to be an Islamic will which gave the sons double the share the daughters received. The testatrix signed the will with her thumbprint because she did not read or write (in any language), nor did she speak very much English. The case was ultimately decided on the basis that the testatrix did not have the capacity to make a will at the time she signed it. In this case, one of the daughters clearly had different expectations, created by the fact that she had lived a considerable part of her life in Australia and she wanted an equal share with her brothers. The will was challenged on the basis of capacity, but, in my opinion, it could also have been challenged on a family provision basis. The general expectation in family provision appears to be equal treatment of children, regardless of sex. The two brothers thought that their mother would have wanted an Islamic will and she signed the will they provided, which was based on a precedent provided by a former Imam. As the judge at first instance said:

> I have come to the view that they arranged for their mother to execute the will which she executed, either well knowing that she did not understand what she was doing or what the effect of her execution of the will would be, or alternatively with indifference to whether or not she understood those matters. I accept that both of the plaintiffs generally believed that it was their mother's duty under Islam to make a will generally leaving full shares to her sons and half shares to her daughters. I accept that they generally believed that if their mother had been asked to make a will at an earlier time in her life, when she knew and understood what she was doing, that she would have made a will generally consistent with those Muslim expectations. … [They] thought that they were doing the right thing.[32]

One of the sons gave evidence that:

> the Muslim faith required an adult with assets to make a will as soon as practicable and not to delay this until old age. The family were conscious of the fact that their mother had not made a will, … and they decided that the time had come to take the question seriously and to prepare the will so that there would be no complications later on, and so that none of the siblings could take advantage of their mother's wealth.[33]

However, the issue which determined the case was her capacity – there was evidence that she had been demented for some time before the will was made and that she entered a facility for dementia some six weeks after the will was made. Although the case was decided on the basis of capacity, press coverage of the case gave prominence to the issue of Islamic wills.[34]

The similarities and differences between the law of wills and intestacy in the Australian Capital Territory (where the *Omari* case was decided) and most other Australian jurisdictions and Muslim law include who is regarded as a spouse or a child (for example Muslim law does not recognise adoption), and the belief that Islamic wills should not give property to non-Muslims, or 'sharers'.[35] The differences between Islamic

[31] *Omari v Omari* [2012] ACTSC 33. The outcome was confirmed by *Omari v Omari* [2016] ACTCA 16.
[32] *Omari v Omari* [2012] ACTSC 33 [63].
[33] ibid [41].
[34] See, eg, D Carrick, I Kahn and P Vines, 'Mariem Omari's Will' (Law Report Broadcast, ABC Radio, 20 March 2012) www.abc.net.au/listen/programs/lawreport/mariem-omari27s-will/3901178.
[35] See generally Thompson (n 23).

rules of inheritance and Australian ones could give rise to confusion for some, and will-drafters would need to be aware of this.

It will be seen immediately that the law of intestacy as it operates in Australian jurisdictions – where the spouse is the largest single inheritor and often inherits alone or with children[36] – does not match the Sunni laws. Similarly, the law of family provision draws on 'community standards' to determine whether a 'wise and just testator' would have drawn the will in the way it had been. Although it is arguable that recent family provision cases have taken more account of the testator's wishes than might have been the case in the past,[37] it is obviously difficult to establish what community standards should be drawn on where cultures appear to be clashing. As Pembroke J commented in 2018:

> We do not simply ride roughshod over the solemn wishes of a testator that have been formally and deliberately expressed in his last will and testament. We do not re-distribute a testator's wealth according to indeterminate and unreliable concepts such as fairness or equality. The law requires courts to respect a testator's freedom of testamentary disposition, to recognise that the making of a will is often the last and most significant decision a person might make, and to interfere only to the extent rendered necessary by the application of the statutory language to the particular circumstances.[38]

As with Jewish testators, the question of how to navigate the Australian legal system and stay true to their own religion is not easily answered by those who follow the teachings of Islam. However, the great advantage of common law wills is their ability to respond to individual situations, so that a good drafter should be able to reflect the needs of the Muslim needing a will in Australia. In *Omari*, the Imam of the Canberra Islamic Centre gave evidence, confirming that:

> the standard expectation is that a Muslim will leave full shares to sons and half shares to daughters. He said that one boy is equal to two girls. … [A] Muslim man in making a will was obliged not to go beyond the limit of Islam, by which he made it clear that he meant that shares to the children of the testator were to be left in the proportions he had explained. He said that a Muslim person with assets was expected to make a will at a relatively early age, and in any event prior to travelling on a haj to Mecca. He conceded that if a Muslim person died not having made a will, the division of their estate would be based on the law of the country where they had been living.[39]

Consideration of the complexity of the Islamic inheritance law shows that this is a simplification, which may not be entirely accurate. Where a male and female are in the same relationship to the deceased – for example, son and daughter, or brother and sister – a double share goes to a male, compared with a female. Otherwise, shares can vary. It is also true that men who receive the larger share are required to use it to support the family, while the share given to women is theirs to do with as they wish.[40] The drafting

[36] See, eg, Succession Act 2006 (NSW) ss 110–113; Administration and Probate Act 1969 (ACT) s 44.

[37] See, eg, *Steinmetz v Shannon* [2018] NSWSC 1090; *Collins v Mutton* [2012] NSWSC 548 [19]; *Andre v Perpetual Trustees WA Ltd* [2009] WASCA 14 [44].

[38] *Steinmetz* (n 37) [33].

[39] *Omari v Omari* [2012] ACTSC 33 [49].

[40] Chaudhry (n 27) 541–42. She notes that 'A woman is always guaranteed sufficient care, and she has no legal obligation to support anyone. This burden of support for all family members falls upon fathers, sons, husbands, and brothers depending on the circumstances': ibid. This is not a principle of Islamic inheritance law, but of Islam generally.

of a will which simply gave one share to the daughter and two shares to the son would not necessarily reflect the complexity of the Islamic law. Drafting it so that part of the sons' share is held on trust for others in the family might reflect the true position better.

The fact that instructions are given according to a set of cultural expectations for groups like Muslims which are very likely to be challenged as inappropriate in a family provision case raises issues for the drafter. It is essential, in such a case, to make it clear to the testator in advance that a challenge could succeed. It may be possible to draft in such a way that cultural expectations of both are met, as in the trust example above.

B. Jewish Inheritance in Australia

The number of Jewish people in Australia is very small, approximately 0.4 per cent of the population according to the 2021 Census. The majority live in Sydney and Melbourne. Jews arrived on the first fleet and so, since the beginning of British colonisation, they have had to navigate the succession law of the colony being different from their religious inheritance law, as they did in Britain beforehand. Although Australia was not settled with an established church, it was clear that not just Christianity, but its specifically Anglican form was favoured for personal status matters such as marriage.[41]

In Australia, it seems that the vast majority of Australian Jews are non-practising Orthodox.[42] They may be relatively secular, but they relate to each other through the Orthodox community, and particularly through Orthodox schools. Australian Jews have been extremely successful as a group in Australia.

Jewish inheritance law's biblical source is Numbers 27, particularly vv 8–11:[43]

> Say to the Israelites, 'If a man dies and leaves no son, give his inheritance to his daughter. If he has no daughter, give his inheritance to his brothers. If he has no brothers, give his inheritance to his father's brothers. If his father had no brothers, give his inheritance to the nearest relative in his clan, that he may possess it. This is to have the force of law for the Israelites, as the Lord commanded Moses.'[44]

[41] The first proper Jewish wedding officiated at by a rabbi in the colony of New South Wales (that of John Moses and Mary Connolly) was not celebrated until 1830, although they had been married earlier by a Christian ceremony: R Apple, 'Mary Connelly Revisited' (2011) 20 *Australian Jewish Historical Society Journal* 183. Note that it was only in 1834 that the Marriage Act 1834 (NSW) was passed, allowing Presbyterian and Roman Catholic priests to celebrate marriage, while earlier only Anglican ministers could do so. The Church Act 1836 (NSW) evened up matters between the three churches by removing Anglican privileges and evening up funding.

[42] G Briner, 'In Australian Jewish Community, Drama Over Fight for Gender Equality' (Website Article, Haaretz, 1 June 2021) haaretz.com/world-news/asia-and-australia/2021-06-01/ty-article/.premium/in-australias-jewish-community-drama-over-fight-for-gender-equality/0000017f-db5f-d3ff-a7ff-fbff95e40000.

[43] The context is given in earlier verses. See Num 27.1–7 NIV: 'The daughters of Zelophehad son of Hepher, the son of Gilead, the son of Makir, the son of Manasseh, belonged to the clans of Manasseh son of Joseph. The names of the daughters were Mahlah, Noah, Hoglah, Milkah and Tirzah. They came forward and stood before Moses, Eleazar the priest, the leaders and the whole assembly at the entrance to the tent of meeting and said, "Our father died in the wilderness. He was not among Korah's followers, who banded together against the Lord, but he died for his own sin and left no sons. Why should our father's name disappear from his clan because he had no son? Give us property among our father's relatives." So Moses brought their case before the Lord, and the Lord said to him, "What Zelophehad's daughters are saying is right. You must certainly give them property as an inheritance among their father's relatives and give their father's inheritance to them"'.

[44] Num 27.8–11 NIV.

The words 'As the LORD commanded Moses', Grunfeld says, is a reminder that the oral law must also be recognised – oral and written law are 'equally binding on the Jew'.[45]

Jewish inheritance law strongly emphasises the male line. So, where there are sons and daughters, the daughters do not inherit – a female descendant of a son will exclude the daughters of the deceased father. The estate owes maintenance to both wives and daughters, so that the estate continues to bear that burden, but a provision in a will to a wife (not yet remarried) or daughter is regarded as invalid, indeed it may be regarded as a theft from the proper ('*halachic*') heir.[46]

This is a pattern which may be difficult for Australian law to accept. Differences between gifts given to sons and daughters are very likely to be struck down in family provision actions, as, despite the currently increasing emphasis on the testator's wishes in family provision claims, courts continue to expect that siblings in similar circumstances will be treated equally to each other. As mentioned in discussing the *Omari* case above, if that case had gone to family provision, rather than being dealt with on the basis of capacity, the differential between the children is most likely to have been struck down.

Jewish inheritance law sees inheritance as immediate. At the moment of death, the estate is transferred to the *halachic* heirs. This is not the Australian system, which sees death as a pivotal point, but the estate exists separately from the testator while debts are paid and until probate is granted. This means that if person makes a will which gives the estate to non-*halachic* heirs, those people are effectively made into thieves from the *halachic* heir. A Jewish Australian man is very likely to want to make a will which benefits his wife, son and daughter after his death. In that situation, if he goes ahead and makes a will in those terms, the *halachic* heir, the son, has effectively had his property stolen by the non-*halachic* heirs, the widow and daughter. If the family is thoroughly Orthodox, this will cause them pain.

What are Jewish people to do in a country which does not practise Jewish law?[47] The first possibility is to rely on the *dina d'malhuta dina* rule (which states that the law of the land is also the Jewish religious law) and simply make an Australian will. The problem is that this has had varying interpretations, so that early commentators on the Talmud accepted that it clearly applies to taxes, customs and fiscal matters. Other early commentators argued that it applied also to civil law, and, in particular, to the validity of documents where the law binds every citizen. The latter sounds as if it could apply to the law of inheritance, including wills; however, sages from the twelfth-century Maimonides and into the nineteenth century were concerned about whether laws of the land, which undermined or contradicted Jewish law, could be accepted under this doctrine. They ultimately came to the conclusion that the rule did not apply to inheritance.[48] For secular Jews (the majority of Australian Jews being non-observant Orthodox) navigating the

[45] I Grunfeld, *The Jewish Law of Inheritance: Problems and Solutions in Making a Jewish Will* (Jerusalem, Targum Press, 1987) 8.

[46] BC Wolf, 'Resolving the Conflict Between Jewish and Secular Estate Law' (2009) 37 *Hofstra Law Rev* 1171, 1172.

[47] For further consideration of this issue, see DC Litman and SH Resnicoff, 'Jewish and American Inheritance Law: Commonalities, Clashes, and Estate Planning Consequences' in L Moscovits and J Revlin (eds), *"Wisdom and Understanding": Studies in Jewish Law in Honour of Bernard S Jackson* (Liverpool, Jewish Law Association, 2012).

[48] Grunfeld (n 45) ch 2.

Australian inheritance law is not very difficult. They are likely to be happy to make wills and may be unconcerned about dying intestate. For practising Orthodox Jews, it is more difficult in that Orthodox Judaism on the whole rejects wills, and the intestacy rules will not meet their needs at all. In particular, the dominance of the spouse in Australian intestacy law is contrary to the rules in Talmudic law that neither a wife, nor a daughter will inherit where there is a male descendant.[49]

Wolf suggests that there are other possibilities, which will not breach the orthodox rules. One of these is to create an *inter vivos* trust with the settlor as trustee and beneficiary with the other beneficiaries.[50] The advantage of this is that it prevents the property from being available to fall into the estate at the time of death and being available for Australian succession law to distribute, which is the problematic aspect for Orthodox Judaism. It thus prevents (mostly) the problem of theft referred to above. However, this would require constant attention to the trust to ensure no after-acquired property was available for the Australian law. To do this, you would have to put all bank accounts and so on into the trust and then monitor it carefully, which may be onerous.

C. Indigenous People and Succession Law in Australia

As is well known, in Australia the Indigenous people are Aboriginal and Torres Strait Islander people. For the most part, this section will only refer to Aboriginal people as the relevant First Nations' people, although many of the points made will also apply to Torres Strait Islanders. It is vitally important to know that, across Australia, there are some 300 language groups of Indigenous people. These have different customary law and customs and cannot be treated as homogeneous.

Since the British arrived in Sydney in 1788, the civil law needs of First Nations people have been mostly ignored by the colonisers. This continued well into the twentieth century and to some extent continues today. Dealing with inheritance was left entirely up to First Nations people. The general perception seems to have been that, if they were living a traditional life, they would not need the common law, and, if they were living an urban life in a city, they did not need the First Nations law. This was based on a continuing misapprehension about the way that Aboriginal people lived their lives. It turns out that many urban Aboriginal people spend times in their lives on country, living fairly traditionally, and vice versa.[51]

During the twentieth century this position continued, with very little attention paid to the inheritance needs of Aboriginal people. A few states set up intestacy legislation specifically for Aboriginal and Torres Strait Islander people,[52] but in most cases the state simply removed any benefit from them and any revenue went into its coffers. However,

[49] ibid 11.

[50] Wolf (n 46) 1183–86.

[51] E Johnston, *Royal Commission into Aboriginal Deaths in Custody National Report*, vol 1 (Canberra, Australian Government Publishing Service, 1991) 39, referring to A Gray 'Aboriginal Migration to the Cities' (1989) 6 *Journal of the Australian Population Association* 122. See also P Vines, 'When Cultures Clash: Aborigines and Inheritance in Australia' in G Miller (ed), *Frontiers of Family Law* (Aldershot, Ashgate, 2003).

[52] See Aboriginal and Torres Strait Islander Communities (Justice, Land and Other Matters) Act 1984 (Qld); Aboriginal Affairs Planning Authority Act 1972 (WA) pt IV. The Administration and Probate Act 1979 (NT) made a real attempt at incorporating customary law into the law of intestacy, but, as with the Queensland and

in a few, small ways, Australian law has made moves towards recognising both the needs and customary law of First Nations people.[53]

Indigenous customary law was not recognised as law at all until the twenty-first century. The Northern Territory Law Reform Committee observed in 2003 that 'Australian law does not recognise traditional law as *"law"*'.[54] The reasons for this are complex, but include the fact that Indigenous customary law is so diverse across communities.

The response of most First Nations people to this and other difficulties in relation to inheritance was to simply ignore the succession law and do an *ad hoc* transfer of property. For example, where a person died, property might be casually distributed to whoever seemed to want it, or to the person who would take it, despite the fact that they were not entitled to it either under customary law, or Australian law. When a person who thought they had a better right appeared, there might be ongoing disagreements for many years, with associated uncertainty about who owned what. This was, not surprisingly, often a recipe for disaster in the form of arguments which could run on for years and split communities.

Using the common law inheritance framework has been problematic for First Nations people in several different ways. The importance of secrecy in Aboriginal culture means that it is necessary to find ways to deal with the need to keep ritual knowledge and objects secret until the right person can receive them. In some groups, it is regarded as important for the deceased's house and belongings to be burnt, which may create problems in a modern city or town. Funerals where smoking of the body needs to be done may meet opposition from councils, whose insurers regard this as a dangerous activity. Burying 'in country' by bringing handfuls of dirt from the country to drop into the grave which is *not* in country, has met opposition from conservationist groups.

One of the most fundamental difficulties is the fact that kinship groupings and names can mean quite different things in the common law of succession, compared with the Aboriginal group's understanding of those names. This can be the same for other immigrant groups, but it is especially difficult with Indigenous Australians. For example, the word 'child' in Australian succession law refers to the next generation down the bloodline from the deceased. However, in many Aboriginal groups, the word 'child' might also refer to what non-Indigenous Australians and the law call 'niece' or 'nephew' (that is, the same sex sibling's child). What should be appreciated is that Indigenous naming practices actually reflect the kinship obligation of mother to child, or father to child, so that, if the succession law norms are applied, children who feel like – and have been treated like – 'children', will not *inherit* like 'children', and dislocation and disgruntlement may result. The terminology is a problem in both wills and intestacy, as it can lead to the wrong people inheriting.

Western Australian provisions, the legislation required that the deceased not have been married under the Marriage Act 1961 (Cth). Many traditional Aboriginal people were married by missionaries on reserves under the Marriage Act and were thereby disqualified: P Vines, 'Consequences of Intestacy for Indigenous People in Australia: The Passing of Property and Burial Rights' (2004) 8(4) *Australian Indigenous Law Reporter* 1.

[53] P Vines, 'Australia's (Slow) Experiment with Indigenous Customary Law in Intestacy' (2023) 4 *Journal of Commonwealth Law* 43.

[54] Northern Territory Law Reform Committee, *Report on Aboriginal Customary Law* (2003) 6 (emphasis in original).

Indigenous people in Australia have often informally adopted people into their family, and many Indigenous children have been adopted into non-Indigenous families. Formal adoption legislation in Australia typically severs all other relationships,[55] but Torres Strait Islander adoption has not been formally recognised by Australian law, and neither has informal Aboriginal adoption. In the Queensland case of *Eatts v Gundy*,[56] an informally-adopted child argued that he should be recognised as a child of the deceased for family provision purposes. This argument was rejected because, unless the formal process under the Adoption Act[57] has been followed, the Queensland court will not recognise the relationship for the purposes of succession law in the absence of legislation recognising Indigenous customary law, as in the Northern Territory, New South Wales and Tasmania.[58] This is another example of the Australian common law ignoring the needs of Indigenous people. However, if the action had been brought in New South Wales, it is likely that Mr Gundy would have succeeded under s 133 of the Succession Act 2006 (NSW), which provides that a person can apply to the court for distribution of the estate 'in accordance with the laws, customs, traditions and practices of the community or group to which the intestate belonged'.[59]

Although there is a burgeoning middle class,[60] it remains true that First Nations people tend to be poorer than the average in the community, and, partly for that reason, they have not been great will-makers. This is now being addressed, partly because of the increasing middle class, but also because there has been a big increase in pro bono will-making so that the will-making rate has risen to about 6 per cent. Drafting wills for Aboriginal people requires some different moves from the ones most drafters are used to dealing with, including determining whether the use of the name of the deceased should be prohibited, not using class gifts to avoid the confusion of kinship terminology, certain ways of allowing secret things to be passed, and so on.[61]

One of the most significant reasons some Aboriginal people wish to make a will is that a will appoints an executor, and an executor has the duty and power to deal with the body of the deceased.[62] There is a massive disproportion of body disposal disputes involving Indigenous people compared with non-Indigenous people – approximately 65 to 70 per cent of the decided cases involve such disputes – and many communities are riven in two by this. The disputes concern where the body is buried, whether it is buried or cremated, who gets to decide what is done with the body and whether the person's body should be dealt with according to customary law (including being buried

[55] See, eg, Adoption Act 2000 (NSW) s 95.

[56] *Eatts v Gundy* [2014] QCA 309.

[57] Adoption Act 2009 (Qld).

[58] See Succession Act 2006 (NSW) pt 4.4; Administration and Probate Act 1969 (NT) pt 4A; Intestacy Act 2010 (Tas) pt 4.

[59] For an example of this provision in action, see *Re Estate of Wilson* [2017] NSWSC 1, (2017) 93 NSWLR 119, discussed in P Vines, '*Re Estate Wilson, Deceased*, (2017): The Last Frontier for Aboriginal Intestacy in Australia?' in B Sloan (ed), *Landmark Cases in Succession Law* (Oxford, Hart Publishing, 2019).

[60] M Langton, *Boyer Lectures 2012: The Quiet Revolution: Indigenous People and the Resources Boom* (Sydney, ABC Books, 2013).

[61] P Vines, 'The NSW Project on the Inheritance Needs of Aboriginal People: Solving the Problem by Making Culturally Appropriate Wills' (2013) 16(2) *Australian Indigenous Law Review* 18; P Vines, *The Aboriginal Wills Handbook: A Practical Guide to Making Culturally Appropriate Wills for Aboriginal People*, 3rd edn (Sydney, NSW Trustee & Guardian, 2019).

[62] See *Williams v Williams* (1882) 20 ChD 659.

on country) or not. Disputes may be between the father and mother of a child, parents and the spouse of a deceased person, some or all of these being First Nations people, or not. The common law treats the executor as the person who decides what happens to the body of a deceased person where they made a will, but, where no will was made, there is no automatic, identifiable person charged with disposing of the body.[63] Being able to appoint an executor[64] and tell them what the testator wants done with their body appears to be much more important to Aboriginal communities than to non-Indigenous communities, and the appointment of someone with the legal right to enforce disposal wishes is seen as a dispute-resolution device. The extent to which customary law should be considered by a court determining how a body should be disposed of is still not settled.[65]

This is the most significant issue concerning death for many Aboriginal people. Both the Queensland Law Reform Commission and the Victorian Law Reform Commission have proposed that it should be possible for a person to specify how they wish for their body to be disposed of,[66] but this has not yet been taken up. If, as the Uniform Succession Law project has suggested, the roles of executor and administrator are assimilated,[67] this problem may well be reduced.[68]

As noted above, Aboriginal customary law or Indigenous customary law as law in intestacy has now been brought into the succession law in the Northern Territory, New South Wales and Tasmania.[69] A number of cases have utilised this in New South Wales,[70] very few in the Northern Territory, and none that I know of in Tasmania.

This recognition of customary law in intestacy, and the increasing take-up of wills has helped somewhat. The doctrine of testamentary freedom has the paradoxical effect of allowing the individual's idiosyncratic wishes and their cultural or religious views to be encapsulated within the will in such a way that the will protects the individual's expression of their wishes. But the law still fails to accommodate the expression of mourning,

[63] See *Jones v Dodd* [1999] SASC 125, (1999) 73 SASR 328 and *South Australia v Smith* [2014] SASC 64, (2014) 119 SASR 247 in relation to intestacy.

[64] *Williams* (n 62).

[65] Compare *Jones* (n 63) and *Britt v Office of the State Coroner* [2022] WASCA 75.

[66] Queensland Law Reform Commission, *A Review of the Law in Relation to the Final Disposal of a Body* (Report No 69, 2011) 129; Victorian Law Reform Commission, *Funeral and Burial Instructions* (Report, 2016) 40–44.

[67] See New South Wales Law Reform Commission, *Uniform Succession Laws: Administration of Deceased Estates* (Discussion Paper 42, 1999) 17.

[68] There may still be disagreement, of course, as in *Sullivan v Public Trustee for the Northern Territory of Australia* (24 July 2002, unreported), NTSC, where the deceased made a will saying he wanted to be buried in his 'homing place' with his wife and son, but his elder brother argued customary law dictated a different place. The court held that the executor's duty was only to try to comply with the deceased's wishes and that, as it was impractical to follow those wishes, he should be buried as his brother and kinfolk wished. They did not decide they had to follow customary law.

[69] See Succession Act 2006 (NSW) pt 4.4; Intestacy Act 2010 (Tas); Administration and Probate Act 1979 (NT).

[70] See P Vines, 'The Use of Customary Law in Intestacy in Australian Jurisdictions: Access to Justice in Action?' (2021) *Australian Bar Review* 1. The first New South Wales case was *Re Estate of Wilson* (n 59). The court's approach is to determine which country the deceased comes from, and then for those applying for customary law provisions to be used to present evidence from elders in that community to explain to the court what the customary law is. Where there is a dispute about what the customary law is, the court will decide between competing views.

the need for very large funerals, sometimes twice a year apart, and for time to attend them,[71] and all the 'sorry business' which is necessary when an Indigenous person dies. This leaves the burden of negotiation on the individual Indigenous person, who may find the burden of constantly negotiating with employers and others very heavy.

D. Legal System Interactions

One of the questions faced by any legal system which even considers the possibility of allowing another legal system's rules to be in play, is the extent to which this creates a form of plurality which supports or undermines either, or both, sets of rules. Most countries are most concerned about maintaining the power and status of their own laws. Many countries deal with the problem of multiple cultures or religious laws within them by using personal status laws. This is particularly common in former colonies. Personal status law – the law of marriage, legitimacy of children, divorce and inheritance – is often the law most closely related to a person's religious culture. Allowing personal status law to be determined by religious affiliation is an obvious way to allow regulation of these matters without attempting to blend aspects of the law of each culture, or come to new understandings of law where multiculturalism exists.[72] So in India, for example, personal status law is governed by religious affiliation as Hindu, Christian, Muslim, Jain and so on, and succession law is dealt with on the basis of the religion one's parents were married under. Similar arrangements, whereby personal status law is governed by religious affiliation, exist in Malaysia, Morocco, Lebanon, Algeria, Israel and many other countries. By hiving off these issues relating to the family and family values, clashes in these areas are avoided or minimised and, as these are regarded as 'private' rather than public law matters, the public aspects of the legal system are not impeded. But Australia has chosen not to go down this path. Law Reform Commission reports on multiculturalism and the law have not even canvassed the possibility of separating off personal status law as a method of dealing with multiculturalism.[73] The assumption has always been that those immigrating to Australia must take the legal system as they find it. There is little scope for the cultural and religious legal traditions of many immigrants to be used at the time of a loved one's death, when the familiar is extremely comforting. Funeral traditions may have to be negotiated with people who do not understand. Jews and Muslims in Australia both have rules for dealing with the fact that they are living in a non-Muslim or non-Jewish country, although, as we have seen, this is not without difficulty. Other groups also have to negotiate their way around the Australian legal system in order to meet religious requirements which are significant to them.

[71] For the same deceased person. This is the reason that funeral insurance is such a major issue for Indigenous people, and that corrupt practices by funeral insurance salespeople have had to be investigated multiple times without any proper resolution of the problem being found. See L O'Brien et al, 'Putting a Price on Peace of Mind: Funeral Insurance and Consumer Harm' (2021) 48 *University of Western Australia Law Review* 641.

[72] H Tagan, 'Personal Family Law Systems – A Comparative and International Human Rights Analysis' (2012) 8 *International Journal of Law in Context* 231.

[73] See, eg, Australian Law Reform Commission, *Multiculturalism and the Law* (Report No 57, 1992); Australian Law Reform Commission, *Recognition of Aboriginal Customary Law* (Report No 31, 1986); Law Reform Commission of Western Australia, *Aboriginal Customary Laws* (Final Report, Project No 94, 2006).

In countries where personal status law operates to recognise religious laws, the experience and needs of the religious group is recognised and validated, at least to some extent. This is not the position in Australia. Indigenous Australians are in their original country, but find themselves affected by a dominant legal system which has mostly ignored their civil law needs, and in particular their inheritance needs. Arguments about whether Indigenous customary law could be used within the common law have mostly been answered by saying that customary law should be recognised, but only to the extent that it does not impinge on common law.[74]

The culture and customary law of First Nations peoples in Australia bears almost no relationship to the religious cultures described above – Christianity, Islam, and Judaism. Indigenous people in Australia come from two traditions which themselves are divided. Torres Strait Islanders' traditions are quite different from Aboriginal cultures. Torres Strait Islander nations are seafaring nations with distinct trading patterns and strong traditions of agriculture, as well as distinct cultures of gift giving within and between groups. Aboriginal peoples are many nations with continuous cultural histories of 60,000 years or more. These cultures are sustained by a sense of place and country – which is the basis for customary law – and traditions of storytelling, which explain the relationships between people and land and each other. Elders are those who are seen as qualified to speak on particular topics. It is impossible here to adequately describe the depth and background of the differing traditions which make up the customary law traditions which continue to govern the lives of Aboriginal people, whether urban or remote. The small numbers of Indigenous people compared to the general population of Australia has made recognition of their needs and law lag behind. In a legal system which rejects pluralism, and recognises multiculturalism in law rather superficially, it is time to ensure that our Indigenous people across the whole of Australia, get their inheritance needs properly met.

V. Conclusion

In Australia, individuals who are from groups with inheritance needs dictated by religion have been forced to negotiate ways of complying with their own religious laws and the Australian succession law. I have discussed some of the ways in which this negotiation may have to take place, and I have tried to show that there may be personal cost in doing so. The fact that testamentary freedom is a major tenet of Australian law makes this easier than it could have been otherwise. It is remarkable that one can put customary law into a will and then have common law protect that customary law manifestation as it appears in the will. This is one of the saving graces of the Australian inheritance law system, because it does offer some flexibility for those whose religious or other preferences are strongly felt and may be accommodated. But without that doctrine, many groups with strongly-held views about inheritance would be unable to protect their traditional and religious views. It is particularly significant that Indigenous people in Australia, by making a will, can indeed put their customary law into place and have it

[74] See, eg, *Recognition of Aboriginal Customary Law* (n 73), *Aboriginal Customary Laws* (n 73).

protected. This is not the same as recognising customary law as law, but it does provide that the individual's wishes can be met. Thus, paradoxically, Australian succession law, while almost completely ignoring the inheritance needs of other cultural and religious groups living in Australia, manages to provide a mechanism which in many ways will meet their needs.

12

Burial Disputes and the Work of the Dead

KATE FALCONER

I. Introduction

It is something of an orthodoxy of the common law that death is not merely a biological endpoint, but also a legal endpoint.[1] That is to say, the common law sees death as a moment of transition, not only from a body *qua* organism capable of maintaining an internal homeostatic environment to a mere corpse bereft of life, but also from a body *qua* rights-bearing and duty-owing legal person to, what? The absence of such a person. Nothing. Thus, 'the Court speaks of the "rights" of a dead body, … [it] is obviously a popular form of expression – a corpse not being capable of rights'.[2]

Despite this apparent orthodoxy, however, when faced with various types of disputes we would recognise as falling within the broad ambit of private law,[3] courts routinely have recourse to the deceased and their wishes. So, for example, disputes about the posthumous use of reproductive material are at least partly (and at least implicitly) decided on the basis of the deceased's own views about posthumous parenthood,[4] and it is a cardinal rule of the construction of testamentary documents that the intention of the deceased be ascertained and complied with.[5]

This recourse to the deceased's wishes in the resolution of private law disputes is frequently explained on the basis of a need to respect the dead.[6] Drawing on insights from the interdisciplinary field of death studies, however, the central claim of this chapter is that respect for the dead and their wishes is not the entire picture. Instead of, or more likely in addition to, a respect bestowed on the dead by the living, is a simple

[1] Although as Chau and Herring point out, as much as lawyers might 'seek to pass the hot potato of defining death over to the doctors', the issue of biological death is not entirely settled amongst the medical profession: P-L Chau and J Herring, 'The Meaning of Death' in B Brooks-Gordon et al (eds), *Death Rites and Rights* (Oxford, Hart, 2007) 13.

[2] *R v Price* (1884) 12 QBD 247, 253 (Stephens J), referring to *R v Stewart* (1840) 12 Ad & E 773, 779; 113 ER 1007, 1009.

[3] And also, surely, disputes that fall within the broad ambit of public law – but this discussion is limited to private law disputes.

[4] See, eg, *Re H, AE (No 2)* [2012] SASC 177 [25]–[41].

[5] See M Glover, 'A Taxonomy of Testamentary Intent' (2015–16) 23(3) *George Mason Law Review* 569.

[6] See, eg, S McGuiness and M Brazier, 'Respecting the Living Means Respecting the Dead Too' (2008) 28 *OJLS* 297.

premise: the dead continue to be present in private law disputes. They continue to do work in our society (and in our courtrooms). Simply put, the dead continue to make demands of the living, to hold us to account, and to incite us to action.

This chapter examines this previously un(der)explored work of the dead, related to but independent of the respect we feel we owe to the deceased, in the particular context of burial disputes – that is, disputes brought by private parties over how, where, and by whom the deceased's body will be disposed of.[7] It explores these disputes – both in terms of their litigation and the judgments that resolve them – from four different angles, each perspective showing how burial disputes illuminate the work of the dead in private law.

II. What Is the Work of the Dead?

Before we turn to burial disputes, however, let us consider what is meant by 'the work of the dead'. We have already noted that the common law equates biological death with legal death. In this regard, however, the law is somewhat unique. Since its emergence as a discrete area of academic study in the last 50 years, the field of death studies has shown that death and our relationships with the dead are complex and multifaceted phenomena.[8] Against this backdrop, disciplines ranging from sociology, history and memory studies to psychology, archaeology and anthropology are quick to emphasise the distinction, indeed the dichotomy, of biological death and lived reality. In these readings, the dead die not once, but twice. The first death is biological – that of the body. The second death is cultural – that of the deceased as a social being.[9]

The time in between biological and cultural death – that is, the time it takes for a person to become nothing in this world[10] – can vary, both on an individual and a societal level. Regardless of its duration, however, it is this intervening period between first and second deaths that we are interested in. Much more so than at anytime in the past two hundred years, in the twenty-first century the interstices dead – the biologically dead but culturally alive – are pervasive.[11] They are no longer sequestered away.[12] Instead, we are encouraged to continue, even to build upon and develop, our relationships with the deceased.[13] And in their pervasiveness, the dead do work.

[7] This chapter will use the terms 'burial dispute' and 'post-death dispute' interchangeably to refer to this category of cases.

[8] M Radomska, T Mehrabi and N Lykke, 'Queer Death Studies: Death, Dying and Mourning from a Queerfeminist Perspective' (2020) 35 *Australian Feminist Studies* 81, 85.

[9] An early and influential account of this argument can be found in the anthropologist Robert Hertz's interpretation of Indonesian mortuary rituals: see 'A Contribution to the Study of the Collective Representation of Death' in R and C Needham (trans), *Death and the Right Hand* (Glencoe, The Free Press, 1960, essay first published 1907).

[10] TW Laqueur, 'The Work of the Dead in 21st Century America' (Australian Death Studies Society Annual Lecture, online, 24 February 2022).

[11] See T Walter, 'The Pervasive Dead' (2019) 24 *Mortality* 389.

[12] ibid.

[13] P Jalland, *Changing Ways of Death in Twentieth Century Australia: War, Medicine and the Funeral Business* (Sydney, UNSW Press, 2006) 368–69.

But what is this 'work' that the dead do? We can begin an answer by first considering *how* the dead do work. During the interstice period between natural and cultural death, the dead are unquiet.[14] They continue to '[create], [recreate], [represent], or [disrupt] the social order of which they had been a part'.[15] They are unavoidable and inescapable; they reflect ourselves and our communities back to us, sometimes truthfully and sometimes as in a funhouse mirror. They demand our attention as their due.[16] In this way the dead 'distract, deter, or cajole the living',[17] and we in turn invest the dead with meaning.[18] Both this cajoling and this investment of meaning can, and frequently do, inspire (re)action on the part of the living. This, for our purposes, is the work of the dead.

At times this work is firmly linked to the *bodies* of the dead. These bodies can reconfigure space in a very real and material sense. The bodies buried in Samoan graves, for example, make powerful statements about traditional rank and family status.[19] In a complex system of customary and legal land title, they also localise claims to property by asserting that the land of which the grave is a part, and any house built upon it, belongs to the descendents of the individual interred there.[20] Similarly, the (re)burial of 'our' dead (even, or perhaps particularly, the nameless, mass dead of violent conflict) consecrates that soil as 'ours', and can help establish new (or reaffirm old) family groups, communities and even nations:[21] 'Serbia is wherever there are Serbian graves'.[22]

The power to reconfigure nations is not the sole purview of the mass, nameless dead, however. Individual dead are regularly reinvested with meaning in what Verdery calls 'dead-body politics'.[23] In the prolific grave-hopping that took place in Eastern Europe in the immediately post-socialist period, for example, the bodies of particular politically-relevant dead worked to establish and legitimise new political orders. Such was the case of Hungarian Prime Minister Imre Nagy, an anti-Stalinist reformer, who was overthrown in a violent Soviet-backed coup in 1956, promptly hanged, and buried face-down in an unmarked grave. Nagy was revered in Hungary as a national (and nationalist) martyr, and his exhumation and subsequent reburial (this time appropriately encoffined) in a solemn ceremony held at Heroes' Square in Budapest in 1989

[14] C Moffat, 'Politics and the Work of the Dead in Modern India' (2018) 60 *Comparative Studies in Society and History* 178, 178.

[15] TW Laqueur, *The Work of the Dead: A Cultural History of Mortal Remains* (Princeton, Princeton University Press, 2015) 10.

[16] AF Gordon, *Ghostly Matters: Haunting and the Sociological Imagination*, New University of Minnesota Press ed (Minneapolis, University of Minnesota Press, 2008) xvi.

[17] Moffat (n 14) 181.

[18] Laqueur (n 15) 17–18.

[19] See M Meleisea and P Schoeffel, 'The Work of the Dead in Samoa: Rank, Status and Property' (2016) 125 *Journal of Polynesian Society* 149.

[20] ibid 159–63.

[21] See discussion in K Verdery, *The Political Lives of Dead Bodies: Reburial and Postsocialist Change* (New York, Columbia University Press, 1999) ch 3 and RP Harrison, *The Dominion of the Dead* (Chicago, University of Chicago Press, 2003) ch 2. These themes also arise in many of the contributions to F Stepputat (ed), *Governing the Dead: Sovereignty and the Politics of Dead Bodies* (Manchester, Manchester University Press, 2014).

[22] Quote attributed to Vuk Drašković, leader of the Serbian opposition to Slobodan Milošović in the 1990s, cited in Verdery (n 21) 98.

[23] See Verdery (n 21).

was attended by over a quarter of a million people. This intensely public honouring of Nagy's body served to legitimise and invigorate the reformist, nationalist, pro-democrat and anti-Soviet factions of the Hungarian government of the day.[24] A mere seven months after Nagy's reburial, the Hungarian Parliament would vote to transform the country from a one-party state to a multiparty democracy.

Dead bodies can also do work in ways that do not involve the very real and material redrawing of national borders, or the remaking of a national political system. Sometimes the work of the dead – work which takes place on and in our imagination – is more personal and more ephemeral. The fields of granite tombstones that mark the British Empire's uncountable dead of the Great War across Belgium and France arrest our attention now just as much as they did when they were first erected, for example. The location of each of these uniform grave-markers with their uniform inscription was based solely on a determination of which newly established cemetery was closest in proximity to the place where their sole, identified occupant fell, with no care as to class or rank. This speaks to a reclamatation of the individual dead by the nation (indeed, the Empire – it was the task of the Imperial War Graves Commission, after all), and to an equality in rememberance that worked to scuttle the already faltering English class system.[25] At the same time, the individual, nameless body taken from the fields of France and ensconced in the tomb of the so-called 'Unknown Warrior' in Westminster Abbey in 1920 worked to represent, in the imagination of a nation, 'all the mighty inarticulate sacrifice' of the preceding years.[26] This 'great symbolic act' also worked in the imagination of the individual bereaved whose loved ones had never come home, allowing each of them to say, 'That body may belong to me'.[27]

Dead bodies do this work because they are concrete – they are manifestly *there*.[28] And in their undeniable material presence they demand a material, entirely physical and entirely pragmatic response – they must be dealt with, managed, contained. At the same time, dead bodies 'evoke the awe, uncertainty, and fear associated with "cosmic" concerns' such as our own mortality, this in turn imposing some measure of sacrality upon the corpse.[29] The corpse is, after all, the means by which the intangible and unknowable (that is, death) becomes tangible and knowable.[30] At once, however, dead bodies represent – they were in fact once – particular individuals who have departed, these individuals having been part of particular communities and social circles which mourn these individual losses. The body after death is centred at an interplay of presence and absence, which ensures the body remains active in social life.[31] At the same time, the body itself is a powerful symbol of the passage of time and the process of

[24] For a description of this process, see KP Benziger, 'The Funeral of Imre Nagy: Contested History and the Power of Memory Culture' (2000) 12 *History and Memory* 142, 147–55.

[25] See discussion in Laqueur (n 15) 467–74. The unsavoury practicalities of the task of dealing with one nation's war dead are explored in R Fathi, '"We Refused to Work Until we had a Better Means for Handling the Bodies." Discipline at the Australian Graves Detachment' (2018) 9 *First World War Studies* 35.

[26] Unattributed quote cited in Laqueur (n 15) 481.

[27] Unattributed quotations cited in ibid.

[28] Verdery (n 21) 27.

[29] ibid 31.

[30] Laqueur (n 15) 83.

[31] E Hallam, J Hockey and G Howarth, *Beyond the Body: Death and Social Identity* (London, Routledge, 1999) 24.

decay from which nothingness is wrought – a nothingness to which we will all, at some point, go. A dead body, then, is simultaneously a potentially dangerous physical object, a powerful and emotive symbol of mortality, and the locus of both general and specific cultural and social relations to death and to the dead.

But not all of the work of the dead is body-adjacent. Sometimes the dead do their work in spectral form – that is, they do their work simply as a result of being *dead*. So, for example, the invocation of eighteenth-century Greek Catholic bishop Inochentie Micu in modern Romanian religious disputes impels Greek Catholics of the present to defend their faith with the same steadfastness exhibited by Micu, even in the face of rebuke and violence.[32] In the same way, the memory and image of the early twentieth-century Indian revolutionary Bhagat Singh – martyred in his youth by the colonial British state – recalls, for some, the lost glory of a past revolution, inspiring (and demanding) those in the present to particular forms of action, such as hunger strikes.[33] Singh's *body* is doing no work here (in fact it was secretly cremated and the ashes thrown into a river mere hours after his execution). Rather, the deceased Singh, 'supposedly over and done with', continues to make himself known to – that is, continues to haunt – the living.[34]

What does it mean for the dead to haunt the living? In the words of Avery Gordon, 'haunting describes how that which appears to be not there is often a seething presence, acting on and often meddling with taken-for-granted realities'.[35] The ghosts that do this haunting are not the bodies cloaked in white sheets at work in carnival haunted-houses. Rather they are social figures – the means by which something (or someone) supposedly lost makes itself known to us.[36] In this way, the deceased, lost to us in corporeal form, casts their social presence before them, demanding they be acknowledged. And so, for example, some who have lost partners or children continue to maintain relationships with their deceased loved ones, the dead being 'felt to be there' and continuing to 'splice' into the land (and the supposed realities, where the dead are simply dead) of the living.[37]

It is this work of the dead, done both by their bodies and their spectres, that is the focus of this chapter. In the discussions that follow we will explore how the incitement to action that the dead represent is clearly visible in the burial dispute case law. First, however, we will consider how the dead are made to show up for work in the courtroom.

III. Raising the Dead in the Courtroom

As indicated in the Introduction to this chapter, a burial dispute arises when parties are in conflict as to how the body will be disposed of (will it be burial or cremation?),

[32] Verdery (n 21) 78.
[33] Moffat (n 14) 186–87.
[34] ibid 178–79, quoting AF Gordon, 'Some Thoughts on Futurity and Haunting' (2011) 10 *borderlands* 1, 2.
[35] Gordon (n 16) 8.
[36] ibid.
[37] Hallam, Hockey and Howarth (n 31) 11, quoting R Simpson, *Changing Families: An Ethnographic Approach to Divorce and Separation* (Oxford, Berg, 1998).

where the remains will ultimately end up (an issue of particular concern for Indigenous Australians, for whom burial on country is frequently of utmost importance) and, underlying everything else, who will have the authority to make the relevant decisions. As also indicated in the Introduction, against the backdrop of this body of case law, this chapter argues that, in the private law, the dead place demands on us and we place demands on the dead.

But how can those supposedly lost to us make demands on us and of us? The answer is simple: they are not truly lost to us. They are present in the background, encouraging parties to bring their disputes to court, and they are present in the courtroom, as the case is heard. There are also traces of them clearly evident in the judgments handed down to resolve these disputes.

Let us begin at the end, by exploring the latter in some detail. Consider the simple act of naming the deceased. In much the same way as a eulogy, it is common in these post-death dispute decisions for the presiding judge to open their judgment with the calling of the deceased's name. 'Sarina Kelly died peacefully on Sunday 25 February 2007'.[38] 'The Deceased, Patrick Norman Fisher, was an Aboriginal man born on 3 August 1986'.[39] '[Albert Brikha died] on 20 February 1998 as a result of an unlawful killing'.[40] And in much the same way as a eulogy, this epideictic act of introducing the deceased by name serves to integrate them firmly into an ongoing dialogue and cement their place in ongoing relationships.[41] The deceased is no longer amorphous – one of the seething mass of uncountable nameless dead – but a distinct person, an individual, called by name in an act of necronominalism to attend to the proceedings.

The power which this act of naming the deceased invokes is not unproblematic. For Australia's First Nations peoples, for example – for whom death is already a marker of disadvantage,[42] and who are far more likely to find themselves a party to a burial dispute than non-Indigenous Australians[43] – the act of naming the deceased can be highly disrespectful. This is so for the exact reason just now set out – by naming the deceased, the deceased is called back to attend the dispute. They are prevented from continuing on their journey, and instead recalled to the present. The deceased might be angry or vengeful at having to return, and may take this out on the still-living.[44] It is for these reasons that some judges deciding burial disputes involving Indigenous Australians refrain from naming the deceased entirely.[45]

So some deceased remain unnamed. And even in those cases where the deceased *is* introduced by name, after this initial naming event they are frequently referred to

[38] *Keller v Keller* [2007] VSC 118, (2007) 15 VR 667 [1].
[39] *White v Williams* [2019] NSWSC 437 [1].
[40] *Escott v Brikha* [2000] NSWSC 458 [1].
[41] T Walter, 'A New Model of Grief: Bereavement and Biography' (1996) 1 *Mortality* 7.
[42] A Kellehear and I Anderson, 'Death in the Country of Matilda' in K Charmaz, G Howarth and A Kellehear (eds), *The Unknown Country: Death in Australia, Britain and the USA* (Basingstoke, Macmillan, 1997) 12.
[43] P Vines, 'Testamentary Freedom and Customary Law: The Impact of Succession Law on the Inheritance Needs of Aboriginal and Torres Strait Islanders in Australia' (2017) 91 *Australian Law Journal* 360, 362.
[44] For a discussion of this name avoidance practice in the community of Coen in Queensland, Australia (albeit from a non-Indigenous perspective), see BR Smith, '"We Don't Want to Chase 'Em Away": Hauntology in Central Cape York Peninsula' in K Glaskin et al (eds), *Mortality, Mourning and Mortuary Practices in Indigenous Australia* (Farnham, Ashgate, 2008).
[45] See, eg, *Nayakacalou v Vincent* [2020] NSWSC 24 [1]; *McKenzie v McKenzie* [2023] SASC 71 [1] fn 1.

only as 'the deceased'. The act of naming the deceased, however, is not required in order to call the deceased to be present in burial dispute judgments. Judges deciding disputes regarding the disposal of the deceased's body are, almost as a rule, at pains to write the deceased into their decision. Information about the deceased's birth, their family and what they did for work, along with, of course, at least their date (if not also their cause) of death, are frequently canvassed in detail in any given burial dispute judgment.[46]

Thus, we know that James Lindsey Laing was born in Scotland in 1929 and studied law in Glasgow. 'A highly intelligent and educated man', he worked for the Attorney-General's department in Canberra after emigrating to Australia in the early 1970s. In Canberra, he and his family lived in the same house for 40 years.[47] We know Mr Laing married his first wife in 1960, and visited her grave every Friday after she died in 2002.[48] We know he had three children and (at the time of judgment) eight grandchildren.[49] We know that, once a 'capable and able lawyer, a prudent and conservative man and a devoted and loving husband and father',[50] Mr Laing's health and personality began to deteriorate, making him vulnerable to the influence of others.[51] And we know that, after suffering a stroke and being intubated and mechanically ventilated for several hours, he died at the age of 84 at Ipswich Hospital in Queensland at 4:15pm on 24 July 2014.[52]

Not all burial dispute judgments write the dead into existence this clearly, of course. And so we know little about Betty Batson beyond the fact that she made a will in September of 2004, that she was the mother of five surviving children, that she died in December of 2020 and that she wanted to be cremated and to have a modest, private funeral in the hope that this would reduce inter-family tension.[53] We know even less about Cyril Michael Roma Snr: only that he was a First Nations man who died on 8 December 2009, had at least seven children and was separated from his former partner.[54] But, as we will see, even the barely-acknowledged dead are still present in the courtroom.

This recourse to the deceased's life story, as abbreviated and bare bones as it is at times, is perhaps the ultimate adherence to our desire for narrative in legal discourse.[55] It also raises a spectre of the deceased in the courtroom. This setting out of their life and death is a written instantiation of the deceased that allows, if not requires, the deceased to be present in the decision. It recalls the deceased to the here-and-now and allows them to make themselves known. Importantly, and as we will see in the

[46] Again, in much the same way as a eulogy, these biographical statements cannot contain everything that is known about the deceased, and so they are necessarily edited and present a particular version of the deceased that some might not recognise: see G Caswell, 'Personalisation in Scottish Funerals: Individualised Ritual or Relational Process?' (2011) 16 *Mortality* 242, 251.

[47] *Laing v Laing* [2014] QSC 194 [10].

[48] ibid [8].

[49] ibid.

[50] ibid [12].

[51] ibid [13]–[15].

[52] ibid [1].

[53] See *McCredie v Batson* [2020] NSWSC 1913.

[54] See *Roma v Ketchup* [2009] QSC 442.

[55] On this, see, eg, JM Van Dunné, 'Narrative Coherence and its Function in Judicial Decision Making and Legislation' (1996) 44 *American Journal of Comparative Law* 463.

discussions below, this written summoning of the dead allows the deceased to make demands of the living – that their own wishes regarding the disposal of their body be complied with, for example – at the same time as it allows the living to make demands of the dead.

In these ways, burial dispute judgments are a very particular form of what Hallam and Hockey call 'death writing'.[56] We have already compared them to eulogies. They also share the same biographical bent as the engraved tombstone (although, as we have seen, are frequently far more detailed), whilst bearing the same ritual force as a will.[57] At the same time, they materialise the dead in the present in a way similar to a photograph,[58] or a film.[59] From these judgments emanate outlines of the deceased. The shading within that outline is as heavy or opaque as the judge sees fit, but the outline of the deceased is always there. Post-death dispute judgments are no dime-novel piece of detective fiction, with the deceased a non-character known only by their absence.[60] Instead they centre the deceased, not merely by virtue of the nature of the dispute, but because the deceased is an unavoidable player in that dispute's resolution.

So far we have focused on the judgments that resolve burial disputes, and how these judgments raise the dead in the courtroom. But the argument of this chapter is that the dead also do work in the act of *bringing* the dispute and in the arguments made in the *litigation* of that dispute by the living. Locating the presence of the dead is harder here, without a concrete text to guide us.[61] But even on this broader and more general level, it can be said that burial disputes are a practice associated with death that bring the living and the dead into proximity.[62] They are a powerful cultural strategy that constitute a system of recall on the part of the living.[63] The formality and ritual of the court combines with the intensely personal and emotional nature of the conflict itself. As we will see below, parties to burial disputes use these conflicts to institutionalise their relationships to and with the deceased. In this process, memory – of the dead, and their relationships with the still living – is used to make the absent (that is, the deceased) present in the courtroom.[64] Simply put, burial disputes conjure the deceased into the courtroom and invite them to haunt the living. And once the dead have been raised, they are put to work.

IV. Putting the Dead to Work in the Courtroom

This section explores burial disputes – both as individual cases and as a body of case law – from four different angles.

[56] See E Hallam and J Hockey, *Death, Memory and Material Culture* (Oxford, Berg, 2001) ch 7.

[57] ibid.

[58] See P Stokes, *Digital Souls: A Philosophy of Online Death* (London, Bloomsbury, 2021) 55–58; Hallam, Hockey, and Howarth (n 31) 35–38.

[59] See the discussion of the various film depictions of Bhagat Singh in Moffat (n 14).

[60] On this issue, see A Bennett, 'Unquiet Spirits: Death Writing in Contemporary Fiction' (2009) 23 *Textual Practice* 463.

[61] Although here court transcripts, where available, present one potential avenue of analysis.

[62] Hallam and Hockey (n 56) 6.

[63] ibid 7.

[64] ibid 3.

A. 'Nothing Is More Dangerous Than to Ignore Them': Complying with the Wishes of the Deceased

Burial disputes are replete with references to the wishes of the deceased regarding the disposal of their body. 'The deceased made clear that any similarity to the public funeral aspect of the service for her husband was not what she wanted'.[65] 'Joan says that the deceased has always expressed a desire to return home and be buried with his nanna in Narrogin'.[66] 'The second defendant heard the deceased tell the second defendant's mother that, if anything happened to him, he wanted to come back to Port Augusta'.[67] With the deceased having no *legal* right to demand that their body be disposed of in any particular way,[68] it is unsurprising that it is here that calls for a need to respect the wishes of the dead regarding the posthumous treatment of their body are perhaps strongest.[69]

Putting respect to one side, however, and in the absence of any legal right to require their wishes be complied with, this chapter argues that the dead push the living into action on their behalf. Their ongoing presence compels the living to act in their interests. To be clear, this goes beyond the accepted societal belief that the wishes of the deceased should be the primary consideration when arranging for the disposal of the deceased's body.[70] The argument here is that the still-present dead, in their haunting of the living, *demand* that the living assert the deceased's wishes on their behalf. This is not merely the living bestowing respect upon the absent dead, but rather the still-present dead inciting the living into action.[71] Thus, in burial disputes, parties can be compelled to action, not (just) to give effect to their own wishes and beliefs, but to ensure the deceased's desires are complied with. In burial disputes, the living stand in the place of the deceased.

Thus, in *Sullivan v Public Trustee*,[72] the plaintiff, a close, personal confidant of the deceased, was compelled to bring an action to require the Public Trustee (as executor of the deceased's estate) to comply with the deceased's wishes regarding the disposal of his body. The deceased, a famous Indigenous artist, was clear in his desire for his body to be buried at Napperby Downs Station in Australia's Northern Territory. He had repeatedly articulated his wishes, which were born of deep emotional, spiritual and

[65] *McCredie* (n 53) [17].

[66] *Bertani v Bertani* [2017] WASC 78 [9].

[67] *South Australia v Smith* [2014] SASC 64, (2014) 119 SASR 247 [45].

[68] '[It] is trite law that there is no property in a corpse': *AB v Attorney-General (Vic)* (21 July 1998, unreported), VSC. As a result, '[i]f there be no property in a dead body it is impossible that by will or any other instrument the body can be disposed of': *Williams v Williams* (1882) 20 ChD 659, 665. Requests for cremation can provide one exception, as to which, see the discussion later in this section.

[69] So much so that the topic has been considered by several law reform commissions: see Victorian Law Reform Commission, *Funeral and Burial Instructions* (Report, 2016); Queensland Law Reform Commission, *A Review of the Law in Relation to the Final Disposal of a Dead Body* (Report No 69, 2011) ch 5.

[70] *Funeral and Burial Instructions* (n 69) 28 para 4.3.

[71] Despret gives the example of purgatory, a period during which the dead demand the living pray for them in order to shorten their time spent in the probationary space: V Despret, *Our Grateful Dead*, trans S Muecke (Minneapolis, University of Minnesota Press, 2021) 32.

[72] The only version of this judgment I have been able to locate is: Transcript of Proceedings, *Sullivan v Public Trustee for the Northern Territory of Australia* (24 July 2002, unreported), NTSC.

cultural need. Napperby Downs was the deceased's 'borning place' and the country of his possum dreaming. It regularly featured in his paintings, and he frequently spoke of the importance of this place and its stories.[73] In the face of opposition from the deceased's family regarding his proposed burial place, however, the Public Trustee had instead made alternative disposal arrangements.[74]

The plaintiff was compelled to act. In doing so, as the court noted, '[she was] not seeking the implementation of her own wishes, rather she is seeking the implementation of the deceased's wishes. She [was] only trying to respect and implement the wishes he so clearly expressed'.[75] Much as the ongoing spectral presence of Bhagat Singh inspires Indian students to acts of revolution in the twenty-first century,[76] the deceased's ongoing social presence in *Sullivan* compelled the plaintiff to step in to his shoes, to adopt his wishes as her own and to advocate for them vigorously. As the plaintiff herself said, 'Well, someone had to support his wishes, and no-one else seemed to be doing it'.[77]

Conway and Stannard see the vindication of the deceased's wishes regarding the disposal of their body by the living as a desire on the part of the living to 'do right' by the deceased.[78] I think it can be put in more stark terms. Simply put, for the living to fail to comply with the demands of the dead and assert the deceased's wishes on their behalf is to ignore the power of obligation that links the departed with the still here;[79] it is a betrayal of the dead. Thus, for the plaintiff in *Sullivan* to fail to act, to fail to take the dispute to court, would be to wrong the deceased, to let him down, to abandon him. The deceased continued to 'splice' into the plaintiff's life and to interrupt her lived reality. When the court sided with the Public Trustee, it was 'absolutely sad for Clifford [the deceased]'.[80] That is, not (or at least, not solely), for the plaintiff, but rather for the deceased as one still present in the dispute. It was 'heartbreaking'.[81]

Further evidence of the work of the dead on the minds of the living can be found in the various pieces of legislation governing cremation in each Australian state and territory. In Queensland, for example, a decedent's request to be cremated must be complied with (if possible) by the person charged with the disposal of the deceased's body, regardless of that person's own thoughts on the matter.[82] This requirement remains in place even in the case of objection by the deceased's family.[83] These provisions were apparently enacted with the express goal of furthering the rights of the deceased[84] – that is to say, in full acknowledgement of the continued presence of the deceased as one entitled to certain actions on the part of the living even after their death.

[73] ibid 7–10.
[74] The wishes of the deceased's family were also deeply grounded in culture and lore.
[75] *Sullivan* (n 72) 6.
[76] See Moffat (n 14) 193–201.
[77] M Sullivan, '7:30: Tjapaltjarri Finally Allowed to Rest in Peace' (ABC, 25 July 2002) <www.web.archive.org/web/20100110044402/http://www.abc.net.au/7.30/content/2002/s629828.htm>.
[78] H Conway and J Stannard, 'The Honour of Hades: Death, Emotion and the Law of Burial Disputes' (2011) 34 *University of New South Wales Law Journal* 860, 870.
[79] Despret (n 71) 25.
[80] Sullivan (n 77).
[81] ibid.
[82] See Cremations Act 2003 (Qld) s 7.
[83] See ibid s 8.
[84] *Parliamentary Debates*, Queensland Legislative Assembly, 1054 (1 April 2003, Keech).

Importantly, these provisions allow the deceased to demand a particular action of the living in a way that would not necessarily be countenanced in life. One generally cannot in life, for example, demand that another provide you with a service or an item of property (other than those services or items of property to which the demandor has a legal claim, of course). But in death the deceased can exhort their will loudly – no going gentle into that good night here! – and see it imposed on others.

With all that said, however, it should be noted that neither the relevant Queensland provision, nor its equivalents in other jurisdictions, appear to have been tested in court.[85] But then, anecdotally, the desire to heed a deceased loved one's call to action regarding the disposal of their body is usually so strong,[86] and the thought of litigating in relation to that disposal so objectionable,[87] so as to remove the need for recourse to the relevant statutory provisions. In this way, the provisions in the Queensland Cremations Act (and their mere existence is sufficient) serve only to remind us that we ignore the unquiet dead at our peril.[88] Instead, we are, rather forcefully, cajoled into action.

B. 'This Macabre Dispute': A Judicial Discourse of Revulsion

It is not only the parties to a dispute who are cajoled into action by the dead. As Verdery notes, 'an unburied body is a source of things being not quite right in the cosmos'.[89] Judges deciding post-death disputes appear to have taken this to heart. Apparently shocked at the 'extraordinary'[90] and 'macabre'[91] cases in which parties cannot agree as to how the disposal of the deceased's remains will be effected, these judges engage in what Conway and Stannard have termed a 'discourse of revulsion'.[92]

Representative of this discourse, in *Keller v Keller*, Hargrave J opened his reasons with the following:

> Sarina Keller died peacefully on Sunday 25 February 2007, aged 81 years. The aftermath of her death has been anything but peaceful. A bitter and spiteful dispute between her two children has led to the wholly undesirable situation – disrespectful of the deceased and offensive to ordinary standards of common decency – that Sarina's body has yet to be disposed of, by burial or cremation.[93]

[85] There appear to be no cases that even mention the equivalent Western Australian provision (Cremation Act 1929 (WA) s 13), and Cremations Act 2003 (Qld) s 7 was not relevant on the facts of the three cases in which it has been mentioned: see *Laing* (n 47); *Tufala v Marsden* [2011] QSC 222; *Reid v Crimp* [2004] QSC 304.

[86] *Funeral and Burial Instructions* (n 69) 29–30 paras 4.11–4.16 (describing the prevalent community value that is the need to respect the wishes of the bereaved).

[87] At least in the eyes of the courts, as the discussion in section IV.B below explores.

[88] That said, there does not appear to be any penalty attached to the Queensland provision requiring compliance with the deceased's wishes to be cremated. In Western Australia, in contrast, failing to comply with the deceased's wishes to be cremated carries a maximum penalty of a $400 fine or one year imprisonment: Cremation Act 1929 (WA) s 15(1).

[89] Verdery (n 21) 45.

[90] *Derwen v Ling* [2008] FamCA 644 [14].

[91] *Rutherford v Wallace* [1999] NSWCA 299 [41].

[92] Conway and Stannard (n 78) 886.

[93] (n 38) 668 [1].

Conway and Stannard suggest this judicial discourse of revulsion stems from two factors: first, distaste at the thought that the deceased's body must be kept 'on ice' throughout the weeks (if not months or years) that the dispute is ongoing, and second, a sense that the parties to the dispute are 'bad people' for being in conflict at a time (ie the death of the deceased) that is expected to bring people together.[94] Underpinning both of these themes is the perceived societal need to respect the dead, and the closely-related idea that lengthy periods of non-disposal fail to accord the dead this respect, and are otherwise indecent.[95]

A need to protect the deceased and their body from any disrespect or indecency is certainly present in burial dispute decisions.[96] As Conway and Stannard point out, however, judges deciding these disputes do not seek to actively explore the emotions underpinning these sentiments.[97] Taking up the task on their behalf, I argue that, rather than judicial disgust at the ongoing non-disposal of the body representing merely an affront to societal standards of decency and respect (perhaps based on notions of how we would like our own dead bodies to be treated), this disgust reflects a more basic – what we might call primeval – concern. A response to the undisposed-of dead that can be found deep in our human history. I argue that the body of the deceased itself demands that it be disposed of, and that this requires action by the still-living (including judges faced with burial disputes).

The desire (need?) to dispose of our dead that their bodies invoke in us is so deeply engrained in the human psyche that some anthropologists and archaeologists consider it to be a unique marker *of humanness*.[98] It is said that every human society across time and geography of which there exists some record has (had) at least some practices relating to the disposal of the dead. And by the same token, the act of leaving the dead to decompose to nothing where they fall is considered the mark of a society in crisis. This need to dispose of the bodies of the dead is a subliminal pull that is felt even towards those decidedly *outside* of our own communities. And so, for example, international law requires belligerents to inter the bodies of *all* dead honourably, including those of enemy soliders and prisoners of war, not merely the bodies of those they fought alongside.[99]

There is, of course, truth to the public health rationale that is frequently said to explain our primeval need to dispose of our dead. Our very ancient ancestors may have buried their dead in order to limit the smell of decay, or to avoid attracting scavengers.[100]

[94] Conway and Stannard (n 78) 887–88. They also note a sense of embarrassment and discomfort on the part of judges faced with a dispute as to the disposal of the deceased's body: at 888. The emotions at the centre of burial disputes are explored in detail in Heather Conway's contribution to this collection: see ch 10.

[95] Conway and Stannard (n 78) 888–91.

[96] See, eg, *South Australia v Smith* (n 67) [21].

[97] Conway and Stannard (n 78) 889–91.

[98] See discussion in Laqueur (n 15) 8–10.

[99] See volume 2, rule 115 of the ICRC's study on customary international humanitarian law, available at ICRC, 'International Humanitarian Law Databases' https://ihl-databases.icrc.org/customary-ihl/eng/docindex/v2_rul_rule115.

[100] W Dunham, 'Did Neanderthals Bury Their Dead With Flowers? Iraq Cave Yields New Clues' *Washington Post* (25 February 2020) www.washingtonpost.com/national/health-science/did-neanderthals-bury-their-dead-with-flowers-iraq-cave-yields-new-clues/2020/02/21/0815e340-5415-11ea-929a-64efa7482a77_story.html.

And very similar concerns can be seen in the development of the modern common law duty to dispose of a body that is imposed on particular individuals close to the deceased in life, and owed to society at large:[101] 'the dead body could not remain on the surface of the earth. It became necessary that someone should see it consigned to the grave'.[102] But there is something else at play. The improperly-disposed-of body is a locus of recrimation and accusation; the undisposed-of body even more so. The undisposed-of body is an aberration. It is no longer an embodied person, instead it is a powerful symbol – of both the person that once was and the decay that is inevitable – that works on our imagination and demands disposal.[103] Put another way, the unburied body requires judges to attempt to repair the tear in the cosmos that body represents, and the discourse of revulsion – so calculated as to shame those before them into disposing of the body swiftly – is part of this attempt.

To be very clear, then, the argument here is that the judicial discourse of disgust and revulsion that is evident in the case law reflects something more than societal discomfort at the fact that relatives of the deceased are delaying disposal with the airing of dirty laundry, and thus offering some indignity to the deceased. The claim made in this chapter is that the presence of an undisposed-of body *works on and in the minds of judges* as a deeply cosmic object that is out of place. These are not emotions and responses that the living create amongst their own communities and then reach out and attach to the dead body. They are instead conveyed from the bodies of the dead to the still-living in a transfer of ancient sentiment. They can be explained in part on the basis of public health, in part on the basis of public decency, and in part on the basis of simply being human.

C. 'A Hideous Gathering of Shades, Sorcerers and Monsters': Banishing the Difficult Dead

So far we have seen how the deceased as a haunting presence require the living to take up their cause and fight in their name. We have also seen how the spectre of the deceased's unburied body inspires judges to a discourse of revulsion and the quick resolution of burial disputes. Here, we consider an example in which both the body and the haunting presence of the deceased are the immediate cause of action on the part of the living.

When Ian Stewart-Brady died in May 2017, his intentions regarding the disposal of his body were clear. It was reported that he wished to be cremated, and his ashes emptied into the River Clyde in Glasgow.[104] Action was required. More (and vastly different) action than is usually required in the case of body disposal – because Stewart-Brady, along with Myra Hindley, was one of the infamous Moors murderers responsible for

[101] See K Falconer, 'The Right to Possession of the Body of the Deceased: A History' (2021) 8 *law&history* 1, 14.

[102] *Tugwell v Heyman* (1812) 3 Camp 298, 299; 170 ER 1389, 1389.

[103] On this, see JR Martel, *Unburied Bodes: Subversive Corpses and the Authority of the Dead* (Amherst, Amherst College Press, 2018).

[104] *Oldham Metropolitan BC v Makin* [2017] EWHC 2543 (Ch), [2018] Ch 543 [17].

the deaths of five teenagers in Manchester, England in the 1960s. Glasgow refused to have him,[105] and concerns that his ashes might be scattered in proximity to where he had committed his crimes led two metropolitan borough councils (Tameside and Oldham) to seek assurances, and ultimately a court order, that this would not take place.[106]

Stewart-Brady's spectre is writ large in Sir Geoffrey Vos' reasons for his decision. More so than the average dead person, he haunted the courtroom. The public – and the court – were revolted by his desire to have the fifth movement of Hector Berlioz's 'Symphonie Fantastique' – which portrays a murderer attending his own funeral in the form of a 'hideous' and 'vulgar' witches' sabbath[107] – played at his cremation.[108] There was public revulsion in communities affected by the murders, with residents concerned that Stewart-Brady's remains would be disposed of in their vicinity, as reports suggested Myra Hindley's remains had been before him.[109] Merseyside Police expressed concerns about public order.[110] Simply put, he could not be allowed to be disposed of as and where he saw fit. Stewart-Brady's wishes regarding his body, and on a more basic level the very fact that his body required disposal, demanded, required, incited action.

What is interesting here is the dual nature of the work done by the dead Stewart-Brady. A quintessential example of the 'difficult dead',[111] he was twice present in the dispute. As a deceased murderer responsible for terrible crimes, he haunted the lives and minds of those affected by his actions. The Deputy Executive Leader of Tameside, speaking for his 220,000 constituents, for example, insisted that '[d]espite these murders happening over 50 years ago, the horror and revulsion has not subsided for the people of Tameside'.[112] Stewart-Brady's social presence was (and likely is) still inescapable, and had to be quelled as much as possible. At the same time, his dead body acted as the physical representation of his crimes and his ability to make himself known in the lives of the living; a unique form of toxic necro-waste.[113] For Tameside and Oldham, the idea that his remains – even in the disembodied and dispersed form of cremated ashes – might persist in the community could not be countenanced. The court must intervene.[114]

And intervene the court did. Ultimately, it was ordered that Stewart-Brady's body be cremated in a spare cremator outside of normal operating hours at a crematorium in the neighbouring borough of Sefton. There were to be no flowers, and no music was allowed to be played. Only a select few (mostly council officials and police) were

[105] ibid.
[106] ibid [18].
[107] ibid [86].
[108] ibid [86]–[87].
[109] ibid [40].
[110] ibid [14], [16].
[111] D Robins and R Smith, 'Hidden Labour in Funeral Directing: Providing Care to "Difficult" Dead Bodies' (2021) 26 *Mortality* 100.
[112] *Oldham* (n 104) [40].
[113] D Robins, 'Toxic Necro-Waste' (2017) 6 *Social Epistemology Review & Reply Collective* 39. See also Robins and Smith (n 111) 102–04.
[114] *Oldham* (n 104) [18].

permitted to attend. His ashes were to be disposed of at sea.[115] Clearly, the strength of his social presence required the court to be cold and clinical in its dealings with Stewart-Brady. And whilst the court acknowledged the existence of a duty to dispose of each and every body decently,[116] his unclean and potentially pollutive presence in the courtroom required the boundaries of that duty to be pushed to the very limit. Thus, whilst other courts have noted that 'it is not possible to conduct a service that is compatible with the most basic norms of human dignity without something being said about the deceased',[117] no service was allowed at Stewart-Brady's cremation, and no words said to commemorate him.[118] He was not to be farewelled so much as banished.

In the context of the existing body of burial dispute case law, this is a unique and emotive obliteration of a dead body, both in practice and in law.[119] In its uniqueness, it is a powerful form of commemorative expression.[120] It is a way of moulding memory, both individually and on a societal level. As McEvoy and Conway point out, '[h]istorically, the physical and symbolic destruction of the body *after* death was an important aspect of the sentence of the court'.[121] The bodies of convicted murderers in eighteenth- and nineteenth-century England, for example, were sent to the dissection table – an infamously terrible punishment considered a fate worse than death.[122] This fate was so feared because it was not merely their bodies that were destroyed. In their not being afforded the dignity of established disposal practices (notably burial in consecrated ground with a Christian service), the convicted dead were denied an acceptable social existence (as a good Christian and a member of a local community of the dead) in death. Instead, their posthumous existence in the minds and memories of the living, if they enjoyed one at all, was as a perpetual outsider, constantly maligned and suffering a social death intended to be as humiliating as possible.[123]

The same can be said for the court's treatment of Stewart-Brady's body. The orders made by Sir Geoffrey Vos were designed to strip Stewart-Brady and his body of the usual trappings of a modern funeral, so as to limit his haunting presence as much as possible. He was to be wiped from the world in an act of 'symbolic [sanitation]',[124] with no trace of his physical self to be left behind, and as little as possible of his social self allowed to endure. His ashes were scattered at sea with only a handful of officials allowed to be present.[125] The spare crematorium used to cremate his body was to be scrubbed clean after the event to remove any trace of him.[126]

[115] ibid [88].
[116] ibid [9].
[117] *McCredie* (n 53) [19].
[118] *Oldham* (n 104) [88].
[119] A point noted by Sir Geoffrey Vos: ibid [84].
[120] K McEvoy and H Conway, 'The Dead, the Law, and the Politics of the Past' (2004) 31 *Journal of Law and Society* 539, 552.
[121] ibid.
[122] R Richardson, *Death, Dissection and the Destitute*, 2nd edn (London, Phoenix Press, 2001) 32–34.
[123] Laqueur (n 15) 347.
[124] Robins and Smith (n 111) 106.
[125] *Oldham* (n 104) [88].
[126] ibid [23].

D. 'Nothing Short of Toxic': Demanding a Relationship with the Dead

In the previous discussions, we focused our attention on the demands the dead make of the living. To conclude our consideration of the work of the dead in burial disputes, we turn our attention to the demands the living make of the dead.

We have already seen that the living are compelled to act on behalf of the deceased in the courtroom, standing in place of the dead and advocating for their wishes. That is to say, we have seen that the dead maintain active relationships with the living, and demand that the living 'live up' to their side of the relationship. These ongoing relationships go both ways, however, and the living can and do make similar demands of the dead. How so? To borrow again from the words of Verdery, '[m]anipulating physical remains is a visual and visceral experience that seems to offer true access to the past'.[127] In bringing post-death disputes, then, the living use the dead, and their relationships with the dead, to access, maintain and project a particular, 'true' view of the(ir) past.

Here, we can return to our comparison of burial disputes and eulogies. In our discussion in section III above we compared the written *judgment* that resolves burial disputes with a eulogy in its acts of naming the deceased and establishing at least an outline of the deceased's life and times. Here, it warrants noting that the person who writes a eulogy controls the narrative of the deceased's life (and their role in it).[128] The same is very much true of the person responsible for arranging the disposal of the deceased's body – the location of that disposal, any associated ceremony, who is invited and who is not. By virtue of making these arrangements, the person responsible receives public acknowledgement that they were the focal point of the deceased's life.[129] In competing for the position of decision-maker in this context, then, parties to burial disputes demand that their relationship with the deceased be recognised as taking priority, and that the deceased support their claim by performing their part in this relationship.

Conway and Stannard refer to this approach to burial disputes as an attempt to 'reclaim' and 'monopolise' the deceased in death.[130] Cases in which parents are in conflict as to the disposal of their deceased child's body are a particularly tragic example of this – the more so when the deceased is a minor child. In these disputes, the two parents frequently attempt to establish that they (and not the other parent) had the closer relationship with their child in the child's lifetime. This is commonly done by emphasising the actions of the parent – the giving of gifts and the payment of financial support on the one hand, and the provision of care and use of a particular last name on the other, for example.[131]

For our purposes, however, we are more concerned with those harder-to-grasp moments in which living parents demand that the deceased perform the role of loving child in the courtroom. We can see this in claims that *the deceased child* had a stronger, more intimate relationship with one parent than the other (as opposed to claims about

[127] Verdery (n 21) 113.
[128] Caswell (n 46) 251.
[129] Conway and Stannard (n 78) 879–80.
[130] ibid.
[131] See *AB v CD* [2007] NSWSC 1474.

the nature of the relationship made from the perspective of the parent). Thus, it is an important factor in the resolution of these disputes that the deceased child chose to '[maintain] close contact' with a parent,[132] or that they 'had a much closer personal relationship with [one parent] prior to [their] death than [they] did with anybody else, including [their other parent]'.[133] In emphasising these points, the deceased's parents are demanding the deceased support their claim of priority in the hierarchy of relationships that continue post-death. The deceased is called to stand witness to the veracity of a particular version of the past in what is, in essence, a post-death custody battle.

There is also an important public-facing aspect here that should not be overlooked (at the same time as it should not be over-emphasised). Ultimately, in at least some of these cases, the legal recognition of one party over the other as decision-maker in arranging the disposal of their child's body becomes a 'prize' awarded by courts to the more involved parent (despite protests by courts to the contrary).[134] That is, the public acknowledgement that is brought about by a decision in one party's favour is not just of the *existence* of a particularly strong relationship with the deceased in a particular family context, but of the *quality* of that relationship as determined by broader community standards. And so, for example, the conscience of a modern community will not favour the claim of a biological mother when the child in question was adopted by another some 20 years ago[135] – the biological mother's relationship with the deceased is simply not of sufficient quality in the eyes of society.

V. Conclusion

In perhaps his second most famous poem, Dylan Thomas tells us that even when our bones are picked clean and the clean bones gone, 'death shall have no dominion' over us. If we take Thomas to be referring to biological death, then we certainly cannot argue. Biological death, as much as legal death, is *an* end, but it is not *the* end. Instead, after biological death (and the legal death with which it corresponds) there is a long, lingering interstice period before the dead finally fade into nothing. This nothingness, this second death, is *the* end.

This chapter has not been concerned with *the* end. It has been concerned with the interstice period that precedes it. Its argument has been founded on the idea, drawn from the interdisciplinary field of death studies, that in this interstice period the dead and their bodies continue to *do work*. They continue to make demands of the living, and to incite us to action. Thus, we have seen that the deceased, deprived of any legal recourse on their own part, turn to the living to demand that their wishes regarding the disposal of their body be enforced.

[132] *Burrows v Cramley* [2002] WASC 47 [6], [10].
[133] *AG v JB* [2022] NSWSC 326 [38].
[134] I Freckleton, 'Disputed Family Claims to Bury or Cremate the Dead' (2009) 17 *Journal of Law and Medicine* 178, 182–83.
[135] *Smith v Tamworth City Council* (1997) 41 NSWLR 680, 697. The deceased in this case was in his early 20s (as opposed to a minor child).

At other times, the demands made by the dead are simpler and more deeply felt. The bodies of the dead demand to be disposed of, not through any particular individual desire on the part of the individual dead to be dealt with in any particular way, but because the very nature of an undisposed-of body makes the demand of disposal of the living. To be human is to dispose of our dead, and to decide a burial dispute is to accord with that demand in the most urgent of ways.

But the living also make demands of the dead. And so we have seen that, in litigating burial disputes, the living call on the dead to affirm and comply with particular views the living have of themselves in their relationships with the deceased. And at times the living are required to banish the dead, to seek to limit the spectral reach of the dead as much as possible.

Underlying all, this chapter has drawn on sociological and historical notions of the pervasiveness of the modern dead and the work that these still-present dead perform in modern society to argue that the deceased themselves, rather than merely a reflexive respect for the deceased on the part of the living, continue to have a real and meaningful presence in burial disputes. And if the dead are at work here, there is no reason to think they are not also at work throughout the entirety of private law.

INDEX

www.ingramcontent.com/pod-product-compliance
Ingram Content Group UK Ltd.
Pitfield, Milton Keynes, MK11 3LW, UK
UKHW020245290926
15470UKWH00002B/754

9 781509 969326